State and Economy in Republican China

A Handbook for Scholars

Harvard East Asian Monographs 193

Supported by

The National Endowment for the Humanities

The Chiang Ching-kuo Foundation for International Scholarly Exchange

The Fairbank Center for East Asian Research, Harvard University

The Institute of Modern History, Academia Sinica, Taiwan

State and Economy in Republican China

A Handbook for Scholars

Edited by

William C. Kirby   Man-houng Lin

James Chin Shih   David A. Pietz

Volume 1

Published by the Harvard University Asia Center
and distributed by Harvard University Press
Cambridge (Massachusetts) and London 2000

Printed in the United States of America

The Harvard University Asia Center publishes a monograph series and, in coordination with the Fairbank Center for East Asian Research, the Korea Institute, the Reischauer Institute of Japanese Studies, and other faculties and institutes, administers research projects designed to further scholarly understanding of China, Japan, Vietnam, Korea, and other Asian countries. The Center also sponsors projects addressing multidisciplinary and regional issues in Asia.

Library of Congress Cataloging-in-Publication Data

State and economy in Republican China : a handbook for scholars / edited by William C. Kirby . . . [et al.]
       p. cm. -- (Harvard East Asian monographs ; 193)
    Includes bibliographical references.
    ISBN 0-674-00367-5 (cl : alk. paper) -- ISBN 0-674-00368-3 (pbk. : alk. paper)
       1. China--Economic conditions--1912-1949--Sources. 2. China--Economic conditions--1912-1949--Archival resources. 3. China--Commerce--History--20th century--Sources. 4. China--Commerce--History--20th century--Archival resources. 5. China--History--Republic, 1912-1949--Sources. 6. China--History--Republic, 1912-1949--Archival resources. 7. Archives--China. I. Kirby, William C. II. Series.

    HC427.8.S73 2000
    338.951'009'04--dc21
                                     00-049855

☺ Printed on acid-free paper

Last figure below indicates year of this printing
10 09 08 07 06 05 04 03 02 01

Assisted by

Shiwei Chen   Hongmin Liang

Jinbao Qian   Hong Sun

Michael S. Weiss

CONTENTS

Part I   Introduction

Part II Business and Economic History Archives of Republican China

4. The Number Two Historical Archives 59

Introduction 59
Economic History Archives 59

Contents

Contents

Part III   Reading Business and Economic History
Documents of Republican China

Contents

VOLUME 2

Part IV   Documents

Contents

State and Economy in Republican China

A Handbook for Scholars

Part I

INTRODUCTION

Chapter 1

Introduction to the Handbook

William C. Kirby

This Handbook is designed for scholars and students of twentieth-century China. It has several related purposes. First, it surveys the holdings of major Chinese archives and collections bearing on the economic and business history of Republican China, including the Republic of China (ROC) on Taiwan. Second, it reproduces, for the purposes of scholarly training, a series of original documents. Third, through its survey of archives and presentation of documents, it aims to encourage further research on a central issue: the relationship between the state and the economy in non-communist China in the twentieth century.

The Handbook has grown out of materials developed for seminars on Republican China at Washington University and at Harvard University. As a genre, however, it has a much longer history. The development of modern China studies in the West has periodically been assisted by the compilation of research aids. Endymion Wilkinson's research guide to Imperial China, updated by James Cole, and now again revised by Wilkinson, remains an invaluable tool.[1] Andrew J. Nathan's 1973 introduction to source materials on modern China made a major contribution in the decade before libraries and archives in the People's Republic of China (PRC) became more generally available to foreign scholars.[2] In the field of modern Chinese history, several generations of Western scholars have initiated their training through the series compiled by John K. Fairbank and Philip A. Kuhn to introduce documents of the Qing period.[3]

Until the mid-1980s, archive-based research on post-imperial (that is, post-1911) Chinese history took place more readily in Japanese, European, and North American holdings than in the

---

1. Endymion P. Wilkinson, *The History of Imperial China: A Research Guide* (Cambridge, Mass.: Harvard University Council on East Asian Studies, 1972); James H. Cole, *Updating Wilkinson: An Annotated Bibliography of Reference Works on Imperial China Published Since 1973* (New York, 1991). See now Endymion Wilkinson, *Chinese History: A Manual, Revised and Enlarged* (Cambridge, Mass.: Harvard University Asia Center, 2000).

2. Andrew J. Nathan, *Modern China, 1840–1972: An Introduction to Sources and Research Aids* (Ann Arbor: University of Michigan Center for Chinese Studies, 1973).

3. John K. Fairbank, *Ch'ing Documents: An Introductory Syllabus,* 3d ed. (Cambridge, Mass.: Harvard University Press, 1965); Philip A. Kuhn and John K. Fairbank, eds., *Introduction to Ch'ing Documents: The Rebellion of Chung Jen-chieh* (Cambridge, Mass.: Fairbank Center for East Asian Research, 1986).

archives of the PRC and the ROC. This situation has now changed. The 1980s and 1990s witnessed a scholarly revolution on several fronts of the modern China field. Officially sponsored projects to publish archival materials, such as the *Zhonghua minguo zhongyao shiliao chubian* of the Party Historical Commission of the Guomindang[4] or the collaborative *Zhonghua minguo shi*[5] of the PRC, were accompanied by the modernization and professionalization of major Chinese archives of the twentieth century.[6] These have rapidly become open to wider scholarly use, not the least in the area of economic history, which both the PRC and the ROC regimes have found politically less problematic than other areas, such as party history or the lives of senior leaders.

A happy result of this opening has been that scholars of Republican China have been confronted with a flood of new materials relating to local, provincial, national, and international history. Introductions to the Chinese archival scene, such as the superb guide edited by Ye Wa and Joseph Esherick and the bilingual directory published by the PRC's Central Archives Bureau, have made information about these archives and their holdings much more available than in the past.[7] An increasing number of archives have published substantial overviews of their holdings.[8] However, many archives have published only the most general description, and some have no printed guides at all.

---

4. Qin Xiaoyi, ed., *Zhonghua minguo zhongyao shiliao chubian* (Important historical documents of the Republic of China, first compilation) (Taipei: Dangshi weiyuanhui, 1981–).

5. Li Xin, ed., *Zhonghua minguo shi* (History of the Republic of China) (Beijing: Chung-hua, 1981–).

6. See, for example, Lu Shouchang, *Xiandai shiyong dang'an guanli xue* (Contemporary archival management) (Taipei, 1983); *Minguo shiqi wenshu gongzuo he dang'an gongzuo* (Work on Documents and Archives of the Republican Period) (Beijing: Dang'an chubanshe, 1987).

7. Ye Wa and Joseph W. Esherick, eds., *Chinese Archives: An Introductory Guide* (Berkeley: University of California, Institute of East Asian Studies, Center for Chinese Studies, 1996); *Zhongguo dang'anguan minglu* (Directory of Chinese national archives) (Beijing: Dang'an chubanshe, 1990), in Chinese and English.

8. Among the earlier guides were *Guoshiguan gaikuang* (Overview of the Academia Historica) (Taipei: Guoshiguan, 1984), updated as *Guoshiguan xiancang guojia dang'an gaishu* (Overview of national archives held at the Academia Historica) (Taipei: Guoshiguan, 1996); *Zhongguo di'er lishi dang'anguan jianming zhinan* (Brief guide to the Second Historical Archives of China) (Nanjing: Dang'an chubanshe, 1987), expanded as *Zhongguo di'er lishi dang'anguan zhinan* (Guide to the Second Historical Archives of China) (Nanjing: Dang'an chubanshe, 1994); *Shanghai shi dang'anguan jianming zhinan* (Brief guide to the Shanghai Municipal Archives) (Shanghai: Shanghai shi dang'anguan, 1991); *Sichuan sheng dang'anguan guancang dang'an gaishu* (Survey of the archival holdings of the Sichuan Provincial Archives) (Chengdu: Sichuan sheng dang'anguan, 1988). The one archive to publish a real catalogue (as opposed to a summary) of part of its holdings is the Institute of Modern History of the Academia Sinica; see its exceptionally useful *Jingji dang'an hanmu huibian* (Catalogue of economic documents) (Taipei: Zhongyang yanjiuyuan, Jindaishisuo, 1987–). For the guides and publications of archives surveyed in this Handbook, see Part I.

None has published a full index or catalogue of all holdings. In addition, there are many collections of original materials in research institutions that are not, in a formal sense, archives, about which little information exists in print. Moreover, none of the available research aids offers a comparative review of holdings—about which collection holds which materials, for which years—of the many official files of the pre-1949 period that were dispersed among Taipei, Nanjing, and various provincial archives. For scholars in need of an overview of available materials on any one field or topic, confronting the mountain of potentially available materials on either side of the Taiwan Strait can be a daunting task.

The first purpose of the Handbook, then, is to provide scholars of Chinese business and economic history with detailed descriptions of major collections in the PRC and on Taiwan. To be sure, these are not the *only* collections: time and space precluded our adding entries on other archives that we surveyed. We have received the assistance of scores of archivists and scholars who know, and have used, each collection surveyed here. Although many individuals contributed particularly to one or another archival description, the archival survey that constitutes Part II of this Handbook is the product of all available information, published and unpublished, and is a truly collaborative, international, scholarly effort.

If Part II aims to assist scholars in locating documents on Chinese business and economic history, Part III tries to help them *read* the variety of materials that they will find. For official documents of the Republican era, there is no greater expert than the late Professor Zhang Wode, of People's University, who kindly gave us permission to translate and edit his authoritative essay, "How to Read Republican Period Documents." We are saddened that Professor Zhang passed away before this Handbook could be completed.

Knowledge of official documentary form, practice, and terminology is essential for the historian of Republican China. But it is not sufficient for studying a period in which the documentary base goes beyond the walls of government to include the private, unofficial, and quasi-official realms of life in twentieth-century China. The Republican era witnessed prodigious efforts at state-building and the rise of a more assertive urban society, a world of both official and private correspondence, of public and private commercial agreements, of diaries as well as draft plans and memoranda. One of the aims of our documents and glossaries is to introduce readers to the structure, organization, and, above all, the *variety* of available historical materials that exist on similar themes, and to assist readers in making professionally competent readings of these materials. We have organized the documents into six sections, telling six different histories of private and public enterprise in Republican China on the mainland and on Taiwan. There is no simple, straightforward structure to each section, but we hope that readers, professors and graduate students alike, will find much to discuss in all of them. To assist with further, original research—the aim of any graduate seminar—we have added to this introductory section a general "Selected Research Aids for the Study of Republican China" developed for the seminar at Harvard.

Taken together, the survey of documentary materials (Part II) and the publication of annotated documents (Part III) seek to further research on the broad theme of "state and economy in Republican China." The Republican era in China has seen great contrasts in attempts by twentieth-century regimes to work out the role of a modern state in a developing economy—ranging from the partial disappearance of the state and the growth of a distinctively Chinese modern capitalism from 1916 to 1927; the promotion of state enterprise at the expense of private capital in the 1930s and 1940s; and the eventually dynamic cohabitation of the Nationalist developmental state with entrepreneurial elites on Taiwan. Only in the past twenty years have scholars begun to investigate the historical evolution of the non-communist Chinese economy in the twentieth century, including the social organization of a distinctively Chinese bourgeoisie; the internationalization of the national economy; the effect of Sino-foreign competition on Chinese business organization; the impact of state controls and the role of economic planning agencies; and the history of specific industries over time.[9] In the last decades of the century, Chinese economies in Taiwan, Hong Kong, and the mainland (where recent structural reform has permitted the return of alternative forms of economic activity) have been among the fastest growing in the world. The study of the roots of that apparent success will be among the most important tasks for scholars of modern China.

*   *   *

Any project such as this has its own history, and there are many people to thank. The initial conception for this endeavor began in 1990 in a graduate seminar on Republican China, co-taught by myself and Professor James Chin Shih at Washington University. We joined with Dr. Lin Man-houng, of the Institute of Modern History of the Academia Sinica, Taiwan, to begin to compile this Handbook in 1993. A Chinese-language survey of Taiwan archives was published by Dr. Lin and the Institute of Modern History in 1995.[10] For many reasons, the larger project has taken much longer. An initial set of formal requests for cooperation, sent to dozens of archives in the PRC and Taiwan, was singularly unsuccessful. The selection and annotation of the documents, overseen by Professor Shih, have gone through many rounds of revision. And, of course, information about individual archives and collections, finally gathered in a much more painstaking fashion than we could have imagined at first, has continued to expand. In the final stages, the collaboration of Professor David Pietz, of Assumption

---

9. See Marie-Claire Bergère, *The Golden Age of the Chinese Bourgeoisie, 1911–37* (Cambridge, Eng.: Cambridge University Press, 1989); Sherman Cochran, *Big Business in China* (Cambridge, Mass.: Harvard University Press, 1980); Parks Coble, *The Shanghai Capitalists and the Nationalist Government* (Cambridge, Mass.: Harvard University, Council on East Asian Studies, 1980); and James Reardon-Anderson, *The Study of Change: Chemistry in China, 1840–1949* (New York: Cambridge University Press, 1991).

10. Lin Manhong (Lin Man-houng), ed., *Taiwan suocang Zhonghua minguo jingji dang'an* (Economic archives in Taiwan of the Republic of China) (Taipei: Zhongyang yanjiuyuan, Jindaishi yanjiusuo, 1995).

College and Harvard's Fairbank Center, whose own research has made extensive use of many of the archives surveyed here, has been essential.

Research for this project has been supported primarily by the National Endowment for the Humanities and by the Chiang Ching-kuo Foundation for International Scholarly Exchange. To these patient patrons, we are most grateful. The project has relied on the institutional support of the Fairbank Center for East Asian Research at Harvard, its directors, Professors James Watson and Ezra Vogel; its Executive Directors, Dr. Robert Murowchick and Ms. Deirdre Chetham; and, critically, the Center's Financial Officer, Ms. Anne Denna. The work of Dr. Lin in Taipei was given strong support by the Institute of Modern History of the Academia Sinica and its former director, Professor Ch'en San-ching.

It is impossible to acknowledge all the institutions and individuals that assisted the archival survey, precisely because so many did. I am grateful in the first instance to Professors Shiwei Chen, Linsun Cheng, and Chuxiong Wei, who assisted in coordinating contacts with archives in the PRC. I am much indebted to the staffs of the Shanghai Academy of Social Sciences, the Shanghai Municipal Archives, the Second Historical Archives, the Suzhou Municipal Archives, and the Beijing Municipal Archives. Professor Kwan Man-bun of the University of Cincinnati generously shared his broad knowledge of the Tianjin Archives. For our Taiwan entries, I am particularly grateful to Dr. Cho Tsun-hung of the Academia Historica, Dr. Kao Shun-shu of the Guomindang Party Archives, and Drs. Chuang Shu-hua, Ch'en Chao-wei, Yeh Lun-hui, Chung Yen-yu, Ch'iu Ching-tun, Chao Yu-chih, Yeh Chen-hui, Chen Chin-man, Chou Hsiu-huan, and Kuo Yun-p'ing, all of whom worked with Dr. Lin in compiling the survey of Taiwan's archives.

Many also worked on the translation of archival reports and the review of glossaries, among them Dr. Hongmin Liang, Dr. Hong Sun, Mr. Paulo Frank, and Dr. Yanming Xiao. Here I should like to offer special thanks to those whose expertise, energy, and good eyesight greatly aided the completion of the Handbook: Professor Shiwei Chen, Mr. Michael Weiss, Mr. Jinbao Qian, and, again, Professor David Pietz, all themselves outstanding young historians of Republican China.

Chapter 2

Notes on the Archives of Republican China[1]

William C. Kirby

Although the existence of state archives has been traced to the fourth and fifth centuries B.C. in the West and perhaps all the way back to the Shang dynasty in China,[2] the establishment of permanent, public, national archival institutions dates only from the French Revolution, with the creation of the Archives Nationales in 1790. The immediate reasons for founding such institutions, such as the British Public Record Office (established 1838), National Archives of the United States (1934), Academia Historica (Guoshiguan) of the Republic of China (1947), or Central Archives (Zhongyang dang'anguan) of the People's Republic of China (1959), have varied, but in their broader purposes they appear to have had several aims in common: to increase bureaucratic efficiency by centralizing the storage of government records, to assist and protect the government by providing an ongoing record of its own activities and commitments, to preserve the cultural/political heritage of the nation as defined by the state, and—finally—to preserve the records of the past for present and future historians.[3] (Arguably, only this last was a main aim of the original Guoshiguan, the State Historiographer's Office under the Qing, whose pre-eminent aim was to manage the dynastic story for posterity.)[4]

Although designed primarily to serve the authorities, modern archives have been best loved by historians. Not long after the founding of the Public Record Office, a report complained: "Our Public Records excite no interest, even in the functionaries whose acts they record, the departments whose proceedings they register; or the proprietors to whose property rights they furnish the most authentic,

---

1. An earlier version of this essay was presented to the Conference on Modern Chinese Historical Archives at the University of California, Berkeley, 1994.

2. See Ernst Posner, *Archives in the Ancient World* (Cambridge, Mass.: Harvard University Press, 1972); *Zhongguo dang'an shiye gaikuang* (The archival endeavor of China) (Beijing: Zhongguo guojia dang'anju, n.d.).

3. See T. R. Schellenberg, *Modern Archives: Principles and Techniques* (Chicago: University of Chicago Press, 1956), pp. 3–10.

4. See Beatrice Bartlett, "Archival Management in the Late Imperial Era," paper presented to the Conference on Modern Chinese Historical Archives at the University of California, Berkeley, 1994.

perhaps the only title-deeds."[5] At the same time, amateur and professional historians in Europe were developing an obsession for unlocking the presumed secrets of archival collections. Thus Ranke wrote passionately of his desire (*Lust*) for the data in archival manuscripts, which he imagined as "so many princesses, possibly beautiful, all under a curse and needing to be saved."[6]

The tension between the purposes of the state, some meant to be kept secret, and the insatiable *Forschungslust* of the modern historical profession, has of course never been resolved. But the very existence of public archives has changed the way historians work. Historians have come to take it for granted that access to archives storing the "primary" materials of history, what Marc Bloch called "the evidence of witnesses in spite of themselves,"[7] is essential to their craft. This is not because primary materials are always superior to narrative sources of earlier generations; nor it is because they are necessarily true—indeed they may be full of lies and distortions. But, as Bloch reminds us, theirs is the "kind of distortion [that] has not been especially designed to deceive posterity."[8]

From the point of view of historians, many of the great advances in archival access in the twentieth century have come when governments have lost their ability to deceive posterity, notably by collapsing in war and revolution. After World War I, European governments competed with each other in the selective publication of documents designed to show how each was innocent of "war guilt"; but it was only after Germany's defeat in World War II, when its archives were seized and microfilmed by the Allies (an event that in turn prompted a fuller opening of Allied archives), that a comprehensive archival investigation of the origins of the first war became possible. More recently, the sudden demise of the Soviet Union and its Eastern European allies—whose archives had been entirely off-limits to scholars—is already having a far-reaching effect on historical research and seems likely to promote greater openness in other archives.[9] Although many governments have adopted policies of unveiling

---

5. House of Commons Select Committee, "On the Perilous State and Neglect of the Public Records," (1848), quoted in Schellenberg, p. 7.

6. Leonard Krieger, *Ranke and the Meaning of History* (Chicago: University of Chicago Press, 1977), p. 105.

7. Marc Bloch, *The Historian's Craft* (New York: Vintage, 1953), p. 61.

8. Ibid., p. 62.

9. See, for example, Mark Kramer, "Archival Research in Moscow," and Kathryn Weathersby, "New Findings on the Korean War," both in *The Cold War International History Project Bulletin,* no. 3 (Fall 1993); Mark Bradley and Robert Brigham, "Vietnamese Archives and Scholarship on the Cold War Period: Two Reports," Working Paper no. 7 of the Cold War International History Project, Woodrow Wilson Center (September 1993); Shuguang Zhang and Jian Chen, *Chinese Communist Foreign Policy and the Cold War in Asia: New Documentary Evidence, 1944–1950* (Chicago: Imprint Publications, 1994); and, most recently, on Sino-Soviet relations, "The Cold War in Asia," *The Cold War International History Project Bulletin,* no. 6/7 (Winter 1995–96); and "Leader

archival materials after the passage of a set amount of time (commonly 30 or 50 years), the historian's best friend remains the government that ceases to govern.

This, after all, is one reason why research in Qing archives has faced fewer political obstacles than has scholarly work on either Nationalist or Communist China. But as the case of the Qing archives demonstrates, the support of governments is essential to the archival endeavor, for the defeat or disappearance of a regime does not by itself open its archive. Early Republican governments were positively lethargic in their approach to records, including their own. The Lishi bowuguan (Historical Museum) founded in the late Qing to house imperial archives was ill-funded and ill-managed under the Qing and then starved under the Republic. The Republican government cared so little about the source materials of its predecessor that tens of thousands of pounds of documents were allowed to be sold for pulp, and more would have been sold had it not been for the determined intervention of private scholars. Matters improved somewhat with the establishment in 1928 of the Institute of History and Philology of the Academia Sinica, but as Lo Hui-min has pointed out, the fact that archival material continued to be measured by weight as late as the Sino-Japanese war was a sign of the "infant state of Chinese archival development."[10] The intervention of the war and civil war meant that it was not until the 1950s that professional archival work would be supported by governments in a manner that ultimately would make the First Historical Archives in Beijing and the National Palace Museum archives in Taipei the world-class institutions that they are today.

Republican archives, too, were neglected in the first half of the century. The Guoshiyuan proposed by Sun Yatsen, renamed Guoshiguan (Academia Historica) under Yuan Shikai (who was seeking no doubt the legitimacy of continuity with the Qing institution), underwent several early incarnations and many false starts before being constituted as the central government archive under the Nationalists. But that did not happen until January 1947. (It says something about the locus of power in Nationalist China that the Nationalist Party Archives were established much earlier, in 1930,[11] perhaps because party archives were deemed more important to the actual working of government.) Even in the 1950s, government ministries in Taiwan were rumored to have sold documentary materials for pulp; it took the passage of legislation to force them to give the Guoshiguan the right of first refusal to their papers. Still, government bodies were free to deposit their archives elsewhere (as the Ministry

---

ship Transition in a Fractured Bloc," *The Cold War International History Project Bulletin,* no. 10 (March 1998).

10. Cyrus Peake, "Documents Available for Research on the Modern History of China," *American Historical Review* 38 (October 1932): 61ff; Lo Hui-min, "Some Notes on Archives on Modern China," in D. Leslie et al., eds., *Essays on the Sources for Chinese History* (Columbia: University of South Carolina Press, 1973), p. 205.

11. *Guoshiguan gaikuang* (Taibei, 1984), pp. 1–3; on the Qing State Historiographer's Office, see Knight Biggerstaff, "Some Notes on the *Tung-hua lu* and the *Shi-lu*," *Harvard Journal of Asiatic Studies* 4, no. 2 (July 1939): 101–15.

of Economic Affairs did with the Institute of Modern History of the Academia Sinica)[12] or to hold on to them themselves, as is the case with the post-1927 materials of the Ministry of Foreign Affairs.

Delay in the opening of Republican, and especially Nationalist-era, historical archives continued after 1949. The lag in systematizing Republican archives on Taiwan reflected the familiar reluctance of governments to release materials about their own recent past, in this case complicated by the continuing state of civil war. Thus the first Nationalist-era documents found in Taiwan to be opened extensively to scholars were captured materials of the Communist movement, housed in the Bureau of Investigation of the Ministry of Justice.[13] Despite prodigious publication projects on Republican history, particularly by the Dangshihui, Guoshiguan, and Institute of Modern History, direct access to archival materials was significantly limited until the 1980s.

For its part, the new PRC government on the mainland showed no interest in promoting scholarship on (as distinct from political study of) Chinese Communist Party (CCP) historical materials. But under the official assumption that the Republican era had definitively ended and that its dynastic history could be written, it devoted its attention to organizing the archives of its Nationalist enemies. The Nanjing Organization Office of the Third Historical Institute of the Academy of Sciences—known later as the Second Historical Archives—was founded in February 1951 to catalogue materials inherited from the Dangshihui, Guoshiguan, and innumerable other collections of Republican archives. Although some materials from these collections would be used in published collections of documents in the 1950s, the enormous scale of the archival work (which centralized Republican records as they had never been under the Republic), the early PRC's official culture of secrecy (which contradicted the very concept of a public archive), and the political disruptions of the years 1958–78 (above all the Cultural Revolution) meant that it was not until 1980 that the collections of the Second Historical Archives could be formally opened to scholarly inquiry.[14]

Since the early 1980s, there has been a revolution in the professional organization and public access of Republican archival materials on both sides of the Taiwan Strait.[15] The Second Archives and

---

12. See *Jingji dang'an hanmu huibian* (Catalogue of economic documents) (Taibei: Zhongyang yanjiuyuan jindaishi yanjiuso, 1987–).

13. See Peter Donovan et al., *Chinese Communist Materials at the Bureau of Investigation Archives, Taiwan* (Ann Arbor: University of Michigan, Center for Chinese Studies, 1976).

14. On the early history of the Second Archives, see *Zhongguo di'er lishi dang'anguan jianming zhinan* (Brief guide to the Second Historical Archives of China) (Beijing: Dang'an chubanshe, 1987), pp. 1–2.

15. See, among other publications, *Dangdai Zhongguo de dang'an shiye* (The archival endeavor in contemporary China) (Beijing: Zhongguo shehui kexue chubanshe, 1988); *Zhongguo dang'an fenlei fa* (Chinese archival classification methods) (Beijing: Dang'an chubanshe, 1987); *Zhongguo dang'an nianjian* (Chinese Archival Yearbook) (Beijing: Dang'an chubanshe, 1992–); Lu Shou-chang, *Xiandai shiyong dang'an guanli xue* (Contemporary archival management) (Taibei, 1983); and *Guoshiguan gaikuang* (Overview of Academia Historica)

several major provincial and municipal archives in the PRC, as well as the Guoshiguan and the Institute of Modern History of the Academia Sinica on Taiwan, now have state-of-the-art storage facilities, preservation programs, cataloguing systems, and retrieval capacities.

Most important for this Handbook, PRC archives—particularly the Second Archives and the Shanghai Archives—have redefined the nature of a state archive, with holdings that extend well beyond those of formal government bodies. If revolutions are a historian's best friend, a Communist revolution must be the best friend of the business historian. The early PRC completed the nationalization of all Chinese and foreign companies, whose assets, including their archives, thereby belonged to the state. As a result, PRC archives are responsible for the papers of non-governmental, Republican-era institutions such as private industrial companies, banks, and educational institutions that came under government (*guoying*) management either in the later stages of Guomindang rule or in the first years of Communist authority. The Shanghai Municipal Archives, for example, holds records of private organizations and firms ranging from chambers of commerce to tobacco companies,[16] and in 1993 received the archives of nine major commercial banks of the Republican era whose papers had been housed with the People's Bank of China. The Business History Archive of the Economics Institute of the Shanghai Academy of Social Sciences, established in 1992, also has major holdings of pre-1949 commercial firms and has quickly become a major resource for historians of Chinese business. As this Handbook suggests, these are but a few of the "private" treasures of PRC archives.

The impact on international scholarship of this newfound archival openness and diversity has been stunning, as old fields are revisited and new ones initiated. In the study of Shanghai alone, Elizabeth Perry has reopened the field of labor history, which had lain dormant in the West since the work of Jean Chesneaux;[17] Frederic Wakeman has brought to light the dark, underworld struggles of the police and their adversaries;[18] Emily Honig has investigated migrant culture, Jeffrey Wasserstrom student culture, Wen-hsin Yeh banking culture—all assisted by archival sources that were not open to

---

(Taibei: Guoshiguan, 1984). Professional and scholarly periodicals reviewing the state of archival work include *Dang'an gongzuo* (Archival work) (Beijing); *Dang'an yanjiu* (Archival research) (Beijing); *Dang'an qingbao* (Archival reports) (Beijing); *Dang'anxue tongxun* (Archival studies newsletter) (Beijing); *Shanghai dang'an gongzuo* (Shanghai archival work) (Shanghai); and *Jindai Zhongguo shi yanjiu tongxun* (Newsletter for modern Chinese history) (Taibei).

16. *Shanghai shi dang'anguan jianming zhinan* (Concise guide to the Shanghai Municipal Archives) (Beijing: Dang'an chubanshe, 1991); Parks M. Coble, "Business History Research in Shanghai," *Chinese Business History* 1, no. 2 (April 1991): 5–7.

17. Elizabeth J. Perry, *Shanghai on Strike* (Stanford: Stanford University Press, 1993); Jean Chesneaux, *The Chinese Labor Movement, 1919–1927* (Stanford: Stanford University Press, 1968).

18. Frederic Wakeman, Jr., *Shanghai Police* (Berkeley: University of California Press, 1996).

research until the mid-1980s.[19] If until then scholars despaired of gaining substantial access to Republican archives, the danger today may be of a surfeit of materials, even if full public access to archives, including their catalogues and finding aids, is still by no means the rule. Certainly few serious research proposals in Republican Chinese history can now omit mention of the multiple archival collections in China and Taiwan that might bear on a topic.

This new situation serves to remind us of how far the practice of archival opening has come in a very short period and, at the same time, how incomplete it remains. It is striking to recall that the major works that defined the field of "Republican China" in the West until around 1990 were based on little or no Chinese archival evidence. For example, influential studies of the Nationalist regime by Qian Duansheng (Tuan-sheng Ch'ien), Lloyd Eastman, and Tien Hung-mao[20] had to be based primarily on published material of the period. Seminal works on social and economic history relied mainly on materials available outside China, for example, the investigations of the north China plain conducted by the Research Bureau of the South Manchurian Railway Company.[21] Indeed, a distinguishing trait of the entire body of Western historiography of Republican China has been its heavy debt to *non-Chinese* archival material. Compared, for example, with modern U.S., British, French, or German history, the use of foreign archives in this field has played an unusually important role.

The historical "archive gap" is now closing fast for historians of Republican China in both its mainland and Taiwan eras—the wealth of materials described in this Handbook simply in the fields of business and economic history makes that clear. For the materials of post-1950 Taiwan, although the ROC has still not passed its much debated Archive Law (now with a Freedom of Information Act attached to it), both the Guoshiguan, which has inherited the Chiang Kai-shek papers, and the Guomindang Dangshihui are following the lead of the Institute of Modern History in making available archival materials of the 1950s and 1960s.

Unfortunately, the same cannot yet be said for archives in the PRC. As a result, a new—or more accurately, a continuing—archive gap exists for those who wish to write the history of the

---

19. Emily Honig, "Migrant Culture in Shanghai: In Search of a Subei Identity"; Jeffrey Wasserstrom, "The Evolution of Shanghai Student Protest Repertoire," both in Frederic Wakeman, Jr., and Wen-hsin Yeh, eds., *Shanghai Sojourners* (Berkeley: University of California, Institute of East Asian Studies, 1992); Wen-hsin Yeh, "Corporate Space, Communal Time: Everyday Life in Shanghai's Bank of China," paper presented at the Luce Seminar on Commerce and Culture in Shanghai, 1895–1937, Cornell University, August 1992.

20. Qian Duansheng, *Minguo zhengzhi shi* (Shanghai: Shangwu, 1946); Lloyd Eastman, *The Abortive Revolution* (Cambridge, Mass.: Harvard University Press, 1974); Hung-mao Tien, *Government and Politics in Kuomintang China* (Stanford: Stanford University Press, 1972).

21. For example, Ramon Myers, *The Chinese Peasant Economy* (Cambridge, Mass.: Harvard University Press, 1970; Philip C. C. Huang, *Peasant Economy and Social Change in North China* (Stanford: Stanford University Press, 1985); and, most recently, Prasenjit Duara, *Culture, Power, and the State* (Stanford: Stanford University Press, 1988).

Communist movement and of the PRC (one reason this Handbook is limited to "Republican China"). Western works that disagreed on the nature of the pre-1949 Communist movement[22] were united in their inability to use the main collections of historical materials in the CCP/PRC Central Archives or Central Military Commission Archives (Zhongyang junwei dang'anguan). This is still the case. Whereas the archives of the Comintern and its activities in China are open and are gradually being published,[23] there is no independent, archive-based scholarship of it emanating from China itself.

History did not end in 1949. To be sure, it is possible to do important work on the CCP and the early PRC in selected provincial and local archives.[24] The PRC has promulgated a high-sounding, and indeed well-meaning, Archive Law that promises the release of most materials after 30 years.[25] Yet in terms of access to most PRC archives, history still ends with "liberation." The archival story of our field seems, then, to be repeating itself: just when the opening of Chinese Republican archives has redressed the international imbalance of historical materials, an even greater imbalance has emerged for the years after 1949.[26] British Foreign Office documents written on (and in) China are declassified through the late 1960s. Those of the German Democratic Republic and its party leadership are catalogued and open through the year 1989 (another happy result of a fallen government); those of the pre-1991 Soviet Union are opening more gradually, but opening nonetheless, led by the former Baltic republics. We know from published guides that the large majority of extant Chinese archival material deals with the years after 1949. But while the archives of the imperialists as well as of the socialist brethren now welcome historians, those of contemporary China remain almost exclusively—true enough to the original purpose of archives—in the service of the state.

---

22. For example, Mark Selden, *The Yenan Way* (Cambridge, Mass.: Harvard University Press, 1971); and Chalmers Johnson, *Peasant Nationalism and Communist Power* (Stanford: Stanford University Press, 1962).

23. See *Die Komintern und die national-revolutionäre Bewegung in China: Dokumente,* vol. 1, *1920–1925,* ed. Russischen Zentrum für Archivierung und Erforschung von Dokumenten zur neuesten Geschichte, Ostasiatischen Seminar der FU Berlin und dem Institut für den Fernen Osten, Russischen Akademie der Wissenschaften (Paderborn: Schöningh, 1966); vol. 2, *1926–27,* 2 pts. (1997).

24. See, for example, Joseph W. Esherick, "Deconstructing the Construction of the Party-State: Gulin County in the Shaan-Gan-Ning Border Region," *China Quarterly,* no. 140 (1994): 1052–79; and Perry, *Shanghai on Strike.*

25. For both the promise and the substantial restrictions in the PRC's recent (1987, revised 1996) Archive Law, see *Zhonghua renmin gongheguo dang'anfa* (Archive Law of the People's Republic of China) (Beijing: Dang'an chubanshe, 1988). For the text of the 1996 law, see *Zhongguo dang'an* (Chinese archives), August 1996.

26. For a reasoned analysis based on quite incompatible source bases, see Gordon H. Chang and He Di, "The Absence of War in the U.S.-China Confrontation over Quemoy," *American Historical Review* 98, no. 5 (December 1993): 1500–1524.

Chapter 3

Selected Research Aids for the Study of Republican China

William C. Kirby

With the Assistance of Jinbao Qian and Michael Weiss

This bibliography was developed for the research seminar on twentieth-century China at Harvard University. It reflects the research priorities of that seminar and covers "Republican China," broadly conceived, including some materials on the early PRC and on the ROC on Taiwan. Such a list, however long, is always incomplete and always out of date.[1] This list aims to introduce students to the variety of reference materials available and to many of the most useful reference tools as of 1999. It is subdivided into the following categories:

I.   Selected Bibliographies and Research Guides
II.   Indexes and Yearbooks
III.   General and Specialized Histories
IV.   Government Gazettes and Journals
V.   Local History and Gazetteers
VI.   Biographical Sources and Memoirs
VII.   Published Documents
VIII.   Newspapers and Periodicals

I. Selected Bibliographies and Research Guides

A. Historical Dictionaries

Chen Xulu. *Zhonghua minguoshi cidian* 中華民國史辭典 (Dictionary of Republican Chinese history). Shanghai: Shanghai renmin chubanshe, 1991.
Shang Hai et al. *Minguoshi da cidian* 民國史大辭典 (Great dictionary of Republican Chinese history). Beijing: Guangbo dianshi chubanshe, 1991.

---

1. To augment this list, see the very useful Modern Chinese History website of the University of California, San Diego: *http://orpheus.ucsd.edu/chinesehistory*.

Yang Liqiang and Liu Qikui. *Jianming Zhonghua minguoshi cidian* 簡明中華民國史辭典 (Concise dictionary of Republican Chinese history). Zhengzhou: Henan renmin chubanshe, 1989.

B. Bibliographies of Reference Works

In English

Fairbank, John K., & Kwang-ching Liu. *An Annotated Bibliography of Selected Chinese Reference Works*. 3d ed. 2 vols. Cambridge, Mass.: Harvard University Press, 1971. Guide to Chinese reference works, including bibliographies.

Nathan, Andrew J. *Modern China 1840–1972: An Introduction to Sources and Research Aids.* Ann Arbor: Center for Chinese Studies, University of Michigan, 1973. An introductory guide to relevant source material. Especially useful for those inexperienced at using Chinese materials.

Teng Ssu-yu & Knight Biggerstaff. *An Annotated Bibliography of Selected Chinese Reference Works*. 3d ed. 2 vols. Cambridge, Mass.: Harvard University Press, 1971. A very useful guide to Chinese reference works in general and bibliographies in particular. Some entries concerning the Republican period.

Tsien Tsuen-hsuin with James K. M. Cheng. *China: An Annotated Bibliography of Bibliographies*. Boston: G. K. Hall, 1978. An extremely useful work for specialized bibliographical materials in all languages. Organized by subject.

In Chinese

Teng Yingjing. *Zhongguo lishi yanjiu gongju shu zhiyin* 中國歷史研究工具書指引 (Guide to research aids on Chinese history). Hong Kong, 1968. Mostly Chinese titles, but some Japanese and English.

Ying Yugang & Xie Yunfei. *Zhongwen gongju shu zhiyin* 中文工具書指引 (Guide to Chinese reference aids). Taibei: Langdai shuju, 1975. Eleven subject headings, partially annotated. Indexed by titles.

C. General Bibliographies

In Western Languages

Bibliography of Asian Studies. Published by the Association of Asian Studies. Formerly *Bulletin of Far Eastern Bibliography,* 1936–40; *Far Eastern Bibliography,* 1941–56; *Journal of*

Asian Studies Bibliography, 1956–69. A comprehensive, annual bibliography of Western-language works on Asia. Organized by subject.

Fairbank, John K., ed. *The Cambridge History of China*, vol. 13, *Republican China, 1912–1949.* 2 vols. Cambridge, Eng.: Cambridge University Press, 1986. Each volume includes useful bibliographies and topical bibliographical essays.

Fairbank, John K., & Merle Goldman. *China: A New History.* Enl. ed. Cambridge, Mass.: Harvard University Press, 1998. Includes a lengthy, annotated "Suggested Reading" list.

Fairbank, John K., & Kwang-ching Liu. *Modern China: A Bibliographical Guide to Chinese Works, 1898–1937.* Cambridge, Mass.: Harvard University Press, 1949; reprinted 1961. An extensive annotated bibliography of materials in Chinese published between 1898 and 1937. Organized by subject.

Fairbank, John K., Masataka Banno, & Sumiko Yamamoto. *Japanese Studies of Modern China.* Cambridge, Mass.: Harvard University Press, 1971. An annotated bibliography of Japanese history and social science works on China published to 1953.

Fogel, Joshua A. *Recent Japanese Studies of Modern Chinese History (II): Translations from Shigaku Zasshi for 1983–1986.* Armonk, N.Y.: M. E. Sharp, 1979. Articles on China from the Ming onward.

Hayford, Charles W. *China.* Cambridge, Mass.: ABC Clio, 1997. World Bibliographical Series 35. An extensive, annotated bibliography, primarily of books in Western languages, covering all fields, with indexes by author, title, and subject.

Kamachi, Noriko, John K. Fairbank, & Chuzo Ichiko. *Japanese Studies of Modern China Since 1953.* Cambridge, Mass.: Harvard University Press, 1975. Same as the Fairbank, Banno, & Yamamoto volume but covering the period 1953–69.

Kiyohara, Michiko. *China Watching by the Japanese from the First Sino-Japanese War to the Unification of China Under the Communist Party: A Checklist of Holdings in the East Asian Collection, Hoover Institution.* Stanford: Hoover Institution Press, 1987.

Lai, Chi-kong. "Enterprise History: Studies and Archives." *Chinese Studies in History* 31, no. 3/4 (Summer 1998): 169–99.

Lee, Don Y. *An Annotated Bibliography of Selected Works on China.* Bloomington: University of Indiana Press, 1981.

Leslie, Donald D., Colin Mackerras, & Wang Gungwu. *Essays on the Sources for Chinese History.* Canberra: Australian National University Press, 1973. Bibliographical surveys and essays on genealogies, gazetteers, newspapers, archival materials, etc. See Jean Chesneaux's interesting study on lexicology as a source for modern Chinese history.

Lust, John, ed. *Index Sinicus.* Cambridge, Mass.: Harvard University Press, 1964. A comprehensive index of articles on China in Western languages published between 1920 and 1955 in periodicals or other collective publications.

Revue Bibliographique de Sinologie, vols. 1–12 (1955–67). An annual bibliography of works on China in Chinese, Japanese, and Western languages with short reviews in French or English.

Skinner, G. William, ed. *Modern Chinese Society: An Analytical Bibliography.* 3 vols. Stanford: Stanford University Press, 1973. A fairly comprehensive bibliography aimed at the social sciences. Separate volumes cover materials in Chinese, Japanese, and Western languages. The system of annotation is complex; so read the introduction carefully.

Tanis, Norman E., et al. *China in Books: A Basic Bibliography in Western Languages.* Greenwich, Conn.: Jai Press, 1979. Not very comprehensive.

Tung, Julia. *Bibliography of Chinese Government Serials, 1880–1949.* Stanford: Stanford University Press, 1979; and *Bibliography of Chinese Academic Serials, Pre-1949.* Stanford: Stanford University Press, 1982. Alphabetical listings of government and academic serials in the library of the Hoover Institution. No annotation or subject headings.

Yu, P. K., ed. *Research Materials on Twentieth Century China: An Annotated List of CCRM Publications.* Washington, D.C.: Association of Research Libraries, Center for Chinese Research Materials, 1975.

In Chinese or Japanese

Bashi nianlai shixue shumu 八十年來史學書目 (Guide to the historiography of the past 80 years). Beijing, 1984. A guide to Chinese-language works published between 1900 and 1980 on Chinese and world history. Arranged by topic; author index.

Beijing xiandai geming shi ziliao mulu suoyin 北京現代革命史資料目錄索引 (Index to bibliographical sources on Beijing's modern revolutionary history). Beijing: Zhonggong dangshi chubanshe, 1981.

Gao Mingshi. *Zhongguo yanjiu zhinan, di wu juan, Jindaishi xiandaishi* 中國研究指南 (第五卷): 近代史現代史 (Guide to China research, vol. 5, modern and contemporary history). Taibei: Lianjing chuban, 1990.

He Dong. *Zhongguo jindai shiliao xuegao* 中國近代史料學稿 (Preliminary compilation of historical source materials for modern China). Beijing: Zhongguo renmin daxue chubanshe, 1990.

Sun Yuesheng & Chen Shumei. *Meiguo Zhongguo xue shouce* 美國中國學手冊 (Handbook for China studies in the United States). Beijing: Zhongguo shehui kexue chubanshe, 1993.

Yang Guoxiong (Peter Yeung) & Li Shutian (Lai Shi Tim). *Xiandai lunwenji wen-shi-zhe lunwen suoyin* 現代論文集 (文史哲) 論文索引 (Chinese studies: an index to collections of essays on literature, history, and philosophy). Hong Kong: University of Hong Kong, Center of Asian Studies, 1979.

Yu Ping-kuen. *Zhongguo shixue lunwen yinde* 中國史學論文引得 (Index to learned articles on Chinese history). 2 vols. Hong Kong: Xianggang yadong xueshe, 1963, 1970. Vol. 1, 1902–62. Articles indexed generally relate to Chinese history, but articles on culture, literature, philosophy, society, and economics are also included.

Zhang Gefei et al. *Zhongguo xiandai shiliaoxue* 中國現代史料學 (Historiography of modern China). Beijing: Qiushi chubanshe, 1987.

Zhang Haihui & Wang Yuzhi. *Jianguo yilai Zhongguo shixue lunwenji pianmu suoyin* 建國以來中國史學論文集篇目索引 (Index of compendia of Chinese history papers since the establishment of the PRC). Beijing: Zhonghua shuju, 1992.

Zhang Xianwen. *Zhongguo xiandaishi shiliaoxue* 中國現代史史料學 (The study of historical materials on modern Chinese history). Ji'nan: Shandong renmin chubanshe, 1985. Provides a comprehensive annotated bibliography of pre-1949 Chinese periodicals.

Zhang Zhuhong. *Zhongguo xiandai gemingshi shiliaoxue* 中國現代革命史史料學 (Historiography of the Chinese revolution). Beijing: Zhonggong dangshi ziliao chubanshe, 1987.

Zhongguo shehui kexue yuan, Lishisuo, Jingjishi zu (Chinese Academy of Social Science, History Institute, Economic History Group). *Bashi nianlai shixue shumu, 1900–1980* 八十年來史學書目, 1900–1980年 (Catalogue of historical works over the past 80 years, 1900–1980). Beijing: Zhongguo shuhui kexue chubanshe, 1984.

———. *Zhongguo shehui jingjishi lunzhu mulu* 中國社會經濟史論著目錄 (List of works on Chinese socioeconomic history). Ji'nan: Qilu shushe, 1988.

Zhongguo shehui kexue yuan, Lishi yanjiusuo. *Guoneiwai youguan jinxiandaishi shumu yilan, 1949–1977* 國內外有關近現代史書目一覽, 1949–1977年 (List of books on modern history published in China and abroad). Beijing: Zhongguo shehui kexue yuan, Lishi yanjiusuo, 1978.

Zhongguo shixue lunwen suoyin 中國史學論文索引 (Index to learned articles on Chinese history). 2 vols. Beijing: Zhongguo kexue yuan, Lishi yanjiusuo, and Beijing daxue lishixi, 1957, 1980. Vol. 1 covers articles published from 1900 to 1937; vol. 2, 1937 to 1949.

Zhongguo xiandaishi shuping xuanji 中國現代史書評選輯 (Collection of reviews of modern Chinese history books). Taibei: Guoshiguan, 1990– .

Zhongyang yanjiuyuan, Jindaishi yanjiusuo tongren zhuzuo mulu 中央研究院近代史研究所同仁著作目錄 (Catalogue of works by fellows of the Institute of Modern History, Academia Sinica). Taibei, 1981.

Zhou Yuanping. *Kangri zhanzheng shi cankao ziliao mulu (1937–1945)* 抗日戰爭史參考資料目錄 (1937–1945) (Bibliography of the history of the War of Resistance Against Japan). Chengdu: Sichuan daxue chubanshe, 1985.

D. Specialized Bibliographies and Research Guides

1. CCP History and Historiography

Feuerwerker, Albert, and S. Cheng. *Chinese Communist Studies of Modern Chinese History.* Cambridge, Mass.: Harvard University, East Asian Research Center, 1967.

Li Yongpu. *Zhongguo gongchandang lishi baokan minglu, 1919–1949* 中國共產黨歷史報刊名錄 (1919–1949) (Index to newspapers and journals of CCP history, 1919–1949).

Lieberthal, Kenneth. *A Research Guide to Central Party and Government Meetings in China, 1949–1975.* New York: Arts and Sciences Institute, 1976.

Wilbur, C. Martin, ed. *Chinese Sources on the History of the Chinese Communist Movement.* New York: Columbia University, East Asia Institute, 1950.

Wu Tien-wei. *The Kiangsi Soviet Republic, 1931–1934: A Selected and Annotated Bibliography of the Ch'en Cheng Collection.* Cambridge, Mass: Harvard-Yenching Library, Harvard University, 1981.

Zhongguo lishixue nianjian 中國歷史學年鑒 (Yearbook of Chinese historical studies). Beijing: Sanlian shudian chubanshe, 1979– . Annual review of current historical work in the PRC.

Zhongguo renmin daxue tushuguan (China People's University Library), comp. *Jiefang qu genjudi tushu mulu* 解放區根据地圖書目錄 (List of books published in the liberated base areas). Beijing: Zhongguo renmin daxue chubanshe, 1989.

2. Foreign Relations, Foreigners in China

Bauer, Wolfgang, ed. *German Impact on Modern Chinese Intellectual History: A Bibliography of Chinese Publications.* Wiesbaden, Germany: Steiner Verlag, 1982. Much more than intellectual history. It lists Chinese works related to Germany and includes works on Germany, Sino-German relations, translations of German works, etc.

Cohen, Warren I. *Pacific Passage: The Study of American–East Asian Relations on the Eve of the Twenty-First Century.* New York: Columbia University, 1996. Several chapters review the historiography of Sino-American relations.

Esser, Alfons. *Biliographie zu den Deutsch-Chinesischen Beziehungen, 1860–1945.* Munich, 1984.

Ichiko, Chuzo, ed. *Kindai Chûgoku: Nitchû kankei toshomokuroku* 近代中國：日中關係圖書目錄 (Bibliograpy of modern China: Sino-Japanese relations). Tokyo, 1979. Supplement published in 1980.

Mote, F. W. *Japanese Sponsored Governments in China, 1937–1945: An Annotated Bibliography Compiled from Materials in the Chinese Collection of the Hoover Library.* Stanford: Stanford University Press, 1954.

Sino-Soviet Conflict: A Historical Bibliography. Santa Barbara, Calif.: ABC-CLIO Information Services, 1985.

Teng Ssu-yu & John K. Fairbank. *Research Guide for China's Response to the West: A Documentary Survey, 1839–1923.* Cambridge, Mass.: Harvard University Press, 1954.

Wang Chi. *History of U.S.-China Relations: A Bibliographical Research Guide.* McLean, Va.: Academic Press of America, 1991.

Yamane Yukio, ed. *Kindai Nitchû kankeishi kenkyû nyumon* 近代日中關係史研究入門 (Research guide to modern Sino-Japanese relations). Tokyo: Kenbun Shuppan, 1996. The most up-to-date and comprehensive guide on the subject.

3. Popular Rebellion, Student Movements, and Secret Societies

Chan, Ming K. *Historiography of the Chinese Labor Movement, 1895–1949: A Bibliography.* Stanford: Stanford University Press, 1981. A critical survey and bibliography of Chinese source materials. Based on the Hoover Institution's collections.

Chow Tse-tsung. *Research Guide to the May Fourth Movement: Intellectual Revolution in Modern China, 1915–1924.* Cambridge, Mass.: Harvard University Press, 1963.

Israel, John W. *The Chinese Student Movement, 1927–1937: A Bibliographical Essay Based on the Resources of the Hoover Institution.* Stanford: Stanford University Press, 1959. Organized by topic; no index.

Teng Ssu-yu. *Protest and Crime in China: A Bibliography of Secret Associations, Popular Uprisings, Peasant Rebellions.* New York: Garland, 1981. Primary and secondary sources on some of the less civilized aspects of Chinese civilization. Divided into sections of Asian- and Western-language materials; with subject index.

Zhongguo huidangshi lunzhu huiyao 中國會黨史論著匯要 (Guide to works on Chinese secret societies). Tianjin: Nankai daxue chubanshe, 1985. Works on secret societies up to the 1911 Revolution. Organized by period with an author index.

4. Women

Cheng, Lucie, Charlotte Furth, & Hong-ming Yip. *Women in China: A Bibliography of Available English Language Materials.* Berkeley: University of California Press, 1984.

Wei, Karen. *Women in China: A Selected and Annotated Bibliography.* Westport, Conn.: Greenwood Press, 1984.

5. Miscellaneous

Attar, Chand. *Tibet, Past and Present: A Select Bibliography with Chronology of Historical Events, 1660–1981.* New Dehli: Sterling, 1981.

Chang Hsu-hsin. *Bibliography of Sun Yat-sen in China's Republican Revolution, 1885–1925.* Lanham, Md.: University Press of America, 1991.

Häggman, Bertil. *Chinese Intelligence and Internal Security, Past and Present: A Bibliographical Selection with Introduction.* N.p.: Foundation for Conflict Analysis, 1979.

Zhongguo nongye jingji wenxian mulu, 1900–1981 中國農業經濟文獻目錄, 1900–1981年 (Catalogue of literature on the Chinese agricultural economy, 1900–1981). Beijing: Nongye chubanshe, 1988. Chinese sources, organized by topic and then chronologically by document date. Mostly journal and newspaper articles.

E. Bibliographies of Dissertations

Gordon, Leonard H. D., and Frank J. Shulman. *Doctoral Dissertations on China: A Bibliography of Studies in Western Languages, 1945–1970.* Seattle: University of Washington Press, 1972. Author, subject, and institutional indexes.

Li Guangyi. *Zhongguo xiandaishi lunwen shumu suoyin: 1949.10-1984.12* 中國現代史論文書目索引, 1949年10月－1984年12月 (Index to articles and books on modern Chinese history, October 1949 to December 1984). Kaifeng: Henan daxue chubanshe, 1986.

Rong, Tianlin. *Zhongguo xiandaishi lunwen zhuzuo mulu suoyin, 1949–1981* 中國現代史論文著作目錄索引, 一九四九年——一九八一年 (Index to articles and books on modern Chinese history, 1949–81). Beijing: Beijing daxue chubanshe, 1986.

Schulman, Frank J. *Doctoral Dissertations on China: A Bibliography of Studies in Western Languages.* Seattle: University of Washington Press, 1978. Useful for checking on dissertations that might not show up in other bibliographies.

University Microfilms International. *China and the Chinese: A Dissertation Bibliography.* Ann Arbor, 1979. Published dissertations.

II. Indexes and Yearbooks

A. <u>Indexes</u>

In Japanese

*Kyûshokuminchi kankei kikan kankôbutsu sogo mokuroku: Taiwan hen*舊殖民地關係機關刊
行目錄：台灣編 (General index of publications by colonial institutions). Tokyo: Ajia
Keizai Kenkyujo, 1973.

Kyûshokuminchi kankei kikan kankôbutsu sogo mokuroku: Manshûkoku Kantôshu hen 舊殖
民地關係機關刊行目錄：滿州・關東州編 (General index of publications by colonial
institutions: Manchukuo and Guandong). Tokyo: Ajia Keizai Kenkyujo, 1975.

In Chinese

Beijing tushuguan. *Minguo shiqi zong shumu* 民國時期總書目 (A general list of books from the
Republican period). Beijing: Shumu wenxian chubanshe, 1994.

Dongfang zazhishe, ed. *Minguo zhiguan biao, 1911–1981* 民國職官表, 1911–1981年 (Tables of
Republican government officials, 1911–1981). Taibei: Wenhai chubanshe, 1981.

Fudan daxue, Lishixi. *Wushier zhong wenshi ziliao pianmu fenlei suoyin* 五十二種文史資料
篇目分類索引 (Catagorized index to 52 compilations of literary and historical materials).
Shanghai: Fudan daxue chubanshe.

Guo Tingyi & Li Minshu, eds. *Zhongguo xiandaishi ziliao diaocha suoyin* 中國現代史資料調
查索引(Index of source materials on modern Chinese history). Taibei: Zhongyang
yanjiuyuan, Jindaishi yanjiusuo, 1969. For Republican China, pp. 9–10, 22–40, 40–52,
and 97–129 are useful; 140 "revolutionary personalities" are listed. The list of martyrs of
the War of Resistance and campaigns for extermination of Communists includes some 700
persons. The checklist provides the names of GMD leaders in Wade-Giles transcription,
arranged in alphabetical order.

Li Yongpu. *Quanguo geji zhengxie wenshi ziliao pianmu suoyin, 1960–1990* 全國各級政協文
史資料篇目索引, 1960–1990年 (National index to literary and historical materials,
1960–90). 5 vols. Beijing: Zhongguo wenshi chubanshe, 1992.

Shanghai tushuguan, comp. *Zhongguo jindai xiandai congshu mulu suoyin* 中國近代現代叢書
目錄索引 (Index to the modern Chinese history series). Shanghai: Shanghai tushuguan,
1982.

Zhonggong zhongyang dangxiao, Yanjiushi, comp. *Xin minzhu zhuyi geming shiqi yingyin
geming qikan suoyin: Kangri zhanzheng shiqi* 新民主主義革命時期影印革命期刊索

引：抗日戰爭時期 (Index to reprinted revolutionary journals of the New Democatic Revolution Period: the War of Resistance Against Japan). Beijing: Zhonggong zhongyang dangxiao chubanshe, 1987.

Zhongguo geming bowuguan, Ziliaoshi, comp. *Ershiliu zhong yingyin geming qikan suoyin* 二十六種影印革命期刊索引 (Index to 26 reprinted revolutionary journals). Beijing: Renmin chubanshe, 1988.

B. Yearbooks

In English

China Handbook. New York: Macmillan, 1937/45–1956/57.

The China Year Book. Ed. H. G. Woodhead. Tianjin and Shanghai, 1912–39, more or less annual. Information on various contemporary topics, such as Chinese government organizations, important events, biographical data on Chinese leaders, the economy, banking, professionals, and foreign affairs.

China Yearbook. Taibei: China Publishing, 1958/59–1980.

The Chinese Year Book. Shanghai: Commercial Press, 1935/36–1944/45.

Republic of China yearbook. Taibei: Guanghua chubanshe, 1989– .

In Chinese

Caizheng nianjian 財政年鑒 (Finance yearbook). Shanghai: Shangwu yinshuguan. 3 issues (1935, 1944, 1948). Materials primarily drawn from the files of the Ministry of Finance, though some were culled from contemporary printed sources. The material in each issue extends up to the time of publication.

Di yi hui Zhongguo nianjian 第一回中國年鑒 (China yearbook, no. 1). Shanghai: Shangwu yinshuguan, 1924; reprinted, 1927. This yearbook emphasizes government organization, but also features sections on population, industry, etc.

Dongbei nianjian 東北年鑒 (Manchuria yearbook). Shenyang: Dongbei wenhuashe nianjian bianyinchu, 1931. Only one issue appeared before the Manchurian Incident of September 1931. It covers political, economic, and geographical information between 1912 and 1931.

Dongbei yaolan 東北要覽 (Manchuria survey). Heilongjiang: Guoli dongbei daxue, 1944. A handbook on Manchuria up to 1944.

Guofang nianjian 國防年鑒 (National defense yearbook). 1948; Hong Kong reprint, 1969. Useful information on the Marshall Mission.

Guomin zhengfu nianjian 國民政府年鑒 (National government yearbook). Chongqing: Guomin zhengfu, Xingzheng yuan, 1943, 1944, 1946. The official source for publicly disclosed data on central and provincial government activities.

Minguo shiba nian Zhongguo Guomindang nianjian 民國十八年中國國民黨年鑒 (GMD yearbook, 1929). Nanjing: Zhongguo Guomindang zhongyang weiyuanhui, Dangshi weiyuanhui, 1930.

Nanyang nianjian 南洋年鑒 (Southeast Asia yearbook). Singapore: Nanyang shangbao, 1939, 1951. Presents information (mostly trade and financial) on various Southeast Asian countries and includes long sections on overseas Chinese in the region.

Neizheng nianjian 內政年鑒 (Internal affairs yearbook). Shanghai: Shangwu yinshuguan, 1936. Contains information regarding central and local government, police adminstration, land policies, ceremonies and customs, public health, and other domestic matters from the beginning of the Republic until 1934/35. Compiled by the Ministry of the Interior.

Renmin shouce 人民手冊 (People's handbook). Shanghai (1950–52), Tianjin (1953, 1955–56), Beijing (1960–65): Dagongbao chubanshe. An important research tool, it contains general information on the early People's Republic, including some official documents unavailable elsewhere.

Shenbao nianjian 申報年鑒 (*Shenbao* yearbook). Shanghai: Shanghai Shenbaoguan, 1933–36; 1944. Emphasis on political and economic affairs. Laws and official regulations are reproduced in its pages; it also covers government, diplomatic affairs, finance, and national defense to intellectual and religious affairs, education, geography, and public health (and numerous other categories). The 1944 edition is a continuation of the 1936 edition and contains useful information about conditions during the Sino-Japanese War.

Shijie nianjian 世界年鑒 (World yearbook). 3 vols. Shanghai: Datong shuju, 1931. Two of the three volumes are devoted to China, with a special emphasis on foreign relations.

Tiedao nianjian, 1931–1932 鐵道年鑒, 1931–1932年 (Railroad yearbook, 1931–32). Nanjing: Tiedao bu, Tiedao nianjian bianzhuan weiyuanhui, 1933. Presents data on the history of Chinese railways and their organization, administration, regulation, condition, activities, and planning. Includes a number of maps and tables.

Wuhan ribao nianjian 武漢日報年鑒 (*Wuhan Daily* yearbook). Hankou.

Yang Jialuo. *Zhonghua minguo zhiguan nianbiao* 中華民國職官年表 (Yearbook of ROC officials). Taibei: Dingwen shuju, 1978. This volume covers the period 1912–28.

Zhang Pengyuan, ed. *Guomin zhengfu zhiguan nianbiao* 國民政府職官年表 (Annual list of Nationalist government officials). Nangang: Zhongyang yanjiuyuan, 1987.

Zhonggong nianbao 中共年報 (Annual report on Chinese communism). Taibei: Zhonggong yanjiu zazhishe, 1967– . Formerly *Feiqing nianbao* 匪情年報 (Annual report on the bandit situation). Material derived from ROC military intelligence.

Zhongguo jiaoyu nianjian 中國教育年鑒 (China education yearbook). Shanghai: Kaiming shudian, 1934; Shanghai: Shangwu yinshuguan, 1948; Taibei: Zhengzhong shuju, 1957. Combined, these three issues contain data relating to the development of education in China from the beginning of the twentieth century down to 1949 and to the mid-1950s in Taiwan.

Zhongguo jingji nianjian 中國經濟年鑒 (China economic yearbook). Shanghai: Shangwu yinshuguan, 1932–36. Compiled by the Chinese Ministry of Industry. Statistical tables and topical studies.

Zhongguo jingji nianjian 中國經濟年鑒 (China economic yearbook). Hong Kong: Taipingyang jingji yanjiushe, 1947; Huanan xinwenshe, 1948. Identical except for advertisements. Published over a decade after the preceding entry, it covers the turbulent years after the Japanese surrender. Information on national and local economic conditions and institutions. Also contains documents, such as international trade agreements, economic regulations, and foreign exchange rates.

Zhongguo laodong nianjian 中國勞動年鑒 (China labor yearbook). Beiping: Beiping shehui diaochasuo, 1928, 1931 (1st and 2d issues); Nanjing: Shiye bu, Zhongguo laodong nianjian bianzuan weiyuanhui, 1933, 1934 (3d and 4th issues). Issue no. 1 covers from 1912 to February 1927, and issue no. 2 from March 1927 to end of 1931. Material in the third and fourth issues came largely from files of the Ministry of Industry. All contain data pertaining to labor conditions, the labor movement, and relevant laws and regulations.

Zhongguo nianjian 中國年鑒 (China yearbook). Shanghai: Shangwu yinshuguan, 1924. One of the earliest yearbooks published in Chinese (with 2,123 pages), it was discontinued after its first issue. Statistical tables with explanations culled from official and private records, foreign sources, and direct investigations made by the compilers. Contains useful information on the last years of the Qing and the early Republic.

Zhongguo waijiao nianjian 中國外交年鑒 (China foreign relations yearbook). Shanghai: multiple publishers, 1933–41. Laws, treaties, and general information concerning China's foreign affairs, including those of the national and local governments. The yearbook also features classified lists of relevant publications (in Chinese and Western languages) and a directory of Chinese diplomatic and consular officials. The 1940–41 issue focuses primarily on the Wang Jingwei government.

Zhongguo wenyi nianjian 中國文藝年鑒 (China literature and arts yearbook). Shanghai: Xiandai chuju, 1933–1937; Taibei: Pingyuan chubanshe, 1966– . The prewar issues are mostly anthologies of current literary productions, but also contain news and information on the contemporary literary scene, as well as classified lists of literary works. The Taibei yearbook focuses on Taiwan literature.

Zhongguo yinhang nianjian 中國銀行年鑒 (Bank of China yearbook). Shanghai: Zhongguo yinhang guanlichu, Jingji yanjiushi, 1934–36. Filled with information related to banking and general economic issues.

Zhonghua minguo nianjian 中華民國年鑑 (Republic of China yearbook). Taibei: Zhonghua minguo nianjianshe, 1951– . A comprehensive political, economic, and cultural survey of the ROC on Taiwan. Includes a "Who's Who" of the ROC on Taiwan.

Zhonghua minguo tongji tiyao 中華民國統計提要 (Statistical abstract of the Republic of China). Nanjing: Xingzhengyuan, 1935-36; Taibei: Xingzhengyuan, 1955–74.

Zhongwai jingji nianbao 中外經濟年報 (Sino-foreign annual economic report). Shanghai: Shijie shuju, 1941. A yearbook that contains monographs prepared by specialists on Chinese economic affairs during the Sino-Japanese War.

Note: There also exist many provincial yearbooks (e.g., *Sichuan nianjian* 四川年鑑, *Hubei nianjian* 湖北年鑑) and municipal yearbooks (e.g., *Shanghai nianjian* 上海年鑑, *Beijing nianjian* 北京年鑑).

III. General and Specialized Histories

A. PRC

Beijing shifan daxue, Zhongguo xiandaishi jiaoyanshi. *Zhongguo xiandaishi, 1919–1949* 中國現代史(1919–1949年) (Modern Chinese history, 1919–49). 2 vols. Beijing: Beijing shifan daxue chubanshe, 1983.

Chen Ruiyun. *Xiandai Zhongguo zhengfu, 1919–1949* 現代中國政府(1919–1949年) (Modern Chinese government, 1919–49). Changchun: Jilin wenshi chubanshe, 1988.

Hu Sheng. *Zhonggguo gongchandang de qishi nian* 中國共產黨的七十年 (Seventy years of the Chinese Communist Party). Beijing: Zhonggong dangshi chubanshe, 1991.

Huang Yuanji & Wang Jinwu. *Zhongguo xiandaishi* 中國現代史 (Modern Chinese history). 2 vols. Zhengzhou: Henan renmin chubanshe, 1982.

Jiang Kefu, ed. *Minguo junshi shi lüegao* 民國軍事史略稿 (A brief draft of the military history of Republican China). Beijing: Zhonghua shuju, 1987.

Jin Chongji & Hu Shengwu, eds. *Xinhai geming shigao* 辛亥革命史稿 (Draft history of the 1911 Revolution). Shanghai: Shanghai renmin chubanshe, 1980.

Junshi kexueyuan, ed. *Zhongguo jindai zhanzheng shi* 中國近代戰爭史 (History of war in modern China). 3 vols. Beijing: Junshi kexue chubanshe, 1984– .

Lai Xinxia, ed. *Beiyang junfa shigao* 北洋軍閥史稿 (Draft history of the Warlord period). Wuhan: Hubei renmin chubanshe, 1983.

Li Shiyue et al. *Sun Zhongshan yu Zhongguo minzhu geming* 孫中山與中國民主革命 (Sun Yat-sen and China's democratic revolution). Shenyang: Liaoning renmin chubanshe, 1981.

Li Xin et al., eds. *Zhonghua minguo shi* 中華民國史 (History of the Republic of China). Beijing: Zhonghua shuju, 1981– . Series 1: vols. 1–2 (end of Qing to March 1912); series 2: vol. 1, pts. 1–2 (1912–16); vol. 2 (1916–20). Zhongguo shehui kexueyuan, Jindaishi yanjiusuo.

Lin Zengping et al., eds. *Xinhai geming shi* 辛亥革命史 (History of the 1911 Revolution). 3 vols. Beijing: Renmin chubanshe, 1980–81.

Mao Lei et al., eds. *Wuhan guomin zhengfu shi* 武漢國民政府史 (History of the Wuhan National Government). Wuhan: Hubei renmin chubanshe, 1986.

Peng Ming. *Wusi yundong shi* 五四運動史 (History of the May Fourth Movement). Beijing: Renmin chubanshe, 1979.

Qian Shifu. *Beiyang zhengfu shiqi de zhengzhi zhidu* 北洋政府時期的政治制度 (The political system of the Warlord period). 2 vols. Beijing: Zhonghua shuju, 1984.

Shang Mingxuan. *Sun Zhongshan yu Guomindang zuopai yanjiu* 孫中山與國民黨左派研究 (Research on Sun Yat-sen and the GMD Left). Beijing: Renmin chubanshe, 1986.

Shi Quansheng, ed. *Zhonghua minguo jingji shi* 中華民國經濟史 (Economic history of the Republic of China). Nanjing: Jiangsu renmin chubanshe, 1989.

———. *Zhonghua minguo wenhua shi* 中華民國文化史 (Cultural history of the Republic of China). Changchun: Jilin wenshi chubanshe, 1990.

Wang Gongan et al., eds. *Guo-Gong liang dang guanxi shi* 國共兩黨關係史 (History of GMD-CCP relations). Wuhan: Wuhan renmin chubanshe, 1989.

———. *Guo-Gong liang dang guanxi tongshi* 國共兩黨關係通史 (Complete history of GMD-CCP relations). Wuhan: Wuhan chubanshe, 1991.

Wang Quanwu, ed. *Zhongguo xiandai zichan jieji minzhu yundong shi* 中國現代資產階級民主運動史 (History of the bourgeois democratic movement in modern China). Changchun: Jilin wenshi chubanshe, 1985.

Wang Zonghua, ed. *Zhongguo da geming shi* 中國大革命史 (History of the Great Chinese Revolution). 2 vols. Beijing: Renmin chubanshe, 1990. Covers the period 1924–27.

Wei Hongyuan. *Zhongguo xiandaishi gao, 1919–1949* 中國現代史稿 (1919–1949年) (Draft history of modern China, 1919–49). 2 vols. Ha'erbin: Heilongjiang renmin chubanshe, 1980–81, 1985–86.

Wu Dongzhi, ed. *Zhongguo waijiao shi* 中國外交史 (History of Chinese foreign policy). 3 vols. (one on the Republican period). Zhengzhou: Henan renmin chubanshe, 1990.

Wu Yannan. *Sun Zhongshan yu xinhai geming* 孫中山與辛亥革命 (Sun Yat-sen and the 1911 Revolution). Guiyang: Guizhou renmin chubanshe, 1986.

Xiao Xiaoqin, ed. *Zhongguo guomindang shi* 中國國民黨史 (History of the GMD). Hefei: Anhui renmin chubanshe, 1989.

Xie Benshu et al., eds. *Huguo yundong shi* 護國運動史 (History of the National Protection movement). Guiyang: Guizhou renmin chubanshe, 1984.

Xinbian Zhongguo xiandaishi 新編中國現代史 (Modern Chinese history, new edition). 3 vols. Nanchang: Jiangxi renmin chubanshe, 1987. General editors: Chen Shanxue (vol. 1); Zhang Qifu (vol. 2); Zhao Shaoquan (vol. 3).

Xinhai geming shi congkan 辛亥革命史叢刊 (1911 Revolution series). Beijing: Zhonghua shuju, 1980– .

Yan Ji & Zhang Dongxin. *Zhongguo Guomindang shigang* 中國國民黨史綱 (Outline history of the GMD). Ha'erbin: Heilongjiang renmin chubanshe, 1991.

Zhang Xianwen, ed. *Zhonghua minguo shigang* 中華民國史綱 (Draft history of the Republic of China). Zhengzhou: Henan renmin chubanshe, 1985. The first semi-official PRC history to give a revisionist assessment of Chiang Kai-shek and the Guomindang's contributions during the Republican period, especially with regard to the Nationalists' anti-Japanese war effort.

Zhongguo gemingshi congshu 中國革命史叢書 (Chinese revolutionary history series). Shanghai: Shanghai renmin chubanshe, 1980s.

Zhongguo jindaishi 中國近代史 (Modern Chinese history). Beijing: Zhonghua shuju, 1983.

Zhonghua minguo shi congshu 中華民國史叢書 (Republic of China history series). 20 vols. Zhengzhou: Henan renmin chubanshe, 1987–93. General editors: Zhang Xianwen & Huang Meizhen.

Zhongguo jindaishi bianxie xiaozu. *Zhongguo jindaishi* 中國近代史 (Modern Chinese history). 7 vols. Beijing: Zhonghua shuju, 1977.

B. ROC

Guo Tingyu. *Zhongguo xiandaishi* 中國現代史 (Modern Chinese history). Taibei: Zhengzhong shuju, 1980.

Huang Dashou. *Zhongguo xiandaishi gang* 中國現代史綱 (Outline of modern Chinese history). Taibei: Wunan tushu chuban, 1980; reprinted 1984.

———. *Zhongguo xiandaishi gangyao* 中國現代史綱要 (Outline of modern Chinese history). Taibei: Da Zhongguo tushu, 1973.

Jiaoyu bu (Ministry of Education). *Zhonghua minguo jianguoshi* 中華民國建國史 (History of nation-building in the Republic of China). 16 vols. Taibei: Guoli bianyiguan, 1985–90.

Li Shougong. *Zhongguo xiandaishi* 中國現代史 (Modern Chinese history). Taibei: Guanghua chubanshe, 1958.

Qin Xiaoyi. *Zhonghua minguo jingji fazhanshi* 中華民國經濟發展史 (History of economic development in the Republic of China). 3 vols. Taibei: Jindai Zhongguo chubanshe, 1983.

———. *Zhonghua minguo wenhua fazhanshi* 中華民國文化發展史 (History of cultural development in the Republic of China). 4 vols. Taibei: Jindai Zhongguo chubanshe, 1981.

Wei Rulin. *Zhongguo xiandaishi* 中國現代史 (Modern Chinese history). Taibei: Huagang chuban, 1977.

Xu Langxuan. *Zhongguo xiandaishi* 中國現代史 (Modern Chinese history). Taibei: Zhengzhong shuju, 1974.

Xu Shishen. *Guomin zhengfu jianzhi zhiminglu* 國民政府建制職名錄 (List of government officials in the ROC). Taibei: Guoshiguan, 1984. Covers the period 1912–48.

Yang Rui. *Zhongguo jindai gemingshi* 中國近代革命史 (Modern revolutionary history in China). Taibei: n.p., 1959.

Zhang Jiyun. *Zhonghua minguo shigang* 中華民國史綱 (Outline history of the Republic of China). 7 vols. Taibei: Zhonghua wenhua chuban shiye weiyuanhui, 1954–56.

Zhang Yufa. *Zhongguo jindai xiandaishi* 中國近代現代史 (Modern Chinese history). Taibei: Donghua shuju, 1978.

———. *Zhongguo xiandaishi* 中國現代史 (Modern Chinese history). Taibei: Donghua shuju, 1977– .

IV. Government Gazettes and Journals

[X] bu gongbao 某某部公報 (Ministry of X gazette). Most ministries had official gazettes (e.g., *Jingji bu gongbao* 經濟部公報 [Ministry of Economic Affairs gazette]).

[X] yuan gongbao 某某院公報 (X *yuan* gazette). Like ministries, the *yuan*s also had official gazettes (e.g, *Lifa yuan gongbao* 立法院公報 [Legislative Yuan gazette]).

(Beiyang) *Zhengfu gongbao* (北洋)政府公報 (Government gazette). Published from 1912 to June 1928, this periodical was the official publication of the Northern Warlord government(s) in Beijing.

Guomin zhengfu gongbao 國民政府公報 (Gazette of the national government). 1925–48.

Linshi gongbao 臨時公報 (Provisional gazette). Official publication of the Provisional Government during Yuan Shikai's term as president.

Linshi zhengfu gongbao 臨時政府公報 (Gazette of the Provisional Government). Official publication of the Provisional Government established by Sun Yat-sen in the wake of the 1911 Revolution (January–April 1912).

Tongji yuebao 統計月報 (Statistics monthly). Nanjing: 1929–. From March 1935 to the end of 1936 published quarterly as *Tongji jibao* (Statistics quarterly). Each issue featured articles on research topics and statistical data.

Zhengfu gongbao 政府公報 (Government gazette). 1938– .

Zongtong fu gongbao 總統府公報 (Office of the President gazette). 1948– .

Note: some provincial governments also published official gazettes.

V. Local History and Gazetteers

Byon, Jae-hoon. *Local Gazetteers of Southwest China: A Handbook.* Seattle: University of Washington, School of International Studies, 1979.

A Checklist of Chinese Local Histories. Stanford: Stanford University Press, 1980.

Chin En-hui. *Zhongguo difangzhi zongmu tiyao* 中國地方志總目提要 (General bibliography of Chinese local gazetteers). Taibei: Hanmei tushu, 1996.

Gao Xiufang. *Beijing-Tianjin difangzhi renwu zhuanji suoyin* 北京天津地方志人物傳記索引 (Index to biographies in Beijing and Tianjin gazetteers). Beijing: Beijing daxue chubanshe, 1987.

Heilongjiang tushuguan. *Dongbei fangzhi renwu zhuanji ziliao suoyin: Heilongjiang juan* 東北方志人物傳記索引:黑龍江卷 (Index to biographical materials in Manchurian gazetteers: Heilongjiang). Ha'erbin: Heilongjiang renmin chubanshe, 1989.

Jilin sheng tushuguan. *Dongbei fangzhi renwu zhuanji ziliao suoyin: Jilin juan* 東北方志人物傳記索引:吉林卷 (Index to biographical materials in Manchurian gazetteers: Jilin). Changchun: Jilin wenshi chubanshe, 1989.

Liaoning tushuguan. *Dongbei fangzhi renwu zhuanji ziliao suoyin: Liaoning juan* 東北方志人物傳記索引:遼寧卷 (Index to biographical materials in Manchurian gazetteers: Liaoning). Shenyang: Liaoning renmin chubanshe, 1991.

Morton, Andrew. *Union List of Chinese Local Histories in British Libraries.* Oxford: China Library Group, 1979.

Wang Deyi. *Zhonghua minguo Taiwan diqu gongcang fangzhi mulu* 中華民國臺灣地區公藏方志目錄 (Catalogue of local gazetteers in libraries in the ROC on Taiwan). Taibei: Hanxue yanjiu ziliao ji fuwu zhongxin, 1985.

Zhongguo difangzhi ziliao gongzuo xiezuozu, comp. *Zhongguo xin fangzhi mulu* 中國新方志目錄 (A catalogue of new gazetteers for China). Beijing: Shumu wenxian chubanshe, 1993.

Zhongguo kexueyuan, Beijing tianwentai, comp. *Zhongguo difangzhi lianhe mulu* 中國地方志聯合目錄 (Unified catalogue of local gazetteers for China). Beijing: Zhonghua shuju, 1986.

Zhu Shijia. *A Catalogue of Chinese Local Histories in the Library of Congress.* Washington, D.C.: U.S. Government Printing Office, 1942.

VI. Biographical Sources and Memoirs

A. <u>Biographical Indexes and Chronologies</u>

1. General

In English

Nunn, G. Raymond. *East Asia: A Bibliography of Biographies.* Honolulu: University of Hawaii Press, 1967.

Wu, Eugene. *Leaders of Twentieth-Century China: An Annotated Bibliography of Selected Biographical Works in the Hoover Library.* Stanford: Stanford University Press, 1956. The index provides a useful alphabetical list of the names of biographers, editors, and compilers as well as of book titles used in this bibliography.

In Chinese

Beijing tushuguan, Shehui kexue cankaozu. *Geming lieshi zhuanji ziliao mulu* 革命烈士傳記資料目錄 (Index to biographical materials on revolutionary martyrs). Beijing: Jiefangjun chubanshe, 1987.

Fudan daxue, Lishixi, Ziliaoshi. *Xinhai yilai renwu zhuanji ziliao suoyin* 辛亥以來人物傳記資料索引 (Index to biographical materials since 1911). Shanghai: Shanghai cishu chubanshe, 1990.

Guofangbu, Qingbaoju (Ministry of National Defense, Bureau of Intelligence), ed. *Fei dangzheng ganbu renshi ziliao huibian* 匪黨政干部人事資料彙編 (Compendium of materials on CCP cadres). Taibei, 1966. Includes over 1,400 entries on high-ranking CCP officials from the provincial level and up.

Lai Xinxia. *Jin sanbai nianlai renwu nianpu zhijian lu* 近三百年來人物年譜知見錄 (List of biographical chronologies of the past 300 years). Shanghai: Shanghai renmin chubanshe, 1983.

Li Zhizhong, comp. *Zhongguo jindai renwu zhuanji ziliao suoyin* 中國近代人物傳記資料索引 (Index to the biographical materials on modern Chinese personalities). Taibei: Guoli zhongyang tushuguan, 1973. Includes biographical source materials on more than 1,500 persons who lived between 1840 and 1973. The 50 genres of materials include journals, diaries, epitaphs, conduct reports, chronologies, memoirs, autobiographies, eulogies, and elegies.

Qin Xiaoyi, ed. *Geming renwuzhi suoyin* 革命人物志索引 (Index to monographs on revolutionaries). Taibei: Zhongyang wenwu gongyingshe, 1983. An index to the

Monographs on Revolutionaries published by the GMD Central Committee's Commission on Party History.

Shao Yanmiao. *Gujin zhongwai renwu zhuanji zhinanlu* 古今中外人物傳記指南錄 (Guide to the biographies of eminent Chinese and foreigners, past and present). Nanjing: Jiangsu jiaoyu chubanshe, 1990.

Wang Baoxian. *Lidai mingren nianpu zongmu* 歷代名人年譜總目 (A general list of biographical chronologies). Taiwan: Donghai daxue tushuguan, 1965.

Wang Deyi. *Zhongguo lidai renwu nianpu zongmu* 中國歷代人物年譜總目 (A general list of Chinese biographical chronologies). Taibei: Huashi chubanshe, 1979.

Yang Dianxun. *Zhongguo lidai nianpu zongmu* 中國歷代年譜總目 (A general list of Chinese chronologies). Beijing: Shumu wenxian chubanshe, 1980.

"Zhuanji wenxue zazhi" zongmulu 傳記文學雜誌總目錄 (General index to the *Journal of Biographical Literature*). Taibei: Zhuanji wenxueshe, 1988.

2. Eminent Individuals

Beijing tushuguan. *Lu Xun yanjiu ziliao suoyin* 魯迅研究資料索引 (Index to research materials on Lu Xun). Beijing: Renmin wenxue chubanshe, 1980.

Shen Pengnian. *Lu Xun yanjiu ziliao bianmu* 魯迅研究資料編目 (Catalogue of research materials on Lu Xun). Shanghai: Shanghai wenyi chubanshe, 1958.

Shoudu tushuguan. *Lao She yanjiu ziliao bianmu* 老舍研究資料編目 (Catalogue of research materials on Lao She). Beijing: Tushuguan xuehui, 1981.

Su Airong et al. *Sun Zhongshan yanjiu zongmu* 孫中山研究總目 (Catalogue of research on Sun Yat-sen). Beijing: Tuanjie chubanshe, 1990.

Zhongshan daxue tushuguan. *Sun Zhongshan zhuzuo ji yanjiu shumu ziliao suoyin* 孫中山著作暨研究書目資料索引 (Index of materials on the works of Sun Yat-sen). Guangzhou, n.p., 1979.

B. Biographical Dictionaries

In English

Bartke, Wolfgang, ed. *Who's Who in the People's Republic of China.* Armonk, N.Y.: M. E. Sharpe, 1981. Intended as a reference guide to the currently active leadership of China, this book includes around 54,000 entries. Data were obtained from the daily Chinese press, using such sources as *People's Daily* or Xinhua News Agency dispatches. Pre-1949 information was collected from Taiwan archives and from the Biographical Service of the

Union Research Institute in Hong Kong. A list of all names alphabetized according to the Wade-Giles system is included.

Bartke, Wolfgang, & Peter Schier. *China's New Party Leadership: Biographies and Analysis of the Twelfth Central Committee of the Chinese Communist Party.* Armonk, N.Y.: M. E. Sharpe, 1985. For the Republican era, see pp. 83–256 for biographical data on all 210 full members and 138 alternative members of the Twelfth CCP Central Committee. This is a revised English version translated from the original German volume, which appeared in 1982–83.

Boorman, Howard L. *Men and Politics in Modern China: Preliminary 50 Biographies*, vol. 1. New York: Columbia University Press, 1960.

———, ed. *Biographical Dictionary of Republican China.* 5 vols. New York: Columbia University Press, 1967–70. Produced by a biographical dictionary project that began in 1955 at Columbia University with the participation of some 79 contributors. The first detailed biographical dictionary of its kind. Volume 5 is a personal name index for the previous four.

Cavanaugh, Jerome, comp. *Who's Who in China, 1918–1950.* 3 vols. Hong Kong: Chinese Materials Center, 1982. This is a reprint from its parent publication, *The China Weekly Review* (pub. 1917–41, 1941–53). The "Who's Who in China" columns of *The Review* were originally published into nine volumes covering the years 1919–50. This fourth edition includes some 3,000 entries of political, diplomatic, financial, business, professional, and religious leaders. Materials were gathered from newspaper articles, official records in Beijing, correspondents, friends, and, in some cases, the biographers themselves.

Editorial Board of *Who's Who in China.* *Who's Who in China's Current Leaders.* Beijing: Foreign Languages Press, 1989.

Fairbank, John K., ed. *Biographies of Guomindang Leaders.* Cambridge, Mass.: Harvard University, Committee on International and Regional Studies, 1948. This book is a translation of a confidential list of alleged "cliques" within the Guomindang leadership. The original list was published by the CCP for its own use in 1945. The names are classified according to "clique" affiliation and arranged alphabetically by the Wade-Giles romanization.

Klein, Donald W., and Anne B. Clark, comps. *Biographic Dictionary of Chinese Communism, 1921–1965.* 2 vols. Cambridge, Mass.: Harvard University Press, 1971. This book contains 433 biographies of CCP activists from 1921 to 1965. Appendixes also provide additional biographical data.

Peleberg, Max. *Who's Who in Modern China.* Hong Kong: Ye Olde Printerie, 1954. Over 2,000 detailed biographical sketches of leading personalities in modern China from 1912 to 1953. The biographies are mostly direct translations from Chinese sources. This book includes detailed histories of political parties and government organizations, a glossary of new terms used in contemporary Chinese, and a dual Chinese and English index.

In Chinese

Beijing fuwenshe. *Zuijin guanshen lüli huilu* 最近官紳履歷彙錄 (Collected records of recent officials and gentry). Beijing: Beijing fuwenshe, 1920.

Cai Kaisong et al. *Ershi shiji Zhongguo mingren cidian* 二十世紀中國名人辭典 (Dictionary of notable twentieth-century Chinese). Shenyang: Liaoning renmin chubanshe, 1991.

Chen Qingzhi. *Zhongguo zhuzuojia cidian* 中國著作家辭典 (Biographical and bibliographical dictionary of Chinese authors). Hanover, N.H.: Oriental Society, 1971.

Ding Disheng, ed. *Ziyou Zhongguo mingren zhuan* 自由中國名人傳 (Biographical dictionary of eminent Chinese in Free China). Taibei: Shijie wenhua fuwu she, 1952.

Fan Yinnan, ed. *Dangdai Zhongguo mingren lu* 當代中國名人錄 (A directory of eminent contemporary Chinese). Shanghai: Liangyou tushu yinshua gongsi, 1931.

Gao Wende. *Zhongguo minzushi renwu cidian* 中國民族史人物辭典 (Biographical dictionary of Chinese ethnic history). Beijing: Zhongguo shehui kexue chubanshe, 1990.

Gongfei zhongyao renwu diaocha 共匪重要人物調查 (Investigation of important figures in the CCP). Taibei: Neizheng bu diaochaju, 1950.

Guoli zhongyang tushuguan. *Zhongguo lidai renwu zhuanji* 中國歷代人物傳記 (Biographies of Chinese through the ages). Taibei: Zhonghua congshu bianshen weiyuanhui, 1973.

Hu Hua, ed. *Zhonggong dangshi renwu zhuan* 中共黨史人物傳 (Biographies of important persons in CCP history). 43 vols. Xi'an: Shaanxi remin chubanshe, 1990. Produced by the Society for the Study of CCP History, this 43-volume series reflects the changing assessments of historical figures that began to occur after 1976 (i.e., after the fall of the Gang of Four).

Hu Zhiwei, ed. *Zhonggong wenhua bairen zhi* 中共文化百人誌 (A hundred cultural figures in the CCP/PRC). Taibei: Zhuanji wenxue zazhishe, 1989.

Huaqiao xiehui zonghui. *Huaqiao mingren zhuan* 華僑名人傳 (Biographies of eminent overseas Chinese). Taibei: Liming wenhua shiye, 1984.

Kunming junqu zhengzhibu, ed. *Jiefangjun jiangling zhuan* 解放軍將領傳 (Biographies of high-ranking officers of the People's Liberation Army). 5 vols. Beijing: Jiefangjun chubanshe, 1987.

———. *Jiefangjun yingxiong zhuan* 解放軍英雄傳 (Biographies of heroes of the People's Liberation Army). Beijing: Jiefangjun chubanshe, 1987.

Li Fangshi. *Zhongguo renwu nianjian* 中國人物年鑒 (Yearbook of eminent Chinese). Beijing: Huayi chubanshe, 1989.

Li Guoqiang et al. *Zhongguo dangdai mingren lu* 中國當代名人錄 (Who's who in contemporary China). 20 vols. Hong Kong: Huafeng shuju, 1988.

Li Kan. *Zhongguo gemingshi renming dacidian* 中國革命史人名大辭典 (Biographical dictionary of Chinese revolutionary history). Changsha: Sanhuan chubanshe, 1992.

Li Shengping. *Zhongguo Gongchandang renming dacidian* 中國共產黨人名大辭典 (Biographical dictionary of the CCP). Beijing: Zhongguo guoji guangbo chubanshe, 1991.

———. *Zhongguo jinxiandai renming dacidian* 中國近現代人名大辭典 (Biographical dictionary of modern China). Beijing: Zhongguo guoji guangbo chubanshe, 1989.

Li Xin, ed. *Minguo renwu zhuan* 民國人物傳 (Biographical dictionary of Republican China). Beijing: Zhonghua shuju, 1978.

Li Xin & Ren Yimin. *Xinhai geming shiqi de lishi renwu* 辛亥革命時期的歷史人物 (Historical figures of the 1911 Revolution period). Beijing: Zhongguo qingnian chubanshe, 1983.

Liao Gailong et al. *Zhongguo renming dacidian: dangdai renwu juan* 中國人名大辭典: 當代人物卷 (Biographical dictionary of China: contemporary figures). Shanghai: Shanghai cishu chubanshe, 1992.

———. *Zhongguo renming dacidian: ishi renwu juan* 中國人名大辭典: 歷史人物卷 (Biographical dictionary of China: historical figures). Shanghai: Shanghai cishu chubanshe, 1990.

———. *Zhongguo renming dacidian: xianren dang-zheng-jun lingdao renwu juan* 中國人名大辭典: 現任黨政軍領導人物卷 (Biographical dictionary of China: currently serving party, government, and military leaders). Shanghai: Shanghai cishu chubanshe, 1989.

Liu Shaotang, ed. *Minguo renwu xiaozhuan* 民國人物小傳 (Biographical sketches of Republican China). 8 vols. Taibei: Zhuanji wenxue chubanshe, 1975.

Nanjing daxue, Lishixi. *Zhongguo lidai mingren cidian* 中國歷代名人辭典 (Biographical dictionary of Chinese history). Nanchang: Jiangxi renmin chubanshe, 1982.

Peng Huaizhen et al. *Zhonghua minguo neige mingren lu* 中華民國內閣名人錄 (Who's who of the cabinet members of the Republic of China). Taibei: Tongcha chubanshe, 1988.

Qin Xiaoyi, ed. *Zhonghua minguo mingren zhuan* 中華民國名人傳 (Biographical dictionary of notables in Republican China). Taibei: Jindai Zhongguo chubanshe, 1984.

Qin Xiaoyi et al. *Zhongguo xiandaishi cidian* 中國現代史辭典 (Dictionary of modern Chinese history). Taibei: Jindai Zhongguo chubanshe, 1985. The biographical section includes eminent Chinese and foreigners from 1894 to 1984.

Satô Saburô, ed. *Minguo zhi jingcui* 民國之精萃 (Elites of Republican China). Taibei: Wenhai chubanshe, 1967. Includes biographies of members of the Upper and Lower Houses in China.

Shijie wenhua fuwushe bianzuan weiyuanhui. *Ziyou Zhongguo mingren zhuan* 自由中國名人傳 (Biographical dictionary of Free China). Taibei: Shijie wenhua fuwushe, 1952.

Song Deci. *Ershi shiji Zhonghua aiguo mingren cidian* 二十世紀中華愛國名人辭典 (Biographical dictionary of twentieth-century Chinese patriots). Jilin: Jilin daxue chubanshe, 1990.

Song Zhemei. *Xingma renwu zhi* 星馬人物誌 (Biographies of notables in Singapore and Malaysia). 3 vols. Hong Kong: Dongnanya yanjiusuo, 1972.

Su Yude, ed. *Xiandai Guangdong renwu cidian* 現代廣東人物辭典 (Biographical dictionary of contemporary Guangdong). Canton: Huanan xianwen zongshe, 1949.

Tian Ziyu, ed. *Zhongguo jindai junfa cidian* 中國近代軍閥辭典 (Biographical dictionary of modern Chinese warlords). Beijing: Dang'an chubanshe, 1989.

Wang Naizhuang et al. *Zhonghua renmin gongheguo renwu cidian* 中華人民共和國人物辭典 (Biographical dictionary of the PRC). Beijing: Zhongguo jingji chubanshe, 1989.

Wu Hailin et al. *Zhongguo lishi renwu cidian* 中國歷史人物辭典 (Biographical dictionary of Chinese history). Ha'erbin: Heilongjiang renmin chubanshe, 1983.

Wu Xiangxiang, ed. *Minguo bairen zhuan* 民國百人傳 (One hundred biographies of the Republic of China). Taibei: Zhuanji wenxue chubanshe, 1971.

———. *Minguo zhengzhi renwu* 民國政治人物 (Political figures of the Republic of China). 2 vols. Taibei: Zhuanji wenxue chubanshe, 1970.

Xiandai Huaqiao renwu zhuan 現代華僑人物傳 (Biographical dictionary of overseas Chinese in the modern period). Taibei: Da Zhonghua chubanshe, 1963.

Xiong Tunsheng, ed. *Zhonghua minguo dangdai mingren lu* 中華民國當代名人錄 (Who's who in Republican China). Taiwan: Zhonghua shuju, 1978. Listings of around 3,700 persons in or affiliated with the Republic of China.

Xu Weimin. *Zhongguo Gongchandang renming cidian* 中國共產黨人名辭典 (Biographical dictionary of the CCP). Shenyang: Liaoning jiaoyu chubanshe, 1988. Over 1,000 entries of communist activists from the founding of the CCP in 1921 until 1988, with *pinyin* index.

Xu Youchun, ed. *Minguo renwu dacidian* 民國人物大辭典 (Biographical dictionary of the Republican period). Shijiazhuang: Hebei renmin chubanshe, 1991. Includes 12,000 succinct entries with an index of important figures in the Republican period.

Yang Jialuo, ed. *Minguo mingren tujian* 民國名人圖鑒 (An illustrated dictionary of notables in Republican China). Nanjing: Zidian guan, 1937.

Zang Lihe. *Zhongguo renming dacidian: lishi renwu juan* 中國人名大辭典: 歷史人物卷 (Biographical dictionary of China: historical figures). Shanghai: Shanghai shudian, 1980.

Zhang Chaowei, ed. *Zhonghua minguo xiandai mingren lu* 中華民國現代名人錄 (Who's who in the Republic of China). Taibei: Zhongguo mingren zhuanji zhongxin, 1982. Includes over 3,500 entries, with indexes in Chinese and English.

Zhonggong dangshi renwu yanjiuhui, comp. *Zhonggong dangshi renwu zhuan* 中共黨史人物傳 (Biographies of CCP figures). 50 vols. Xi'an: Shaanxi renmin chubanshe, 1980– .

Zhonggong renming lu 中共人名錄 (Who's who in the PRC). Taibei: Guoli zhengzhi daxue, Guoji guanxi yanjiu zhongxin, 1983. Data are obtained from a wide combination of archival materials stored in the United States, Japan, Hong Kong, and Taiwan as well as information leaked out of the PRC. Over 6,000 entries give descriptions of CCP officials, the People's government, the PLA, and other organizations.

Zhongguo guomindang, Dangshi bianzuan weiyuanhui (GMD, Party History Compilation Commission). *Geming renwu zhi* 革命人物誌 (Who's who of revolutionaries). Taibei: 1969.

Zhongguo jindai mingren tujian 中國近代名人圖鑒 (Illustrated dictionary of contemporary Chinese). Taibei: Tianyi chubanshe, 1977. Includes an introduction by Zhang Jian. This volume is primarily intended to introduce individuals who contributed to the development of the Chinese Republic. It is printed in both Chinese and English.

Zhongguo renming dacidian, dangdai renwu zhuan 中國人名大辭典: 當人代物卷 (Chinese biographical dictionary: contemporary figures). Shanghai: Shanghai cishu chubanshe, 1992.

Zhongguo renming dacidian, lishi renwu juan 中國人名大詞典：歷史人物卷 (Chinese biographical dictionary: historical figures). Shanghai: Shanghai cishu chubanshe, 1990.

Zhongguo shehui kexue yuan, Jindaishi yanjiuyuan (CASS, Institute of Modern History). *Jindai lai Hua renming cidian* 近代來華人名辭典 (Biographical dictionary of foreigners in China). Beijing: Zhongguo shehui kexue chubanshe, 1981. Some 1,800 enties listing foreigners of various occupations (diplomats, missionaries, journalists, merchants, advisors, explorers, etc.) who came to China between 1840 and 1949.

Zhong-wai mingren yanjiu zhongxin. *Zhongguo dangdai mingren lu* 中國當代名人錄 (Who's who in contemporary China). Shanghai: Shanghai renmin chubanshe, 1991.

C. <u>Biographical Periodicals</u>

Guoshiguan guankan 國史館館刊 (Journal of the Academia Historica). Taibei.

Renwu 人物 (Personalities). Beijing: Sanlian shudian.

Renwu chunqiu 人物春秋 (Historical personalities). Beijing: Renwu chunqiushe.

Renwu zazhi 人物雜誌 (Personalities magazine). Beijing: Renwu zazhishe.

Wenshi ziliao 文史資料 (Literary and historical materials). *Wenshi ziliao (WSZL)* is a whole genre in and of itself. It is a collection of the reminiscences of people who were somehow involved in historical events, large or small, or who knew those involved. *WSZL* is published at the national, provincial, and local levels under the auspices of the China People's Political Consultative Conference. Usually the title will begin with the place-name (as in *Hunan wenshi ziliao* 湖南文史資料 or *Guangzhou wenshi ziliao* 廣州文史資料). The national edition is called *Wenshi ziliao xuanji* 文史資料選輯 (Selections from *Literary and Historical Materials*) and is published in Beijing. For the most comprehensive index to *WSZL*, see Li Yongpu, *Quanguo geji zhengxie wenshi ziliao pianmu suoyin, 1960–1990* 全國各級政協文史資料篇目索引 (National Index to "Literary and Historical Materials," 1960–90), 5 vols. Beijing: Zhongguo wenshi chubanshe, 1992.

Zhuanji wenxue 傳記文學 (Biographical literature). Taibei: Wenhua yishu chubanshe.

Zongheng 縱橫. Beijing: Zhongguo wenshi chubanshe.

D. Alternative Name Indexes

Chen Deyun. *Gujin renwu bieming suoyin* 古今人物別名索引 (An index to alternative names of ancient and contemporary figures). Taibei: Yi wenyin shukuan, 1965.

Chen Yutang, ed. *Zhonggong dangshi renwu bieming lu* 中共黨史人物別名錄 (An index to alternative names of CCP members). Beijing: Hongqi chubanshe, 1985. This edition was for internal circulation (*neibu*) only. Different types of names include style, literary, pen, and secret names.

Miao Shixin. *Zhongguo xiandai zuojia biming suoyin* 中國現代作家筆名索引 (An index to the pen names of contemporary Chinese authors). Ji'nan: Shandong daxue chubanshe, 1986.

Xu Naixiang et al. *Zhongguo xiandai wenxue zuozhe biming lu* 中國現代文學作者筆名錄 (An index to the pen names of contemporary Chinese literary writers). Changsha: Hunan renmin chubanshe, 1988.

Zhang Jingru et al. *Wusi yilai lishi renwu bieming lu* 五四以來歷史人物別名錄 (An index to alternative names of prominent figures since the May Fourth Movement). Xi'an: Shaanxi renmin chubanshe, 1986.

Zhu Baoliang, ed. *Ershi shiji Zhongguo zuojia biming lu* 二十世紀中國作家筆名錄 (Index of twentieth-century Chinese writers' pen names). Taibei: Hanxue yanjiu zhongxin, 1989. The original edition was published in Boston in 1977. This enlarged edition contains over 6,700 entries with some 18,000 pen names. It is arranged alphabetically by Wade-Giles romanization.

VII. Published Documents

A. <u>General</u>

In Western Languages

Brandt, Conrad, Benjamin Schwartz, & John K. Fairbank, eds. *A Documentary History of Chinese Communism.* Cambridge, Mass.: Harvard University Press, 1959.

Die Komintern und die national-revolutionäre Bewegung in China: Dokumente, vol. 1, *1920–1925,* ed. Russischen Zentrum für Archivierung und Erforschung von Dokumenten zur neuesten Geschichte, Ostasiatischen Seminar der FU Berlin, and Institut für den Fernen Osten, Russischen Akademie der Wissenschaften. Paderborn: Schöningh, 1996; vol. 2, *1926–27,* 2 pts. 1997.

Saich, Tony, ed. *The Rise to Power of the Chinese Communist Party.* Armonk, N.Y.: M. E. Sharpe, 1996.

Schram, Stuart, ed. *Mao's Road to Power: Revolutionary Writing, 1912–1949.* 6 vols. to date. Armonk, N.Y.: M. E. Sharpe, 1992– .

Teng Ssu-yu & John K. Fairbank. *China's Response to the West: A Documentary Survey 1839–1923.* Rev. ed. Cambridge, Mass.: Harvard University Press, 1979. For the Republican period, this compilation translates several famous articles by Cai Yuanpei, Li Dazhao, Chen Duxiu, Hu Shi, Sun Yat-sen, and Liang Qichao.

In Chinese

Geming wenxian 革命文獻 (Documents of the revolution). 112 vols. Taibei: Zhongguo guomindang zhongyang weiyuanhui, Dangshi weiyuanhui, 1953–89. With index; contains original documents and letters from the 1911–49 period.

Jindaishi ziliao 近代史資料 (Materials on modern history). Beijing: Zhongguo shehui kexue chubanshe, 1954–67. Contains original documents, especially on the first decade of the Republic (Yuan Shikai, May Fourth, May Thirtieth, political cliques, etc.).

Zhongguo xiandai shiliao congshu 中國現代史料叢書 (Collection of historical materials on modern China). 36 vols. General editor: Wu Xiangxiang. Taibei: Wenxing shudian, 1962–63. Deals especially with the founding of the Republic and the Yuan Shikai period, as well as, to a lesser extent, on the 1930s and 1940s.

Zhonghua minguo kaiguo wushi nian wenxian 中華民國開國五十年獻 (Documents from the first fifty years of the Republic of China). 26 vols. Taibei: Zhongguo guomindang zhongyang weiyuanhui, Dangshi weiyuanhui, 1961–65. Deals mostly with the 1911 Revolution and the early years of the Republic.

Zhonghua minguo shi dang'an ziliao congkan 中華民國史檔案資料叢刊 (Compendium of archival sources on the history of the Republic of China). Beijing: Dang'an chubanshe, 1989.

Zhonghua minguo shi dang'an ziliao huibian 中華民國史檔案資料匯編 (Compendium of archival materials on the history of the Republic of China). 5 series. Nanjing: Jiangsu guji chubanshe, 1979–99. Contains original documents and letters, covering the ROC government from 1911 to 1949. It is one of the major documentary series compiled by the Number Two Chinese Archives.

Zhonghua minguo shishi jiyao 中華民國史事紀要 (Historical accounts of important events in the Republic of China). Multiple volumes. Taibei: Zhonghua mingguo shiliao yanjiu zhongxin, 1971– . The title is slightly deceiving. Instead of a summary, this is a chronologically organized (to the day) multi-volume compilation of official documents, especially speeches and telegrams, from the Republican period. Each volume covers one year or half of one year. Very useful if you know specific dates or are concentrating on a very narrow time period; otherwise it can be difficult to find the desired materials.

Zhonghua minguoshi shiliao changbian 中華民國史史料長編 (Chronological compilation of materials on the history of the Republic of China). 70 vols. Nanjing: Nanjing daxue chubanshe, 1993. Original documents.

Zhonghua minguo zhongyao shiliao: *dui Ri kangzhan* 中華民國重要史料: 對日抗戰 (Important historical materials on the Republic of China: War of Resistance Against Japan). Multiple volumes. Taibei: Zhongguo Guomindang zhongyang weiyuanhui, Dangshi weiyuanhui, 1981. Especially good for the 1937–45 Sino-Japanese war. Volumes arranged thematically (e.g., foreign relations, etc.).

B. Archival Journals

Beijing dang'an shiliao 北京檔案史料 (Beijing archival materials). Beijing: Beijing shi dang'an guan, 1986– .

Dang'an yu lishi 檔案與歷史 (Archives and history). Shanghai: Shanghai shi dang'anguan. Publication of the Shanghai Municipal Archives containing examples of its holdings and articles resulting from secondary research.

Dang de wenxian 黨的文獻 (Party documents). Beijing: Zhongyang wenxian chubanshe, 1988– . Bimonthly. This journal contains original party documents and commentary. It is jointly published by the Central Archives and the CCP Historical Resources Research Institute.

Jiangsu lishi dang'an 江蘇歷史檔案 (Jiangsu historical archives).

Lishi dang'an 歷史檔案 (Historical archives). Beijing: Lishi dang'an zazhishe, 1981– . This journal is published under the auspices of the Number One Archives in Beijing.

Minguo dang'an 民國檔案 (Republican archives). Nanjing: Minguo dang'an zazhishe, 1985– . Published under the auspices of the Number Two Archives in Nanjing, this publication provides a mixture of Republican-era documents stored in the Number Two Archives, including letters, telegrams, official reports, and communications, as well as scholarly essays on historically relevant topics.

Zhonggong dangshi ziliao 中共黨史資料 (Materials on CCP history).

C. <u>Politics</u>

Beiyang junfa shiliao 北洋軍閥史料 (Historical sources on the Beiyang warlords). 33 vols. Tianjin: Tianjin guji chubanshe, 1996.

Beiyang junfa tongzhi shiqi de bingbian 北洋軍閥統治時期的兵變 (Mutinies during the Beiyang Warlord period). Nanjing: Jiangsu renmin chubanshe, 1982.

Beiyang junfa tongzhi shiqi de dangpai 北洋軍閥統治時期的黨派 (Political parties of the Beiyang Warlord period). Beijing: Dang'an chubanshe, 1994.

Fujian shibian dang'an ziliao 福建事變檔案資料 (Archival sources on the Fujian incident). Fuzhou: Fujian renmin chubanshe, 1984.

Guomindang tongzhi shiqi de xiao dangpai 國民黨統治時期的小黨派 (Small political parties during the period of Nationalist rule). Beijing: Dang'an chubanshe, 1992.

Guomindang zhengfu zhengzhi zhidu dang'an shiliao xuanbian 國民黨政府政治制度檔案史料選編 (Selected archival sources on the political system of the Nationalist government). Hefei: Anhui jiaoyu chubanshe, 1994.

Huabei shibian ziliao xuanbian 華北事變資料選編 (Collection of sources on the North China incident). Zhengzhou: Henan renmin chubanshe, 1983.

Minguo dangpai shetuan dang'an shiliao conggao 民國黨派社團檔案史料叢稿 (Archival sources series on political parties and mass organizations of the Republican period). Multiple vols. Beijing: Dang'an chubanshe, 1988– .

Sun Zhongshan feng'an dadian 孫中山奉安大典 (Grand ceremony for the burial of Sun Yat-sen). Beijng: Beijing huawen chubanshe, 1989.

Wusa yundong he Sheng-Gang bagong 五卅運動和省港罷工 (The May Thirtieth incident and the Guangdong–Hong Kong strike). Nanjing: Jiangsu guji chubanshe, 1985.

Wusi aiguo yundong dang'an ziliao 五四愛國運動檔案資料 (Archival materials on the May Fourth Movement). Zhongguo shehui kexue chubanshe, 1980. Compiled from the collection at the Number Two Archives in Nanjing.

Xi'an shibian dang'an shiliao xuanji 西安事變檔案史料選輯 (Selected archival materials on the Xi'an incident). Beijing: Dang'an chubanshe, 1986. These materials were jointly compiled by the Number Two Archives in Nanjing, the Yunnan Provincial Archives, and the Shaanxi Provincial Archives.

Yuan Shikai shiliao huikan 袁世凱史料彙刊 (Compendium of historical materials on Yuan Shikai). 26 vols. Taibei: Wenhai chubanshe, 1966. Includes government gazette materials.

Zhi-Wan zhanzheng 直皖戰爭 (The Zhili-Anfu war). Nanjing: Jiangsu renmin chubanshe, 1980. Materials from the Number Two Archives relating to the confrontation between the Zhili and Anfu warlord cliques.

Zhongde waijiao midang 1927 nian–1947 nian 中德外交密檔 (1927 年–1947 年) (Confidential archives of Sino-German diplomacy, 1927–47). Guilin: Guangxi shifan daxue chubanshe, 1994.

Zhongguo guomindang diyi, er ci quanguo daibiao dahui huiyi shiliao 中國國民黨第一、二次全國代表大會會議史料 (Historical materials on the first and second GMD national congresses). Nanjing: Jiangsu guji chubanshe, 1986.

Zhongguo wuzhengfu zhuyi he Zhongguo shehuidang 中國無政府主義和中國社會黨 (Chinese anarchism and the Chinese Socialist Party). Nanjing: Jiangsu renmin chubanshe, 1981. Divided into two sections, this work contains archival material on (1) the development of Chinese anarchism and (2) the establishment, dissolution, and reconstitution of the Chinese Socialist Party.

Zhongshanling shiliao xuanbian 中山陵史料選編 (Collection of sources on Sun Yat-sen's mausoleum). Nanjing: Jiangsu guji chubanshe, 1986.

D. Business and Economics (Non-communist Areas)

Beijing de Zhongguo yinhang 北京的中國銀行 (The Bank of China in Beijing). Beijing: Zhongguo jinrong chubanshe, 1989.

Beijing dianche gongsi dang'an shiliao, 1921 nian–1949 nian 北京電車公司檔案史料，1921 年–1949年 (Archival sources on the Beijing Electric Tramway Company, 1921–49). Beijing: Yanshan chubanshe, 1988.

Beijing shougongye shehuizhuyi gaizao ziliao 北京手工業社會主義改造資料 (Sources on the socialist transformation of the handicraft industry in Beijing). Beijing: Zhonggong dangshi chubanshe, 1992.

Beijing zilaishui gongsi dang'an shiliao, 1908 nian–1949 nian 北京自來水公司檔案史料，1908年–1949年 (Archival sources on the Beijing Water Works Company, 1908–49). Beijing: Yanshan chubanshe, 1986.

Dasheng qiye xitong dang'an xuanbian 大生企業系統檔案選編 (Selected archives of Dasheng Business Enterprises). Nanjing: Nanjing daxue chubanshe, 1987– .

Guomin zhengfu caizheng jinrong shuishou dang'an shiliao: 1929–1937 國民政府財政金融稅收檔案史料, 1927–1937 (Archival sources on financial, banking and taxation affairs of the National government, 1927–37). Beijing: Zhongguo caizheng jingji chubanshe, 1997.

Hanyeping gongsi dang'an shiliao xuanbian 漢冶萍公司檔案史料選編 (Selected archival sources on the Hanyeping Company). 2 vols. Beijing: Zhongguo shehui kexueyuan chubanshe, 1994.

Jiaotong yinhang shiliao 交通銀行史料 (Historical sources on the Bank of Communications). Beijing: Zhongguo jinrong chubanshe, 1995.

Jincheng yinhang shiliao 金城銀行史料 (Historical sources on the Kincheng Banking Corporation). Shanghai: Shanghai renmin chubanshe, 1983.

Jindai Tianjin zhiming qiye jingying guanli 近代天津知名企業經營管理 (Management of business enterprises in modern Tianjin). Tianjin: Zhonggong Tianjin yinshuachang, 1995.

Jingji wenti ziliao huibian 經濟問題資料彙編 (Compendium of materials on economic issues). Taibei: Ministry of Economic Affairs, 1952.

Jiu Shanghai de zhengquan jiaoyisuo 舊上海的證券交易所 (Stock exchanges in Old Shanghai). Shanghai: Shanghai guji chubanshe, 1992.

Jiu Zhongguo de gufen zhi, 1868 nian–1949 nian 舊中國的股份制, 1868 年－1949 年 (Stock-share system in Old China, 1868–49). Beijing: Dang'an chubanshe, 1996.

Jiu Zhongguo de Shanghai guangbo shiye 舊中國的上海廣播事業 (Broadcasting in old Shanghai). Beijing: Dang'an chubanshe, 1985.

Kangri zhanzheng shiqi guomin zhengfu jingji fagui 抗日戰爭時期國民政府經濟法規 (National government laws and regulations on economic affairs during the War of Resistance Against Japan). Beijing: Dang'an chubanshe, 1992.

Kangzhan houfang yejin gongye shiliao 抗戰後方冶金工業史料 (Historical sources on the metallurgical industry in rear areas during the War of Resistance). Chongqing: Chongqing chubanshe, 1988.

Minguo waizhai dang'an shiliao 民國外債檔案史料 (Archival materials on foreign debt during the Republican period). Beijing: Dang'an chubanshe, 1989.

Shanghai jiefang qianhou wujia ziliao huibian, 1921–1957 上海解放前後物價資料匯編, 1921–1957年 (Materials on prices in Shanghai before and after Liberation, 1921–57). Shanghai: Zhongguo kexueyuan, Shanghai jingji yanjiusuo, 1958. Contains commodity price tables with some analysis and interpretation.

Shanghai qianzhuang shiliao 上海錢莊史料 (Historical sources on native banks in Shanghai). Shanghai: Shanghai shehui kexueyuan chubanshe, 1960.

Shanghai zhuce shangbiao tuji 上海註冊商標圖集 (Pictorial collection of registered trademarks in Shanghai). Shanghai: Beijia chubanshe, 1988.

Silian zongchu shiliao 四聯總處史料 (Historical sources on the joint board for the Bank of China, the Central Bank of China, the Bank of Communications, and the Farmers' Bank of China). Beijing: Dang'an chubanshe, 1993.

Suzhou shanghui dang'an congbian 蘇州商會檔案叢編 (Archival series on the Suzhou Chamber of Commerce). Wuhan: Huazhong shifan daxue chubanshe, 1991– .

Tianjin shanghui dang'an huibian 天津商會檔案匯編 (Selected archives of the Tianjin Chamber of Commerce). Tianjin: Tianjin renmin chubanshe, 1991.

Wu Yunchu yu Zhongguo tianzi huagong qiye 吳蘊初與中國天字化工企業 (Wu Yunchu and China's chemical industry enterprises of the "Tian" Group). Chongqing: Kexuejishu wenxian chubanshe, Chongqing fenshe, 1990.

Yijiu erqi nian de Shanghai shangye lianhehui 一九二七年的上海商業聯合會 (The Shanghai Commercial Association in 1927). Shanghai: Shanghai renmin chubanshe, 1983.

Zhang Jian nongshang zongzhang renqi jingji ziliao xuanbian 張謇 農商總長任期經濟資選編 (Selected sources on the economy during Zhang Jian's term as minister of agriculture and commerce). Beijing: Nanjing daxue chubanshe, 1987.

Zhongguo haiguan midang: Hede Jin Deng'an handian huibian, 1874–1907 中國海關密檔：赫德、金登干函電匯編，1874–1907 (Confidential documents of the Chinese Maritime Customs: correspondence between Robert Hart and James Duncan Campbell, 1874–1907). 9 vols. Beijing: Zhonghua shuju, 1990– .

Zhongguo nongmin yinhang 中國農民銀行 (Farmers' Bank of China). Beijing: Zhongguo caizheng jingji chubanshe, 1980.

Zhongguo yinhang hangshi ziliao huibian 中國銀行行史資料匯編 (Selected archival sources on the history of the Bank of China). Beijing: Dang'an chubanshe, 1991.

Zhongguo ziben zhuyi gongshang qiye shiliao congkan 中國資本主義工商企業史料叢刊 (Historical sources on capitalist industry and commerce in China). Beijing: Zhonghua shuju, 1963– .

Zhonghua minguo jinrong fagui dang'an ziliao xuanbian 中華民國金融法規檔案資料選編 (Selected archival documents on the financial regulations of Republican China). 2 vols. Beijing: Dang'an chubanshe, 1990.

Zhonghua minguo shangye dang'an ziliao huibian 中華民國商業檔案資料匯編 (Selected archival sources on commerce during Republican China). Beijing: Zhongguo shangye chubanshe, 1991.

E. Social Movements

Guangdong funü yundong shiliao (1924–1927) 廣東婦女運動史料 (1924–1927) (Historical documents of the women's movement in Guangdong). Guangzhou: Guangdong sheng dang'anguan, 1983.

Jiangsu sheng funü yundong shiliao xuan 江蘇省婦女運動史料選 (Selected historical documents of the women's movement in Jiangsu province). Nanjing, Jiangsu sheng funü lianhehui 1984.

Jiangxi suqu funü yundong shiliao xuanbian 江西蘇區婦女運動史料選編 (Collection of archival sources on the women's movement in the Jiangxi Soviet area). Nanchang: Jiangxi renmin chubanshe, 1982.

Jiefang zhanzheng shiqi Beiping xuesheng yundong 解放戰爭時期北平學生運動 (Student movements in Beiping during the Civil War). Beijing: Guangmin ribao chubanshe, 1995.

Kangri zhanzheng shiqi de Guangdong qingnian yundong 抗日戰爭時期的廣東青年運動 (The youth movement in Guangdong during the War of Resistance Against Japan). N.p.:Guangdong dang'anguan et al., 1981.

Minguo banghui yaolu 民國幫會要錄 (Essential records of secret societies in Republican China). Beijing: Dang'an chubanshe, 1993.

Qingmo minchu de jinyan yundong he wanguo jinyanhui 清末民初的禁煙運動和万國禁煙會 (The anti-opium movement and the International Anti-Opium Association in the late Qing and early Republic). Shanghai: Shanghai kexuejishu wenxian chubanshe, 1996.

Shanghai gonghui lianhehui 上海工會聯合會 (The Shanghai Associated Labor Unions). Beijing: Dang'an chubanshe, 1989.

Zhongguo qingnian yundong lishi ziliao 中國青年運動歷史資料 (Historical sources on the Chinese youth movement). Multiple volumes. Beijing: Zhonggong dangshi ziliao chubanshe, 1988– .

F. CCP and Base Areas (General)

Guomindang zhuidu hongjun changzheng dang'an shiliao huibian 國民黨追堵紅軍長征檔案史料匯編 (Compendium of archival materials on the GMD's pursuit and blockade of the Red Army during the Long March). Beijing: Dang'an chubanshe, 1987.

Shaan-Gan-Ning bianqu kangri minzhu genjudi 陝甘寧邊區抗日民主根据地 (The Democratic Base Area of the Shaanxi-Gansu-Ningxia Border Region during War of Resistance Against Japan). Beijing: Zhonggong dangshi ziliao chubanshe, 1990.

Shaan-Gan-Ning bianqu minzu zongjiao shiliao xuanbian 陝甘寧邊區民族宗教史料選編 (Collection of historical sources on ethnic and religious affairs in the Shaanxi-Gansu-Ningxia Border Area). Xi'an: Shaanxi renmin chubanshe, 1991.

Shaan-Gan-Ning bianqu zhengfu wenjian xuanbian 陝甘寧邊區政府文件選編 (Collection of documents of the Shaanxi-Gansu-Ningxia Border Area government). 14 vols. Beijing: Dang'an chubanshe, 1986–89.

Shaan-Gan-Ning geming genjudi shiliao xuanji 陝甘寧革命根据地史料選輯 (Collection of historical sources of the Shaanxi-Gansu-Ningxia Revolutionary Base Area). Multiple vols. Lanzhou: Gansu renmin chubanshe, 1981–.

Zhedong dihou kangri genjudi shiliao 浙東敵后抗日根据地史料 (Historical sources on the East Zhejiang Base Area behind enemy lines). Beijing: Zhonggong dangshi ziliao chubanshe, 1987.

Zhonggong Jiangxi suweiai ziliao 中共江西蘇維埃資料 (Materials on the CCP Jiangxi Soviet) (also known as the Chen Cheng collection). 21-reel microfilm collection from Taiwan containing original documents captured by General Chen Cheng during campaigns against the Jiangxi Soviet, 1930–34. A helpful bibliography for this collection is Wu Tien-wei, *The Kiangsi Soviet Republic, 1931–1934: A Selected and Annotated Bibliography of the Ch'en Ch'eng Collection.* Cambridge, Mass.: Harvard-Yenching Library, 1981.

Zhonggong Wuhan shiwei wenjian xuanbian (1949–1951) 中共武漢市委文件選編 (1949–1951). (Selected documents of the CCP Wuhan Committee, 1949–51). Wuhan: Wuhan shi dang'anguan, 1989.

Zhonggong zhongyang kangri minzu tongyi zhanxian wenjian xuanji 中共中央抗日民族統一戰線文件選編 (Collection of the CCP Central Committee documents on the United Front for Resisting Japan). 3 vols. Beijing: Dang'an chubanshe, 1984–86.

Zhonggong zhongyang wenjian xuanji 中共中央文件選集 (Collection of documents of the CCP Central Committee). Multiple vols. Beijing: Zhongyang dangxiao chubanshe, 1988– .

Zhongguo xin minzhu zhuyi geming shiqi genjudi fazhi wenxian xuanbian 中國新民主主義革命時期根据地法制文獻選編 (Collection of documents on the legal system in the base areas during the Chinese New Democratic Revolution). 5 vols. Beijing: Zhongguo shehui kexueyuan chubanshe, 1981.

Zhongyang geming genjudi shiliao xuanbian 中央革命根据地史料選編 (Collection of historical documents on the Central Revolutionary Base Area). Nanchang: Jiangxi renmin chubanshe, 1983.

G. <u>CCP and Base Areas</u> (Economic and Financial)

Anhui geming genjudi caijing shiliao xuan 安徽革命根据地財經史料選 (Collection of financial and economic documents of the Anhui Revolutionary Base Area). Hefei: Anhui renmin chubanshe, 1983.

Anhui geming genjudu gongshang shuishou shiliao xuan 安徽革命根据地工商税收史料選 (Collection of historical sources on industrial and commercial taxation in the Anhui Revolutionary Base Area). Hefei: Anhui renmin chubanshe, 1984.

Binhai diqu tudi gaige shiliao xuanbian 濱海地區土地改革史料選編 (Archival documents on land reform in the Binhai area of Shandong). Shandong sheng Linyi diqu dang'anguan, 1990.

Dongjiang geming genjudi caizheng shuishou shiliao xuanbian 東江革命根据地財政税收史料選編 (Collection of financial and tax documents of the Dongjiang Revolutionary Base Area). Guangzhou: Guangdong renmin chubanshe, 1986.

E-Yu-Wan geming genjudi caizheng jingjishi ziliao xuanbian 鄂豫皖革命根据地財政經濟史資料選編 (Collection of financial and economic documents of the Hubei-Henan-Anhui Revolutionary Base Area). Wuhan: Hubei renmin chubanshe, 1989.

Hebei jianzu jianxi dang'an shiliao xuanbian 河北減租減息檔案史料選編 (Archival documents on rent and interest reduction in Hebei). Shijiazhuang: Hebei renmin chubanshe, 1989.

Hebei tudi gaige dang'an shiliao xuanbian 河北土地改革檔案史料選編 (Archival sources on land reform in Hebei). Shijiazhuang: Hebei renmin chubanshe, 1990.

Huabei geming genjudi gongshang shuishou shiliao xuanbian 華北革命根据地工商税收史料選編 (Collection of historical sources on industrial and commercial taxation in the North China Revolutionary Base Area). 4 vols. Shijiazhuang: Hebei renmin chubanshe, 1987.

Huazhong jiefangqu caijing shiliao xuanbian 華中解放區財經史料選編 (Selected historical sources on finance and the economy of the Central China liberated areas). 7 vols. Nanjing: Nanjing daxue chubanshe, 1987–89.

Huazhong kangri genjudi caijing shiliao xuanbian (Jiangsu bufen) 華中抗日根据地財經史料選編（江蘇部分） (Selected historical sources on finance and the economy of the Central China base areas during the War of Resistance Against Japan: Jiangsu). 4 vols. Beijing: Dang'an chubanshe, 1986.

Huazhong kangri genjudi caijing shiliao xuanbian (E-Yu bianqu xinsijun wushi bufen) 華中抗日根据地財經史料選編（鄂豫邊區、新四軍五師部分） (Selected historical sources on finance and economy of the Central China base areas during the War of Resistance Against Japan: Hubei/Henan border area, 5th division of New Fourth Army). Wuhan: Hubei renmin chubanshe, 1989.

Jiefang zhanzheng shiqi Shaan-Gan-Ning bianqu caizheng jingji shi ziliao xuanji 解放戰爭時期陝甘寧邊區財政經濟史資料選輯 (Historical documents on financial and economic history in the Shaanxi-Gansu-Ningxia Border Area during the War of Liberation). Xi'an: Sanqin chubanshe, 1989.

Jiefang zhanzheng shiqi tudi gaige wenjian xuanbian 解放戰爭時期土地改革文件選編 (Collection of documents on land reform during the War of Liberation). Beijing: Zhonggong zhongyang dangxiao chubanshe, 1981.

Jinggangshan geming genjudi shiliao xuanbian 井岡山革命根据地史料選編 (Collection of historical sources of the Jinggangshan Revolutionary Base Area). Nanchang: Jiangxi renmin chubanshe, 1986.

Jin-Ji-Lu-Yu kangri genjudi caizheng jingji shiliao xuanbian 晉冀魯豫抗日根据地財政經濟史料選編 (Collection of historical sources on finance and the economy in the Shanxi-Hebei-Shandong-Henan base areas). Beijing: Dang'an chubanshe, 1985– .

Jin-Sui bianqu caizheng jingji ziliao xuanbian 晉綏邊區財政經濟資料選編 (Historical sources on financial and economic affairs in the Shanxi-Suiyuan Border Area). Taiyuan: Shanxi renmin chubanshe, 1986.

Jin-Sui geming genjudi gongshang shuishou shiliao xuanbian 晉綏革命根据地工商稅收史料選編 (Selected historical documents on industrial and commercial taxation in the Shanxi-Suiyuan Revolutionary Base Area). Taiyuan: Shanxi renmin chubanshe, 1986.

Kangri zhanzheng shiqi Jin-Cha-Ji bianqu caizheng jingji shiliao xuanbian 抗日戰爭時期晉察冀邊區財政經濟史料選編 (Collection of historical sources on finance and the economy in the Shanxi-Chahaer-Hebei Border Area during the War of Resistance Against Japan). Tianjin: Nankai daxue chubanshe, 1984.

Kangri zhanzheng shiqi Jin-Ji-Lu-Yu bianqu caizheng jingji shi ziliao xuanbian 抗日戰爭時期晉冀魯豫邊區財政經濟史資料選編 (Collection of historical sources on financial and economic affairs in the Shanxi-Hebei-Shandong-Henan Border Area during the War of Resistance Against Japan). Beijing: Zhongguo caizheng jingji chubanshe, 1990.

Kangri zhanzheng shiqi Shaan-Gan-Ning bianqu caizheng jingji shiliao zhaibian 抗日戰爭時期陝甘寧邊區財政經濟史資料摘編 (Selected sources on the financial and economic history of the Shaanxi-Gansu-Ningxia Border Area during the War of Resistance Against Japan). Multiple vols. Xi'an: Shaanxi renmin chubanshe, 1981.

Min-Zhe-Gan geming genjudi caizheng jingji shiliao xuanbian 閩浙贛革命根据地財政經濟史料選編 (Collection of financial and economic documents of the Fujian-Zhejiang-Jiangxi Revolutionary Base Area). Xiamen: Xiamen daxue chubanshe, 1988.

Shaan-Gan-Ning bianqu jiaoyu ziliao 陝甘寧邊區教育資料 (Sources on education in the Shaanxi-Gansu-Ningxia Border Area). 12 vols. Beijing: Jiaoyu kexue chubanshe, 1981.

Shaan-Gan-Ning geming genjudi gongshang shuishou shiliao xuanbian 陝甘寧革命根据地工商税收史料選編 (Collection of historical sources on industrial and commercial taxation in the Shaanxi-Gansu-Ningxia Revolutionary Base Area). 9 vols. Xi'an: Shaanxi renmin chubanshe, 1985–87.

Shandong de jianzu jianxi 山東的减租减息 (Rent and interest reduction in Shandong). Beijing: Zhonggong dangshi chubanshe, 1994.

Shandong geming genjudi caizheng shiliao xuanbian 山東革命根据地財政史料選編 (Selected historical sources on financial and economic affairs in the Shandong Revolutionary Base Area). 1985.

Taiyue geming genjudi caizheng shiliao xuanbian 太岳革命根据地財政史料選編 (Selected historical sources on financial and economic affairs in the Taiyue Revolutionary Base Area). 2 vols. Taiyuan: Shanxi jingji chubanshe, 1990.

Tudi geming shiqi Guangxi Zuoyoujiang geming genjudi caizheng jingji shiliao xuanbian 土地革命時期廣西左右江革命根据地財政經濟史料選編 (Collection of financial and economic documents of the Zuoyoujiang revolutionary base areas in Guangxi during the Land Revolution period). Guilin: Guangxi renmin chubanshe, 1989.

Zhonggong Ji-Lu-Yu bianqu dangshi ziliao congshu: Caijing gongzuo ziliao xuanbian 中共冀魯豫邊區黨史資料叢書：財經工作資料選編 (Party history sources for the CCP Hebei-Shandong-Henan Border Area: selected sources on financial and economic affairs). 2 vols. Ji'nan: Shandong daxue chubanshe, 1989.

Zhongyang geming genjudi gongshang shuishou shiliao 中央革命根据地工商税收史料 (Historical sources on industrial and commercial taxation in the Central Revolutionary Base Area). Fuzhou: Fujian renmin chubanshe, 1985.

Zhongyuan jiefangqu gongshang shuishou shiliao xuanbian 中原解放區工商税收史料選編 (Historical sources on industrial and commercial taxation in the Zhongyuan Liberated Area). Zhengzhou: Henan renmin chubanshe, 1989.

H. Sino-Japanese Conflict and "Puppet" Governments

Guandongjun wenjian ji 關東軍文件集 (Documents on the Japanese Guandong Army).

Jidong Riwei zhengquan 冀東日偽政權 (East Hebei Japanese puppet regime). Beijing: Dang'an chubanshe, 1992.

Kangri zhanzheng shiqi Guomindangjun jimi zuozhan riji 抗日戰爭時期國民黨軍機密作戰日記 (Confidential war journals of Nationalist troops during the War of Resistance Against Japan). Beijing: Dang'an chubanshe, 1995.

Kangri zhanzheng zhengmian zhanchang 抗日戰爭正面戰場 (Major campaigns in the War of Resistance Against Japan). 2 vols. Nanjing: Jiangsu guji chubanshe, 1987.

Nanjing datusha 南京大屠殺 (The Nanjing Massacre). Beijing: Zhonghua shuju, 1995.

Qinhua Rijun Nanjing datusha dang'an 侵華日軍南京大屠殺檔案 (Archival records on the Nanjing Massacre). Nanjing: Jiangsu guji chubanshe, 1987.

Riben diguozhuyi qinhua dang'an xuanbian: Dongbei jingji lüeduo 日本帝國主義侵華檔案選編：東北經濟掠奪 (Selected archival documents on the Japanese invasion of China: economic conquest in the Northeast). Beijing: Zhonghua shuju, 1991.

Riben diguozhuyi qinhua dang'an xuanbian: Dongbei lici da can'an 日本帝國主義侵華檔案選編：東北歷次大慘案 (Selected archival documents on the Japanese invasion of China: major massacres in the Northeast). Beijing: Zhonghua shuju, 1989.

Riben diguozhuyi qinlüe Shanghai zuixing shiliao huibian 日本帝國主義侵略上海罪行史料匯編 (Selected historical sources on the Japanese invasion of Shanghai). (Shanghai: Shanghai renmin chubanshe, 1997.

Riben diguozhuyi zai Min zuixing lu 日本帝國主義在閩罪行錄 (Records of Japanese crimes in Fujian). Fuzhou: Fujian renmin chubanshe, 1995.

Riben qinhua zuixing shizheng: Hebei, Tianjin diqu diren zuixing diaocha dang'an xuanji 日本侵華罪行實證：河北、天津地區敵人罪行調查檔案選輯 (Evidence of Japanese crimes in China: selected archival documents concerning the investigation of enemy crimes in Hebei and Tianjin). Beijing: Renmin chubanshe, 1995.

Riben qinlüe Zhejiang shilu 日本侵略浙江實錄 (Records on the Japanese invasion of Zhejiang). Beijing: Zhonggong dangshi chubanshe, 1995.

Riwei Beijing Xinminhui 日偽北京新民會 (Japanese-puppet Beijing: the New Citizen Society). Beijing: Guangmin ribao chubanshe, 1989.

Riwei de qingxiang 日偽的清鄉 ("Village clearance" campaigns by the Japanese and their puppets). Beijing: Zhonghua shuju, 1995.

Riwei Shanghai shi zhengfu 日偽上海市政府 (The Japanese-puppet Shanghai municipal government). Beijing: Dang'an chubanshe, 1986.

Riwei zai Beijing diqu de wuci qianghua zhian yundong 日偽在北京地區的五次強化治安運動 (Five campaigns by the Japanese and their puppets to tighten public order in the Beijing area). Beijing: Yanshan chubanshe, 1987.

Shenxun Wangwei hanjian bilu 審訊汪偽漢奸筆錄 (Records on the interrogations and trials of traitors from the Wang Jingwei regime). 2 vols. Nanjing: Jiangshu chubanshe, 1992.

Wangwei zhengfu Xingzhengyuan huiyilu 汪偽政府行政院會議錄 (Minutes of the Wang Jingwei puppet government's Executive Yuan). Beijing: Dang'an chubanshe, 1992.

Weiman kuilei zhengquan 偽滿傀儡政權 (The puppet Manchurian regime). Beijing: Zhonghua shuju, 1994.

Weiman xianjing tongzhi 偽滿憲警統治 (Military policing in puppet Manchuria). Beijing: Zhonghua shuju, 1993.

Xijunzhan yu duqizhan 細菌戰與毒氣戰 (Germ and chemical warfare). Beijing: Zhonghua shuju, 1989.

Xinsijun wenxian 新四軍文獻 (Documents on the New Fourth Army). Beijing: Jiefangjun chubanshe, 1988– .

I. Tibet, Taiwan, and Other Areas

Huang Musong, Wu Zhongxin, Zhao Shouyu, Dai Chuanxian fengshi banli Zangshi baogaoshu 黃慕松，吳忠信，趙守鈺，戴傳賢，奉使辦理藏事報告書 (Reports by Huang Musong, Wu Zhongxin, Zhao Shouyu, and Dai Chuanxian as commissioners of Tibetan affairs). Beijing: Zhongguo Zangxue chubanshe, 1993.

Jindai Kangqu dang'an ziliao xuanbian 近代康區檔案資料選編 (Collection of archival sources on Xikang in modern times). Chengdu: Sichuan daxue chubanshe, 1990.

Jiushi banchan yuanji zhiji he shishi banchan zhuanshi zuochuang dang'an xuanbian 九世班禪圓寂致祭和十世班禪轉世坐床檔案選編 (Selected archival documents on mourning the death of the ninth Panchan Lama and inaugurating the tenth Panchan Lama). Beijing: Zhongguo Zangxue chubanshe, 1991.

Min-Tai guanxi dang'an ziliao 閩臺關係檔案資料 (Archival sources on relations between Fujian and Taiwan). Xiamen: Lujiang chubanshe, 1993.

Minyuan Zangshi diangao 民元藏事電稿 (Draft telegrams on Tibetan affairs in 1912). Lhasa: Xizang renmin chubanshe, 1983.

Neimenggu zizhi yundong lianhehui dang'an shiliao xuanbian 內蒙古自治運動聯合會檔案史料選編 (Selected documents of the Association for Inner Mongolia Autonomy). Beijing: Dang'an chubanshe, 1989.

Qingdai yilai zhongyang dui Xizang de zhili yu huofo zhuanshi zhidu shiliao huibian 清代以來中央對西藏的治理與活佛轉世制度史料匯編 (Collected historical documents on the central government's control over Tibet and the Buddhist incarnation and transmigration system since the Qing dynasty). Beijing: Huawen chubanshe, 1996.

Shisanshi dalai yuanji zhiji he shisishi dalai zhuanshi zuochuang dang'an xuanbian 十三世達賴圓寂致祭和十四世達賴轉世坐床檔案選編 (Selected archival documents on mourning the death of the thirteenth Dalai Lama and inaugurating the fourteenth Dalai Lama). Beijing: Zhongguo Zangxue chubanshe, 1991.

Taiwan "Er er ba" shijian dang'an shiliao 臺灣 ″二。二八″ 事件檔案史料 (Archival sources on the February 28th incident). Beijing: Dang'an chubanshe, 1991.

Xinjiang yu Su'e shangye maoyi dang'an shiliao 新疆與蘇俄商業貿易檔案史料 (Archival sources on commercial trade between Xinjiang and Russia). Urumqi: Xinjiang renmin chubanshe, 1994.

Xizang difang lishi dang'an congshu 西藏地方歷史檔案叢書 (Archival series on Tibetan history). Multiple vols. Beijing: Zhongguo Zangxue chubanshe, 1985– .

Xizang dizhen shiliao huibian 西藏地震史料匯編 (Historial sources on earthquakes in Tibet). 2 vols. Lhasa: Xizang renmin chubanshe, 1982.

Xizang lishi dang'an huicui 西藏歷史檔案會萃 (Collection of archival documents on Tibet). Beijing: Wenwu chubanshe, 1995.

Yuan yilai Xizang difang yu zhongyang zhengfu guanxi dang'an shiliao huibian 元以來西藏地方與中央政府關係檔案史料匯編 (Collected archival sources on the relationship between the central government and Tibet since the Yuan dynasty). Beijing: Zhongguo Zangxue chubanshe, 1995.

Zhongguo gongchandang Xizang zizhiqu zuzhishi ziliao, 1950–1987 中國共產黨西藏自治區組織史資料，1950–1987 (Sources on CCP organizational history in Tibet, 1950–87). Lhasa: Xizang renmin chubanshe, 1993.

J. The Transition to Communist Rule; Early PRC

Beiping de heping jieguan 北平的和平接管 (The peaceful takeover of Beiping). Beijing: Beijing chubanshe, 1995.

Beiping heping jiefang qianhou 北平和平解放前後 (Before and after the peaceful liberation of Beiping). Beijing: Beijing chubanshe, 1989.

Guomin jingji huifu shiqi de Beijing 國民經濟恢復時期的北京 (Beijing during the recovery period of the national economy). Beijing: Beijing chubanshe, 1995.

Jianguo yilai zhongyao wenxian xuanbian 建國以來重要文獻選編 (Collection of important documents since the founding of the PRC). Multiple vols. Beijing: Zhonggong zhongyang wenxian chubanshe, 1991– .

Jiefang chuqi Tianjin chengshi jingji hongguan guanli 解放初期天津城市經濟宏觀管理 (Macro-management of the urban economy in Tianjin in the early years after Liberation). Tianjin: Zhonggong, Tianjinshi yinshuachang, 1995.

Liaoning dui zi gaizao dang'an xuanbian 遼寧對資改造檔案選編 (Archival documents on transforming capitalism in Liaoning). Liaoning sheng dang'anguan, 1987.

Nanjing jiefang 南京解放 (Liberation of Nanjing). Nanjing: Jiangsu guji chubanshe, 1990.

Shanghai jiefang 上海解放 (Liberation of Shanghai). Beijing: Dang'an chubanshe, 1989.

Tianjin jieguan shilu 天津接管史錄 (Historical records on the takeover of Tianjin). Beijing: Zhonggong dangshi chubanshe, 1991.

Xi'an jiefang dang'an shiliao xuanji 西安解放檔案史料選輯 (Archival documents on the liberation of Xi'an). Xi'an: Shaanxi renmin chubanshe, 1989.

Zhongguo ziben zhuyi gongshangye de shehuizhuyi gaizao 中國資本主義工商業的社會主義改造 (The socialist transformation of industry and commerce in China). Multiple vols. Beijing: Zhonggong dangshi chubanshe, 1992– .

Zhonghua renmin gongheguo jingji dang'an zilioa xuanbian, 1949–1952 中華人民共和國經濟檔案資料選編 (1949–1952) (Selected archival documents on the PRC economy, 1949–52). Beijing: Shehui kexueyuan chubanshe, 1989– .

VIII. Newspapers and Periodicals

A. Bibliographies

Chinese Newspapers in the Library of Congress. Washington, D.C., 1985.

Chinese Periodicals in the Library of Congress. Washington, D.C., 1978.

Guoli zhongyang tushuguan guancang qikan mulu 國立中央圖書館館藏期刊目錄 (Catalogue of periodicals in the National Central Library). Nanjing, 1933.

Qikan suoyin 期刊索引 (Index of periodicals). Nanjing: Sun Yat-sen Institute for the Advancement of Culture and Education, 1933–37.

Ribao suoyin 日報索引 (Index to Chinese newspapers). Nanjing: China Library Service, 1934–37. Issued monthly by the Sun Yat-sen Institute for the Advancement of Culture and Education.

Shanghai tushuguan. *Zhongguo jindai qikan pianmu huilu* 中國近代期刊遍目匯錄 (Catalogue of modern Chinese periodicals). 6 vols. Shanghai: Shanghai renmin chubanshe, 1980–84.

Zhongwen zazhi suoyin 中文雜志索引 (Index of Chinese periodicals). Guangzhou: Lingnan daxue, 1935.

B. Surveys of Primary Print Sources

In English

China Press Review. Postwar and pre-Liberation, translation of selected articles, GMD and non-GMD. Put out by U.S. consulates: Chongqing, 1945–48 (spotty); Canton (Guangzhou), 1946–58; Kunming, 1945–48; Mukden (Shenyang), 1947–48; Beijing-Tianjin, January 1946–July 1948; Shanghai, September 1945–February 1950.

China Weekly Review, July 25, 1924–Nov. 1, 1951. Weekly. International, national, and local news, NYSE quotes, Chinese writers, pro-GMD. Incorporated in the United States.

The Chinese Recorder, Shanghai, June 1, 1868–1940. Monthly. Articles by foreign missionaries and Chinese Christians on missionary activities, government policy, etc.

Current Background, June 13, 1950–July 7, 1977. U.S. Consulate, Hong Kong. Translation of selected Mainland newspaper articles and news releases.

North China Herald, Shanghai, 1850–1941. Weekly. National and international news, local stories ("news from the outposts").

Survey of the China Mainland Press (*SCMP*), November 1, 1950–September 30, 1977. Put out by the U.S. Consulate in Hong Kong. Selected articles from Mainland newspapers. International and regional issues.

US Consulate Translation of Radio Broadcast of Communist Hsin Hua Station, North Shensi. Peking, November 20, 1947–July 10, 1949.

US Foreign Broadcast Information Service (*FBIS*), 1948–74. FBIS daily reports, translations of selected radio broadcasts, worldwide. Table of contents.

In Chinese

Newspapers

Da gong bao 大公報 (L'Impartial). Tianjin, 1902–25. Changed management in 1926–49, with various editions (Hong Kong, 1938–41, 1948–64; Chongqing, 1941–46; Beijing, 1957–66; Shanghai, 1937–52; Tianjin, 1929–56). It was initially a pro-imperialist publication; when sold to the warlord government in 1916, it began espousing pro-Japanese sentiments.

Jiefang ribao 解放日報 (Liberation daily). Yan'an, May 1941–February 1947. Anti-GMD stories on Communist successes and military victories, examples of successful CCP policies in action.

Jiuguo ribao 救國日報 (National salvation daily). Nanjing, August 1932–37. Nationalist publication. Main function was to rally protest against Japanese incursions.

Nongbao 農報 (Agriculture). Beijing. August 1916–June 1928. Ed. Li Dazhao. Reformist and bourgeois, following the ideals of Liang Qichao.

Renmin ribao 人民日報 (People's daily), Beijing, 1949– .

Shenbao 申報. Shanghai. From April 1872 to 1909, controlled by U.S. and English business interests (Ernest Major) with limited shareholding by Chinese. In 1912, publishing rights sold to Shi Liangcai, who managed it until his death in late 1934. The GMD took over its operation from the end of the Pacific War until 1949. There is a comprehensive index to it.

Shishi xinbao 時事新報 (The China times). Shanghai, Nanjing, Chongqing, 1907–49. Early on it was the mouthpiece for the Progress Party; seized in 1934 by H. H. Kung.

Xinhua ribao 新華日報 (New China daily). Wuhan & Chongqing, 1938–47. This was a CCP-sponsored newspaper published in GMD-controlled areas.

Zhonghua ribao 中華日報 (China daily). Nanjing, April 1942–45. Collaborationist government-owned newspaper, controlled by Wang Jingwei.

Zhongyang ribao 中央日報 (Central daily). Nanjing, November 1932–September 1937; Chongqing, September 1938–42; Shanghai, Feb. 1928–April 1949; Taibei, October 1949–70. Pro-GMD. National policies, victories over Communist forces.

Journals

Dongfang zazhi 東方雜志 (Eastern miscellany). Shanghai: Shanghai shangwu yinshuguan, March 1904–December 1948. Published in Changsha, Hong Kong, and Chongqing during the Pacific War. It has an index.

Gongshang banyuekan 工商半月刊 (Industry and commerce biweekly). 1929–36.

Guoji maoyi daobao 國際貿易導報 (International trade report). April 1930–December 1938.

Guomin 國民 (Citizen). Beijing: Beijing daxue, Guogu zazhishe, January 1919–?. Ceased publication shortly after the May Fourth movement.

Guowen zhoubao 國聞周報 (National news weekly). Shanghai: Guowen tongxunshe, August 1924–December 1937. It has an index.

Jingji banyuekan 經濟半月刊 (Economics biweekly). November 1927–November 1928.

Renwen yuekan 人文月刊 (Humanities monthly). Shanghai, 1930–37.

Xin chao 新潮 (New tide). Shanghai, 1919–22.

Xin qingnian 新青年 (New youth). Shanghai, April 1915–July 1926.

Xin Zhonghua 新中華 (New China). Shanghai: Zhonghua shuju, January 1933–May 1949.

Xue heng 學衡. Nanjing: Nanjing dongnan daxue, January 1922–July 1933.

Yinhang zhoubao 銀行周報 (Banking weekly). 1917–50.

Zhonghang yuekan 中行月刊 (Bank of China monthly). August 1938–December 1938.

Zhongwai jingji zhoukan 中外經濟周刊 (Economics weekly). March 1923–October 1927.

Part II

BUSINESS AND ECONOMIC HISTORY ARCHIVES

OF REPUBLICAN CHINA

Chapter 4

The Number Two Historical Archives
中國第二歷史檔案館

Introduction

The Number Two Historical Archives in Nanjing (Zhongguo di'er lishi dang'anguan 中國第二歷史檔案館) is a national archive directly administered by the Chinese State Archives Bureau. Its primary mission is to acquire, arrange, and preserve records of the Republican period (1912–49). It has a total of 1,560,000 volumes (*juan* 卷) of documents. The holdings consist mainly of records concerning the following: the Republic of China (ROC) Provisional Government in Nanjing and other revolutionary governments in the south, the ROC Government in Beijing, the Nationalist Party (Guomindang, or GMD) and its National Government in Nanjing and Chongqing, the Chinese collaborationist governments in Japanese-occupied areas, and important individuals.

Economic History Archives

I. The Republic of China Provisional Government and Other Revolutionary Governments in the South

Between 1912 and 1927, revolutionaries in South China set up three governments: the Provisional Government in Nanjing (1912), the Military Government in Guangzhou (1923–25), and the National Government, first in Guangzhou and later in Wuhan (1925–27). Though incomplete, the records of these governments are now kept in the Number Two Archives.

The Provisional Government (Linshi zhengfu 臨時政府) founded by Sun Yat-sen (孫逸仙, also known as Sun Zhongshan 孫中山) in Nanjing on January 1, 1912, lasted only three months. Of the nine ministries and other offices over which Sun presided, the archives contain documents from the Office of the President (Zongtong fu 總統府), Ministry of the Interior (Neiwu bu 內務部), Ministry of Finance (Caizheng bu 財政部), Ministry of the Army (Lujun bu 陸軍部), and the Liaison Office (Liushou fu 留守府).

More than a decade after the Provisional Government was disbanded, Sun became generalissimo of the Military Government (Lu-Hai jun dayuanshuai dabenying 陸海軍大元帥大本營), which operated in Guangzhou from March 1923 to June 1925. This position gave him a broad range of powers over military and civil affairs and personnel appointments. The Number Two Archives holds numerous documents concerning the Nationalist Party; the state; military affairs of the Military Government, including the Nationalist Party Central Executive Committee's resolutions and policy statements; party recruitment papers; army deployment and provisions; and written communications from important political figures such as Sun Yat-sen, Hu Hanmin 胡漢民, and Tan Yankai 譚延闓.

The Military Government ended two weeks after the GMD Central Executive Committee's June 15, 1925, decision to organize the National Government (Guomin zhengfu 國民政府). On July 1, the Guangzhou National Government was established under the supervision and guidance of the Guomindang. As the forces of the Northern Expedition projected GMD military power to the Yangzi River in late 1926, the National Government moved its main offices to Wuhan, where it remained from December until relocating to Nanjing in August 1927. In addition to historical materials focusing on the internal and external affairs of the GMD regime, state, and military, the archives contains a large assortment of documents relating to specific events, such as the May Thirtieth incident of 1925 and various labor incidents (e.g., strike by workers against the Canton Sincere Company 廣州先施公司 and other Guangdong companies).

II. The ROC Government in Beijing (1912–28)

A. *Ministry of Finance*

The Beiyang Government's Ministry of Finance (Caizheng bu) was established in Beijing in March 1912 to manage and supervise accounting, revenue and expenditures, taxes, government bonds, currency, state monopolies, public savings, and banks and other fiscal concerns. It was composed of a General Affairs Office and five departments. In July 1927, the government expanded the ministry with the creation of the Salt Office, the Tobacco and Alcohol Office, the Stamp Tax Section, and the Official Assets Section.

The Number Two Archives' holdings of Ministry of Finance records are substantial. These include regulations governing each department and office; appointment notices; state, provincial, and military budgets; bond contracts; and documents relating to currency smuggling, overseas Chinese, joint ventures, and foreign banks.

B. *Ministry of Agriculture and Commerce*

The Ministry of Agriculture and Commerce (Nongshang bu 農商部) grew out of a merger between the Ministry of Agriculture and Forestry (Nonglin bu 農林部) and the Ministry of Industry and Commerce (Gongshang bu 工商部) in December 1913. Its duties were to regulate agriculture, forestry, fisheries, livestock, industry and commerce, and mining. In July 1927, the ministry was divided into two new ministries: the Ministry of Agriculture and Industry (Nonggong bu 農工部) and the Ministry of Industry (Shiye bu 實業部).

The Number Two Archives has over 3,000 volumes of documents from the Ministry of Agriculture and Commerce. Besides regulations, appointment papers, and other general documents, the collection contains surveys of commodities, insurance, and pawnshop prices; reports from international labor conferences; land survey tables; and weather reports for 1913–20. In addition, there are mining licenses issued by offices in Shanxi, Jiangsu, Zhejiang, Zhili (Hebei), Rehe, and Jingzhao.

III. The Guomindang (GMD) Party (1924–47)

A. *The Secretariat of the Guomindang Central Executive Committee*
Established in January 1924, the Secretariat of the GMD Central Executive Committee (CEC) (Zhongyang zhixing weiyuanhui, Mishuchu 中央執行委員會秘書處) was responsible for routine affairs. Prior to creating the position of secretary general (*mishuzhang* 秘書長) in March 1929, the Secretariat was directed by the CEC's three-member standing committee. Below the Secretariat were numerous departments and sections in charge of, among other things, documents, statistics, finance, accounting, and personnel.

The Number Two Archives possesses an extensive collection of documents from the Secretariat including those on party regulations, organization, propaganda, and training, as well as materials reflecting relations between the GMD and the CCP. The collection also contains intelligence reports, handbooks, party periodicals, minutes of meetings, proposals, and resolutions from important GMD congresses.

B. *Supreme National Defense Council (1939–47)*
In February 1939 the Supreme National Defense Council (Guofang zuigao weiyuanhui 國防最高委員會) replaced the GMD Central Political Council (Zhongyang zhengzhi weiyuanhui 中央政治委員會) as the paramount executive organ with control over party, government, and military affairs during the war against Japan. The leader of the party served concurrently as the council's head executive and, along with eleven other officials, made up its standing commission. The council was dissolved in April 1947.

The collection at the Number Two Archives contains documents from the Supreme National Defense Council between 1938 and 1946. These include work reports, budgets, fiscal reports for 1942–44, and reports on the GMD's economic blockade of CCP-controlled areas.

IV. The Nationalist Government in Nanjing and Chongqing (1927–49)

A. *The National Government (1927–49)*
The National Government (Guomin zhengfu) was established in Nanjing on April 18, 1927, as the highest institution of national government. The term *Guomin zhengfu* was commonly used in two senses: first, to refer to the central government in Nanjing (the national government); and second, to refer to a distinct organization that held supreme power atop the administrative structure of the central government (the National Government, sometimes referred to as the

National Government Committee [Guomin zhengfu weiyuanhui]). The chairman (*zhuxi*) of the National Government (Committee) was Chiang Kai-shek (Jiang Jieshi 蔣介石). In 1928 the government established an administrative structure composed of five *yuan* beneath the National Government: Legislative Yuan (Lifa yuan 立法院), Executive Yuan (Xingzheng yuan 行政院), Judicial Yuan (Sifa yuan 司法院), Examination Yuan (Kaoshi yuan 考試院), and Control Yuan (Jiancha yuan 監察院). This organizational structure remained essentially unchanged after the National Government moved to Chongqing. In March 1948 the government held a general election in accordance with the 1946 constitution. On May 20, Chiang Kai-shek and Li Zongren 李宗仁 were formally elected president and vice-president, respectively; and the National Government was reorganized as the Office of the President (Zongtong fu 總統府); the five-yuan system remained.

Over 11,000 volumes of National Government documents have been preserved at the Number Two Archives and provide a wealth of material on all aspects of the government and its subordinate organizations. Some general subtopics include regulations, organizational structure, personnel, planning, fiscal management, military affairs, foreign relations, local administration, education, public health, transportation and communications, water conservancy, grain administration, Mongolian and Tibetan affairs, relations with overseas Chinese, and the 1927 purge of the Communists.

B. The National Reconstruction Commission (1928–38)

As a key organization in the GMD program to rebuild the national economy, the National Reconstruction Commission (Guomin zhengfu jianshe weiyuanhui 國民政府建設委員會) was responsible for researching and initiating projects in water management, electricity, and mining. Following its creation in February 1928, the Reconstruction Commission expanded to include numerous sections and committees (e.g., the Enterprises Section, the Economic Committee). The commission was disbanded in January 1938 following the outbreak of the war with the Japanese.

National Reconstruction Commission documents in the Number Two Archives relate to conferences, water management, electricity, and mining.

C. The National Defense Planning Commission (1932–35)

The National Defense Planning Commission (Guofang sheji weiyuanhui 國防設計委員會) was created in November 1932, approximately a year after the Japanese invasion of Manchuria in September 1931. As its name indicates, the commission was responsible for formulating policies for national security. In addition, matters involving the arms trade, mining and metallurgy, chemicals, petroleum, defense technology, and border issues fell under its purview. In March 1935, the commission merged with the Department of Resources (Ziyuan si 資源司) of the Department of Ordnance (Binggong shu 兵工署) to become the National Resources Commission (Ziyuan weiyuanhui 資源委員會) under the Military Commission (Junshi weiyuanhui 軍事委員會).

The Number Two Archives has a small collection of National Defense Planning Commission documents, including reports on foreign military activity, diplomatic problems, data on military expenditures covering 1929–34, and reports written by Weng Wenhao 翁文灝 and others concerning plans for the development of national defense industries.

D. The Department of Ordnance (1928–49)

The Department of Ordnance (Binggong shu 兵工署), established under the Ministry of Military Administration (Junzheng bu 軍政部) in November 1928, oversaw the management of munitions technology, arms manufacturing, and ordnance administration. A reorganization in 1946 expanded the responsibilities of the Department of Ordnance to include acquiring and developing armaments and provisions; training special forces of the Ordnance Department; testing, researching, and experimenting with weapons and raw materials; managing armories; and formulating principles governing chemical warfare strategy.

Documents from the Department of Ordnance cover the period 1932–49. Besides materials relating to regulations, organization, conferences, personnel, and expenditures, the collection also contains documents concerning arms research and development, weapons production, arms and provisions purchases, and management of its subordinate organizations (e.g., munitions works, armories).

E. The National Resources Commission (1935–49)

Resulting from a merger of the National Defense Planning Commission and the Resources Section of the Ordnance Department in April 1935, the National Resources Commission (NRC) (Ziyuan weiyuanhui 資源委員會) was responsible for planning the natural and human resources related to industrial development and national defense. Initially under the control of the Military Commission (Junshi weiyuanhui 軍事委員會), the commission came under the jurisdiction of the Ministry of Economic Affairs in March 1938. The main functions of the NRC were to develop and manage key industrial sectors including electricity and mines. In May 1946 it became directly subordinate to the Executive Yuan. Three years later (1949), the commission again was placed under the Ministry of Economic Affairs, and its functions expanded to include developing and managing enterprises in agriculture, forestry, animal husbandry, and fishing. Overall, the NRC developed over 200 different enterprises, the infrastructure to manage them, numerous branch offices, and a telecommunications network. In 1949, the commission's enterprises were taken over by the government of the People's Republic.

There are over 30,000 volumes of NRC documents stored at the Number Two Archives. These include letters to and from important NRC leaders such as Weng Wenhao 翁文灝, Qian Changzhao 錢昌照, Sun Yueqi 孫越崎, and Wu Zhaohong 吳兆洪; work reports; investigation and research surveys; financial records; documents regarding the expropriation of industries formerly in Japanese-occupied areas; and management records of industrial, mining, and power facilities.

F. The National Economic Council (1933–38), Supreme Economic Council (1945–47), and the National Economic Council (1947–48)

The National Economic Council (NEC) (Quanguo jingji weiyuanhui 全國經濟委員會) was established under the National Government in September 1933 after a two-year preparatory phase. The Council's primary task was to map out plans for economic development. Specifically, the Council oversaw road construction, water conservancy, public health, education, rural reconstruction, sericulture, and the cotton industry. The NEC set up three branch offices, in Shanghai, Jiangxi, and in the Northwest. When the council ceased operations in 1938 after the outbreak of the Sino-Japanese War its organs were incorporated into various ministries (e.g., the Roads Commission came under the jurisdiction of the Ministry of Communications, and the Water Conservancy Commission was subordinated to the Ministry of Economic Affairs).

In November 1945, the government established the Supreme Economic Council (Zuigao jingji weiyuanhui 最高經濟委員會). Initially it was under the National Government, but later it came under the jurisdiction of the Executive Council. Like its predecessor, this new body formulated economic policy and coordinated implementation with other agencies concerned with economic development. The president of the Executive Yuan served as the council's chairman, with the vice president of the Executive Yuan and various heads of ministries as members. In May 1947, the Supreme Economic Council was reorganized as the National Economic Council (Quanguo jingji weiyuanhui 全國經濟委員會) under the Executive Yuan. The council was disbanded in August 1948.

The Number Two Archives has combined the documents of these three institutions into one collection.

G. War Production Board (1944–45)

The War Production Board (Zhanshi shengchan ju 戰時生產局) oversaw military and civilian wartime production, handled international and domestic equipment purchases, and assigned priority to emergency imports and exports. Although officially subordinate to the Executive Yuan, the bureau also received instructions from the Military Commission.

Despite its brief existence, a large number of documents from the War Production Board are stored at the Number Two Archives. The collection includes documents on the production of weapons, machinery, steel, oil, and other goods necessary for the war effort.

H. China Industrial Cooperatives ("CIC" or "Indusco") (1938–50)

The China Industrial Cooperatives (Zhongguo gongye hezuo xiehui 中國工業合作協會) was founded in Hankou on August 5, 1938, to raise capital, help localities organize industrial associations, increase production, and give financial assistance to the war against Japan. After the war, Indusco played a role in coordinating industrial development. In May 1950, it was merged into the Central Cooperative Enterprise Management Bureau (Zhongyang hezuo shiye).

I. Ministry of Finance (1927–49)

The Ministry of Finance (Caizheng bu 財政部) was established in May 1927. In November 1928, it was placed under the administrative aegis of the Executive Yuan. The ministry's main functions were to manage the national treasury, levy taxes, regulate issuance of public bonds, and supervise and direct local finance.

The Number Two Archives has over 50,000 volumes of Ministry of Finance documents, catalogued in thirteen categories: national treasury, general finance, local finance, bonds, taxation, salt administration, customs, smuggling, trade, monopolies, opium suppression, textile controls, and miscellaneous (e.g., regulations, organization, personnel, planning, statistics).

J. Treasury Administration (1940–49)

The Treasury Administration (Guoku shu 國庫署) grew out of the reorganization of the Ministry of Finance's Treasury Department (Guoku si 國庫司) in March 1940. Remaining under the Ministry of Finance, it was assigned to formulate, review, explain, and implement the public treasury system; manage income and expenditures; and register, circulate, store, and transfer all legal tender.

The Treasury Administration documents at the Number Two Archives include information on treasury revenue and outlays, special funds (*tezhong jijin* 特種基金), internal and external debt, and other relevant functions.

K. Customs Administration (1927–49)

The Number Two Archives has nearly 2,000 volumes of documents from the Customs Administration (Guanwu shu 關務署) covering its activities from 1927 until 1949.

L. Directorate General of the Salt Administration

The evolution of the Directorate General of the Salt Administration (Yanwu zongju 鹽務總) during the Nationalist period was complex. Initially, the Salt Affairs Office (Yanwu chu 鹽務處) was placed under the Ministry of Finance in 1927 and reorganized a few months later as the Salt Administration (Yanwu shu 鹽務署) in charge of salt production, transportation, sale, and taxation. In January 1929 the Ministry of Finance established a separate division, the Inspectorate General of the Salt Gabelle (Yanwu jihe zongsuo 鹽務稽核總所), to collect salt taxes and to clear foreign debts resulting from Yuan Shikai's Reorganization Loan of 1913. Many of its staff, including the inspector general, were foreigners. In a structural reorganization in 1936, the Salt Administration became the Ministry of Finance's Salt Affairs Department (Yanzheng si 鹽政司), with the Inspectorate General of the Salt Gabelle being replaced by the Directorate General of Salt Administration (Yanwu zongju 鹽務總局). The Salt Affairs Department's function was to audit tax receipts and revenue, whereas the Directorate General of Salt Administration was responsible for managing production, transportation, sales, and taxation. These organizations merged in early 1945.

The Number Two Archives has combined documents from both organizations into one collection, totaling more than 17,000 volumes. These documents can be divided into the following categories: general affairs, inspection, salt production, salt transportation and sale, accounts and auditing, saltpeter management, and supervision.

M. Central Water Conservancy Experimentation Department (1935–49)

Originally called the Central Hydraulics Experimentation Institute (Zhongyang shuigong shiyan suo 中央水工實驗所) at its inception in January 1935, the Central Water Conservancy Experimentation Department (Zhongyang shuili shiyan chu 中央水利實驗處) conducted hydraulic surveys and experiments. Documents include survey reports, charts, tables, construction contracts, and data from experiments.

N. Ministry of Industry and Commerce (1928–30)

The Ministry of Industry and Commerce (Gongshang bu 工商部) was created in February 1928. It consisted of four departments: the General Affairs Department, the Industry Department, the Commerce Department, and the Labor Department. In January 1931 the ministry was combined with the Ministry of Agriculture and Mining (Nongkuang bu 農礦部) to form the Ministry of Industry (Shiye bu 實業部). Documents include personnel records, industrial and commercial surveys, records of labor unrest, and budgets.

O. Ministry of Industry (1931–38)

Created from the merger of the Ministry of Industry and Commerce and the Ministry of Agriculture and Mining in 1931, the Ministry of Industry (Shiye bu 實業部) had eight departments: Agriculture, Mining, Cooperatives, Fishing, Livestock, plus four departments of the former Ministry of Industry and Commerce. The Number Two Archives has more than 22,000 volumes of documents from the Ministry of Industry covering 1931–38.

P. Ministry of Economic Affairs (1938–49)

The Ministry of Industry was reorganized and expanded in January 1938 as the Ministry of Economic Affairs (Jingji bu 經濟部), subordinate to the Executive Yuan. In May 1948, the ministry was again reorganized, this time under the name Ministry of Industry and Commerce (Gongshang bu 工商部), but its scope of responsibilities remained much the same. In March 1949, the Ministry of Industry and Commerce was combined with the Ministry of Agriculture and Forestry (Nonglin bu 農林部), the Ministry of Water Conservancy (Shuili bu 水利部), and the National Resources Commission (Ziyuan weiyuanhui 資源委員會) to again form the Ministry of Economic Affairs.

The Ministry of Economic Affairs collection has more than 38,000 volumes of documents covering agriculture, forestry, mining, industry, commerce, international trade, and electricity production. The documents of the Ministry of Industry and Commerce (May 1948–February 1949) are also in this collection.

Q. Public Offices for Road Construction and Maintenance (1932–49)

During the mid- to late Republican period, the Nationalist government set up offices in various commissions and departments to oversee the construction and maintenance of public roads. Between 1932 and 1949, at least sixty administrative reorganizations and transfers of these offices occurred. Of primary concern to these offices was managing overland cargo and military supplies and postal services.

Unfortunately, documents on road construction and maintenance offices at the Number Two Archives are not systematically arranged. Researchers interested in specific information may have to wade through the twenty or so archival subcollections on road-construction organizations.

R. Chinese National Aviation Corp. (1930–49) and Central Air Cargo Company (1943–49)

1. The Chinese National Aviation Corp. (Zhongguo hangkong gufen youxian gongsi 中國航空股分有限公司, or "Zhong hang" 中航) was founded in August 1930 as a joint venture between the Ministry of Communications (Jiaotong bu 交通部) and Pan American Airlines of the United States. The company focused on air freight and trained Chinese civilian pilots.

2. Originally the Eurasia Aviation Corporation (Ou-Ya hangkong gongsi 歐亞航空公司), the Central Air Cargo Company (Zhongyang hangkong yunshu gongsi 中央航空運輸公司, or "Yang hang" 央航) was a state-run civilian airline company under the Ministry of Communications. Reorganized in March 1943, the company engaged in passenger transport, mail delivery, and the manufacturing, assembly, and repair of aviation equipment.

The Number Two Archives has separate holdings for these two companies. They include Chinese- and English-language documents such as contracts, board meeting minutes, progress reports, communications with foreign companies, records of labor strikes, and routes and schedules.

V. Banks and Companies

The Number Two Archives has an extensive collection of documents from most of the major financial institutions of the Republican period. The following is a partial list of these organizations:

The Trade Commission (Maoyi weiyuanhui 貿易委員會) (1938–46)

Fuxing Commercial Company (Fuxing shangye gongsi 復興商業公司) (1939–46)

Fuhua Trade Company (Fuhua maoyi gongsi 富華貿易公司) (1937–42)

Central Bank of China (Zhongyang yinhang 中央銀行) (1928–49)

Bank of China (Zhongguo yinhang 中國銀行) (1912–49)

Bank of Communications (Jiaotong yinhang 交通銀行) (1908–49)

Farmers' Bank of China (Zhongguo nongmin yinhang 中國農民銀行) (1933–49)

Joint Board of the Four Banks 四聯總處 (1937–48). The four banks are the Bank of China, the Central Bank of China, the Bank of Communications, and the Farmers' Bank of China.

Manufacturers' Bank of China (Zhongguo guohuo yinhang 中國國貨銀行) (1929–49)

Central Trust of China (Zhongyang xintuo ju 中央信託局) (1935–49)

Postal Remittances & Savings Bank (Youzheng chujin huiye ju 郵政儲金匯業局) (1930–49)

Central Cooperative Bank of China (Zhongyang hezuo jinku 中央合作金庫) (1946–49)

VI. Railroads

The Number Two Archives has a large collection pertaining to railways and railway administration in China. The following is a partial list of these holdings:

The Ministry of Railroads (Tiedao bu 鐵道部) (1928–38)

Beiping-Tianjin Railroad Administration (Ping-Jin qu tielu guanliju 平津區鐵路管理局) (1946–49)

Beijing-Nanjing Railroad Administration (Bei-Ning tielu guanliju 北寧鐵路管理局) (1906–49)

Tianjin-Pukou Railroad Administration (Jin-Pu qu tielu guanliju 津浦區鐵路管理局) (1913–49)

Beijing-Shanghai (Shanghai-Nanjing) Shanghai-Hangzhou-Ningbo Railroad Administration (Jing-Hu [Hu-Ning] Hu-Hang-Yong tielu guanliju 京滬(滬寧) 滬杭甬鐵路管理局) (1914–49)

Merchants' Jiangnan Railroad Company, Ltd. (Shangban Jiangnan tielu gufen youxian gongsi 商辦江南鐵路股分有限公司) (1932–49)

Zhejiang-Jiangxi Railroad Administration (Zhe-Gan tielu guanliju 浙贛鐵路管理局) (1934–49)

Beiping-Hankou Railroad Administration (Ping-Han tielu guanliju 平漢鐵路管理局) (1906–49)

Guangdong-Hankou Railroad Administration (Yue-Han qu tielu guanliju 粵漢區鐵路管理局) (1936–49)

VII. Official History Bureaus

The Number Two Archives also houses documents of official history organizations of the Nationalist Government era. These include:

The Guomindang Central Party History Commission (Guomindang zhongyang dangshi shiliao bianzuan weiyuanhui 國民黨中央黨史史料編纂委員會) (1930–)

Academia Historica (Guoshi guan 國史館) (1940–49)

The Ministry of Defense History Compilation Bureau (Guofang bu shizheng ju 國防部史局) (1946–49) and the War History Compilation Commission (Zhanshi bianzuan weiyuanhui 戰史編纂委員會) (1934–49)

VIII. Archives of the Chinese Government in Japanese-Occupied Areas (1937–45)

Ministry of Finance (1940–45) and Ministry of Industry (1941–45)
The government of Wang Jingwei set up a Ministry of Finance (March 1940) and Ministry of Industry (August 1941) to administer regions occupied by Japanese forces. The Number Two Archives has preserved a small collection of documents from these two ministries. These documents primarily relate to financial and economic policies and conditions in occupied China.

IX. The Inspectorate General of the Customs

The Inspectorate General of Customs (IGC; Haiguan zongshuiwu si 海關總稅務司) was established in Shanghai in 1859 and moved to Beijing in 1864. During the Qing dynasty, it was under the nominal jurisdiction of the Office in Charge of Foreign Affairs (Zongli geguo shiwu yamen 總理各國事務衙門), which became the Ministry of Foreign Affairs (Waiwu bu 外務部) in 1901. In 1906–27 the IGC was subordinate to the Ministry of Finance's Taxation Department (Caizheng bu, Shuiwu ju 財政部稅務司). Under the Nationalist government, the IGC came under the jurisdiction of the Finance Ministry's Customs Administration and moved back to Shanghai in 1928. After the outbreak of the Pacific War, the Japanese assumed control over the IGC, and the Nationalist government had to establish another IGC in Chongqing. After the war, the Chongqing IGC moved to Shanghai and took over all customs offices in the former Japanese-occupied areas.

The IGC's primary functions were to collect customs duties, administer navigation and harbors, construct and maintain lighthouses, and manage postal services. In the Qing dynasty the IGC consisted of four departments: Taxation, Maritime Affairs, Education, and Postal Administration. In the Republican period, it consisted of two major departments: Taxation and Maritime Affairs. The post of inspector general of customs was controlled first by Great Britain and later by the United States.

The records of the IGC are the largest documentary collection in the Number Two Archives, with a total of 53,874 volumes of documents covering a span of almost ninety years from 1861 to 1949. Most documents are in English. This collection is a rich source of information for the study of Chinese maritime trade during this period. In addition to tax regulations, it contains valuable information about customs administration, duties and income, smuggling, navigation, shipping, accounting, foreign trade, and postal administration, as well as intelligence reports.

Publications

In the 1950s, the Number Two Archives compiled two reference works intended for domestic circulation among research organizations and institutes of higher learning. These were *Zhongguo xiandai zhengzhishi ziliao huibian* 中國現代政治史資料匯編 (Collected sources on modern Chinese political history) and *Zhongguo xiandai zhengzhishi dashi yuebiao* 中國現代政治史大事月表 (Monthly chronology of major events in modern Chinese political history). Scholars have found the former publication, a large, multivolume collection of documents spanning the period from the May Fourth movement in 1919 until the end of the Republic in 1949, very useful. However, the collection is not without flaws. For instance, its emphasis on "directing all endeavors toward the needs of class struggle" precluded an objective selection of documents that would have ensured a more comprehensive presentation of that period's history. As a consequence,

certain documents, such as those reflecting the economic achievements of the Nationalist government during the Nanjing Decade or its role in the war against the Japanese, did not receive
adequate representation. A second defect lies in the collection's narrow focus on political history,
resulting in the neglect of economic, social, and cultural developments.

After Chinese archives reopened to researchers in 1980, the publication of document
collections has increased. Since then, the Number Two Archives has compiled and published
more than forty collections of selected documents. These can be subsumed under two general
categories: comprehensive and topical. One example of a comprehensive series is the multivolume
Zhonghua minguo shi dang'an ziliao huibian 中華民國史檔案資料匯編 (Collection of archival
sources on Republican China). It includes material from the Nanjing Provisional Government,
the Beiyang Government, and the Southern Revolutionary Government under Sun Yat-sen, as
well as biographical data on Chiang Kai-shek, Zhang Jingjiang (張靜江), and other important
figures. The first two volumes, published in 1979 and 1982, contain documents chiefly on
politics, with only a few related to finance, banking, or culture. When the series was expanded in
the late 1980s and early 1990s, greater attention was given to other types of documents, such as
those pertaining to finance, education, industry, commerce, and economic and social reform.
Each thematic topic constitutes one or two volumes. Among the volumes on economic development
are *Nanjing guomin zhengfu shiqi caizheng jingji* 南京國民政府時期財政經濟 (Finance and the
economy of the Nanjing National Government period), 9 vols.; *Beiyang zhengfu shiqi caizheng*
北洋政府時期財政 (Fiscal administration of the Beiyang government period), 2 vols.; *Beiyang
zhengfu shiqi jinrong* 北洋政府時期金融 (Banking and finance during the Beiyang government
period), 2 vols.; *Beiyang zhengfu shiqi gongkuangye* 北洋政府時期工礦業 (Industry and mining
during the Beiyang government period); and *Beiyang zhengfu shiqi nongshang* 北洋政府時期農
商 (Agriculture and commerce during the Beiyang government period).

Aside from the comprehensive series, the Number Two Archives has, since 1980, begun
publishing topical volumes usually organized around a specific historical event, person, or
organization. One rationale for publication of these volumes is to revisit and reassess important
topics in modern Chinese history. An example is *Kangri zhanzheng zhengmian zhanchang* 抗日
戰爭正面戰場 (Battlefront of the War of Resistance Against Japan), 2 vols. (Nanjing: Jiangsu
guji chubanshe, 1987). Earlier historiography in the PRC emphasized communist-organized
guerrilla resistance in Japanese-occupied areas and paid little attention to the Nationalist
government's role in the war. In contrast, these volumes, with documents on major battles fought
by Chiang's troops, acknowledge his government's role in the resistance effort. A second purpose
for the Number Two Archives to compile and publish documents on particular subjects is to
open new avenues of research and make public hitherto unpublished materials. One such example
is the multi-volume *Minguo dangpai shetuan dang'an shiliao conggao* 民國黨派社團檔案史料
叢稿 (Archival sources on political parties and mass organizations during the Republican period)
(Beijing: Dang'an chubanshe, 1988–).   The volumes of this project include documents on small
political parties of the Republican period that have been overlooked by scholars. A third purpose

of the Number Two Archives' publication efforts is to address issues of contemporary significance. *Nanjing datusha* 南京大屠殺 (The Nanjing Massacre) (Beijing: Zhonghua shuju, 1995) is one example. The Nanjing Massacre, or the "Rape of Nanking," continues to be a significant issue in contemporary Sino-Japanese relations. The purpose of publishing these documents is to refute certain Japanese denials of the incident. Additional examples of publication of historical documents to serve contemporary political interests are *Jiushi banchan yuanji zhiji he shishi banchan zhuanshi zuochuang dang'an xuanbian* 九世班禪圓寂致祭和十世班禪轉世坐床檔案選編 (Selected archival documents on ceremonies for mourning the death of the ninth Panchan Lama and selecting and inaugurating the tenth Panchan Lama) (Beijing: Zhongguo Zangxue chubanshe, 1991) and *Shisanshi dalai yuanji zhiji he shisishi dalai zuochuang dang'an xuanbian* 十三世達賴圓寂致祭和十四世達賴轉世坐床檔案選編 (Selected archival documents on ceremonies for mourning the death of the thirteenth Dalai Lama and selecting and inaugurating the fourteenth Dalai Lama) (Beijing: Zhongguo Zangxue chubanshe, 1991).

Important for the purpose of this survey are the thematic or topical volumes on the economic history of the Republican period. Most of these volumes were compiled and published in cooperation with institutions interested in compiling their professional gazetteers (行業志). The following is a selected list of published collections related to financial and economic developments during the Republican period:

Jiaotong yinhang shiliao 交通銀行史料 (Historical sources on the Bank of Communications). Beijing: Zhongguo jinrong chubanshe, 1995.

Zhongguo yinhang hangshi ziliao huibian 中國銀行行史資料匯編 (Selected archival sources on the history of the Bank of China). Beijing: Dang'an chubanshe, 1991.

Riben diguozhuyi qinhua dang'an ziliao xuanbian: Dongbei jingji lüeduo 日本帝國主義侵華檔案選編：東北經濟掠奪 (Selected archival documents on the Japanese imperialist invasion of China: economic conquest in the Northeast). Beijing: Zhonghua shuju, 1991.

Zhonghua minguo jinrong fagui dang'an ziliao xuanbian 中華民國金融法規檔案資料選編 (Selected archival documents on financial regulations of Republican China). Beijing: Dang'an chubanshe, 1990.

Minguo waizhai dang'an shiliao 民國外債檔案史料 (Archival sources on foreign debts of Republican China). Beijing: Dang'an chubanshe, 1989–92.

Zhonghua minguo shangye dang'an ziliao huibian 中華民國商業檔案資料匯編 (Selected archival documents on commerce in Republican China). Beijing: Zhongguo shangye chubanshe, 1991.

Zhongguo haiguan midang: Hede Jin Denggan handian huibian, 1874–1907 中國海關密檔 赫德、金登干函電匯編, 1874–1907 (Confidential documents of the Chinese Maritime Customs: correspondence between Robert Hart and James Duncan Campbell, 1874–1907). Beijing: Zhonghua shuju, 1990– .

Zhang Jian nongshang zongzhang renqi jingji ziliao xuanbian 張謇農商總長任期經濟資料 選編 (Selected sources on the economy during Zhang Jian's term as minister of agriculture and commerce). Nanjing: Nanjing daxue chubanshe, 1987.

In addition, the Number Two Archives published a new guide, *Zhongguo dier lishi dang'anguan zhinan* 中國第二歷史檔案館指南 (Guide to the Number Two Chinese Archives), in 1994, replacing the 1987 edition of *The Brief Guide to the Number Two Chinese Archives*. It has also published *Jiangsu diqu dang'an anjuan mulu* 江蘇地區檔案案卷目錄 (Index to archival sources relating to the Jiangsu area).

The National Catalog Center for Republican Archives (Quanguo minguo dang'an mulu zhongxin 全國民國檔案目錄中心) is based at the archives. Its primary mission is to collect, compile, and publish catalogs of Republican-era documents preserved in the PRC. It has completed a three-volume project entitled *Quanguo minguo dang'an quanzong yilan* 全國民國檔案全宗一 覽 *(*Concise national guide to archival collections of Republican China). The center also plans to compile and publish catalogs and indexes on special topics. Projects in progress include *Xizang he Zangzu zhuanti wenjian mulu* 西藏和藏族專題文件目錄 (Index to documents on Tibet and Tibetans), *Dongnanya Huaqiao Huaren zhuanti wenjian mulu* 東南亞華僑華人專題文件目錄 (Index to documents on Overseas Chinese in Southeast Asia), *Guancang zhaopian mulu* 館藏照 片目錄 (Index to archival photographs), *Guancang lishi ditu mulu* 館藏歷史地圖目錄 (Index to historical maps), and *Minguo shiqi shaoshu minzu zhuanti mulu* 民國時期少數民族專題目錄 (Index to documents on ethnic minorities during the Republican period).

Chapter 5

Beijing Municipal Archives
北京市檔案館

Introduction

The Beijing Municipal Archives (BMA) (Beijing shi dang'anguan 北京市檔案館) was established in December 1957. BMA holdings include government documents, communications from non-governmental organizations (e.g., schools, companies, associations), and land contracts dating from the early Qing dynasty. The BMA maintains 407 documentary collections, totaling 1.1 million volumes. It contains a substantial number of Republican-period documents relating to important Beijing historical events such as the May Fourth movement (1919) and the Marco Polo Bridge incident (1937). Documents generated by the governments of Wang Jitang 王揖唐, Wang Kemin 王克敏, and Jin Bihui 金璧輝 (best known as 川島芳子) can also be found in the archives.

During the Republican era, Beijing experienced significant economic development. Many of the major companies that contributed to the city's development are represented in the BMA's collection. Documents from public and private businesses such as the Beiping Waterworks Company (Beiping zilaishui gongsi 北平自來水公司), Beijing Electric Tramway Company (Beijing dianche gongsi 北京電車公司), Ruifuxiang Shoe Company (Ruifuxiang 瑞蚨祥), and Quanjude Restaurant (Quanjude 全聚德) reflect the burgeoning level of economic activity in the capital during the early to mid-twentieth century. These materials are supplemented by the records of state and private banks and other financial institutions.

Economic History Archives

I. The Beijing Chamber of Commerce

Formed in 1906, the Beijing Chamber of Commerce (Beijing shanghui 北京商會) grew out of the Beijing Chamber of Remittance and Exchange Banks (Beijing shi huidui zhuangjin yinhao shanghui 北京市匯兌莊金銀號商會), an organization originally established by the Qing Ministry of Commerce as part of the New Policy reforms of 1905. Among other things, the New Policy entailed the formulation of a commercial law, the reorganization of government administration, and the abolition of the Confucian civil service examinations. In this atmosphere of reform, merchants and entrepreneurs in urban areas began to organize interest groups.

Up to 1950, the Beijing Chamber of Commerce changed its name several times: Beijing Commerce Association (Beijing shi shangwu zonghui 北京市商務總會), the Beiping Chamber of Commerce (Beiping shi shanghui 北平市商會), the Beijing Association of Industry and

74

Commerce (Beijing shi gongshang lianhehui 北京市工商聯合會). By any name, the organization perceived its main purpose as spurring the development of commerce, industry, foreign trade, and promoting public welfare. Toward these ends, the chamber engaged in compiling statistics and carrying out market surveys, researching legal questions pertaining to commerce and industry, searching for new trade opportunities, assessing and certifying commercial transactions, putting together (and, in cases of overseas involvement, inspecting translations of) legal contracts, assisting in commercial registration, and other activities along these lines. Although membership was mostly private, consisting largely of independent shopkeepers and members of various public associations (*gonghui* 公會), the Beijing Chamber of Commerce remained a part of the government bureaucratic structure. During the Qing the Chamber fell under the jurisdiction of the Ministry of Commerce (Shang bu 商部); during the early part of the Republican era, it was subordinate to the Ministry of Agriculture, Industry, and Commerce (Nonggongshang bu 農工商部); and by the Nanjing Decade (1927–37), the Chamber was placed under the administrative superintendency of the Beiping Municipal Bureau of Social Affairs (Beiping shi shehui ju 北平市社會局).

The Beijing Chamber of Commerce collection covers the organization's activities up to 1949. Materials include regulations, organizational charts, membership lists, conference minutes, budgets, work reports, accounts, and letters reflecting the chamber's relationship with the government and other sectors of society. Other collections in the BMA also contain documents directly or indirectly related to the chamber, such as those of the Bank of Communications (Jiaotong yinhang 交通銀行), the Chung Foo Union Bank (Zhongfu yinhang 中孚銀行), the Sin Hua Savings Bank (Xinhua chuxu yinhang 新華儲蓄銀行), the Bank of China (Zhongguo yinhang 中國銀行), the Beijing Finance Bureau (Beijing caizheng ju 北京財政局), the Beiping Waterworks Company (Beiping zilaishui gongsi 北平自來水公司), and the Beijing Street Car Company (Beijing dianche gongsi 北京電車公司).

II. Beijing Association of Industry and Commerce

The records of the Beijing Association of Industry and Commerce represent an extension of the Beijing Chamber of Commerce Archives beyond the year 1949. Before 1949, the chamber was operated by private citizens, but after 1949 it became an arm of the Beijing Municipal Government, a tool by which the authorities could manage commercial activity.

III. Beiping Waterworks Company

Founded in 1908 under the name of the Capital Waterworks Company, Ltd. (Jingshi zilaishui gufen youxian gongsi 京師自來水股份有限公司), the Beiping Waterworks Company officially registered with the Ministry of Industry and Commerce in 1929. Over the years the company changed names several times and generated numerous historical documents.

The BMA collection contains materials relating to the company's formative period, including documents related to its approval by the Qing government, the original public stock offering, purchases of equipment from overseas distributors, the building of waterworks, and company management practices. In response to growing consumer demand during the early Republican period, the Beiping Waterworks Company planned to expand through foreign debt. However, the chaotic climate of the Warlord era following Yuan Shikai's death in 1916 and internal management problems prevented the implementation of the expansion program. Nevertheless, many documents illustrate the company's modernization efforts through the hiring of foreign engineers and consultants, purchases of foreign technology, help to customers with the installation of water meters, and the enlisting of police to restrain demonstrations by well operators.

During the Nanjing Decade, the company hired a large cadre of technical personnel to undertake surveys to establish a foundation for further development. When the Japanese Army occupied Beiping in 1937, Tokyo deputed a group of "advisors" to assume control of the company. In 1948, the Beijing Municipal Government permitted the company to be privatized. This experiment lasted one year. When the Communists took Beijing in March 1949, the city government reassumed managerial control over the waterworks.

The BMA houses a substantial body of letters, telegrams, orders, reports, plans, regulations, secret communiqués, contracts, and other documents that can provide insight into the development of the Beiping Waterworks Company.

IV. Beijing (Beiping) Electric Tramway Company

The Beijing Electric Tramway Company, Ltd. (Beijing shi dianche gufen youxian gongsi 北京市電車股份有限公司) was formed through cooperation between the Ministry of Finance and private merchants in 1921. Each sector, public and private, contributed half of the company's starting capital. In 1936, the Beiping Municipal Government took over management duties. After 1949 the Beijing Military Control Commission (Beijing junguanhui 軍管會) of the People's Liberation Army managed the tramway.

The Beijing Electric Tramway Company had a clearly delineated organizational structure governed at the top by a shareholders' association and a board of directors. The Ministry of Finance and the private shareholders' group each deputed a supervisor to conduct occasional joint accounting inspections.

The Beijing Electric Tramway Company exhibited a certain degree of functional diversification and concern for the livelihood of its employees. In addition to providing local freight services, the company also operated a power plant and ran the city's mass transit system. For its employees, it extended bonuses, severance pay, pensions, and provided free or partial health care and other welfare benefits, such as haircuts, admittance to bathing facilities, and free rides on company vehicles. Despite such perquisites, successive years of war and inflation exacerbated disputes between company workers and management.

The documents of the Beijing Electric Tramway Company include reports, contracts, statistical charts and tables, incoming and outgoing communications, and rules and regulations.

V. Beijing Private Businesses, 1861–1958

As the imperial capital, Beijing attracted branches or franchises from many of the major business establishments around the country. After 1949, when the PRC government collectivized or nationalized commercial enterprises, many of their records were transferred to the BMA and to the Beijing Association of Industry and Commerce Archives.

VI. Beijing Municipal Finance Bureau

From its inception in 1912, the Beijing Municipal Finance Bureau was responsible for regulating the city's expenditures, levying and collecting taxes, issuing municipal bonds, and managing enterprises jointly owned by the state and private merchants. Unfortunately, the time period and volume numbers of the Finance Bureau's collection are unknown. However, the collection is still valuable for research on the economic history of Republican-era Beijing (Beiping). The archives include budgets, directives from the Ministry of Finance and the Beijing Municipal Government, name lists, rules and regulations, taxation policies, and more.

A small collection of Beijing's finance-related documents is stored in the Beijing East District Archives (Beijing dongchengqu dang'anguan 北京東城區檔案館). This collection primarily contains pre-1949 publications, including *Zhengfu gongbao* 政府公報 (Government gazette), *Zhengfu caizheng, jingji, faling huibian* 政府財政經濟法令匯編 (Collection of government regulations concerning finance and the economy), *Zhanshi jingji dongtai jiyao* 戰時經濟動態輯要 (Important collection on the wartime economic situation), and *Jingji nianjian* 經濟年鑒 (Economic yearbooks). In addition, there are over 80 different Republican-period periodicals, journals, and published works concerning social and economic conditions in Beijing and China.

As the capital of the late imperial period and the early republic, Beijing developed into a financial and commercial center. Banks, finance associations, pawnshops, and currency dealers were found throughout the city. As a result, the BMA has amassed a sizable collection of materials on the Beijing financial community. In 1990, the Finance Research Institute of the People's Bank of China–Beijing Branch and the BMA began a project to arrange and compile these materials. The result is the multi-volume *Beijing jinrong shiliao* 北京金融史料 (Historical sources on Beijing finance). Each volume features brief histories and documents for one or several Chinese financial institutions (e.g., the Shanghai Commercial & Savings Bank [Shanghai shangye chuxu yinhang 上海商業儲蓄銀行], vol. 1; the Bank of Communications [Jiaotong yinhang 交通銀行] and the Bank of China [Zhongguo yinhang 中國銀行], vol. 5).

Publications

The guide for the Beijing Municipal Archives is entitled *Beijing shi dang'anguan zhinan* 北京市檔案館指南 (Guide to the Beijing Municipal Archives) (Beijing: Dang'an chubanshe, 1996).

The BMA has also published collections of selected documents. In addition to the multivolume *Beijing jinrong shiliao*, these documentary surveys include *Beijing zilaishui gongsi dang'an shiliao, 1908 nian–1949 nian* 北京自來水公司檔案史料，1908 年–1949 年 (Archival sources on the Beijing Waterworks Company, 1908–49) (Beijing: Yanshan chubanshe, 1986), and *Beijing dianche gongsi dang'an shiliao, 1921 nian–1949 nian* 北京電車公司檔案史料 (1921 年–1949 年) (Archival sources on the Beijing Electric Tramway Company, 1921–49) (Beijing: Yanshan chubanshe, 1988).

In addition to Republican-era collections, the BMA has published selected economic documents of the post-1949 period. Two such volumes are *Beijing shougongye shehuizhuyi gaizao ziliao* 北京手工業社會主義改造資料 (Sources on the socialist transformation of the handicraft industry in Beijing) (Beijing: Zhonggong dangshi chubanshe, 1992) and *Guomin jingji huifu shiqi de Beijing* 國民經濟恢復時期的北京 (Beijing during the period of national economic recovery) (Beijing: Beijing chubanshe, 1995).

The BMA also sponsors a quarterly journal, *Beijing dang'an shiliao* 北京檔案史料 (Beijing archival sources), as a regular channel for publishing selected documents.

Chapter 6

Shanghai Municipal Archives
上海市檔案館

Introduction

The Shanghai Municipal Archives (SMA) (Shanghai shi dang'anguan 上海市檔案館) was established in December 1959. Although disrupted during the Cultural Revolution (1966–76), most services were restored by late 1979. The SMA is currently under the jurisdiction of the Shanghai Municipal Government, but receives professional advice and supervision from the State Archives Bureau.

Economic History Archives

The SMA has 1,158 collections with more than 1.1 million volumes of documents, some dating back to the Qing dynasty. The SMA also houses documents formerly held by the People's Bank of China–Shanghai Branch Archives (Zhongguo renmin yinhang, Shanghai fenhang dang'anchu 中國人民銀行上海分行檔案處). This collection is particularly rich in documents on financial institutions in Shanghai. The collection at the SMA can be broken down into seven categories:

1. Pre-1949 documents of CCP underground organizations in Shanghai and other CCP-sponsored organizations, such as workers' unions, youth leagues, and women's federations

2. Post-1949 documents on CCP organizations, municipal people's governments, and mass organizations in Shanghai

3. East China Administrative Region documents

4. Records of foreign agencies in pre-1949 Shanghai

5. Archives of the Shanghai municipal governments and their military and police forces under the Nationalists (1927–37, 1945–49) and Japanese occupation (1937–45)

6. Economic records, including those of various industrial and commercial enterprises and trade associations in Shanghai

7. Records of Shanghai's most important banking, financial, and insurance companies

The SMA is particularly strong in documentary collections on commercial associations, chambers of commerce, and financial institutions. The following is a survey of holdings related to commercial associations and banks.

Same-Trade Associations 同業公會

Same-trade associations (*tongye gonghui* 同業公會) first appeared in Shanghai in the late Qing. After the Beiyang government promulgated same-trade association regulations (i.e., *Gongshang tongye gonghui guize* 工商同業公會規則) in 1917, their numbers increased only slightly. Only after the Nanjing National Government promulgated the *Gongshang tongye gonghui fa* 工商同業公會法 (Industrial and commercial trade association law) in 1929 did trade associations develop rapidly. By the end of 1936 the number of trade associations in Shanghai had increased to 236, and by 1947 to 297. They were incorporated into the Shanghai Municipal Industrial and Commercial Association (Shanghai shi gongshangye lianhehui 上海工商業聯合會) after 1949.

Trade association documents were initially kept in the Shanghai Municipal Industrial and Commercial Association but were later transferred to the SMA. The SMA now has 440 documentary collections on trade associations, the largest of its kind in China. The vast majority of them are pre-1949 documents covering various businesses in Shanghai; some 20 percent relate to the post-1949 period. No collections extend beyond 1958. Of the pre-1949 holdings, some collections date back to the late Qing: those of ironware (documents beginning 1909), silk-reeling (1908), native banks (1904), cotton cloth (1904), shoes (1880), tea export (1876), jewelry (1873), cigarettes (1868), ceramics (1867), handwoven cloth (1810), and the fur trade (1773) associations. The size of these collections ranges from a few volumes to several hundred. The largest collection is that of the Machine Industry Trade Association, with 753 volumes.

I. The Shanghai Silk-Reeling Industry Trade Association

Silk reeling was one of the first indigenous industries in China to employ modern machinery. Mechanization of the industry occurred largely in the late nineteenth century when China's handwoven silk faced tough competition in international markets. By the turn of the century, modern silk reeling in China had achieved a considerable scale. One development that reflected this change was the founding in April 1909 of the General Sericulture Industry Guild (Sichang canye zong gongsuo 絲廠蠶業總公所). The guild's membership reached beyond Shanghai to include members from neighboring Jiangsu, Zhejiang, and Anhui provinces. The guild evolved into the Shanghai Silk-Reeling Industry Trade Association (Shanghai saosi gongye hui 上海繅絲工業公會) in 1929. The association underwent a number of subsequent name changes before it was disbanded in November 1949. Its main business was to coordinate silk purchases and production in Jiangsu, Shanghai, Anhui, and Zhejiang.

The Shanghai Silk-Reeling Industry Trade Association collection contains 757 volumes of records for the 1911–49 period. These documents record the organizational structure, functions, and regulations of the trade association at various developmental stages. They include its charters, member registrations, bylaws, and the minutes of conferences and meetings. But the majority of the collection consists of business records. These include silk production and sales plans, trade surveys, regulations regarding cocoon management, prices, and silk inspection rules and procedures. Also included are letters, loan applications, tax reduction petitions, professional and technical exchanges with foreign countries, and records of participation in international trade fairs. The collection also includes data on revenues and expenditures, as well as original account books.

II. The Shanghai Cotton-Spinning Merchants Association

The Chinese Cotton-Spinning Merchants Association (Huashang shachang lianhehui 華商紗廠 聯合會) was established in March 1917 to represent cotton-spinning businesses in Shanghai, Jiangsu, Zhejiang, and Anhui. It was one of the earliest transprovincial trade associations in China. With merchants and businessmen in Shanghai as its core members, the association had charters in Jiangsu, Zhejiang, and Anhui provinces, as well as in other areas. Later it changed its name several times. After the Communists took over Shanghai, it was reorganized as the Shanghai Municipal Cotton-Spinning Industry Trade Association (Shanghai shi maofang zhiye tongye gonghui 上海市棉紡織業同業公會).

The Shanghai Cotton-Spinning Industry Trade Association collection contains 954 volumes of records covering 1917 to 1958. Of these materials, over 60 percent are from the Republican period. Pre-1937 documents are particularly rich. Among other things, the collection details board meetings of the association, as well as annual conference reports.

III. The Shanghai Banking Industry Trade Association

The banking industry grew up in Shanghai on the foundation laid by native banks (*qianzhuang* 錢莊). After its establishment in 1918, the Shanghai Banking Industry Trade Association (Shanghai yinhang shangye tongye gonghui 上海銀行商業同業公會) became influential not only in industrial, commercial, and financial circles but also in the social realm. Although it was a member of the Shanghai Chamber of Commerce (Shanghai shanghui 上海商會), the Shanghai Banking Industry Trade Association often embarked on independent initiatives. It issued political statements in its own name, participated in social and economic activities, and intervened in domestic as well as foreign affairs.

The Shanghai Banking Industry Trade Association collection covers 1917 to 1952 and totals 776 volumes. The holdings include the union's organizational regulations and documents regarding its chairmen, boards of directors, and members. Other records include reports on professional meetings, business guidelines, and letters and telegrams. Some communications were made directly with officials, such as Chiang Kai-shek, T. V. Soong 宋子文, and Sun Ke 孫科.

The records also reflect the trade association's participation in domestic and foreign politics. For example, there are documents that show how political groups solicited financial support from the association. The association also requested political assistance from the Nationalist government, petitioning for protection from industrial and commercial competition in exchange for financial contributions.

IV. The Shanghai Native Bank Trade Association

Native banks (*qianzhuang* 錢莊) in Shanghai were traditional financial institutions. For a long time they played an important financial role, although the scope of their business was initially limited to the exchange of money. Later, however, the rapid growth of trade in Shanghai stimulated demand for more and better commercial financing, and some native banks expanded their services correspondingly. Soon they became intermediaries between powerful foreign banks and local businesses badly in need of capital. The contemporary term for this new type of native bank was "commercial native bank" (*huihua qianzhuang* 匯劃錢莊 or *datong hang* 大同行). As a result, the original association of native banks in Shanghai underwent several organizational changes. It was finally reorganized into the Shanghai Native Bank Trade Association (Shanghai qianzhuangye tongye gonghui 上海錢莊業同業公會) in 1917.

The association's records, totaling 693 volumes, cover 1904 to 1952. Most of the documents focus on the post-1917 period. Documents prior to 1917, although few in number, shed considerable light on the evolution of native banks in Shanghai.

As these documents show, before the outbreak of the Sino-Japanese War (1937–45), the growth of the modern banking industry was accompanied by a decline of native banks in Shanghai, although a few still managed to endure. To survive, native banks carried out many reforms and learned new management methods from modern banks. In this sense, the Shanghai Native Bank Trade Association collection serves as a supplement to that of the Shanghai Banking Industry Trade Association.

V. The Shanghai Silk and Satin Commercial Association

The silk and satin trade has a long history in Shanghai. The origin of the Silk and Satin Commercial Association can be traced to the founding of the Profound Prosperity Hall (Zhanhua tang 湛華堂) in 1850. In 1930 a number of individual guilds were united and organized into the Shanghai Silk and Satin Commerce Trade Association (Shanghai chouduan shangye tongye gonghui 上海綢緞商業同業公會).

Totaling 330 volumes, the collection covers the period 1908 to 1956. Although many of the early records were lost, documents of subsequent periods are quite comprehensive. Among these are business regulations, market plans, lists of committee members, conference reports, management reports, industrial relief committee reports, customs figures, and mediation records. There are also letters requesting the government to adjust taxes on silk and satin exports and to reduce import duties, as well as documents designed to encourage silk and satin merchants to participate in international trade fairs.

VI. The Shanghai Yarn Commercial Trade Association

The Shanghai Yarn Commercial Trade Association (Shanghai shashangye tongye gonghui 上海紗商業同業公會) was initially called the Shanghai Yarn Guild (Shanghai shaye gongsuo 上海紗業公所). Merged with the Shanghai Native Cotton Commercial Association (see below) during the Japanese occupation of Shanghai, the association was renamed the Yarn and Cotton Association (Shabu lianhe hui 紗布聯合會), which was under the control of the Asia Development Board (Xing Ya yuan 興亞院) of the Japanese occupation authorities. Following Japan's defeat, the organization was formally called the Shanghai Yarn Commercial Trade Association.

Since much of the organization's work was once closely associated with the Japanese authorities, many of its records were destroyed by the Japanese before they surrendered. The collection has only 146 volumes, covering the period 1928 to 1954, with the majority of the documents related to the post-war period (1946–49). The collection includes the association's charter, organizational regulations, membership registration, conference minutes, business reports, and financial records.

VII. The Shanghai Native Cotton Commercial Trade Association

The history of the Shanghai Native Cotton Commerce Trade Association (Shanghai tubu shangye tongye gonghui 上海土布商業同業公會) can be traced back to the mid-Qing period and the founding of the Qizaotang Cotton Guild (Qizaotang buye gongsuo 綺藻堂布業公所) in 1792. Subsequently renamed several times, the organization assumed its final name in 1930. By that time, however, the native cotton industry had already undergone a dramatic decline due to the rapid rise of the modern textile industry in Shanghai. Reflecting this trend, membership in the association shrank to several dozen by the 1940s.

Only 81 volumes of the association's records survive. Early documents illustrate the evolution of the Qizaotang Cotton Guild, including lists of its board members, membership registrations, tax payments, and prohibitions on illegal business practices. Records of the Republican period include the association's organizational charters, reports on trade fairs, exports to Southeast Asian countries, marketing information, and pricing and product standards.

VIII. Miscellaneous

There were many other industrial and commercial trade associations in Shanghai. The SMA includes holdings on more than twenty trade associations, including the following examples.

Trade Association Names	Volumes	Years Covered
Machine Industry	753	1943–56
Electrical Equipment	494	1940–57
Cotton Dye	878	1917–58
Shipping	503	1926–52
Insurance	361	1926–52
Cotton Cloth	333	1904–58
Food Processing	334	1921–58

Banks , Insurance Companies, and Other Enterprises

The SMA and the Records Office of the People's Bank of China (PBC)–Shanghai Branch were the two principal institutions that kept documentary collections on modern banks in Shanghai. As noted above, the PBC collection has been transferred to the SMA.

The bulk of the banking-related documents held in the SMA belonged to banks often referred to as representing "bureaucratic capital" (*guanliao ziben* 官僚資本). By contrast, those in the PBC Shanghai Branch's Records Office were largely from private banks, as well as trust, investment, and insurance companies (domestic and foreign). Overall, the banking records from both institutions are significant in size and scope.

I. Original SMA Banking Archives

The core holdings of the SMA consist of a total of 10,500 volumes in 38 categories. These documents can roughly be divided into four groups:

Group 1: Records of central government banks such as the Shanghai branches of the Central Bank of China (Zhongyang yinhang 中央銀行), the Bank of China (Zhongguo yinhang 中國銀行), the Farmers' Bank of China (Zhongguo nongmin yinhang 中國農民銀行), the Bank of Communications (Jiaotong yinhang 交通銀行), the Central Cooperative Bank of China (Zhongyang hezuo jinku 中央合作金庫), the Postal Remittance & Savings Bank (Youzheng chujin huiye ju 郵政儲金匯業局), and the Central Trust of China (Zhongyang xintuo ju 中央信託局). These collections include conference minutes, loan regulations, business proposals, personnel reports, exchange rates, and mortgage documents.

Group 2: Local banks such as the Shanghai City Bank (Shanghai shi yinhang 上海市銀行), the Shanghai branches of the Farmers' Bank of Jiangsu (Jiangsu sheng nongmin yinhang 江蘇省農民銀行), the Jiangsu Local Provincial Bank (Jiangsu sheng difang yinhang 江蘇省地方銀行), the Bank of Canton (Guangdong yinhang 廣東銀行), the Bank of Taiwan (Taiwan yinhang 臺灣銀行), and many other provincial banks. Not surprisingly, the Shanghai City Bank has the largest collection with a total of over 1,550 volumes covering 1930–49.

Group 3: Financial banks, trusts, and insurance companies such as the Seng Dah (Shengda) Trust Company (Shengda xintuo gongsi 生大信託公司).

Group 4: Other financial institutions, with nearly 3,500 volumes of documents.

II. Recently Transferred Banking and Financial Holdings from the PBC–Shanghai Branch Archives

A. Modern Banks

Banking documents constitute the bulk of financial records originally housed in the Shanghai PBC. The holdings include materials from private and state as well as domestic and foreign banks.

Bank Name	Volumes	Years Covered
Private Commercial Banks		
Shanghai Commercial & Savings Bank (Shanghai shangye chuxu yinhang 上海商業儲蓄銀行)	2946	1915–52
Kincheng Banking Corporation (Jincheng yinhang 金城銀行)	1383	1917–52

Sin-Hua [Xinhua] Trust & Savings Bank (Xinhua xintuo chuxu yinhang 新華信託儲蓄銀行)	1010	1917–52
Continental Bank (Dalu yinhang 大陸銀行)	885	1919–52
National Commercial Bank (Zhejiang xingye yinhang 浙江興業銀行	772	1907–52
Ningpo Commercial & Savings Bank (Siming shangye chuxu yinhang 四明商業儲蓄銀行)	5687	1908–53
National Industrial Bank of China (Zhongguo shiye yinhang 中國實業銀行)	871	1915–52

State Banks

Bank of Communications (Jiaotong yinhang 交通銀行)	2360	1912–49
Bank of China (Zhongguo yinhang 中國銀行)	506	1912–49
Four Banks and Two Bureaus (Sihang Erju 四行二局)	440	1929–56
Central Trust of China (Zhongyang xintuo ju 中央信託局)	303	1934–50
Joint Board of Four Banks (Silian zongchu 四聯總處)	75	1908–49
Central Bank of China (Zhongyang yinhang 中央銀行)	55	N/A

B. Native Banks

Documents from 71 native banks were formerly kept in the Shanghai PBC. These include records from the Ching Dah Bank (Qingda qianzhuang 慶大錢莊) and the Foo Yuan Native Bank (Fuyuan qianzhuang 富源錢莊). Most of the other native banks have less than 20 volumes in their documentary collections.

C. Trust Companies

The former Records Office of the PBC–Shanghai Branch kept a total of 291 volumes of documents from fifteen trust companies. These include the records of the Shanghai Trust Company (Shanghai xintuo gongsi 上海信托公司), the First Trust Company of China, Ltd. (Zhongguo diyi xintuo gongsi 中國第一信托公司), and the China Trust Company (Zhongguo xintuo gongsi 中國信托公司).

D. Insurance Companies

The insurance company collections transferred to the SMA from the former Records Office of the PBC–Shanghai Branch contain approximately 3,500 volumes of records from 51 firms (47 Chinese and 4 foreign). The collection of the Shanghai Insurance Association (Shanghai shi baoxianye tongye gonghui 上海市保險業同業公會) has 72 volumes covering 1929 to 1951. The collection of Mixed Records of Joint and Private Insurance Companies (Shanghai shi heying siying baoxianye lianhe dang'an 上海市合營私營保險業聯合檔案) has another 39 volumes covering 1921 to 1949. The collections of other insurance companies are listed below.

Name	Volumes	Years Covered
China Insurance Corporation, Ltd. (C.A.C.) (Baofeng baoxian gongsi 寶豐保險公司)	911	1931–52
Tai Shan Property Insurance Company, Ltd. (Taishan chanwu baoxian gongsi 泰山產物保險公司)	634	1930–56
Tai Shan Life Insurance Company, Ltd. (Taishan renshou baoxian gongsi 泰山人壽保險公司)	450	1932–56

China United Issuance Society, Ltd.   343   1911–58
 (Hua'an hequn baoxian gongsi 華安合群保險公司)

Tai Ping Property Insurance Company, Ltd.   318   1930–58
 (Taiping chanwu baoxian gongsi 太平產物保險公司)

Tai Ping Life Insurance Company, Ltd.   30   N/A
 (Taiping renshou baoxian gongsi 太平人壽保險公司)

E. Investment Companies and Other Enterprises

The SMA also received a number of collections from the Shanghai PBC including those of investment firms, real estate companies, transportation, and other business enterprises. There are also some records of stock and security companies. For instance, the collection of the Shanghai Securities Exchange (Shanghai zhengquan jiaoyi suo 上海證券交易所) has over 800 volumes of documents, covering 1946 to 1951. The archives also holds biographical collections of prominent investors and bankers. Six volumes cover Zhu Shiming (朱世明) and Fan Songyao (範誦堯) between 1939 and 1943, with another 109 volumes concerning Xi Demao (席德懋) between 1928 and 1946, and 47 volumes concerning Bei Zuyi (貝祖詒) between 1927 and 1937.

Publications

The SMA has published a guide to its documentary holdings entitled *Shanghai shi dang'anguan zhinan* 上海市檔案館指南 (Guide to the Shanghai Municipal Archives) (Beijing: Dang'an chubanshe, 1991). It also publishes *Dang'an yu lishi* 檔案與歷史 (Archives and history), a bimonthly journal that contains selected documents from the archives.

The SMA has also published many collections of documents. In the early 1980s, it undertook two projects on the role of Shanghai's commercial and working classes during the Nationalist government's 1927 purge of Communists. These two collections are *Yijiu erqi nian de Shanghai shangye lianhehui* 一九二七年的上海商業聯合會 (The Shanghai Commercial Association in 1927) (Shanghai: Shanghai renmin chubanshe, 1983), and *Shanghai gongren sanci wuzhuang qiyi* 上海工人三次武裝起義 (The three armed uprisings of Shanghai workers) (Shanghai: Shanghai renmin chubanshe, 1983). Other publications on labor movements include *Wusa yundong* 五卅運動 (May Thirtieth movement) (Shanghai: Shanghai renmin chubanshe, 1991) and *Shanghai gonghui lianhehui* 上海工會聯合會 (The Shanghai Workers' Association) (Beijing: Dang'an chubanshe, 1989).

Other publications related to economic history include *Jiu Shanghai de zhengquan jiaoyisuo* 舊上海的證券交易所 (Stock exchanges in Old Shanghai) (Shanghai: Shanghai guji chubanshe,

1992), *Zhongguo zibenzhuyi gongshangye de shehuizhuyi gaizao: Shanghai juan* 中國資本主義
工商業的社會主義改造：上海卷 (The socialist transformation of capitalist industry and
commerce in China: Shanghai) (Beijing: Zhonggong dangshi chubanshe, 1993), *Jiu Zhongguo de
gufen zhi, 1868 nian–1949 nian* 舊中國的股份制，1868年–1949年 (The share system in Old
China: 1868–1949) (Beijing: Dang'an chubanshe, 1996), and *Wu Yunchu qiye shiliao* 吳蘊初企
業史料 (Historical sources on Wu Yunchu's business enterprises), 2 vols. (Beijing: Dang'an
chubanshe, 1989), with one volume covering the Tien Yuan Electro-Chemical Works (Tianyuan
dianhua chang 天原電化廠卷) and the other the Tien Chu Vei Ching Manufacturing Company
(Tianchu weijing chang juan 天廚味精廠卷).

Documents on economic history during the Japanese occupation of Shanghai can be found in
Riwei Shanghai shi zhengfu 日偽上海市政府 (The Japanese-puppet Shanghai Municipal
Government) (Beijing: Dang'an chubanshe, 1986) and *Riben diguozhuyi qinlüe Shanghai zuixing
shiliao huibian* 日本帝國主義侵略上海罪行史料匯編 (Selected historical sources on the crimes
of the Japanese imperialist invasion of Shanghai) (Shanghai: Shanghai renmin chubanshe, 1997).

Publications of the PBC–Shanghai Branch

When the Shanghai PBC started to compile documents from its archival holdings in the mid-1950s,
its primary interest was in a few big banks whose history represented the development of
banking institutions in modern China. These compilation projects covered Shanghai native banks
(Shanghai *qianzhuang* 上海錢庄); the Hongkong & Shanghai Banking Corporation (Huifeng
yinhang 匯豐銀行), one of the most important foreign banks in modern China; the Commercial
Bank of China (Zhongguo tongshang yinhang 中國通商銀行), the first modern bank created
with Chinese capital; the Kincheng Banking Corporation (Jincheng yinhang 金城銀行); the
Shanghai Commercial & Savings Bank (Shanghai shangye chuxu yinhang 上海商業儲蓄銀行);
and two Chinese state banks, the Bank of Communications (Jiaotong yinhang 交通銀行) and the
Central Bank of China (Zhongyang yinhang 中央銀行).

The first major publication project was *Shanghai qianzhuang shiliao* 上海錢莊史料 (Historical
sources on native banks in Shanghai) (Shanghai: Shanghai renmin chubanshe, 1960). Since its
publication, it has been one of the most widely used sources for the study of native banks in
modern China. It was reprinted in 1978.

The second major publication of banking documents was *Zhongguo diyi jia yinhang:
Zhongguo tongshang yinhang de chuchuang shiqi (1897 nian zhi 1911 nian)* 中國第一家銀行：
中國通商銀行的初創時期（一八九七年至一九一一年）(The first bank in China: the early years
of the Commercial Bank of China, 1897–1911) (Beijing: Zhongguo shehui kexueyuan chubanshe,
1982).

The third project was *Jincheng yinhang shiliao* 金城銀行史料 (Historical sources on the
Kincheng Banking Corporation) (Shanghai: Shanghai renmin chubanshe, 1983). It covers the

35–year history of this corporation from its founding in 1917 to collectivization in 1952. The corporation not only offered such banking services as savings, loans, and remittances but extended its activities to such areas as industrial investment, commercial management, stock exchanges, insurance, transportation, and warehouses. In addition, a subsidiary, Chengfu Trust Company (Chengfu xintuo gongsi 誠孚信託公司), managed several textile mills, a machine tools factory, and an institute of textile research.

Apart from documentary compilations, the Shanghai People's Bank also published *Shanghai jinrong shihua* 上海金融史話 (Historical tales of Shanghai banking and finance) (Shanghai: Shanghai renmin chubanshe, 1978).

Chapter 7

Shanghai Association of Industry and Commerce Archives and Other Collections in Shanghai
上海市工商業聯合會檔案室

Introduction

The Shanghai Association of Industry and Commerce (Shanghai shi gongshangye lianhehui 上海市工商業聯合會) was established in 1951 when the original Shanghai Chamber of Commerce (Shanghai shi shanghui 上海市商會) and the Shanghai Chamber of Industry (Shanghai shi gongyehui 上海市工業會) merged. The association's archival holdings include materials from more than 350 trade associations, and other commercial and industrial entities. The extant documents, still extensive despite destruction during the Sino-Japanese War, reflect political and economic conditions in Shanghai. The following is a selected description of collections of the Shanghai Association of Industry and Commerce.

Economic History Archives

I. The Shanghai General Chamber of Commerce

The Shanghai General Chamber of Commerce (Shanghai zong shanghui 上海總商會) evolved from the Shanghai Commercial Association (Shanghai shangye huiyi gongsuo 上海商業會議公所), which was founded in early 1902. The association was reorganized as the Shanghai Associated Commercial Associations (Shanghai shangwu zonghui 上海商務總會) in 1904. It merged with the Shanghai Trade Port Association (Shangbu gongsuo 商埠公所) in 1902 to form the Shanghai General Chamber of Commerce. It was disbanded by the Nationalist government in 1929. The Shanghai General Chamber of Commerce collection covers the years 1902–29.

II. The Shanghai Commercial Association

The Shanghai Commercial Association (Shanghai shangye lianhehui 上海商業聯合會) was established on March 22, 1927, in response to the belief that the chairman of the Shanghai General Chamber of Commerce had sided with warlords when the Guomindang's Northern Expedition appeared likely to succeed. The association was chaired by Yu Qiaqin 虞洽卿, Wang Yiting 王一亭, and Wu Yunzhai 吳蘊齋. The association supported Chiang Kai-shek and called for cooperation between him and the southeastern warlord Sun Chuanfang 孫傳芳 in suppressing Communists and expressed the hope of collaboration with the GMD in industrial development.

91

In early April the association received approval from the Guomindang Shanghai Provisional Committee. Soon it replaced the Shanghai General Chamber of Commerce. Although the association existed for only eight months, its records are an important source for the study of state-business relations at this critical historical moment. The collection has only 49 volumes, but they include the association's constitution, conference records, and letters and telegrams with important politicians, such as Chiang Kai-shek and Bai Chongxi 白崇禧. The collection also contains documents from the Municipal Council of the foreign concessions and on labor-management disputes.

III. The Chamber of Commerce of Shanghai Special Municipality

The Chamber of Commerce of Shanghai Special Municipality (Shanghai tebieshi shanghui 上海特別市商會), commonly known as the Shanghai Municipal Chamber of Commerce (Shanghai shi shanghui 上海市商會, was established in June 1930. It was under the jurisdiction of the Shanghai Bureau of Social Affairs (Shanghai shi shehuiju 上海市社會局). It also received political directives from the Mass Training Commission of the GMD Shanghai Executive Committee. After the Japanese invasion in 1937, the chamber set up an office in Chongqing. At the same time an organization was established with the same name by Chinese commercial interests in Japanese-controlled territory. After the war, the organization was taken over by the Nationalists and reorganized.

The collection has nearly 1,500 volumes of documents, dating from 1945 to 1949. A majority of the prewar records were destroyed during the war. Documents of the Chamber of Commerce under Japanese occupation are not included in this collection. The holdings include meeting minutes, annual budgets, work reports, documents regarding the takeover of the Japanese-controlled chamber of commerce and factories, correspondence concerning Japanese war criminals, worker surveys, and communication with social organizations such as labor unions, peasant associations, and women's associations.

IV. The Shanghai Chamber of Industry

The Shanghai Chamber of Industry (Shanghai shi gongye hui 上海市工業會), a city-wide association, was established in August 1948 and ended its operations one year later. Its purpose was to plan industrial reform and development and to promote the common interests of industry.

The collection has approximately 600 volumes. Documents include the organizational charter, meeting minutes, business reports and correspondence, and letters to Chiang Kai-shek. To a considerable extent, these documents reflect industrial and commercial conditions on the eve of the communist takeover.

Publications

A selection of documents from the Shanghai Commercial Association (上海商業聯合會) was published in Shanghai Municipal Archives, comp., *Yijiu erqi nian de Shanghai shangye lianhehui* 一九二七年的上海商業聯合會 (The Shanghai Commercial Association in 1927) (Shanghai: Shanghai renmin chubanshe, 1993).

Since 1985 the Shanghai Association of Industry and Commerce, with assistance from the Fudan University History Department, has been compiling a ten-volume documentary collection of the Shanghai General Chamber of Commerce entitled *Shanghai zong shanghui shiliao congbian* 上海總商會史料叢編 (Historical sources series on the Shanghai General Chamber of Commerce), covering 1902–29. Part I of the series covers the chamber's organizational evolution (*Zuzhi yan'ge bian* 組織沿革編) and consists of three volumes. Part II is a collection of meeting minutes (*Yishi lu bian* 議事錄編) in three volumes, covering the three periods 1912–19, 1920–25, and 1926–29, respectively. Part III concerns the chamber's participation in political events (*Huodong bian* 活動編). This part consists of four volumes, covering the four periods 1902–11, 1912–19, 1920–25, and 1926–29, respectively.

Shanghai Municipal Industry and Commerce Administration Archives
上海市工商行政管理局檔案室

The Shanghai Municipal Industry and Commerce Administration (Shanghai shi gongshang xingzheng guanliju 上海市工商行政管理局) has one of the best collections on industrial and commercial administration in China. It contains some 200,000 volumes of records, 190,000 of which are business-related. These archives reflect many aspects of China's economy during the 1950s, including the role of the new government. Many of the documents are business registration records and include almost all private businesses in Shanghai during the 1950s. Other material concerns trademark registrations and product brands.

The administration's archival holdings of the 1950s are open to researchers. It has recently compiled an official history of its own organizational evolution, *Shanghai gongshang xingzheng guanli zhi* 上海工商行政管理志 (Gazetteer of the Shanghai Municipal Industry and Commerce Administration) (Shanghai: Shanghai shehui kexueyuan chubanshe, 1997).

Since the 1960s the administration has published several documentary surveys, often in cooperation with other institutions. One example is *Shangye zibenjia shi zenyang boxue dianyuan de? jiu Shanghai xiedaxiang choubu shangdian de "diangui"* 商業資本家是怎樣剝削店員的？舊上海協大祥綢布商店的"店規" (How did commercial capitalists brutally exploit shop employees? the "shop rules" of the Shanghai Xiedaxiang Silk Cloth Shop in Old Shanghai) (Shanghai: Shanghai renmin chubanshe, 1966).

The administration has also contributed several volumes to *Zhongguo ziben zhuyi gongshang qiye shiliao congkan* 中國資本主義工商企業史料叢刊 (Historical sources series on capitalist industrial and commercial business enterprises in China) (Beijing: Zhonghua shuju, 1963–). These volumes include *Shanghai minzu maofangzhi gongye* 上海民族毛紡織工業 (Shanghai's native silk-reeling industry), *Shanghai minzu xiangjiao gongye* 上海民族橡膠工業 (Shanghai's native rubber industry), *Shanghai minzu jiqi gongye* 上海民族機器工業 (Shanghai's native machine industry), and *Shanghai shi mianbu shangye* 上海市棉布商業 (Shanghai's cotton cloth commerce). An additional archival publication is *Shanghai zhuce shangbiao tuji* 上海註冊商標圖集 (Pictorial collection of registered trademarks in Shanghai) (Shanghai: Beijia chubanshe, 1988).

Besides publications of archival sources, the administration has also used its documentary holdings to write histories of individual trades. These volumes form part of a series produced with the cooperation of other institutions entitled *Shanghai shi congshu* 上海史叢書 (Shanghai history series) (Shanghai: Shanghai shehui kexueyuan chubanshe). Two volumes in this series are *Shanghai jindai xiyao hangye shi* 上海近代西藥行業史 (History of Western medicine in modern Shanghai) and *Shanghai jindai baihuo shangye shi* 上海近代百貨商業史 (History of department stores in modern Shanghai). Both were published in 1988.

Shanghai Academy of Social Sciences, Economics Institute, Chinese Business History Resource Center
中國企業史資料研究中心

Introduction

The Chinese Business History Resource Center (Zhongguo qiye shi ziliao yanjiu zhongxin 中國企業史資料中心) of the Shanghai Academy of Social Sciences (SASS) was founded in May 1992 with support from the Luce Foundation and Cornell University. Its purpose is to collect, catalogue, and preserve archival material related to business history in modern China. The center also compiles and publishes selected documents and books on Chinese business history.

The Economics Institute at SASS has conducted business history research since the 1950s. It has published over 30 business history document collections, including those on the Oriental Engineering Works, Ltd. (Dalong jiqi chang 大隆機器廠), the Hengfeng Textile Mill (Hengfeng sha chang 恆豐紗廠), the Nanyang Brothers' Tobacco Company (Nanyang xiongdi yancao gongsi 南洋兄弟煙草公司), the Rong Family Enterprises (Rong jia qiye 榮家企業), Liu Hongsheng's Enterprises (Liu Hongsheng qiye 劉鴻生企業), the Wing On Company (Yongan gongsi 永安公司), the Kiangnan Dock and Engineering Works (Jiangnan zaochuan chang 江南

造船廠), the British-American Tobacco Company (Ying Mei yancao gongsi 英美煙草公司), Sassoon Sons & Co., Ltd. (Shasun yanghang 沙遜洋行), Butterfield and Swire (Taigu yanghang 太古洋行), and many others. Other document collections cover areas such as machinery, paper making, silk reeling, silk weaving, flour milling, rubber production, pharmaceuticals, hardware, retailing, fabrics, and other industrial and commercial activities. The institute recently compiled and published the *Zhonghua qiyeshi congshu* 中華企業史叢書 (Republican Chinese business history series). This series includes research or documents on the Shanghai Ball Bearings Company (Shanghai zhoucheng gongsi 上海軸承公司), the New Light Underwear Factory (Xinguang neiyi chang 新光內衣廠), China Pharmaceuticals (Zhonghua zhiyao chang 中華製藥廠), and New Asia Pharmaceuticals (Xinya zhiyao chang 新亞製藥廠).

Many of these materials were placed in the Chinese Business History Resource Center when it opened in 1992. The center also keeps the records of more than twenty other companies (Chinese and foreign) operating in China prior to the CCP victory in 1949. These include the Chartered Bank of India, Australia, and China (Maijiali yinhang 麥加利銀行), the National City Bank of New York (Huaqi yinhang 花旗銀行), the Equitable Eastern Banking Corporation (later the Chase Bank) (Datong yinhang 大通銀行), American Commercial Bank (Meiguo shangye yinhang 美國商業銀行), American Asiatic Insurance Bank (Mei Ya baoxian yinhang 美亞保險銀行), Zhengxin Accounting and Law Office (Zhengxin kuaijishi lüshi shiwusuo 正信會計師律師事務所), and the China Institute of Economic Statistics (Zhongguo jingji tongji yanjiu suo 中國經濟統計研究所). Moreover, the center holds many clippings on economic affairs from Chinese and foreign newspapers of the Republican period, as well as commercial and industrial surveys of post-1949 Shanghai.

Economic History Archives

I. The Rong Family Enterprises

The Rong family business enterprises (Rongjia qiye 榮家企業) consisted mainly of the Mow Sing Flour Mills (Rongxin mianfen chang 榮新麵粉廠), the Foh Sing Flour Mills (Fuxin mianfen chang 福新麵粉廠), and the Sung Sing Textile Mills (Shenxin fangzhi chang 申新紡織廠), and other related businesses. These businesses were largely financed and controlled by Rong Zongjing (榮宗敬) and Rong Desheng (榮德生). Beginning with investments in flour and textile ventures, the Rong family economic interests expanded rapidly to become one of the most extensive business networks controlled by Chinese capitalists. In 1980 the Economics Institute at SASS published a documentary selection, *Rongjia qiye shiliao* 榮家企業史料 (Historical sources on Rong family business enterprises), which covers the years 1915–60. Unfortunately, original copies of many documents included in this 41-volume project were lost after the documents had been published. Documentary holdings of the Rong family enterprises cover (1) headquarters;

(2) Shenxin; (3) Rongxin and Fuxin; (4) personnel; (5) labor; and (6) miscellaneous affairs. These materials include company records, statistics, correspondence, accounting reports, work reports, newspaper clippings, reports on working conditions, memoranda, and industry reports.

II. Liu Hongsheng's Enterprises

Liu Hongsheng (劉鴻生) got his start as a comprador in the Kaiping Engineering and Mining Company (Kaiping kuangwu ju 開平礦務局) based in Shanghai. He invested his earnings in warehouses, coal mines, banks, and match-making, cement, textile, charcoal briquet, and enamel companies. In 1981 the Economics Institute at SASS compiled a three-volume collection entitled *Liu Hongsheng qiye shiliao* 劉鴻生企業史料 (Historical sources on Liu Hongsheng's business enterprises). Materials pertaining to Liu's activities in match making, cement, and banking are currently available. The library at the Business History Center also keeps a good collection of interviews with personnel who worked in Liu's businesses. In all, these records cover 1920–64.

III. Liu Hong Accounting Office

Liu Hongsheng originally set up the Liu Hong Accounting Office (Liu Hong juzhang ju 劉鴻記帳房) as his personal accounting office, but it gradually developed into the internal accounting section of his business empire. It kept Liu's private letters, business documents, and correspondence with other commercial and industrial organizations. The office hired consultants, drafted outgoing documents, drew up regulations, and coordinated the allocation and use of the Rong family members' savings. The center has over 1,200 volumes of Liu's business documents and correspondence between 1914 and 1950. These documents concentrate on Liu's match factories, cement factories, charcoal briquette factories, and coal mining, transportation, warehouse, real estate, and banking ventures.

IV. The British-American Tobacco Company

The British-American Tobacco Company (BAT) (Ying Mei yancao gongsi 英美煙草公司) was organized in 1902 by six major tobacco firms in the United States and Britain. In the same year, BAT began to invest in China. In 1919 BAT established the British-American Tobacco Company (China), Ltd. (Zhu-Hua Ying Mei yancao youxian gongsi 駐華英美煙草有限公司), in Shanghai. On the eve of the Sino-Japanese War, BAT had set up 25 tobacco factories and related businesses in China and had more than 25,000 employees.

In 1983 the SASS Economics Institute compiled a four-volume collection of BAT documents entitled *Yin Mei yancao gongsi zai-Hua qiye ziliao huibian* 英美煙草公司在華企業資料匯編 (Collected historical sources on BAT enterprises in China). Currently, the center's holdings contain a large number of documents of the BAT (China), Ltd., in Shanghai and its business branches in other parts of China. These materials include company records, trademark registrations, biographies, trade reports, accounts and balances, reports on worker organizations, and sales statistics.

V. Butterfield and Swire

Butterfield and Swire (Taigu yanghang 太古洋行) was one of the earliest foreign firms in China. It opened its business in Shanghai in 1867 and developed into one of the region's major shipping companies. It withdrew from China when the Communists took control of Shanghai in 1949. The center has a holding of 1,669 items (or 3,979 pages) of Butterfield and Swire documents, all hand-copied or photcopied from the records of the Shanghai Harbor Bureau. They are arranged in several categories: (1) business enterprise organization; (2) activities in China; (3) comprador system; and (4) worker conditions.

VI. The China Institute of Economic Statistics

The China Institute of Economic Statistics (Zhongguo jingji tongji yanjiusuo 中國經濟統計研究所) grew out of the Research Committee of the China Economics Society (Zhongguo jingji xueshe yanjiu weiyuanhui 中國經濟學社研究委員會). It took its final name in 1933. In the 1930s it conducted two large-scale statistical surveys of domestic industry, one in 1931–32 covering industry in Shanghai, and the second in 1933–34 covering factories throughout China (except Gansu, Xinjiang, Yunnan, Guizhou, Ningxia, Qinghai, and Japanese-occupied Manchuria). Before the outbreak of the Pacific war in December 1941, the institute published *Shanghai gongye baogao* 上海工業報告 (Report on industry in Shanghai), *Shanghai zhi sichang* 上海之絲廠 (Silk factories in Shanghai), *Zhongguo gongye diaocha baogao* 中國工業調查報告 (Survey report on Chinese industry), *Shanghai gongyehua yanjiu* 上海工業化研究 (Research on Shanghai industrialization), *Shanghai zhi fazhan yu gongye baogao* 上海製發展與工業報告 (Report on Shanghai's development and industry), and *Woguo diannong jingji zhuangkuang* 我國佃農經濟狀況 (The state of the tenant economy in China).

The China Institute of Economic Statistics collection consists of 1,200 volumes of industrial and economic surveys conducted in the 1930s. These surveys cover local economic conditions, mining, industry, agriculture, communication, and trade.

VII. Zhengxin Accounting and Law Office

The Chinese Business History Resource Center holds over 1,000 documents of the Zhengxin Accounting and Law Office (Zhengxin kuaijishi lüshi shiwusuo 正信會計師律師事務所) between 1931 and 1951. These materials are arranged into categories such as accounting, law, enterprise records, government organizations, and miscellaneous. The documents mainly concern accounting records, asset verifications, and audits (for more than 900 Chinese and foreign factories, firms, banks, schools, government agencies, and public organizations in Shanghai, Zhejiang, and Jiangsu as well as in other areas of China). The collection also contains documents related to commercial disputes and lawsuits, business registrations, trademarks, company reorganizations, and asset assessments.

VIII. Newspaper Clippings

The Economics Institute acquired a substantial collection of newspaper clippings from the Shanghai Commercial & Savings Bank's Library (Shanghai shangye chuxu yinhang ziliao shi 上海商業儲蓄銀行資料室). In the 1930s and 1940s the bank library clipped important articles from more than 40 major Chinese, Japanese, and English newspapers, such as *Shen bao* 申報 (Shen Bao daily news), *Dagong bao* 大公報 (*L'Impartial*), *Xinwen bao* 新聞報 (China daily newspaper), *Zhongyang ribao* 中央日報 (Central daily), *Shishi xinbao* 時事新報 (China times), *Riri xinwen* 日日新聞 (Daily news), *Shang bao* 商報 (Business newspaper), and *Jinrong shibao* 金融日報 (Finance daily). The clippings are mainly news reports and reviews of economic and financial conditions in Shanghai.

Chapter 8

Jiangsu Provincial Archives
江蘇省檔案館

Introduction

The Jiangsu Provincial Archives (JPA) (Jiangsu sheng dang'anguan 江蘇省檔案館) stores nearly 200,000 volumes of records produced by the Nationalist provincial government and CCP local authorities during the Republican period. The collection is organized into two basic categories: National governmental records and revolutionary records. The following is a brief survey of the JPA collection with a primary focus on the first category of documents.

Economic History Archives of the Nationalist Government in Jiangsu

I. Provincial Governmental Organs

A. The Jiangsu Provincial Government Secretariat

The Jiangsu Provincial Government Secretariat (Jiangsu sheng zhengfu mishu chu 江蘇省政府秘書處) was established in May 1927. It was responsible for drafting and storing communications, using official seals, preparing and announcing regulations, and conducting special judicial affairs. The 1,300-volume collection includes documents on land tax regulations, taxation, budgets, meeting minutes, banking, airport construction, military rations, agricultural surveys, and the economic blockade of CCP-controlled areas.

B. Jiangsu Provincial Finance Department

The Jiangsu Provincial Finance Department (Jiangsu sheng caizheng ting 江蘇省財政廳) was established in 1927. The department was subordinate to the Jiangsu provincial government but received technical supervision and advice from the Ministry of Finance. Its main functions were to administer provincial taxes and public bonds, examine fiscal budgets, supervise income and expenditures, and manage public properties. The collection totals 3,271 volumes, but covers only the 1946–49 period. Documents relate to fiscal planning, publicly managed enterprises, price indices, taxes (including the land tax), statistics, public bonds, county debt, banking reports and statistics, native banks (*qianzhuang* 錢莊), provincial and local treasuries, and agricultural loans. Issues of the *Jiangsu caizheng gongbao* 江蘇財政公報 (Jiangsu financial gazette) are also a part of the collection.

The records of the Finance Department's subordinate organ, the Jiangsu Provincial State-Land Administration (Jiangsu sheng guoyou dichan guanli ju 江蘇省國有地產管理局), consists of

1,938 volumes spanning 1946–49. Most documents concern investigations of land development, ownership, and prices.

In addition, the collection of the Ministry of Finance's Jiangsu District State-Tax Collectorate (Caizheng bu, Jiangsu qu guoshui guanli ju 財政部江蘇區國稅管理局) contains 4,844 volumes of records covering 1945–49.

C. Jiangsu Provincial Reconstruction Department and Its Subordinate Organs

The Jiangsu Provincial Reconstruction Department (Jiangsu sheng jianshe ting 江蘇省建設廳) was established in 1927, but suspended activity during the war with Japan. After the war, it resumed operations. Its responsibilities included constructing public roads, railways, and ports, and developing agriculture, mines, industry, and commerce. Although the 8,603-volume collection covers only 1945–49, the range of topics is broad. These include radio stations, utilities, tele-communications, road and railway construction, river projects, flood relief, agriculture, forestry, animal husbandry, sericulture, fisheries, urban planning, industry, commerce, mining, banks, meteorological data, and the takeover of enemy properties.

The collection also contains the records of several affiliated agencies of the Reconstruction Department. These include the Jiangbei Canal Engineering Bureau (Jiangbei yunhe gongchengju 江北運河工程局), the Jiangsu Water Conservancy and Sea Embankment Construction Office (Jiangsu shuili haitang gongchengchu 江蘇水利海塘工程處), the Jiangsu Sericulture Improvement Management Commission (Jiangsu canye gaijin guanli weiyuanhui 江蘇蠶業改進管理委員會), the Jiangsu Agriculture Improvement Institute (Jiangsu nongye gaijinsuo 江蘇農業改進所), and the Jiangnan Water Conservancy Engineering Office (Jiangnan shuili gongchengchu 江南水利工程處).

D. Jiangsu Provincial Office of Social Affairs

The Jiangsu Provincial Office of Social Affairs (Jiangsu sheng shehui chu 江蘇省社會處) was established in December 1945. Its main functions were to administer social welfare, relief, and other public service functions. Records cover the period 1945–49 and include information on labor disputes, standard of living indices for workers, unemployment, flood relief affairs, land reform, and land-tax reductions.

The collection for a subordinate organization, the Jiangsu Cooperative Office of Supplies (Jiangsu sheng hezuoshe wupin gongxiao chu 江蘇省合作社物品供銷處), contains records for 1938–49, including documents on sugar, salt, cloth, and the grain supply.

E. Jiangsu Provincial Statistics Office

The Jiangsu Provincial Statistics Office (Jiangsu sheng tongji chu 江蘇省統計處) evolved in 1947 out of the Statistics Office of the Jiangsu Provincial Secretariat (Jiangsu sheng mishu chu, Tongji shi 江蘇省秘書處統計室), which was initially established in 1934. Its archival collection covers 1942–49. The collection includes meeting minutes, labor surveys, cost of living surveys, budgets, expenditures, and issues of *Jiangsu sheng tongji tiyao* 江蘇省統計提要 (Jiangsu statistical abstracts) and *Jiangsu sheng tongji jianbao* 江蘇省統計簡報 (Brief bulletin of Jiangsu statistics).

F. The Yellow River Flood Rehabilitation Bureau–Jiangsu Branch

The Yellow River Flood Rehabilitation Bureau–Jiangsu Branch (Huangfan qu fuxing ju, Jiangsu sheng yewu guanli chu 黃泛區復興局江蘇省業務管理處), established in March 1938, was charged with the task of rehabilitating the Yellow River valley in Jiangsu. In addition to records from the Jiangsu Branch, the collection also contains the records of another branch: the Henan-Anhui-Jiangsu Branch (Huangfan qu fuxing ju Yu-Wan-Su yewu guanli chu 黃泛區復興局豫皖蘇業務管理處). The collection covers 1948–49 and includes information on project plans, irrigation works, American loans, model farms, forestation, and budgets.

II. Banks

A. Provincial Bank of Jiangsu

The Provincial Bank of Jiangsu (Jiangsu sheng yinhang 江蘇省銀行) was called the Jiangsu Bank (Jiangsu yinhang 江蘇銀行) when it was first established in 1912. The bank offered savings, loans, remittances, mortgages, transferable securities, trust, and other services. Although its 141–volume collection covers 1911–49, the majority of records are from the 1930s and 1940s. The collection includes annual reports, treasury reports, and statistics on savings, loans, and remittances. A bank with a similar name was the Local Bank of Jiangsu (Jiangsu sheng difang yinhang 江蘇省地方銀行). Its 53-volume collection covers 1940–45.

B. Farmers' Bank of Jiangsu

The Farmers' Bank of Jiangsu (Jiangsu sheng nongmin yinhang 江蘇省農民銀行) was established in 1928. It was subordinate to the Jiangsu provincial government but supervised by the Farmers' Bank of China (Zhongguo nongmin yinhang 中國農民銀行). Its business included extending credit for agricultural development and collecting land taxes. Its archival collection has 305 volumes covering 1929–49. The Jiangnan branch has a separate collection of records covering 1940–45.

III. Companies

A. The Capital Electricity Works

The Capital Electricity Works (Shoudu dianchang 首都電廠) was the result of a merger in 1928 of the Jiangsu Provincial Nanjing Power Plant (Jiangsu shengli Nanjing diandeng chang 江蘇省立南京電燈廠) and the Nanjing Municipal Power Plant (Nanjing shi diandeng chang 南京市電燈廠). It was placed under the control of the National Reconstruction Commission (Jianshe weiyuanhui 建設委員會), but in 1937 was transferred to the Yangtse Power Co., Ltd. (Yangzi dianqi gufen youxian gongsi 揚子電氣股份有限公司). The archival collection has 340 volumes covering 1935–49. These records include information about personnel, construction projects, and rural electricity.

B. The China Sericulture Company–Wuxi Branch
The China Sericulture Company–Wuxi Branch was set up in March 1946 to collect and process silkworm cocoons. Its collection has 151 volumes from 1946–49 covering acquisition of silkworm cocoons, rice prices, and loans to farmers.

C. China Salt Company–Nanjing Branch
The China Salt Company–Nanjing Branch (Zhongguo yanye gongsi, Nanjing banshi chu 中國鹽業公司南京辦事處) was established in 1947 to conduct salt transportation and sale in and around Yangzi River ports. It was taken over by the PLA Military Control Committee (Renmin jiefang jun junguanhui 人民解放軍軍管會) in July 1949. The archival collection has 90 volumes of records concerning transport, sales, prices, taxes, and the PLA takeover.

Archives on the Economic History of Communist-Controlled Areas

Only a limted number of records held at the JPA concerning pre-1949 CCP economic policy in the Jiangsu area are accessible. An exception is the records of the CCP Jiangsu Provincial Committee, which are organized into three different periods.

I. The Land Revolution Period (1927–37)

The CCP Jiangsu Provincial Committee
The CCP Jiangsu Provincial Committee (Zhonggong Jiangsu sheng weiyuanhui 中共江蘇省委員會) was established soon after the CCP-GMD split in 1927. The collection has 2,806 volumes, but its time span is unclear. The records contain information on labor and peasant movements, resolutions regarding unemployed workers, and minutes of meetings on land issues, famines, and other subjects.

II. The Sino-Japanese War Period (1937–45)

A. The CCP Central Jiangsu District Committee
The collection of the CCP Central Jiangsu District Committee (Zhonggong Suzhong qu weiyuanhui 中共蘇中區委員會, March 1941–October 1945) has approximately 200 volumes. Documents

include resolutions on land-tax reductions; instructions regarding unemployed peasants; information on finance, trade, industry and commerce; grain collection and storage; and surveys of land quality and production.

B. The CCP Huaibei Jiangsu-Anhui Border Region Committee

The CCP Huaibei Jiangsu-Anhui Border Region Committee (Zhonggong Huaibei Su-Wan bianqu weiyuanhui 中共淮北蘇皖邊區委員會, August 1941–October 1945) collection contains records pertaining to agricultural production, harvests, loans, efforts to strengthen financial and economic work, and resolutions on textile production.

Other records concerning CCP economic policies in Jiangsu province during the Sino-Japanese War can be found in small collections such as the CCP Central Jiangsu District No. 4 Local Committee (Zhonggong Suzhong qu disi difang weiyuanhui 中共蘇中區第四地方委員會, March 1941–October 1945), the Southern Jiangsu District Government (Sunan qu xingzheng gongshu 蘇南區行政公署, March 1943–October 1945), the Central Jiangsu District Government (Suzhong qu xingzheng gongshu 蘇中區行政公署, March 1943–October 1945), the Central Jiangsu No. 4 District Government (Suzhong disi xingzheng qu zhuanyuan gongshu 蘇中第四行政區專員公署, March 1941–October 1945), and the Yancheng-Funing District Government (Yan-Fu qu xingzheng gongshu 鹽阜區行政公署, September 1941–July 1945).

III. The Post-War Period (1945–49)

A. The CCP Central Committee Central China Office and the CCP Central China Work Commission

The CCP Central Committee Central China Branch Office (Zhonggong zhongyang Huazhong fenju 中共中央華中分局) was set up in the Jiangsu-Anhui Liberated Area (Su-Wan jiefang qu 蘇皖解放區) in October 1945 with the task of supervising CCP organizations in central and northern Jiangsu, the southern and northern Huai River areas, and CCP underground activities in the Jiangsu-Zhejiang-Anhui Border Area (Jiangnan Su-Zhe-Wan bianqu 江南蘇浙皖邊區). In November 1947, the branch office was replaced by the CCP Central China Work Commission (Zhonggong Huazhong gongzuo weiyuanhui 中共華中工作委員會). The latter was discontinued in April 1949. The collections of these organizations have over 300 volumes. Documents reflect information about budgets and expenditures, local currency, grain production and purchase, trade, land reform, land tax reduction, salt administration, and military industries.

More information on CCP economic policy in central and northern Jiangsu during the GMD-CCP Civil War era can be found in the collections of subordinate local committees. These collections, which vary in size, include the CCP Central Jiangsu District Committee (Zhonggong Suzhong qu weiyuanhui 中共蘇中區委員會), the CCP Northern Jiangsu District Committee (Zhonggong Subei qu weiyuanhui 中共蘇北區委員會), the CCP Jiang-Huai District Committee (Zhonggong Jiang-Huai qu weiyuanhui 中共江淮區委員會) and its No. 2 Local Committee (Zhonggong Jiang-Huai qu dier difang weiyuanhui 中共江淮區第二地方委員會), and the CCP

Central China nos. 1, 2, 5–7, and 9–11 local committees (Zhonggong Huazhong di yi, er, wu, liu, qi, jiu, shi, shiyi difang weiyuanhui 中共華中第一、二、五、六、七、九、十、十一地方委員會).

B. The Jiangsu-Anhui Border Area Government and the Central China Administrative Office

The Jiangsu-Anhui Border Area Government (Su-Wan qu zhengfu 蘇皖區政府) was established in November 1945. Its jurisdiction included eight administrative districts (with some later adjustments), extending over 51 cities and counties in Jiangsu province, nineteen counties in Anhui, and three in Henan. The border area government was discontinued in November 1947, when the Central China Administrative Office (Huazhong xingzheng banshichu 華中行政辦事處) was set up in its place to lead the local communist governments in the Jiangsu area. The collections of these organizations contain records about ship management, postal services, construction projects, grain, finance, trade, taxes (including import-export tax), currency (including exchange rates), commodity prices, river projects, and other relevant topics.

The archival collections of district governments also contain many records concerning the economy during 1945–49. Such collections include the records of the Jiangsu-Anhui Border Area nos. 1, 2, 5, and 9 administrative district governments (Su-Wan bianqu di yi, er, wu, jiu, xingzheng qu zhuanyuan gongshu 蘇皖邊區第一、二、五、九行政區專員公署) and the Jiang-Huai No. 2 Administrative District Government (Jianghuai dier xingzheng qu zhuanyuan gongshu 江淮第二行政區專員公署).

C. Biographical Collection of Deng Kesheng 鄧克生

Deng Kesheng (1911–76) held a variety of official posts in CCP-controlled areas of Jiangsu during the 1940s. His biographical collection at the JPA contains several of his articles on finance and the economy.

Publications

The JPA has published a guide to its documentary holdings entitled *Jiangsu sheng dang'anguan zhinan* 江蘇省檔案館指南 (Guide to the Jiangsu Provincial Archives) (Beijing: Dang'an chuban-she, 1994).

The JPA has also compiled more than 60 volumes of documentary sources, most concerning the history of the CCP in Jiangsu. Among these are two surveys of the financial and economic history of the Jiangsu communist areas. One is *Huazhong kangri genjudi caijing shiliao xuanbian* 華中抗日根據地財經史料選編 (Selected historical materials on finance in Central China base areas during the War of Resistance Against Japan), 4 vols. (Beijing: Dang'an chubanshe, 1986). The other is *Huazhong jiefangqu caijing shiliao xuanbian* 華中解放區財經史料選編 (Selected historical sources on finance in the Central China liberated areas), 7 vols. (Nanjing: Nanjing daxue chubanshe, 1987–89). Other relevant publications of archival materials are *Jiangsu nongmin yundong dang'an shiliao xuanbian* 江蘇農民運動檔案史料選編 (Selected archival sources on peasant movements in Jiangsu) (Beijing: Dang'an chubanshe, 1983); *Subei kangri gengjudi* 蘇北 抗日根据地 (Resist-Japan base areas in northern Jiangsu) (Beijing: Zhonggong dangshi ziliao chubanshe, 1987–89); and *Suzhong kangri genjudi* 蘇中抗日根据地 (Anti-Japanese base areas in central Jiangsu) (Beijing: Zhonggong dangshi ziliao chubanshe, 1989).

In 1992, the Archives began a quarterly journal entitled *Jiangsu lishi dang'an* 江蘇歷史檔案 (Jiangsu historical archives), which serves as a channel for publishing archival material.

Chapter 9

Suzhou Municipal Archives, Suzhou Chamber of Commerce Collection
蘇州市檔案館蘇州商會檔案

Introduction

The Suzhou Municipal Archives (Suzhou shi dang'anguan 蘇州市檔案館) was established in 1959. It was closed during the Cultural Revolution and reopened in May 1980. Today, the archive houses over 130,000 volumes of material, covering a wide array of subjects, including politics, culture, military affairs, and foreign relations.

Of particular value to the study of economic history during the Republican period are the collections of the Suzhou Chamber of Commerce (described below) and the Suzhou Textile Factory (Sulun shachang 蘇輪紗廠). In recent years, editorial staffs of Chinese local gazetteers have used the archive for research on the history of sericulture and handicraft textile industries, and on important individuals and organizations such as Sheng Xuanhuai (盛宣懷) and the Suzhou Urban Commune (Suzhou shimin gongshe 蘇州市民公社). Although the Suzhou Municipal Archives has many valuable documentary collections on economic history, the following survey concentrates on the Suzhou Chamber of Commerce collection.

Economic History Archives

I. Suzhou Chamber of Commerce

The Suzhou Chamber of Commerce (Suzhou shanghui 蘇州商會) was established in 1905. With approval from the Board of Commerce (Shang bu 商部) of the Qing dynasty, it shared responsibility with the general chambers of commerce of Shanghai and Nanjing for commercial affairs in Jiangsu province. It maintained branches in Songjiang (淞江), Changzhou (常州), and Zhenjiang (鎮江) prefectures and Taicang (太倉) district. The chamber also controlled a merchant militia corps and supported urban communes (Shimin songshe 市民公社). Between 1931 and 1949, its official name was the Wu County Chamber of Commerce (Wuxian shanghui 吳縣商會). During its 45–year history, the Suzhou Chamber of Commerce played a significant part in commercial activities, as well as major political events, in the lower Yangzi area.

The Suzhou Chamber of Commerce collection is one of the two best archival collections of chambers of commerce in China, second only to the Tianjin Chamber of Commerce collection at the Tianjin Municipal Archives. The majority of documents in the Suzhou Chamber of Commerce collection date from 1905 to the 1930s. The records include material on local branches, mining businesses, banking institutions, trade guilds, merchant militia corps, and the Suzhou Urban Commune.

106

The collection has about 90 types of documents, mostly petitions, instructions, and correspondence. Most documents are in Chinese, but some are in foreign languages. In addition, the collection contains imperial edicts and rescripts, orders, instructions, communications from the central government and yamen at the provincial, prefectural, and county levels, correspondence from other major chambers of commerce and social organizations, petitions and reports from local branches, telegraphs, bulletins, and correspondence from Overseas Chinese chambers of commerce.

The documents can roughly be divided into 30-odd categories: secretarial and administrative affairs, organization and personnel, commercial laws and regulations, political events, fire fighting and public order, finance and banking, industry and trade, transportation, urban construction and public utilities, agriculture, water conservancy, relief aid, education, public health, taxation, riots, foreign trade, survey and statistics, business disputes, public philanthropy, war damage, Japanese occupation, food prices and supply, anti-imperialist movements, labor disputes, mass movements, government agencies, social organizations, correspondence with other chambers of commerce, meetings, merchant militia, Suzhou Urban Commune, revenue and expenditures, and social life. The collection also contains newspapers, tablet inscriptions, account books, scrolls, and photographs.

II. Special Documents

A. *Suzhou Merchant Militia Corps*
The Suzhou Merchant Militia Corps (Suzhou shangtuan 蘇州商團) collection covers the period 1906–36. The holdings include documents on the corps' evolution from the Suzhou Merchant Sports Association (Sushang tiyu hui 蘇商體育會) through the Merchant Militia Association (Shangtuan gonghui 商團公會) to the Merchant Militia Corps Headquarters (Shangtuan tuan benbu 商團團本部). The Merchant Corps had a regular force of more than 2,000 members. It controlled more than 30 brigades in Suzhou and surrounding areas, including Wu County (Wuxian 吳縣), Wujiang (吳江), Wuxi (無錫), and Taicang (太倉). As the records of the earliest and longest-running merchant militia group in the lower Yangzi area, this material is important to our understanding of the relationship between business and politics in the region.

B. *Suzhou Urban Commune*
An important collection of documents at the Suzhou Municipal Archives concerns urban communes, or *shimin gongshe*. The urban commune was first set up in 1909 as a self-government organization and continued until 1927 or so. Its organization was based on street patrol wards, and members were drawn mainly from industrial and commerce circles and were called *shimin* 市民 (urban resident) instead of *shangren* 商人 (merchant). The commune's membership and organizational structure transcended the traditional limits of commercial guilds and same-trade associations.

Documents in the Suzhou Chamber of Commerce include petitions to establish urban communes, membership qualifications, lists of members, commune regulations, and documents about organizational structure, revenue, and expenditure. The commune's activities reflect priorities in urban administration and educational and political participation. This kind of urban commune was found only in the Suzhou region; its uniqueness as a type of self-government organization makes its documents particularly valuable for the study of the relationship between state and society as China underwent the transition from an imperial system to a republic.

C. Banks

A third group of important documents are banking records, which reflect the growth and decline of financial institutions in Suzhou. The oldest document in the collection dates from 1889 and deals with the establishment of the Forever Prosperity Bank (Yong feng qianzhuang 永豐錢莊), one of the earliest native banks in Suzhou. In 1908, the Bank of Communications–Suzhou Branch (Jiaotong yinhang, Suzhou fenhang 交通銀行蘇州分行), the first joint-venture bank between Chinese merchants and the government, opened for business. In 1912 the Jiangsu Bank–Suzhou Branch (Jiangsu yinhang, Suzhou fenhang 江蘇銀行蘇州分行), the first provincial bank, was set up. By 1945, Suzhou had 95 banks, of which 60 were native banks. By the eve of the communist victory in 1949, the number of banks in Suzhou had declined to 36, of which 12 were native banks.

One bank deserving special attention is the Suzhou Land Bank (Suzhou tianye yinhang 蘇州田業銀行). It was sponsored by the Lands and Estate Association (Tianye gonghui 田業公會), whose members were all landlords. The bank's headquarters were located in Suzhou, with branches in Wuxi (吳錫) and other major towns of the region. This bank provided loans for peasants and invested in rice-hulling mills, water pumping stations, and land.

D. Silk Industry

The fourth and largest group of documents at the Suzhou Chamber of Commerce concerns the silk industry. With approximately 100,000 items, the collection is one of the most extensive of its kind in China. Although the collection contains some tablet inscriptions dating to the early sixteenth century, most documents were produced after the founding of the Suzhou Chamber of Commerce in 1905. They mainly cover organizational history, silk production, raw material, equipment, cocoon purchases, silk reeling, technical innovation, foreign trade, domestic markets, silk taxes, business registration, and surveys and statistics.

Publications

Between 1980 and 1994, the Suzhou Municipal Archives compiled and published a number of documentary surveys of the Suzhou Chamber of Commerce. These include *Suzhou shimin gongshe dang'an xuanji* 蘇州市民公社檔案選輯 (Selected documents of the Suzhou Urban Commune) and "Suzhou changmen bingbian" 蘇州閶門兵變 (Mutiny in Changmen, Suzhou), in *Xinhai geming shi congkan* 辛亥革命史叢刊 (Revolution of 1911 history series), vols. 4 and 6 (Beijing: Zhonghua shuju, 1982, 1986). In addition, the archives published a separate volume of the chamber's documents, in *Suzhou shanghui dang'an congbian di yi ji, 1905–1911* 蘇州商會檔案叢編, 第一輯, 1905–1911 (Suzhou Chamber of Commerce archives series, vol. 1, 1905–11) (Wuhan: Huazhong shifan daxue chubanshe, 1991). This volume contains documents relating to economic history (e.g., mining, banking, factories, taxation, and public health) up to 1911, amounting to about one-sixth of the entire collection of the Suzhou Chamber of Commerce.

Chapter 10

Nantong Municipal Archives, Dasheng Business Enterprises Collection
南通市檔案館大生企業檔案

Introduction

The Nantong Municipal Archives (Nantong shi dang'anguan 南通市檔案館) was established in 1959. It has more than 260 collections, with a total of 100,655 volumes of documents. The archive is particularly noted for its documentary collection on Zhang Jian 張謇 (1853–1926) and his Dasheng business enterprises.

Zhang Jian and His Dasheng Business Enterprises

Zhang Jian (*zi*: Jizhi 季直; *hao*: Se'an 嗇庵) earned a reputation for his activities in business, education, and politics. Despite receiving the highest honor in the Qing metropolitan civil service examination, Zhang's faith in commerce as a means to national salvation (as signified in the phrase "enterprise to save the nation" *shiye jiuguo* 實業救國) prompted him to seek a career outside the imperial bureaucracy. In 1895, Zhang returned to Nantong from Beijing hoping to raise capital for a textile factory. Four years later, his Dasheng Textile Mill (Dasheng shachang 大生紗廠) was in full operation. Although most Chinese capitalists struggled during the years before and after the Revolution of 1911, Zhang's mounting profits encouraged him to invest in a second mill in 1913.

Although Zhang's goals of political reform and local self-government met with disappointment, his economic success continued. The years during and after World War I were particularly profitable, and he opened two more mills in 1922 and 1923. But Zhang's business interests were not confined to industrial production. In 1901 he formed the Tonghai Reclamation Company (Tonghai kenmu gongsi 通海墾牧公司) to transform the Nanhuai salt-yard region of Jiangsu's coastal Tonghai district into farmland. Between 1914 and 1922, almost half of the 45 companies operating in the Tonghai area either belonged to Zhang's Dasheng consortium or had some kind of relationship with it.

Besides commerce, Zhang also viewed education as an essential building block of national development. He founded China's first teacher-training institution, Tongzhou Normal School (Tongzhou shifan xuexiao 通州師範學校), in Nantong in 1902 and the country's first modern museum, the Tongzhou Museum (Tongzhou bowuyuan 通州博物苑), in 1905. Furthermore, over the years he set up dozens of technical schools and institutes specializing in agriculture, textiles, medicine, and other professions and assisted in establishing over 300 public and private elementary schools in Nantong county alone. In terms of higher education, Zhang played an instrumental role in the founding of China's first teacher's college, Three Rivers Normal School

(Sanjiang shifan xuetang 三江師範學堂)—the earliest precursor to Nanjing University—and helped finance Zhendan Public School (Zhendan gongxue 震旦公學), also called Fudan Public School (Fudan gongxue 復旦公學), which later became Fudan University in Shanghai; Hehai Special School (Hehai zhuanmen xuexiao 河海專門學校), later Nanjing Hehai University (Nanjing hehai daxue 南京河海大學); Shanghai Wusong Commerce and Shipping School (Shanghai wusong shang chuan xuexiao 上海吳淞商船學校); and the Suzhou Railroad School (Suzhou tielu xuexiao 蘇州鐵路學校), among others.

The Nantong Municipal Archives holds an estimated 10,000 volumes of Dasheng documents. In addition, the Nantong Library has a small collection of published books and periodicals related to Zhang Jian and his enterprises. Part of the Nantong Library's documentary collection has recently been published in the six-volume *Zhang Jian quanji* 張謇全集 (Comprehensive collection of Zhang Jian) (Nanjing: Jiangsu guji chubanshe, 1994).

Economic History Archives

I. Zhang Jian

This collection contains correspondence between Zhang Jian and important historical figures such as Sun Yat-sen, Yuan Shikai, Han Guojun 韓國鈞, and high officials of the late Qing. Some of these letters, for example, reveal Zhang's attitudes toward the Sino-Japanese War, Empress Dowager Ci Xi, and the Reform Movement of 1898. The collection also contains information on his Dasheng businesses, a three-volume set of paternal instructions to his son, Zhang Xiaoruo (張孝若), and collections of Zhang's personal inscriptions, couplets, and notes. In addition, the Nantong Municipal Archives houses published works relating to Zhang Jian's life. These include *Zhang Jian riji* 張謇日記 (Zhang Jian's diaries), *Zhang Jizhi zhuanji* 張季直傳記 (Biography of Zhang Jizhi), *Zhang Jizhi jiulu* 張季直九錄 (Nine records on Zhang Jizhi), *Se Weng kenmu shoudie* 嗇翁墾牧手牒 (The Venerable Se's correspondence on land reclamation and livestock raising), *Tongzhou xingban shiye zhi lishi* 通州興辦實業之歷史 (The industrial history of Tongzhou), and *Ershinian lai zhi Nantong* 二十年來之南通 (Nantong in the past twenty years).

The Nantong Municipal Archives also houses records pertaining to Zhang Jian's activities in agriculture and water conservancy. In fact, the records of the Huainan salt-yard companies are the only extant papers in China documenting the transition from traditional small-scale farming methods to large-scale agricultural production. In terms of water conservancy, in 1911 Zhang funded technical teams to survey the Huai River system. He also served terms as superintendent of the Huai River (*dao-Huai duban* 導淮督辦). Plans, maps, charts, and other papers related to Zhang's Huai River projects are available at the Nantong Municipal Archives and the Nantong Library.

II. Dasheng Business Enterprises

This collection contains documents collected from three different sources: the Dasheng Textile Company (transferred to the archives in 1952), the Shanghai headquarters of Dasheng Enterprises, and the enterprises and employees of the Dasheng group. This material includes letters, accounts, annual summaries, minutes of shareholder and board of directors meetings, work reports, contracts, regulations, proposals, telegrams, trademarks, stock certificates, shareholder name lists, business cards, seals, and other items from Dasheng's numerous subsidiary companies and schools. About half the collection consists of accounting documents. These documents cover over half a century between the conglomerate's founding in the 1890s and its transformation into a joint state-private enterprise in 1952. The Dasheng collection has been listed by the Chinese State Archives Bureau as a "key archives for national conservation" (*quanguo zhongdian baohu dang'an* 全國重點保護檔案).

III. Other Holdings at the Nantong Municipal Archives

In addition to the documentary collection of Zhang Jian and his Dasheng enterprises, the Nantong Municipal Archives houses over 35,000 volumes of local government documents for the years 1912 to 1949.

Publications

Selected documents of the Nantong Municipal Archives have been published in *Dasheng qiye xitong dang'an xuanbian* 大生企業系統檔案選編 (Selected archival documents of the Dasheng Enterprises group) (Nanjing: Nanjing daxue chubanshe, 1987–).

Chapter 11

Sichuan Provincial Archives
四川省檔案館

Introduction

The Sichuan Provincial Archives (Sichuan sheng dang'anguan 四川省檔案館) officially opened in April 1966, but its work was partially interrupted during the Cultural Revolution (1966–76). A preparatory committee began to acquire archival materials in the 1950s, and over the next decades, the archives acquired more than 1.14 million volumes of documents, making it one of the largest provincial archives in China. The majority of documents relate to the provincial government, political parties, mass organizations, and businesses based in Sichuan and Xikang provinces. Its collection of Baxian (Ba county) documents 巴縣檔案, with about 113,000 volumes, is the largest and best-known archival collection of Qing local government material available in China. In addition, the collection of the Sichuan-Yunnan frontier affairs commissioner (*Chuan Dian bianwu dachen* 川滇邊務大臣, with more than 1,100 volumes covering the years 1906–12, is a good source for the study of aborigines and Chinese-Tibetan relations in the first decade of the twentieth century.

Economic History Archives

I. Sichuan Provincial Finance Department

The Sichuan Provincial Finance Department (Sichuan sheng caizheng ting 四川省財政廳) was established in June 1914 to administer tax collection efforts and manage revenues for the province. The Finance Department had several subordinate organizations, including the Local Tax Bureau (Difangshui ju 地方稅局), the Business Tax Bureau (Yingyeshui ju 營業稅局), the Printing Factory (Yinshua suo 印刷所), the Printing Bureau (Yinshua ju 印刷局), the Taxation Inspection Office (Shuiwu ducha chu 稅務督察處), and the Land Registry Office (Tudi chenbao banshi chu 土地陳報辦事處).

Although the 8,300-volume collection of the Finance Department covers the years 1912–49, the majority of the documents date from after 1935. Besides regulations, fiscal plans, and work reports, the collection contains documents on taxation, GMD funds, military and local police, budget inspections, audits of publicly owned enterprises, and banking records.

II. Land Tax and Grain Administrative Agencies

The first provincial grain administration agency in Sichuan was not established until after the National Government moved its wartime capital to Chongqing in 1938. This was the Sichuan Provincial Grain Administration Commission (Sichuan sheng liangshi guanli weiyuanhui 四川省糧食管理委員會). In 1940 it was reorganized as the Sichuan Provincial Grain Management Bureau (Sichuan sheng liangshi ju 四川省糧食管理局), and in 1941 as the Sichuan Provincial Grain Administrative Bureau (Sichuan sheng liangshi zhengju 四川省糧食政局).

The land tax was initially under the jurisdiction of the provincial Finance Department and retained for provincial use. After the land tax was remitted to the National Government, the Ministry of Finance established the Sichuan Land Tax Office (Caizheng bu, Sichuan tianfu guanli chu 財政部四川田賦管理處) in August 1941 and incorporated into it the Sichuan Provincial Land Registration Office (Sichuan sheng tudi chenbao banshi chu 四川省土地陳報辦事處) a few months later. In May 1945, the Sichuan Land Tax Office was merged with the Sichuan Provincial Grain Administration Bureau to form the Sichuan Provincial Land Tax and Grain Office (Sichuan sheng tianfu liangshi guanli chu 四川省田賦糧食管理處) under the jurisdiction of the Sichuan provincial government.

The Sichuan Provincial Archives has organized the records of land-tax organizations into a single collection, totaling 8,900 volumes. These documents are a good source for the study of the relationship between center and locality. The collection's holdings can roughly be divided into four parts. First are administrative documents dealing with such issues as the founding and reorganization of land tax and grain agencies, laws and regulations on land tax and grain administration, personnel appointments and transfers, meeting minutes, plans and reports, and correspondence with GMD party, military, and police units. A second group comprises the records of the Sichuan Land Tax Office, mainly documents on land tax rates, granaries, the deeds tax, tax disputes and complaints, tax evasion, and tax reductions and exemptions. The third component is the Sichuan Provincial Grain Administration Bureau's records. These include data on grain allotments to employees in government and public organizations, grain investigations, production reports, rice prices, grain purchases, storage and transportation, and price regulations. The fourth part is the records of the Sichuan Provincial Land Tax and Grain Office. In addition to documents on grain collection, purchase, storage, transportation, processing, and distribution, these records also contain information on grain administration, grain merchant registration, debt clearance, the food supply, and grain distribution. The collection also contains documents on tax and grain administration in Xikang province.

III. Salt Administration Agencies

Early in the Republican period, Sichuan established a Department of Salt Administration (Yanzheng bu 鹽政部) to administer production, transportation, and sales. Soon it was reorganized as the Salt Administration Bureau (Yanzheng ju 鹽政局), which was replaced in 1914 by the Office of Salt Commissioner (Yanyun shishu 鹽運使署). In the mid-1930s, the Office of Sichuan Salt Commissioner and the Sichuan Office of the Salt Gabelle were merged to form the Sichuan Salt Administration (Sichuan yanwu guanli ju 四川鹽務管理局), which later became the Sichuan-Xikang Salt Administration (Chuan-Kang quyanwu guanli ju 川康區鹽務管理局). Similarly, local offices of the salt gabelle were also organized into the salt administration system.

The Sichuan Provincial Archives has more than 8,400 volumes on the salt monopoly in Sichuan province and and a smaller number for Xikang. The collection consists of the records of three bureaus: the Northern Sichuan Salt Administration (Chuanbei yanwu guanli ju 川北鹽務管理局, 1936–42), the Sichuan-Xikang Salt Administration, Chengdu Office (Chuan-Kang qu yanwu guanli ju, Chengdu zhiju 川康區鹽務管理局成都支局, 1942–49), and the Sichuan-Xikang Salt Administration, Kangya Office (Chuan-Kang qu yanwu guanli ju, Kangya zhiju 川康區鹽務管理局康雅支局, 1942–49). In addition, the collection also has documents of the Directorate General of Salt Administration, which was relocated to Wutongqiao 五通橋 in Sichuan during the war against Japan.

IV. Sichuan-Xikang Taxation Agencies

Major tax agencies in the Sichuan and Xikang area included the Sichuan-Xikang Region Direct Tax Administration (Chuan-Kang qu zhijieshui ju 川康區直接稅局), the Sichuan-Xikang Region Excise Tax Administration (Chuan-Kang qu huowushui ju 川康區貨物稅局), and the Sichuan-Xikang Region State Tax Collectorate (Chuan-Kang qu guoshui guanli ju 川康區國稅管理局). In 1943 the first two offices were merged to form the Eastern Sichuan Tax Administration (Dongchuan shuiwu guanli ju 東川稅務管理局) and the Western Sichuan Tax Administration (Xichuan shuiwu guanli ju 西川稅務管理局). But two years later they reverted to the Sichuan-Xikang Region Direct Tax Administration and the Sichuan-Xikang Region Excise Tax Administration. The former was responsible for collecting income, probate, land, deeds, stamp, and business taxes, and the latter was in charge of the taxes on state monopolies such as tobacco, liquor, matches, and sugar. In 1948 these two administrations were merged to form the Sichuan-Xikang Region State Tax Collectorate.

The Sichuan Provincial Archives contains 456 volumes of records on these three tax agencies, covering 1936–49. Most of the documents pertain to organizational structure and personnel.

V. Sichuan Financial Institutions

The Sichuan Provincial Archives has over 42,000 volumes of banking records. The following is a list of major financial institutions represented in this group:

Provincial Bank of Sichuan
(Sichuan sheng yinhang 四川省銀行)

Sichuan Provincial Cooperative Bank
(Sichuan sheng hezuo jinku 四川省合作金庫)

Central Bank of China, Chengdu Branch
(Zhongyang yinhang, Chengdu fenhang 中央銀行成都分行)

Bank of China, Chengdu Branch
(Zhongguo yinhang, Chengdu zhihang 中國銀行成都支行)

Bank of Communications, Chengdu Branch
(Jiaotong yinhang, Chengdu zhihang 交通銀行成都支行)

Farmers' Bank of China, Chengdu Branch
(Zhongguo nongmin yinhang, Chengdu fenhang 中國農民銀行成都分行)

Chengdu Office of the Joint Board of the Bank of China, the Central Bank of China, the
    Bank of Communications, and the Farmers' Bank of China
(Sihang lianhe banshichu, Chengdu fenchu 四行聯合辦事處成都分處)

Central Trust of China, Chengdu Branch
(Zhongyang xintuo ju, Chengdu fenju 中央信託局成都分局)

The Central Mint, Chengdu Branch
(Zhongyang zaobichang, Chengdu fenchang 中央造幣廠成都分廠)

Provincial Bank of Xikang, Chengdu Office
(Xikang sheng yinhang, Chengdu banshi chu 西康省銀行成都辦事處)

VI. Accounting and Auditing Agencies

Sichuan's provincial-level accounting agencies during the Republican period included the Sichuan Provincial Accounting Office (Sichuan sheng kuaiji chu 四川省會計處), the Sichuan Provincial Auditing Office (1939–49, Sichuan sheng shenji chu 四川省審計處), and the Sichuan Statistics Office (1941–49, Sichuan sheng tongji chu 四川省統計處). On October 1, 1949, the Accounting Office and the Statistics Office were merged to form the Sichuan Provincial Accounting and Auditing Office (Zhuji chu 主計處).

The Sichuan Provincial Accounting Office collection has 3,700 volumes of records, covering 1939–49. The Sichuan Provincial Statistics Office collection has about 500 volumes of documents dated 1937–49. The Sichuan Provincial Auditing Office and the Sichuan Provincial Accounting and Auditing Office do not have individual collections. Instead, documents of these two agencies are scattered throughout other collections.

VII. Reconstruction Department

Formed in May 1930, the Sichuan Provincial Reconstruction Department (Sichuan sheng jianshe ting 四川省建設廳) took charge of agriculture, forestry, land reclamation, mining, electricity, communications, transportation, water conservancy, industry, commerce, cooperatives, and surveys in Sichuan province. In addition to its internal offices, the Reconstruction Department administered the Agriculture Improvement Institute (Nongye gaijin suo 農業改進所), the Public Roads Bureau (Gonglu ju 公路局), the Public Roads Transportation Company (Gonglu yunshu gongsi 公路運輸公司), the Geological Survey Institute (Dizhi diaocha suo 地質調查所), the Measurements Inspection Office (Duliangheng jianding suo 度量衡檢定所), the Cooperative Enterprises Administrative Office (Hezuo shiye guanli chu 合作事業管理處), the Mining Industry Inspection Office (Kuangye zhidao chu 礦業指導處), the Meteorology Office (Qixiang suo 氣象所), the Radio Broadcasting Station (Wuxiandian zongtai 無線電總臺), the Sichuan Silk Improvement Farm (Sichuan cansi gailiang chang 四川蠶絲改良場), the Pingbei Land Reclamation Bureau (Pingbei kenwu guanli ju 平北墾務管理局), and the Telephone Management Office (Dianhua guanli chu 電話管理處).

The Sichuan Provincial Archives has more than 11,300 volumes of documents of the Sichuan Provincial Reconstruction Office, spanning 1925–49. These can be subdivided into the following categories:

1. Commerce: includes documents related to Sichuan's foreign trade, city and county enterprises, industry, replies to registration applications from companies and banks, and monthly price reports.

2. Industry: includes city and county investigations, replies to factory registration applications (e.g., cement, pharmaceuticals, paper, fertilizer, and textile firms), personnel, organization, finance, and operation files from county power plants and electric companies.

3. Geological surveys and mining: documents concern mining applications, mining disputes, petroleum research, maps, and accounts of mine surveys.

4. Postal services and communications: material pertains to radio stations, postal services, transportation infrastructure (construction, maintenance, plans), transportation prices, railroad surveys, accident reports, and bicycle and rickshaw registrations.

5. Urban utilities: contains files on the Chengdu branch of the China Urban Administration Society (Zhongguo shizheng xuehui 中國市政學會), Chengdu and Chongqing water companies, urban reconstruction plans, construction, and public utilities (parks, restrooms, road lights).

6. Agriculture and reclamation: includes surveys of Sichuan agricultural production, land use, reclamation, loans, natural disasters, agrarian industries, and papers from Sichuan University Agriculture College (Sichuan daxue nongxue yuan 四川大學農學院).

7. Forestry: contains documents related to various forestry agencies (e.g., Sichuan Provincial Forestry Society, Sichuan sheng linxue hui 四川省林學會), reforestation, and lumber and charcoal supply surveys.

8. Livestock husbandry: contains papers concerning livestock insurance, veterinary training, livestock purchase loans, and related issues.

9. Water conservancy: includes documents pertaining to the Water Conservancy Bureau (Shuili ju 水利局), budgets, projects, surveys, periodicals from government offices (e.g., Yangtze River Water Conservancy Commission, Changjiang shuili weiyuanhui 長江水利委院會), and county water conservancy loans.

This collection also contains papers on airports in Chengdu 成都, Chongqing 重慶, and Mianyang 綿陽.

VIII. Communications Agencies

Records of communications agencies in the Sichuan Provincial Archives are included in the following four collections: the Sichuan Public Roads Bureau (Sichuan sheng gonglu ju 四川省公路局, 1926–49), the Sichuan Public Roads Truck Transportation Company (Sichuan sheng gonglu qiche yunshu gongsi 四川省公路汽車運輸公司, 1946–49), the Sichuan Post Courier Bureau (Sichuan sheng yiyun guanli chu 四川省驛運管理處, 1940–49), and the Directorate General of Public Roads, Fifth District Public Roads Works Bureau (Jiaotong bu, Gonglu zongju, Diwu qu gonglu gongcheng ju 交通部公路總局第五區公路工程局, 1940–49). These four collections have approximately 33,200 volumes. To give one example, materials concerning the Public Roads Transport Company include wage schedules, budget reports, monthly expenditure and income reports, vehicle rental agreements, papers on the management of horse couriers and carriage routes, documents relating to vehicle maintenance, inspections, and work reports, as well as conference minutes.

IX. Measurements Inspection Office

The Sichuan Measurements Inspection Office (Sichuan sheng duliangheng jianding suo 四川省度量衡檢定所) was established under the Provincial Reconstruction Department (Jianshe ting 建設廳) in 1935, when Sichuan was officially brought under the control of the Nationalist government. The Sichuan Provincial Archives holds more than 1,600 volumes of documents from this office covering 1935–49.

X. Water Conservancy Bureau

Water conservancy in Sichuan province was initially the responsibility of the Provincial Reconstruction Department, which set up the Water Conservancy Bureau (Shuili ju 水利局) in late 1935, and the Sichuan Provincial Agricultural Irrigation Loan Commission (Sichuan nongtian shuili daikuan weiyuanhui 四川農田水利貸款委員會) in 1939. The latter was reorganized into the Sichuan-Xikang Irrigation Loan Commission (Chuan-Kang huili daikuan weiyuanhui 川康水利貸款委員會) in 1939. In late 1940 it merged with the Reconstruction Department's Water Conservancy Bureau to form the Sichuan Provincial Water Conservancy Bureau (Sichuan sheng shuili ju 四川省水利局), directly subordinate to the Sichuan provincial government.

The Sichuan Provincial Water Conservancy Bureau collection has 5,400 volumes of documents (including those of its predecessors), covering 1932–49. The collection contains personnel records, meeting minutes, resolutions, plans and reports, and data on irrigation loans, budgets, expenditures, and water conservancy training. The collection also has some documents from the Xikang Provincial Water Conservancy Bureau (Xikang sheng shuili ju 西康省水利局).

XI. Agriculture Improvement Institute

Established in September 1938, the Sichuan Agriculture Improvement Institute (Sichuan nongye gaijin suo 四川農業改進所) was composed of eight different provincial agencies: the Livestock Nursery Institute (Jiachu baoyang suo 家畜保養所), the Silk Improvement Farm (Cansi gailiang chang 蠶絲改良場), the Rice and Wheat Improvement Institute (Daomai gaijin suo 稻麥改進所), the Cotton Crop Experiment Farm (Mianzuo shiyan chang 棉作實驗場), the Number One Forestry Farm (Diyi linchang 第一林場), the Agricultural and Botanical Disease and Insect Prevention Institute (Nonglin zhiwubing chonghai fangzhi suo 農林植物病蟲害防治所), the Horticulture Experiment Farm (Yuanyi shiyan chang 園藝實驗場), and the Forestry Experiment Farm (Linye shiyan chang 林業實驗場).

The Sichuan Provincial Archives holds nearly 10,000 volumes of documents of the Agriculture Improvement Institute covering 1935–49. Beside regulations, appointments, dismissal records, resumés, and budgets, the collection contains documents on sericulture, cotton, grain, sugarcane, livestock breeding, veterinary medicine, pest and disease prevention, farm management, agricultural prices, natural disasters, and productivity.

XII. Postal Services and Telecommunications

The Sichuan Provincial Archives has more than 24,400 volumes of documents concerning postal services and telecommunications. These are primarily held in the following collections:

1. The West Sichuan Postal Administration Bureau (Xichuan youzheng guanli ju 西川郵政管理局): established in Chengdu in 1923 when Sichuan was divided into two postal districts, East Sichuan and West Sichuan. Documents cover 1930–49.

2. The Chengdu Telecommunications Bureau (Chengdu dianxin ju 成都電信局): grew out of the Chengdu Telegraph Bureau (Chengdu dianbao ju 成都電報局) in 1944. This collection covers 1930–49.

3. The Sichuan Telecommunications Bureau (Sichuan dianxin guanli ju 四川電信管理局) resulted from a merger of the Provincial Telephone Bureau (Dianhua guanli ju 電話管理局) and the Provincial Radio Station (Wuxiandian zongtai 無線電總台) in 1948. Records cover 1939–49.

XIII. Industrial Enterprises Managed by the National Resources Commission

The National Resources Commission (NRC; Ziyuan weiyuanhui 資源委員會), established in 1935, took over and managed factories and mining operations throughout China. Its affiliated businesses in Sichuan and Xikang provinces included the Sichuan-Xikang Development Company (Chuan-Kang xingye gongsi 川康興業公司), the Dujiang Power Plant (Dujiang dianchang 都江電廠), the Sichuan-Xikang Copper Mining Bureau (Chuan-Kang tongye guanli ju 川康銅業管理局), the Preparatory Office of the Peng County Copper Mining Bureau (Peng xian tongkuang ju, Choubei chu 彭縣銅礦局籌備處), and the Huachang Development Company (Huachang xingye gongsi 華昌興業公司).

The Sichuan Provincial Archives houses over 1,500 volumes of these and other NRC-sponsored businesses between 1925 and 1950. Below is a brief description of these records.

1. The Sichuan-Xikang Development Company: founded in March 1942, its documents include name lists of employees and board directors, wage schedules, market surveys, meeting minutes, investment and asset adjustment records, company plans, weekly work reports, and records from the following subsidiary companies: the Sichuan Silk Company (Sichuan siye gongsi 四川絲業公司, the Sichuan Machinery Company (Sichuan jixie gongsi 四川機械公司), the Sichuan Agriculture Company (Sichuan nongye gongsi 四川農業公司), the Chengdu Waterworks Company (Chengdu zilaishui gongsi 成都自來水公司), the Wan County Hydroelectric Power Plant (Wan xian shuidian chang 萬縣水電廠), and the Xikang Wool and Rawhide Company (Xikang maoge gongsi 西康毛革公司).

2. The Dujiang Power Plant: preparations for the plant began in 1945, and it was completed in 1947. Documents include employee lists, resumés, work plans, reports, budgets, accounting reports, agreements with customers in Chengdu, Guan County 灌縣, and Pujiang 蒲江, purchase and inspection agreements, and correspondence with other Sichuan-based power plants.

3. The Sichuan-Xikang Copper Mining Bureau and the Preparatory Office of the Peng County Copper Mining Bureau: the former was set up in 1939; the latter was started by private capital in 1923, but taken over jointly by the NRC and the Chongqing Office of the Military Commission in 1935. Documents include appointment records, medical records, accounts, monthly work reports, correspondence, records of mining rights, geological surveys, output reports, equipment and vehicle purchase reports, transport and distribution reports (including shipping contracts and duty exemption and shipping applications), mine maps, and excavation plans.

4. The Huachang Development Company: founded in 1942, its documents include information on the Huachang 華昌, Shixi 石溪, and Jianwei 犍為 coal mines, chemical analyses, company rules, name lists, and employment agreements.

5. Other NRC businesses: the Sichuan Provincial Archives contain materials from or pertaining to the following companies and agencies subordinate to the NRC: Sichuan Mining Industry Advisory Office (Sichuan kuangye zhidao chu 四川礦業指導處), Sichuan Mining Company (Sichuan kuangye gongsi 四川礦業公司), Sichuan Longsheng Chemical Company (Sichuan longsheng huaxue gongsi 四川隆聖化學公司), Sichuan Sugar Company (Sichuan tangye gongsi 四川糖業公司), and Sichuan Livestock Trade Company (Sichuan chuchan maoyi gongsi 四川畜產貿易公司).

XIV. Companies Managed by the Ministry of Finance Trade Commission

Prior to the Sino-Japanese War (1937–45), the Ministry of Finance Trade Commission set up a Consignment Office (Shouhuo chu 收貨處) in Chengdu. The office was granted a monopoly on wool, tea, silk, pig bristles (*zhuzong* 豬鬃), tung oil (*tungyou* 桐油), and other local products. With the outbreak of the war, the Trade Commission expanded some of its subordinate companies, such as the Fuxing Trading Company (Fuxing shangye gongsi 復興商業公司) and Fuhua Trading Company (Fuhua maoyi gongsi 富華貿易公司), and reorganized the Tea Shipping Department (Chayun chu 茶運處) into the China Tea Company (Zhongguo chaye gongsi 中國茶業公司). These three companies had branches in Chengdu. The Sichuan Provincial Archives keeps about 2,100 volumes of documents from these companies.

Publications

The Sichuan Provincial Archives' guide, *Sichuan sheng dang'anguan guancang dang'an gaishu* 四川省檔案館館藏檔案概述 (General guide to holdings in the Sichuan Provincial Archives) (Chengdu: Sichuan shehui kexueyuan chubanshe, 1988), was one of the first of its kind published in China.

As one of the largest local archives in China, the Sichuan Provincial Archives has published many documentary compilations, most concerning political subjects. Documents pertaining to Sichuan's economic history during the Qing dynasty can be found in collections such as *Qingdai Qian Jia Dao Baxian dang'an xuanbian* 清代乾嘉道巴縣檔案選編 (Selected archival documents of Ba county during the Qianlong, Jiaqing, and Daoguang reigns of the Qing dynasty), 2 vols. (Chengdu: Sichuan daxue chubanshe, 1989, 1997); *Qingdai Baoxian dang'an huibian: Qianlong juan* 清代巴縣檔案匯編：乾隆卷 (Selected archival documents of Ba county during the Qianlong

122

reign) (Beijing: Dang'an chubanshe, 1991); *Qingmo Chuan Dian bianwu dang'an shiliao* 清末川滇邊務檔案史料 (Archival sources on frontier affairs in Sichuan and Yunnan during the late Qing) (Beijing: Zhonghua shuju, 1989); and *Jindai Kangqu dang'an ziliao xuanbian* 近代康區檔案資料選編 (Selected archival sources on the Xikang region in modern times) (Chengdu: Sichuan daxue chubanshe, 1990).

Documents on the economic history of the Republican period can be found in *Sichuan gongren yundong shiliao xuanbian* 四川工人運動史料選編 (Selected historical sources on the labor movement in Sichuan) (Chengdu: Sichuan daxue chubanshe, 1988); and *Chuan-Shaan suqu baokan ziliao xuanbian* 川陝蘇區報刊資料選編 (Selected sources from newspapers and journals from the Sichuan-Shaanxi Soviet area) (Chengdu: Sichuan daxue chubanshe, 1987).

The *Sichuan dang'an shiliao* 四川檔案史料 (Sichuan archival sources) is a quarterly journal sponsored by the Sichuan Provincial Archives and devoted to publishing archival material.

Chapter 12

Chongqing Municipal Archives
重慶市檔案館

Introduction

Established in 1960, the Chongqing Municipal Archives (CMA; Chengdu shi dang'anguan 城都市檔案館) contains many collections of pre-1949 Republican-era documents from government bureaus in the Chongqing region. It also houses a large number of government documents from the post-1949 period. The documents of the CCP Chongqing Municipal Committee are currently stored in the committee's General Office rather than in the CMA. Of the more than 600,000 volumes preserved at the archives, over 80 percent date from after 1937 when the Nationalist government relocated to Chongqing.

Documents in the CMA cover a wide range of topics, including those relating to party and administrative affairs, education, the military, police activity, judicial matters, finance, and industry and commerce.

Economic History Archives

I. Finance

From the early years of the Republican period, Chongqing was the financial center of China's southwest region. Financial and taxation records are therefore especially plentiful at the CMA. These include documents from the Chongqing State Revenue Service (Taxation Bureau), the Excise Tax Bureau, the Direct Tax Bureau, the Finance Bureau, the Grain Administration Bureau, Chongqing branch offices of foreign banks, domestic post and remittance bureaus, the China Trust Company (Zhongguo xintuo ju 中國信托局), banking trade associations, and war industry trade associations. Among these materials, a substantial proportion pertain to the Young Brothers Banking Corporation (Juxingcheng yinhang 聚興城銀行) and 24 other commercial banks.

II. Industry and Commerce

After the outbreak of the Sino-Japanese War in 1937, much of China's coastal industry accompanied the Nationalist government in its move to Chongqing. This stimulated Chongqing's development and enhanced its role as an economic center. Included in the CMA collections on economic history are records from the Chongqing Chamber of Commerce, other chambers of commerce, relocated factory associations, textile factories (e.g., the Yuhua Textiles Factory [Yuhua fangzhi chang 裕華紡織廠] and the China Textiles Factory [Zhongguo maofang chang 中國毛紡廠]), steel companies (e.g., Yuxin Iron and Steel Company [Yuxin gangtie chang 渝鑫鋼鐵廠]), steel and mining companies (e.g., the Tianfu Coal Mines [Tianfu meikuang 天府煤礦]), electric companies (e.g., Chongqing Municipal Electricity Company [Chongqing shi dianli gongsi 重慶市電力公司] and Tien Yuen Electro-Chemical Works [Tianyuan dianhua chang 天源電化廠]), shipping companies (e.g., Ming Sung Shipping Company [Mingsheng lunchuan gongsi 民生輪船公司] and the Qianghua Steamship Company [Qianhua lunchuan gongsi 強華輪船公司]), and trading companies (e.g., Baoyuantong Trading Company, Ltd. [Baoyuantong maoyi youxian gongsi 寶元通貿易有限公司]).

Publications

The CMA has published an archival guide entitled *Chongqing shi dang'anguan jianming zhinan* 重慶市檔案館簡明指南 (Guide to the Chongqing Municipal Archives) (Chongqing: Kexue jishu wenxian chubanshe, Chongqing fenshe, 1990).

The archives has also compiled more than 20 collections of selected documents on economic subjects. These include *Silian zongchu shiliao* 四聯總處史料 (Historical sources of the Joint Board of the Bank of China, the Central Bank of China, the Bank of Communications, and the Farmers' Bank of China) (Beijing: Dang'an chubanshe, 1993); *Kangri zhanzheng shiqi guomin zhengfu jingji fagui* 抗日戰爭時期國民政府經濟法規 (Economic laws and regulations of the National Government during the War of Resistance Against Japan) (Beijing: Dang'an chubanshe, 1992); and *Kangzhan houfang yejin gongye shiliao* 抗戰後方冶金工業史料 (Historical sources on metallurgical industry in rear areas during the War of Resistance) (Chongqing: Chongqing chubanshe, 1988). Documents on wartime economic damage caused by the Japanese bombardment can be found in *Chongqing da hongzha* 重慶大轟炸 (Massive bombing of Chongqing) (Chongqing: Chongqing chubanshe, 1992).

Part of the CMA's holdings on the Young Brothers Banking Corporation can be found in *Juxingcheng yinhang* 聚興城銀行 (Young Brothers Banking Corporation) (Xi'an: Xi'an shifan daxue chubanshe, 1988). The corporation was founded by the Young (Yang) family (楊氏家族) in Chongqing and later became the largest private commercial bank in Sichuan province, with more than 30 branches. This collection includes documents and memoirs about the corporation's organizational evolution, business management, finance, personnel, and investments.

Chapter 13

Tianjin Municipal Archives and Other Collections in Tianjin
天津市檔案館

Introduction

During the late Qing and Republican periods, Tianjin developed into a major commercial and industrial center in North China. This section surveys archival material held at the Tianjin Municipal Archives, the Nankai Institute of Economics, the Tianjin Municipal Museum, Tianjin Municipal Library, the Tianjin Academy of Social Sciences, and other institutions.

Tianjin Municipal Archives

Established in 1964, the Tianjin Municipal Archives (Tianjin shi dang'anguan 天津市檔案館) has been under the administrative control of the Tianjin Municipal Government and the National Archives Bureau (Guojia dang'an ju). Closed to most Chinese and foreign researchers until it was relocated to its current quarters on Weijin Road in 1990, the archive is now open for public use. A guidebook is available. With over 600 complete files (*quanzong* 全宗) in over 1.2 million folders (*juan* 卷), it ranks among the largest municipal and provincial archives in China. The oldest document in the collection is a title patent (*gaoming* 誥命) issued in 1722, but much of the archive's material dates from the Republican period.

The archive's major collections include holdings on the Tianjin Special Municipality (Tianjin tebieshi 天津特別市) from 1937 to 1945, which contains material on company registrations and surveys; the postwar Tianjin Municipal Government (Tianjinshi zhengfu 天津市政府) from 1945 to 1949; the Tianjin Municipal Social Affairs Bureau (Tianjinshi shehuiju 天津市社會局) from 1928 to 1949, which includes company registers as well as materials on trade unions and labor disputes; the Tianjin Chamber of Commerce (Tianjin shanghui 天津商會) from 1903 to 1949, a treasure trove of materials on commerce and industry; 148 trade associations (Tianjinshi gehangye tongye gonghui 天津市各行業同業公會) from 1912 to 1949; and the Executive Yuan's Administrative Bureau for Japanese and Puppet Enterprises and Property in Hebei, Beiping, and Tianjin (Xingzhengyuan Hebei-Ping-Jin qu diwei chanye chuli ju 行政院河北平津區敵偽產業處

理局) from 1937 to 1949, which, with over 50,000 juan, is by far the largest collection of economic history materials in the archives.

Smaller municipal holdings include those of individual offices (such as the wartime Municipal Finance Bureau) and of the Tianjin xian (縣) government from 1916 to 1949. In addition, materials of some Tianjin-based offices of national ministries, commissions, or corporations may be found. These include documents of the Ministry of Finance, Tianjin Tax Bureau (Caizheng bu, Tianjin huoshuiju 財政部天津貨稅局), 1945–49; the Ministry of Finance, Tianjin Direct Tax Bureau (Caizheng bu, Tianjin zhijieshuiju, 財政部天津直接稅局), 1937–49; Bank of China, Tianjin Branch (Zhongguo yinhang, Tianjin fenhang 中國銀行天津分行), 1912–49; and the National Resources Commission's Beiping-Tianjin Office (Ziyuan weiyuanhui, Ping-Jin banshi chu 資源委員會平津辦事處), 1947–48, and its Northern Hebei Power Generating Company, Tianjin Branch (Jibei dianli youxian gongsi, Tianjin fengongsi 冀北電力有限公司天津分公司), 1945–49.

Archives of individual companies are plentiful and include those of the Santai (三泰) Spinning Mill (1887–1949), renamed in 1945 as China Weaving Development Corporation, Tianjin Mill No. 4; the No. 1 Tianjin Paper Mill (Tianjin zhiye gufan youxian gongsi diyi fenchang 天津紙業股份有限公司第一分廠), 1939–49; and the East Asia Tobacco Company (Dongya yancao chang 東亞煙草廠), 1941–45.

Other collections include the archives of the Maritime Customs of Tianjin (1861–1949) and the Huabei Postal Administration (1877–1949). In addition, papers left by foreign companies make up a sizable portion of the archives. Foreign researchers collaborating with Chinese scholars have been granted limited access to these foreign-language materials on a case-by-case basis.

Taken as a whole, the holdings of the Tianjin Municipal Archives cover every facet of the city during the Republican period. Land deeds, court cases, and collection of land taxes from the files of the District Office and the Land Bureau offer materials for the study of urban land use and development. Contracts and surveys of various trades from the Municipal Trades Assembly or company papers and their personnel records provide detailed information on merchant activity and business. Archival materials are still being transferred from the Public Security Bureau, courts, and banks, making this an underutilized but important archive.

The Nankai Institute of Economics Collection at Nankai University

The Nankai Institute of Economics Collection, long inaccessible to both Chinese and foreign researchers due to earthquake damage and other reasons, has been incorporated into the Nankai University Library. Headed by Franklin Ho (He Lian 何廉), H. D. Fong (Fang Xianting 方顯庭), and Chen Xujing (陳序經), the institute became one of China's leading centers of economic research during the Republican period. Although part of the collection was lost during World War II, it still includes a number of rare documents and government archival material, including H. H. Kung's (Kong Xiangxi 孔祥熙) confidential national financial report of 1939 and reports compiled by the Nationalist Special Economic Survey Office (Tezhong jingji diaocha chu 特種經濟調查處) in Japanese-occupied territory. Even during the war years, when the university moved to Sichuan, the collection continued to expand, supplemented by survey reports of dyeing mills and soap factories in Tianjin under Japanese occupation, as well as the papers of the Tianjin Wine Trade Guild (1936–45). After 1949, the institute continued its research on the Republican-era economy, focusing on the Chee Hsin (啓新) Cement Co., Ltd., the Kailan Mining Administration, and the Salt Gabelle Administration.

The institute is widely known for its compilation of statistical series on the Republican economy. Although the original ledgers upon which the price data series were compiled have been lost, remittance rates between Shanghai and Tianjin from 1898 to 1927, indices of wholesale prices, cost of living records, and foreign trade data have all been reprinted. Local newspapers and periodicals, as well as a number of unpublished master theses on credit unions and cotton-marketing cooperatives in North China, are also available at the Nankai University Library.

Tianjin Municipal Museum

A repository of material artifacts as well as written materials, the Tianjin Municipal Museum has long been neglected and closed to both Chinese and foreign researchers. Of major importance to students of the Republican period is the personal correspondence of Wu Jinglian, speaker of the Parliament from 1912 to 1923, and three presidents of the Republic: Yuan Shikai, whose family settled in Tianjin after his death, and his successors Li Yuanhong and Xu Shichang, who spent their retirement in the city. These letters and telegrams, reproduced under the series title of *Beiyang junfa shiliao* (see Bibliography, section VII.C), not only cover public and official matters but also detail how they and their Northern warlord brethren became capitalists through investments in industrial enterprises. Recent urban renewal has yielded some twenty steles from various guilds and native place organizations. In addition, the museum holds some 30,000 photographs of Tianjin, deposit slips (*zhezi* 折子), bank drafts (*yinpiao* 銀票), and a folio of native-cloth trade-marks.

Tianjin Municipal Library

Among the largest municipal libraries in the country, the Tianjin Municipal Library contains collections of company and bank annual reports, minutes of board meetings (for example, of the Yung Lee [永利] Soda Co., Ltd.), business manuals, and manuscript ledgers of the Association of Charitable Organizations (Cishan shiye lianhehui 慈善事業聯合會). It is also the repository of the family papers of Yan Xiu (嚴修, 1860–1929), an educator-reformer, salt merchant, and stockholder in various industrial enterprises.

Tianjin Academy of Social Sciences

Focusing on local history, the Tianjin Academy of Social Sciences' Institute of History houses an extensive collection of historical material, including the meeting minutes of the Tianjin Provisional Government (1900–1902), membership lists of the Tianjin Special Municipality Industrial Federation, 1942 and 1943, documents of Sino-foreign companies such as the annual audit reports of the Yee Loong Real Estate Co. (1922–41) (Yilong fangchang gongsi 義隆房產公司, known also as the Société foncière Franco-Chinoise de Tientsin), and Japanese materials from the library of the South Manchurian Railroad, Tianjin Office (Mantie Tianjin shiwuchu 滿鐵天津事處).

Other Archives and Libraries

Although state archival law mandates the transfer of documents from most major enterprises and state organs to municipal archives, not all state organs, enterprises, or institutions follow this practice. The Tianjin Municipal Bureau on Land and Real Estate (Tianjinshi fangdichan guanli ju 天津市房地產管理局) is the repository of a large number of land deeds and contracts, a selection of which has recently been published. Major state enterprises such as the No. 2 National Cotton Mill, successor to the Yu Yuan Cotton Mill established in 1918, or the Tianjin Dongya Woolen Mill (Tianjin dongya maofang chang 天津東亞毛紡廠), formerly the Oriental Wool Manufacturers, Ltd., Tientsin, maintain their own archives. Material from defunct enterprises may also be found outside official archives. For example, the Santiaoshi Museum (Santiaoshi bowuguan 三

條石博物館) holds the ledgers of several ironsmithing and engineering workshops instrumental in the development of Hebei's rural cotton-spinning and weaving industry.

Memoirs of entrepreneurs constitute another important source of information for the period. Although some have appeared in the National and Tianjin Wenshi ziliao (文史資料) series published by the city's various people's political consultative conferences, and the *Gongshang shiliao congkan* (工商史料叢刊) compiled by the Commercial and Industrial Alliance (Gong-shang lianhehui 工商聯合會, the successor to the Republican-era Chamber of Commerce), the bulk of such material remains unpublished.

Publications

For a convenient research guide to the holdings of various institutions in Tianjin, see *Tianjin difangshi lianhe mulu* 天津地方史聯合目錄 (Union catalogue of Tianjin local history), 3 vols. (Tianjin: Tianjin difangshi lianhe mulu bianjizu, 1980–84); *Tianjinshi baokan lunwen ziliao suoyin, 1949–1980* 天津市報刊論文資料索引 (Index to periodical literature on Tianjin local history, 1949–80) (Tianjin: Tianjin shehui kexueyuan, 1982); and Kishi Toshihiko, Liu Haiyan, et al., comps., *Tenshinshi bunken mokuroku* 天市文獻目綠 (A catalog of sources on Tianjin history) (Tokyo: Tôkyô daigaku, Tôyô bunka kenkyûjo, 1998). For an overview, see Brett Sheehan, "Archives and Libraries in Tianjin," *Chinese Business History* 6.1 (1995): 9–11. For updates and for newly published documentation, see the archives' journal, *Tianjin dang'an shiliao* 天津檔案史料 (Tianjin archival materials).

The authoritative guide to the Tianjin Municipal Archives is the Tianjinshi dang'anguan, comp., *Tianjinshi dang'anguan zhinan* 天津市檔案館指南 (Guide to the Tianjin Municipal Archives) (Beijing: Zhongguo dang'an, 1996). Documentary materials published by the archive include Tianjinshi dang'anguan, ed., *Tianjin shanghui dang'an huibian, 1903–1911* 天津商會檔案匯編 (Selected archival materials of the Tianjin Chamber of Commerce), 2 vols. (Tianjin: Tianjin renmin, 1989); *Tianjin shanghui dang'an huibian, 1912–1928*, 4 vols. (Tianjin: Tianjin renmin, 1992); *Tianjin shanghui dang'an huibian, 1929–1936*, 2 vols. (Tianjin: Tianjin renmin, 1995); and *Tianjin shanghui dang'an huibian, 1937–1945*, 2 vols. (Tianjin: Tianjin renmin, 1998); Tianjinshi dang'anguan et al., eds., *Qingmo Tianjin haiguan youzheng dang'an xuanbian* 清末天津海關郵政檔案選編 (Selected archival materials of the Tianjin Maritime Customs Postal Administration in the late Qing) (Beijing: Jiyou chubanshe, 1988); and Tianjinshi dang'anguan, ed., *Tianjin youzheng shiliao* 天津郵政史料 (Historical materials on the Tianjin Postal Administration), 4 vols. (Beijing: Hangkong hangtian daxue, 1988–96).

Selected records from foreign concessions in Tianjin have been published as Tianjinshi dang'anguan, ed., *Tianjin zujie dang'an xuanbian* 天津租界檔案選編 (Selected archival materials on foreign concessions in Tianjin) (Tianjin: Tianjin renmin, 1992). Selected materials from various companies have been published in Lan Changyun, ed., *Tianjin jindai zhiming qiye jingying guanli, 1860–1949* 天津近代知名業企經營管理 (The management and operations of notable enterprises in modern Tianjin) (Tianjin: Tianjin dang'an guan, 1995).

The Nankai Institute's indices are available in Nankai daxue jingji yanjiusuo et al., eds., *Nankai jingji zhisu huibian* 南開經濟指數匯編 (Nankai economic indices) (Beijing: Zhongguo shehui kexueyuan, 1988). Parts of the Nankai Institute's post-1949 projects have been published as Nankai daxue jingji yanjiusuo, ed., *Qixin yanghui gongsi shiliao* 啟新洋灰公司史料 (Historical materials on the Chee Hsin Cement Co., Ltd.) (Beijing: Sanlian shudian, 1963); and *Zhongguo jindai yanwushi ziliao* 中國近代鹽務史資料 (Historical materials on salt in modern China), 4 vols. (Tianjin: Nankai daxue, 1985–91).

For land deeds and contracts, see Tianjinshi fangdichan chanquan shichang guanli chu, comp., *Tianjin lidai fangdi qizheng* 天津歷代房地契証 (House and land deeds from Tianjin) (Tianjin: Tianjin renmin, 1995).

The Department of History of Nankai University conducted a historical survey of the local cotton-spinning and weaving industry, which was presented in an unpublished report entitled "Tianjinshi Santiaoshi zaoqi gongye ziliao diaocha baogao" 天津市三條石早期工業資料調查報 (Survey report on the early industries of Santiaoshi in Tianjin), held in the History Department's library.

For memoir material, see Li Yongpu, ed., *Quanguo geji zhengxie wenshi ziliao bianmu suoyin* 全國各級政協文史資料編目索引 (An index to historical materials published by the national and local-level political consultative conferences), 5 vols. (Beijing: Zhongguo wenshi, 1992), especially vol. 2.

Chapter 14

The Academia Historica
國史館

Introduction

The Academia Historica (AH, Guoshi guan 國史館) was established in January 1947 in Nanjing. According to the Organizational Law passed by the Legislative Yuan in Taiwan in 1956, the Academia Historica is directly subordinate to the Office of the President (Zongtongfu 總統府). At present, the Academia Historica holds around 250,000 volumes and publishes 30 to 40 volumes of historical material every year.

Economic History Archives

I. Executive Yuan

The Executive Yuan (Xingzheng yuan 行政院) was established in January 1928. Subordinate to it were the Interior, Foreign, Defense, Finance, Mining Industry, Trade, Education, Communications, Railways, and Public Health ministries, as well as the Commissions of Mongolian and Tibetan Affairs, Overseas Chinese Affairs, and Opium Suppression.

Archival holdings from the Executive Yuan can be divided into eight categories:

1. General: This material pertains to executive policies transmitted to the National Government, administrative reports delivered by the premier (head of the Executive Yuan), inquiries and replies sent to the Legislative Yuan, Guomindang proposals, the People's Political Council (Guomin canzhenghui 國民參政會), Sanminzhuyi Youth Corps, National Policy Consultative Committee (Guoce guwen weiyuanhui 國策顧問委員會) and the Advisory Committee on War Strategy (Zhanlüe guwen weiyuanhui 戰略顧問委員會), petitions from ministries and municipalities, the Outline of National Reconstruction during the War of Resistance, constitutional outlines for the "period of mobilization against the communist rebellion," elections to the National Assembly, organizational laws and regulations, and local investigation reports.

2. Finance: Material concerns the Ministry of Finance and agencies subordinate to it, annual income and expenditure reports, the premier's proposals on financial crises, wartime expenditures, proposals for improving the tax system, customs tariffs, provincial and county finances, land

expenditures, wartime taxation plans, bylaws for financial administration, local taxation, surveys of national property, central and local banks, currency and currency reform, foreign currency markets, military expenditures, and salt administration.

3. Economy: Records on economic summits and meetings, National Production conferences (Quanguo shengchan huiyi 全國生產會議), economic development, provincial financial administration, National Congress economic proposals, wartime economy, capital management, enemy industries, Finance Ministry wartime three-year plans, postwar national defense and economic reconstruction plans, War Production Board (Zhanshi shengchan ju 戰時生產局) work plans, capital auctions, transportation, foreign export agencies, trade commissions (*maoyi weiyuanhui* 貿易委員會), wartime economic superintendencies (*jingji duchatuan* 經濟督察團), economic intelligence reports, land reclamation, agricultural credit contracts, Sino-Japanese trade associations, national defense plans, industrial experimental centers, irrigation plans, and investment by overseas Chinese.

4. Education: Documents include information on the establishment and reform of schools at all levels, expenditures by the Academia Sinica (Zhongyang yanjiuyuan 中央研究院), National Palace Museum, scientific institutions, student strikes, National Taiwan University, middle school education and mass education, overseas study, military discipline, educational expenses, personnel education, appointments and dismissals, and salaries.

5. Transportation: Records of construction plans, demobilization, air transportation, railroad construction, postal administration, telegraph services, cooperation between the China National Aviation Corporation (Zhongguo hangkong gongsi 中國航空公司) and American airlines, links between China and Japan, port and airport construction, shipping, reparations, Sino-foreign postal agreements, draft telegraph laws, broadcasting, construction of the Wuhan bridge, and the central meteorological bureau and other meteorological agencies.

6. Public Health: Records include material on health inspections, drugs, public health, public health administration, disease prevention, summer public health work plans, work reports, management, importation and storage of drugs and narcotics, opium addiction and suppression, hospitals, public health agencies, and prenatal nutrition and support.

7. Overseas Chinese Affairs: Documents on overseas Chinese organizations, returned overseas students, passports, remittances, and registration.

8. Accounting: Materials pertain to the National Government Accounting Office, national budgets, draft national treasury laws, public funds, annual accounting reports, supplementary budgets, annual statements, revenue and expenditure reports by government agencies, wartime budgets,

management of the Sun Yat-sen mausoleum, provincial and municipal assemblies, election bureaus, police, Ministry of the Interior, Bureau of Land Administration (Dizheng bu 地政部), and official appointments.

II. Ministry of Finance

The Ministry of Finance (Caizheng bu 財政部) was the highest government organ charged with managing financial administration. In addition, it was also responsible for providing leadership and supervising local financial administrators. Since 1912, the Ministry of Finance has undergone many organizational reforms, but its functions have remained largely unchanged. When the Nationalist government retreated to Taiwan in 1949, it took a portion of the Ministry of Finance's records. The records of the Ministry of Finance are the single largest collection housed by the AH. Documents are held in some 37,970 volumes containing 1,193,594 items, dating from 1912 to 1983.

The records of the Ministry of Finance held at the AH are catalogued and divided into ten categories: state taxation, personnel affairs, State Treasury, currency, local financial administration, research into financial affairs, Secretariat, statistics, salt administration, and general affairs. The following is a brief introduction to each of these categories.

1. State Taxation: Comprising approximately two-fifths of the Ministry of Finance collection, these materials are valuable sources for the study of Nationalist government tax administration. Included are regulations and orders governing taxes on tobacco, sugar, liquor, matches, minerals, cotton, stamps, income, inheritances, and merchandise. Materials pertain to tax collection, subsidies, exemptions, rebates, rates, credits, accounting, smuggling, monopoly rights and profits, lawsuits, tax reform, and intelligence reports. There are also materials relating to the management of state tax organizations and revisions of the tax system.

2. Personnel affairs: These are the records of the Personnel Department (Renshi bu 人事部) of the Ministry of Finance. The collection (1940–44) contains documents relating to examinations, employment, training, salaries, backgrounds, evaluation and registration, citations and disciplinary actions, promotions, transfers, disability compensation, pensions, retirement, subsidies, fringe benefits, dereliction of duty, investigations, corruption, lawsuits, arrest warrants, layoffs, staff quotas, relief, and transfer of offices. In addition, these materials include work plans, records of official functions, minutes of recruitment meetings, and personnel management reports from provincial tax bureaus.

3. State Treasury: This group contains documents from the State Treasury Administration (Guoku shu 國庫署) dated 1928–48. They mainly include material on central and provincial income and expenditures. Also included are materials on administrative planning, regulations and bylaws,

fines, indemnities, monopoly rights, government fees, donations from overseas Chinese, public enterprises, expenditures of the various *yuan*, provincial income and expenditure reports, subsidies for government agencies, Treasury Administration statistics, central government resolutions, People's Political Council (Guomin canzheng hui 國民參政會) budgets, relief committees, publicly held lands, foreign advisors, military supplies, military labor, domestic debt, national defense, foreign debt, list of payments for American goods, reparations and indemnities, wartime losses, grain price controls, shipping, and marketing. The State Treasury records also contain material on food provisions for the police, military, prisoners, and foreigners.

4. Currency: This collection contains documents from the original Currency Department (Qianbi si 錢幣司), dated 1925–48. Records include the Currency Department's yearly administrative plans, work reports, currency and financial institutions, meeting minutes, currency reform, proposals to replace the tael (*liang* 兩) with the *yuan* 元 (Chinese dollar), the "silver question," interdiction of silver exports, inflation, subsidies, loans, foreign exchange, *fabi* 法幣 (China's national currency issued by the Nationalist government from November 1935 to August 1948), preparatory management committees (*zhunbei guanli weiyuanhui* 準備管理委員會), counterfeit money, bribery, provincial currencies, currency transportation, inflation, disaster relief, Sino-Japanese currency exchange disputes, financial stabilization, the Currency Research Commission (Bizhi yanjiu weiyuanhui 幣制研究委員會), financial affairs advisory committees, currency management methods, coinage, Tibetan currency, enterprise control, bank and native bank investigation reports, the Central Bank, Bank of China, Farmers' Bank of China, commercial banks, local banks, public debt, savings societies' savings certificates, Central Trust of China (Zhongyang xintuo ju 中央信託局), the Currency Administration Commission (Bizheng weiyuanhui 幣政委員會), compensation and indemnity guarantees, and takeover of enemy banks.

5. Local Financial Administration: This group contains the records of local financial administrative departments (*difang caizheng si* 地方財政司), dating from 1930 to 1948. The materials relate to local tax regulations, ordinances, provincial tax administration, local budgets, annual revenue and expenditure plans, annual reports from local financial administration agencies, wartime financial administration, provincial tax collection, land taxes, land sales taxes (*dijia shui* 地價稅), business taxes (*yingye shui* 營業稅), miscellaneous losses, entertainment taxes, land deed taxes (*qishui* 契稅), public construction, construction taxes, highway maintenance taxes, tax remission, abolition of license taxes, slaughter tax (levied on slaughtered animals), 25 percent rent reduction, local tax losses, public property rental, budgets, provincial self-government financial administration reports, Ministry of Finance's investigation reports, public debt, relief, local tax exemption petitions, and explanations of laws and decrees.

6. Research into Financial Affairs: When the Nationalist government moved to Nanjing, it began to sponsor research into financial affairs. It established numerous special investigative organiza-

tions, such as the Ministry of Finance Investigation Committee, Finance Research Committee, Currency System Investigation Committee, Currency Reform Investigation Committee, and a committee to investigate replacing the *liang* (tael) with the *yuan*. The archives of these research organizations date from 1929 to 1948 and include materials following the outbreak of the Sino-Japanese war, such as research conducted by the Japanese-controlled financial administration, economic and financial developments of the Wang Jingwei government, wartime economic policy, surrender of enemy resources, grain and land requisition, tax investigations, wartime losses, mobilization plans, production plans, Ministry of Finance plans for wartime reconstruction, and postwar national defense and reconstruction plans.

7. Secretariat: These were originally the Secretariat (Mishu chu 秘書處) archives, dating from 1912 to 1949. Material from the 1937–45 period is the most numerous and pertains to Ministry of Finance plans, reports by the Ministry of Finance for important meetings of the Guomindang, inquiries and replies, resolutions, reports and resolutions of the National People's Convention (Guomin huiyi 國民會議) and the National Assembly (Guomin dahui 國民大會), National Finance Conference (Quanguo caizheng huiyi 全國財政會議) reports, war zone economic councils, revenue and tax loss estimates, wartime economic plans, and resolutions from the Second National Financial Administration Conference.

8. Statistics: These records date from 1915 to 1968 and originated from the Statistical Bureau (Tongji chu 統計處). These materials pertain to wartime financial statistics, local tax collection, annual reports, national tax monopoly profit and losses, registration books, and regulations.

9. Salt Administration: These are the records of the Bureau of Salt Administration, dating from 1915 to 1968. Documents are divided into two types: (1) *business operations*: meeting minutes, work reports, salt administration reform plans, tax rates, salt storage, monthly salt price reports, maps, salt storage facilities, registers, tax rate tables, provincial and district-level salt administration including Guangzhou and Guangxi, Fujian, eastern and western Zhejiang, the region south of the Huai River (Huainan), Shandong, Changlu, Hunan and Hubei, Jiangxi, Shaanxi and Shanxi, Yunnan, the Northeast, and Taiwan; and (2) *general affairs*: Salt Administration Bureau yearly revenue and expense estimates, preliminary budgets, financial statements, personnel examinations, employment, dismissals and retirements, transfer and arrest of communist personnel, buildings, roads, bridges, and airfields.

10. General Affairs: These documents originated from the General Affairs Department (Zongwu ting 總務廳) and date from 1941 to 1949. They include documents on affairs, such as the procurement of supplies and materials, daily necessities, property valuation tables, building repairs, military equipment, annulments, government stores and cooperatives, decommissioned troops, revenues and expenditures, subsidies, travel expenses, engineering fees, donations, insurance

fees, rents, purchases, equipment and installation fees, fines, bid invitations, telecommunications (telegraphs, telephone, and radio stations), personnel (appointments, dismissals, number of employees, examinations, transfers, promotions, awards, evaluations, and salaries). In addition there is material from radio stations, the Agricultural Bureau (Nongben ju 農本局), Materials Department (Wuzi ju 物資局), and the Cotton Cloth and Yarn Management Bureau.

The AH has published introductions to these collections, such as *Kangzhan qian shi nian huobi shi ziliao* 抗戰前十年貨幣史資料 (Materials on the monetary history of the decade preceding the Sino-Japanese war), 3 vols. (1985-88); *Kangzhan shiqi de zhuanmai shiliao* 抗戰時期的專賣史料 (Historical materials on monopolies during the Sino-Japanese war) (June 1992); and *Guomin zhengfu shiqi de yanzheng shiliao* 國民政府時期鹽政史料 (Historical material on the Salt Administration during the National Government period) (June 1993).

III. Ministry of Food (Liangshi Bu 糧食部)

During the Japanese invasion of China, agricultural disruption led to grain shortages and high prices. In order to meet military and civilian demands for grain, the National Government set up the National Grain Control Bureau (Quanguo liangshi guanli ju 全國糧食管理局) in August 1941 under the Executive Yuan. Initially, the bureau was charged with managing food supplies, but in November 1940, provinces and counties set up their own grain administration organizations. With worsening war conditions, the government considered returning to the old system of tax collection, in order to gain overall control of grain prices and distribution. In April 1941, the central government passed a resolution putting the collection of local land taxes under central government control. In July the National Grain Administration Bureau was abolished and the Ministry of Grain Provisions was established under the Executive Yuan. In October provincial grain management departments (*sheng liangshi guanli ju* 省糧食管理局) were changed into provincial grain administration departments (*sheng liangzheng ju* 省糧政局), increasing provincial responsibility for grain administration.

In April 1981, the Ministry of Finance transferred the archives of the Ministry of Food (Liangshi bu 糧食部) to the AH. These archives contain materials from the National Grain Administration Bureau beginning from 1940 and the Ministry of Food (established in May 1941). There are 7,955 volumes, with documents originating from nearly all provinces and major cities such as Nanjing, Shanghai, Beiping, Chongqing, Hankou, and Shenyang. These materials are divided into eight categories:

1. General: Documents include implementation plans from the Ministry of Food and grain administration agencies, provincial and municipal grain administration work reports, proposals to improve grain administration, rules and regulations on the management of personnel involved in

grain administration, and the organizational bylaws of the Ministry of Food and subordinate agencies. These documents also contain information on employment, training, salaries, subsidies, examinations, evaluations, awards and sanctions, social security, vacations, dismissals, retirement, and pensions.

2. Storage: Materials pertain to grain administration policies, collection, and provincial and county procurement, grain receipt and balance reports, construction, repair, maintenance and renting of granaries, storage, grain-processing plans and contracts, granary construction, grain purchases, grain contributions, procurement and manufacture of grain bags, grain donations by overseas Chinese, provincial standards for grain payment cash, grain stockpiling, and vegetable cultivation.

3. Control: Records on provincial and county plans to increase grain production, provincial grain supply, price stabilization and control, Control Department work reports and newsletters, national and local grain price investigations, provincial grain production, provincial expenses, provincial grain administration annual reports, grain consumption, provincial supply and marketing, local eating habits, grain and rice consumption, schools, news agencies, party branches, civilian organizations, relief for overseas Chinese and refugees, provincial interdiction of grain exports, rent reduction in disaster areas, interprovincial grain trade, private breweries, private liquor sales, and grain plunder.

4. Allocation: These documents include information on the regulation of military grain provisions, procurement, transportation, government and school grain allocations, grain market investigation reports, provincial grain distribution, prison rations, provincial grain transportation contracts (water and land transport), annual reports of grain losses through storage and transportation, procurement and transportation of rice and wheat, expense reports from grain transport stations in Jiangxi, grain transport in Sichuan, and local collection of inferior grain.

5. Supervision and Management: Materials on grain administration meetings, work reports, purchase of American fertilizer, corruption and bribery, rewards and punishments, international transportation, and the Food Price Control Commission (Pingtiao weiyuanhui 平調委員會).

6. Financial Affairs: Information on agricultural loans, the Financial Affairs Department's dissolution of provincial land and grain agencies, personnel, provincial grain transportation, the Chinese Food Company (Zhongguo liangshi gongsi 中國糧食公司), grain purchase and storage, and procurement of grain by the Sichuan No. 1 Public Grain Supply Department (Sichuan minshi diyi gongyingchu 四川民食第一供應處).

7. Accounting: Documents on provincial grain administration expenditures, personnel, local agricultural loans, relief of poor fishermen and salt workers, and accounting reports from grain administration agencies.

8. Land taxes (*tianfu* 田賦): Material relating to provincial land tax collection, monthly reports, land tax collection expenses, tax exemptions following natural disasters, land tax management committees, propaganda, and training and expenses of land tax collectors.

IV. National Resources Commission

The National Resources Commission (NRC; Ziyuan weiyuanhui 資源委員會) was set up in April 1935 under the Military Affairs Commission to manage the development of China's natural resources. In February 1938 it came under the direction of the Ministry of Economic Affairs, and its responsibilities expanded to include management of engineering, mining, and electric industries. During the Sino-Japanese war, it was instrumental in the development of electric power stations, petroleum, gas, tungsten, lead, zinc, and other minerals and metals.

In 1945 the NRC took over mineral operations from the Japanese in northern and eastern China and Taiwan. In May 1946 it came under the direction of the Executive Yuan. By 1948 the NRC managed numerous production enterprises, including electrical power, gas, oil, steel, machinery, and chemicals, and had some 387 agencies and 220,000 personnel under its direction. In 1949, the NRC again came under the direction of the Ministry of Economic Affairs. When the NRC followed the Nationalist government to Taiwan in 1949, it continued to operate until 1952, when it was replaced by the State Enterprises Company (Guoying shiye gongsi 國營實業公司).

The NRC archives were originally stored in 304 boxes in Chongqing. In 1946, these archives were transferred to Nanjing, with the exception of 120 boxes (dating from before 1942), which remained in Chongqing and are now held at the Number Two Historical Archives in Nanjing. In 1949, the NRC archives that were stored in Nanjing were transported to Taiwan via Guangzhou. The archives were first stored in Jiayi at the China Petroleum Company's (Zhongguo shiyou gongsi 中國石油公司) solvent plant. In November 1961, the Ministry of Economic Affairs transferred the greater part of these archives to the AH. The remaining materials were transferred to the Institute of Modern History of the Academia Sinica.

The NRC archives have suffered losses due to war and dislocation prior to and after 1949. Further losses were incurred during floods in 1959 when the archives were stored in Jiayi. The archives were arranged and cataloged by the AH as follows: 19,616 volumes of Chinese-language materials, divided into general affairs, public works, business activities, financial affairs, transportation, materials, and miscellaneous; 7,979 volumes of English-language materials.

A. Chinese-Language Documents (19,616 volumes)

The NRC Chinese-language documents (including internal [*neibu*] documents) date from 1938 to 1952, with most from 1942 to 1948.

1. General Affairs (*zongwu* 總務): Documents on a wide scope of subjects, such as orders and regulations, meeting minutes, and personnel data (examinations, appointments, training, promotions, transfers, dismissals, layoffs, salaries, evaluations, fringe benefits). Documents include information on political trends, health care, issuance of official seals, issuance and receipt of telegrams, handling of official documents, postal matters and delivery of official communications, factory and house rentals, vehicle and equipment procurement, fuel, communications, security, maps, charts, books, and publications.

2. Public Works (*gongwu* 工務): Engineering agreements, construction plans, construction reports, allocation charts, factory equipment installation and maintenance reports, inspection reports, mineral and oil exploration reports, and patent applications.

3. Business Activities (*yewu* 業務): Official orders, regulations, work reports, inspection reports, costs, procurements, purchases, domestic sales, foreign sales, smuggling, production and supply reports, plant registration and inspection, mineral rights for state-owned enterprises, applications, trademarks, licenses, research and development, survey and development of mineral resources, transportation losses, property theft, fire and flood losses, wartime losses, Sino-foreign enterprises, technological cooperation, American aid, foreign advisors, removal of local factories and plants, takeover of properties and enterprises held by the Japanese, demobilization plans, and progress reports.

4. Financial Affairs (*caiwu* 財務): Accounting and financial regulations, annual reports, accounting reports, budgets, financial statements, accounting reports, cash and credit balances, property inventories, expenditures receipts, procurement of funds, tax payments, donation account books, foreign exchange applications, foreign currency purchases, insurance, transportation insurance, and asset reports.

5. Transportation (*yunshu* 運輸): Material dating from 1941 to 1948 on the purchase, maintenance, and dispatch of vehicles, fuel procurement and distribution, financial statements, transportation management contracts (public roads, water transportation, etc.), applications, and expenses.

6. Materials (*cailiao* 材料): Documents dating from 1941 to 1948 and pertaining to regulations for the management of materials, loading and transportation, collection and procurement of

machinery and materials, equipment use, raw materials, procurement procedures and bid invitations, negotiations, order forms, contracts, monthly reports, record books, monthly inventories, income and losses, equipment purchases, and lending and transfer of property and equipment to various agencies.

7. Miscellaneous (*zonghe* 綜合): Records from the Business Activities Committee Joint Group (Yewu weiyuanhui zonghe zu 業務委員會綜合組), dating from 1946 to 1949. They are quite random and include government directives, organizational rules, work reports, advisory reports, meeting minutes, work plans, Legislative Yuan inquiries, appointments and dismissals of directors and supervisors, employee rosters, and payment for goods by foreign banks. Other areas include technical cooperation, labor unrest, personnel, transfer of vehicles, takeover of enterprises in former communist- and Japanese-occupied areas, war damages, the February 7th Incident of 1947, and equipment and transportation.

B. English-Language Documents (7,979 volumes)

The English-language documents from the NRC collection at the AH archives consist of communications between the NRC and foreign organizations dating from 1940 to 1952 (the most numerous from 1944 to 1949). There are around 287,939 documents divided as follows:

1. Purchases, Sales, and Procurement: Most of this material consists of communications with foreign governments and companies, including an index of materials on foreign companies, telegrams, letters, contracts, market reports, personnel investigation reports, price reports, negotiations, and inquiries and replies regarding business transactions. The principal foreign organizations and companies involved were the U.S. Congress, the U.S. Departments of Commerce, Interior, Defense, Army, and Navy, the Chinese Embassy in the United States, American Telephone and Telegraph Corporation, Radio Corporation of America, U.S. Steel Corporation, American Plastics Corporation, Reo Motors Inc., Universal Trading Corporation, American Cyanamid Company, Aluminum Company of America, and Canadian Misecorres.

2. Training and Overseas Internships: Records of agreements and negotiations to send personnel to receive training and participate in technical cooperation programs with companies such as South Pennsylvania Oil Company, N.R.K. Manufacturing and Engineering Company, Bethlehem Steel Export Company, Westinghouse Electrical and Manufacturing Company, and the North American Fertilizer Company. In addition, there are personal reports from men such as Sun Yunxuan, Cai Tongyu, Liu Zengshi, and Wei Yongning.

3. Miscellaneous: Material includes international correspondence, import and export applications, industrial development investigation reports, and the correspondence of leading NRC figures such as Weng Wenhao, Qian Changzhao, Du Dianying, and Lu Zuzhi.

C. Publications of NRC Documents

Although the records of the NRC are dispersed throughout mainland China and Taiwan, the AH collection is relatively comprehensive. To date the AH has published five volumes of material: *Ziyuan weiyuanhui dang'an shiliao chubian* 資源委員會檔案史料初編 (Collected historical material on the National Resources Commission, 1st ed.), 2 vols. (1984); *Ziyuan weiyuanhui jishu renyuan fumei shixi shiliao* 資源委員會技術人員赴美實習史料 (Historical materials on National Resources Commission technical personnel who underwent training in the United States), 3 vols. (1988); *Ziyuan weiyuanhui dang'an shiliao huibian: dianye bufen* 資源委員會檔案史料匯編: 電業部分 (Collected historical material on the National Resources Commission: electrical power industry) (1992); *Ziyuan weiyuanhui dang'an shiliao huibian: guangfu chuqi Taiwan jingji jianshe, shang* 資源委員會檔案史料匯編: 光復初期臺灣經濟建設 (Collected historical materials on the National Resources Commission: economic reconstruction during the initial period of the recovery of Taiwan, vol. 1) (1993); *Taiwan tudi ziliao huibian diyiji: guangfu chuqi tudi zhi jieshou yu chuli* (yi) 臺灣土地資料匯編第一輯: 光復初期土地之接收與處理 (Collection of material on land in Taiwan, series I, the takeover and handling of land in the early period of the recovery of Taiwan, vol. 1) (1993).

Chapter 15

The Institute of Modern History, Academia Sinica
中央研究院近代史研究所

Introduction

The Institute of Modern History (Zhongyang yanjiuyuan, Jindai shi yanjiusuo 中央研究院近代研究所) stores documents on economic history dating from the late Qing to the present. These records can be divided into four general periods: from the late empire to the early Republic; the Nanjing government period before the Sino-Japanese War; the period of the Sino-Japanese war; and from 1949 to the present. Materials on water conservancy and mining, as well as personnel records, dominate the records from the pre-1949 period. Documents from the post-1949 period are by comparison more complete.

Economic History Archives

I. Ministry of Industry and Commerce (Gongshang bu 工商部)
Although formally established in March 1911, its records cover 1905–13. Documents pertain mostly to mining and total seven folders (*hantao* 函套)

II. Ministry of Agriculture and Commerce (Nongshang bu 農商部)
Founded in 1913. The documents in this collection cover 1913–29. With a relatively large collection (569 folders), the holdings are predominantly mining and water conservancy records. Mining records include licenses and geological surveys; water conservancy records include documents on Huai River conservancy and provincial-level projects.

III. Ministry of Commerce (Shang bu 商部)
The Ministry of Commerce documents cover 1901–43 and consist mainly of records related to mining. Included are a variety of provincial-level licenses for mining ventures. The size of the collection is only six folders.

IV. Ministry of Agriculture, Industry, and Commerce (Nonggongshang bu 農工商部)
The documents cover 1905–11 and include records on mining, water conservancy, and irrigation. Mining records include documents on state-owned companies and mining licenses. The holdings on water conservancy are comparatively limited. These include budgets, personnel reports, project reports, and memos from various departments. The collection contains 23 folders.

V. National Water Conservancy Bureau (Quanguo shuili ju 全國水利局)

Established in 1913. The bureau's records cover 1913–26. In 33 folders, the collection includes documents on provincial water conservancy councils, the Ocean and River Charting Bureau, the American Engineering Technical Group, the Huai River Project, and the Water Irrigation Construction and Maintenance Plan.

VI. Ministry of Interior (Neizheng bu 內務部)

Established in 1911. The collection contains 14 folders from 1912 to 1925. Documents cover the Yongding River project, Tianjin floods, budgets, and proposals.

VII. Huai River Control Commission (Dao Huai weiyuanhui 導淮委員會)

Established in 1929. The collection contains 607 folders with documents from 1929 to 1948. Included are administrative records, the organizational charter, survey reports, personnel records, budgets, conference reports, meeting records, project studies and reports, surveys, contracts for construction projects, records of machinery and materials, and landholding and water conservancy records from provincial agencies.

VIII. National Reconstruction Commission (Jianshe weiyuanhui 建設委員會)

Established in 1928. Documents cover predecessor and successor agencies from 1907 to 1938 and relate primarily to water conservancy, electricity, and coal. Documents include personnel records, budgets, and project reports. Personnel records and personnel surveys are the most extensive and complete. Also included are documents on national and provincial electrical enterprises, generators, power plants, organizational charters, stockholder records, and business records. The collection consists of 484 folders.

This collection includes certain materials of the Postal Ministry (Youzhuan bu 郵傳部) and the Ministry of Communications (Jiaotong bu 交通部). The Institute of Modern History also holds documents from the following subordinate organizations of the National Reconstruction Commission: the Model Irrigation Control Bureau (Mofang guan'gai guanli ju 模範灌溉管理局), Electric Appliance Manufacturing Plant (Dianji zhizao chang 電機製造廠), the Capital Electricity Plant (Shoudu dianchang 首都電廠), and the National Electrical Industries Guidance Committee (Quanguo dianye zhidao weiyuanhui 全國電業指導委員會), as well as documents from 519 private electrical enterprises.

IX. National Economic Council (Quanguo jingji weiyuanhui 全國經濟委員會)

Established in 1931, the National Economic Council was charged with planning a wide array of economic-related matters. The council was also responsible for the planning, financing, and implementation of projects. The records of the council consist of 653 folders covering 1928–37. The institute's collections on administrative records and issues relating to water conservancy are the most complete. Administrative records include organizational charters, personnel records, budget records, records of foreign advisors, surveys of the Chinese economy made by the League of Nations, and work reports. Documents on water conservancy projects include personnel records, budgets, and surveys. There are also records relating to the council's activities in agricultural research, public health, and highway construction.

The records in the following areas are the most complete:

Secretariat (Mishu chu 秘書處): Organizational charters, regulations, personnel records, information regarding foreign advisors, League of Nation surveys, water conservancy reports, and meeting records.

Agriculture (*nongye* 農業): Records of the Northwest Farm Stock Improvement Station and the Shandong Cotton Planting Instruction Center.

Water conservancy: (shuili 水利): Documents concerning administration, and budgets and reports from the Jiangsu-Jiangxi Enginering Bureau (Jiang-Gan gongcheng ju 江贛工程局), the Anhui Huai River Engineering Bureau (Wan-Huai gongcheng ju 皖淮工程局), and others.

X. Ministry of Industry (Shiye bu 實業部)

Established in 1930, the Ministry of Industry was a leading agency of the Nationalist government before the Sino-Japanese War. The ministry divided its responsibilities among the departments of Agriculture, Forestry, Fishery, Mining, Commerce, and Industry. Organized in 1,467 folders, documents range from 1928 to 1938 and focus on agriculture, forestry, industry, commerce, and mining. The Ministry of Industry was one of the first Chinese ministries to keep complete archival records. These records include personnel records, organizational charters, budget records, and project reports. In addition, the Institute holds documents from the following subordinate departments:

Agriculture: The Agriculture Department (Nongye si 農業司) was in charge of research and development of silk production, soil improvement, pest and disease prevention, seed improvement, farm tool improvement, irrigation, agricultural surveys, and monitoring and regulating farmer associations. The Agricultural Department controlled a variety of organizations, including the Central Agricultural Experimentation Institute (Zhongyang nongye shiyansuo 中央農業實驗所), the Central Agricultural Extension Commission (Zhongyang nongye tuiguang weiyuanhui 中央農業推廣委員會), the Management Commission of the Central Model Agricultural Extension District (Zhongyang mofang nongye tuiguang qu guanli weiyuanhui 中央模範農業推廣區管理委員會), the National Grain Improvement Institute (Quanguo daomai gaijin suo 全國稻麥改進所), and the Jiangxi Rural Assistance Office (Jiangxi nongcun fuwu chu 江西農村服務處), as well as provincial cotton and silk experimention centers.

Industry: The Industry Department (Gongye si 工業司) had jurisdiction over state-owned as well as private industrial and chemical manufacturing plants. It controlled management, oversight, and certification.

Commerce: The Commerce Department (Shangye si 商業司) controlled state-owned and private enterprise management, oversight, and protection. Documents from the department include commercial regulations, records of the Commercial Dispute Mediation Center (Shangshi gongduan chu 商事公斷處), same-trade associations, stock exchanges, and company registrations.

Mining and Fisheries: These departments had jurisdiction over the regulation of their respective industries.

XI. National Resources Commission (Ziyuan weiyuanhui 資源委員會)

As noted in chapters 4 and 14, The National Resources Commission was responsible for developing and managing national resources for national security. The commission was charged with developing heavy and light industries, mining, and electrical works during the Sino-Japanese war. After the war, the commission was also charged with the administration of industrial assets in former Japanese-occupied territories. The commission had jurisdiction over state-owned, joint state- and private-owned, and provincial and private industries.

This collection contains 1,418 folders covering 1938–52. The documents focus on electricity, mining, machinery, chemicals, paper, cement, sugar, salt, and textiles. The Institute of Modern History stores documents from the National Resources Commission under fifteen broad categories: administration, research, and services (28 folders, 1940–52), electricity (52 folders, 1936–53), fuel (62 folders, 1937–53), iron and steel (30 folders, 1938–52), mining (46 folders, 1938–54), machinery (14 folders, 1939–52), electrical equipment (6 folders, 1938–50), chemical (44 folders, 1939–54), paper (3 folders, 1946–52), cement (8 folders, 1941–48), sugar (3 folders, 1942–53), salt (1 folder, 1950–52), textiles (2 folders, 1946–52), and miscellaneous (5 folders, 1941–52).

XII. Ministry of Economic Affairs (Jingji bu 經濟部), 1938–49

In 1938 the Nationalist government consolidated a number of departments under the new Ministry of Economic Affairs. The ministry was responsible for water conservancy, agriculture, forestry, industry, resource management during the Sino-Japanese war, commerce, electricity, and mining. The institute's records cover 1938–71 and are filed in 3,198 folders. The large majority of those available for research are on the pre-1945 period. Administrative documents include organizational charters, property records, personnel records, conference records, policy reports, budgets, and statistics.

Documents of the following subordinate organizations are included in the ministry's archives:

Business Department (Qiye si 企業司): The Business Department oversaw investment activities and joint state- and private-owned enterprises of the Ministry of Economics. Documents from this department include regulations and organizational charters, reports from economic councils during the Sino-Japanese War, plans for economic reconstruction after the war, and basic information on 30 public and private enterprises.

Department of International Trade (Guoji maoyi si 國際貿易司): Documents include trade regulations, tariff agreements, and registries.

Department of Economic Control (Guanzhi si 管制司): The Department of Economic Control was instrumental in the Nationalist government's effort to coordinate economic policy during the Sino-Japanese war. The records of the following subordinate bureaus are filed in the department's holdings: the Materials Bureau (Ziwu ju 物資局 [administrative and personnel records]), the Equipment and Material Warehouse (Qicai zongku 器材總庫 [personnel records]), the Daily Necessities Management Bureau (Riyong bixupin guanli chu 日用必需品管理處 [administrative and personnel records, plans]), and councils controlling individual industrial sectors, such as textiles and fuel.

Department of Mining (Kuangye si 礦業司): Documents on administration (regulations, records of same-trade associations and private mining enterprises, conference records, project plans), Mining Research Center (Kuangzhi yanjiusuo 礦治研究所 [personnel, work, and survey records]), Gold Bureau (Tanjin ju 探金局 [personnel records, project plans, project reports, and survey reports]), Central Geological Survey Institute (Zhongyang dizhi diaocha suo 中央地質調查所 [administrative, budgetary, and personnel records; and geological surveys]), and provincial enterprises (particularly from Sichuan).

Department of Electrical Enterprises (Dianye si 電業司): Documents are arranged in the following categories: administration (regulations, policy proposals, and statistical records) and electrical enterprises (registration records). Enterprise records include registrations, trademarks, finances, output, and performance evaluations.

Department of Commerce (Shangye si 商業司): Regulations, trade association records, foreign investments, product inspection reports, stock exchange records, trademark registrations, and enterprise registrations (including information on organization and capital).

Department of Industry (Gongye si 工業司): Administrative records (regulations, conference records, industrial plans, industry surveys, foreign investment records, international conferences), industrial council reports (e.g., Industrial Council [Gongye weiyuanhui 工業委員會], Labor-Management Dispute Resolution Council [Laozi jiufen pingduan weiyuanhui 勞資糾紛評斷委

員會], Labor Recruitment Council [Zhenggong shiwu weiyuanhui 征工事務委員會]), personnel training records, factory registrations (including name, location, products), records of the Central Standards Bureau (Zhongyang biaozhun ju 中央標準局), and records of the Central Industrial Research Institute (Zhongyang gongye shiyan suo 中央工業試驗所), including project reports, plans, and personnel records.

Agriculture and Forestry Department (Nonglin si 農林司): Documents from the following agencies: Farmers' Associations, including organizational and membership information from Zhejiang, Fujian, Sichuan, and several other provinces, the Central Agricultural Research Institute (Zhongyang nongye shiyan suo 中央農業實驗所), the Jinshuiliuyu Farm (金水流域農場), and the Jiangxi Agricultural Service Administration (Jiangxi nongcun fuwu qu guanli chu 江西農村服務區管理處).

Water Conservancy Department (Shuili si 水利司): Administrative, budget, personnel, and project records from organizations such as the Yellow River Conservancy Commission (Huanghe shuili weiyuanhui 黃河水利委員會), Yangzi River Conservancy Commission (Yangzijiang shuili weiyuanhui 揚子江水利委員會), and the Huai River Control Commission (Daohuai weiyuanhui 導淮委員會). Also included are documents from the following agencies: Jianghan Engineering Bureau (Jianghan gongcheng ju 江漢工程局), Zhujiang Conservancy Bureau (Zhujiang shuili ju 珠江水利局), Jin Sha Jiang Engineering Office (Jin Sha Jiang gongcheng chu 金沙江工程處), Sichuan and Tibet Water Conservancy Loan Commission (Chuan Kang shuili daikuan weiyuanhui 川康水利貸款委員會), Hubei Dike Protection Fund Commission (Hubei tigong zhuankuan baoguan weiyuanhui 湖北堤工專款保管委員會), Central Hydraulic Experimentation Institute (Zhongyang shuigong shiyan suo 中央水工試驗所), Water Conservancy Design and Survey Team (Shuili sheji celiang dui 水利設計測量隊), Water Conservancy Aerial Survey Team (Shuili hangkong celiang dui 水利航空測量隊), and the Climate and Atmospheric Research Institute (Qixiang yanjiusuo 氣象研究所).

Xichang Office (Xichang banshi chu 西昌辦事處): The Xichang Office was established to promote small-scale agricultural manufacturing during the Sino-Japanese war. Personnel, budget, and operating records.

Industrial and Mining Coordinating Office (Gongkuang tiaozheng chu 工礦調整處): This office was charged with coordinating industrial and mining capital, resources, raw materials, equipment, and marketing. There are two types of documents from the office: (1) administrative documents including organization, regulations, plans, reports, and (2) documents concerning individual enterprises. Documents from the Hengyang Textile Factory (Hengyang fangzhi chang 衡陽紡織廠) are the most complete. Most of the enterprises coordinated by the office were in the paper, textile, and cement industries.

Industry and Commerce Assistance Office (Gongshang fudao chu 工商輔導處): The duties of this office were similar to those of the Industrial and Mining Office. Documents include personnel records, operational records, budgets, and work-project reports.

Special Economic Investigation Office (Tezhong jingji diaocha chu 特種經濟調查處): This collection includes documents on personnel, budget, organization, and important projects.

XIII. Ministry of Economic Affairs (Jingji bu 經濟部), 1949–71

The 490 boxes of documents in this collection concern administration, personnel, industry, commerce, mining, state-owned enterprises, fisheries, and water conservancy. The National Resources Commission files are available for research, but other files from the ministry are still being catalogued or await sorting. This collection includes meeting and conference records, committee reports, statistical records, budget records, outlines for economic construction, surveys of technical personnel in the Taiwan region, surveys of labor conditions, records of provincial-level industries, records of the conversion of state-owned industries to private ownership, telegrams supporting the re-election of President Chiang Kai-shek, and records from the GMD Central Committee.

XIV. Ministry of Agriculture and Forestry (Senlin bu 農林部)

This ministry was established in 1940. Covering 1940–48, the 3,976 folders in the collection include documents on forestry, fisheries, pasturing, and land reclamation.

XV. Ministry of Water Conservancy (Shuili bu 水利部)

Established in 1947. Records held in 1,062 folders covering 1947–48.

XVI. Water Conservancy Council of the Executive Yuan (Xingzheng yuan, Shuili weiyuanhui 行政院水利委員會)

This collection has 1,600 folders containing documents from 1941 to 1948. The council was formally established in 1945.

XVII. Salt Administration Organizations (Yanwu jiguan 鹽務機構)

The documents in this collection date from the Qing dynasty to 1970. Documents from the Qing period are organized separately. Pre-1949 Republican-era records consist mainly of published pamphlets, brochures, and booklets, as well as personnel records. Taiwan documents include those on the Japanese colonial administration's Taiwan salt monopoly, personnel records, production research, market surveys, labor surveys, and reports on trade associations.

XVIII. Commodity Price Control Committee Reports (Wujia dudaohui bagao 物價督導會報告)

Dated 1969–91, this collection includes personnel records, laws and regulations, policy plans, meeting and conference records, research, testimony in the Legislative Yuan, and records of agricultural and industrial prices.

XIX. Wang Jingwei Regime (Wang Jingwei zhengfu 汪精衛政府)

This collection contains 40 boxes of material from 1938 to 1945. Documents are from the Agricultural and Mining Ministry, the Ministry of Industry, and the Ministry of Food. Most of the documents are from the Ministry of Industry, which had jurisdiction over forestry, industry, commerce, mining, water conservancy, and cooperatives. Water conservancy documents are limited to activities in Anhui, Zhejiang, Jiangsu, and Shanghai. Agricultural documents include data on allocation of resources, loans, training, planning, and agricultural improvement, as well as 74 agricultural cooperatives.

XX. Commerce Department Company Files (Shangye si gongsi dang'an 商業司公司檔案)

Containing 10,000 files, the collection covers ca. 1920–40.

XXI. Disaster Relief Commission (Shanhou shiye weiyuanhui 善後事業委員會)

In 50 boxes, documents cover 1946–50.

XXII. Japanese Reparations Management Commission (Riben peichang ji guihuan wuzi jieshou weiyuanhui 日本賠償及歸還物資接收委員會)

Established in 1946. The collection contains 22 boxes of material covering 1946–52. Documents include reports, correspondence, trade records, and records of Japanese businesses on Taiwan.

XXIII. Materials Bureau (Wuzi ju 物資局)

Established in 1946. Only one box of documents can be found at the Institute of Modern History; it consists mainly of plans and charts from 1946 to 1951.

XXIV. Economic Stabilization Board (Jingji anding weiyuanhui 經濟安定委員會)

The board was established in 1953. Documents cover 1953–58 and are held in sixteen boxes. The collection consists of organizational records, meeting and conference records, reports by American economic advisors, records of the United Nations Conference on the Asian and Far Eastern Economy, records of managed trade in staples, cement, and textiles, taxation reports, and programs to encourage purchase of domestic products.

XXV. Council on U.S. Aid (Meiyuan hui 美援會)

Comprising five boxes, documents cover the period 1952–54. The collection consists of meeting records, documents on the managed sale of raw cotton, textile conferences, and tourism reports.

XXVI. The Joint Commission on Rural Reconstruction (Zhongguo nongcun fuxing lianhe weiyuanhui 中國農村復興聯合委員會)

The Joint Commission on Rural Reconstruction (JCRR) was established by a Sino-American agreement in 1948. It was originally set up as a temporary and unofficial joint organization to plan and coordinate agricultural policies in China. The JCRR was originally conceived to encourage agricultural development, economic and technological assistance, and to coordinate planning between the government and the private sector. In 1979, the JCRR was reorganized as the Agricultural Development Council of the Executive Yuan (Xingzheng yuan, Nongye fazhan weiyuanhui 行政院農業發展委員會), formally becoming a part of the executive branch of the government.

In 1990 the Academia Historica took possession of the JCRR documents dating from 1948 to 1979. The entire collection numbers over 20,000 *juan* (卷). The Academia Historica has compiled a general guide to the collection entitled *Nongfuhui dang'an* 農復會檔案. Since most of the JCRR's business was conducted in English, over 90 percent of the documents are in English.

There are four general types of JCRR documents stored at the Academia Sinica:

A. Administrative: 6,904 folders organized by the eighteen administrative units of the JCRR. Administrative documents include personnel reports, work reports, meeting minutes of implementation groups, conference reports, loan information, and published materials. Documents on financial affairs include regulations, budgets, loans, audit reports, and personnel information from the Sino-American Economic and Social Development Fund. Administrative records also contain documents from the Program and Budget Office, the Office of Information and Education, the Livestock Production Group, the Agricultural and Plant Improvement Group, the Water Conservancy Group, the Project Review Office, the Farmers Association Group, the Fishermen Associations Group, the Rural Health and Hygiene Group, the Land Group, the Agricultural Promotion Group, and the International Cooperation Group.

B. Projects: documents are organized by individual projects. These include development projects in agricultural production and improvement, water resources, rural health and hygiene, livestock production, forestry, fisheries, food products, fertilizers, land reform, and the offshore islands (Quemoy, Matsu, Penghu).

C. Official correspondence

D. Special documents: These include plans for rural reconstruction and cover the years from 1948 to 1979. The collection includes 1,880 files and 314 attached items.

Publications

The Institute of Modern History has published several catalogs relevant to economic history, including a catalog of 15,000 maps stored at the institute. These catalogs are *Jingji dang'an hanmu huibian* 經濟檔案函目彙編, vol. 1 (1903–37); vol. 2 (1936–52) (Taibei: Zhongyang yanjiuyuan jindaishisuo, 1987–); and *Jinshisuo dang'an guancang Zhongwai ditu mulu huibian* 近史所檔案館藏中外地圖目錄彙編, 2 vols. (1991).

Chapter 16

Taiwan Historical Materials Commission: The Taiwan Area Productive Industries Management Council Collection (1949–1953)
台灣省文獻委員會：台灣區生產事業管理委員會

The Taiwan Area Productive Industries Management Council (Taiwan qu shengchan shiye guanli weiyuanhui 台灣區生產事業管理委員會)was created in June 1946 and absorbed into the Stabilization Council (Anding weiyuanhui 安定委員會) of the Ministry of Economic Affairs in 1953. Before the creation of the Management Council, there were three types of state-owned industries on Taiwan. The first were industries owned by the central government (administered by the National Resources Commission). The second were industries administered by the Taiwan provincial government. The third were industries jointly administered by the central and provincial governments. The Management Council was created to secure control by the Nationalist government over all state-owned industries on Taiwan, which comprised around 70 percent of all industries on the island in the postwar period. Originally subordinate to the Taiwan provincial government, the council came under central government control, with its administrative domain expanded to include supervision of private industries and financial and foreign trade policies. The council became a lead agency in coordinating industry, communications, foreign trade, finance, and resources. Its membership consisted of the major economic policy makers in Taiwan.

The Management Council formed working groups (*gongzuo xiaozu* 工作小組) to focus on individual issues such as equipment and supplies, electric power, electrical engineering, cement, railroad ties, pineapples, tea, timber, coal, pharmaceuticals, fisheries, textiles, foreign trade, industry, finance, technical cooperation, trade with Japan, and Japanese reparations.

The Taiwan Provincial Historical Materials Commission's collection includes the following general categories:

1. itemized list (*qingce* 清冊) of documents
2. functions (*yiban yewu*一般業務): 4,446 files (*juan* 卷)
3. business reports: eighteen cases (*he* 盒) of industry reports
4. accounting reports: ten cases
5. correspondence: nineteen cases
6. budgets: three cases
7. accounts: thirteen bundles (*bao* 包)

State-owned industries under the supervision of the Management Council were involved in petroleum, sugar, forestry, agricultural, industry, mining, cement, paper, machinery, shipping, aluminum, iron and steel, shipbuilding, fertilizer, salt, chemicals (sulfuric acid), camphor, gold and copper mining, vegetable oil, textiles, and medicine. Business and financial reports include production records, financial reports, and personnel records. These documents also include company charters and information on capital, boards of directors, and shareholders. The collection also contains important economic and industrial surveys, such as the industrial policy report submitted to the United Nations Far Eastern Economic Conference in 1953. There are also documents from conferences that reviewed the state-owned industrial sector and assessed the performance of individual state-owned enterprises. These records consist of enterprise business records, assets, finances, debt, and budgets. Besides records on review and discussion conferences on state-owned industries, there are also documents from a variety of special conferences, such as discussions on American financial aid, trade with Japan, trade with the Ryukyu Islands, and industrial assistance and protection.

The records of the Management Council's Standing Committee are scattered among the collection. The collection as a whole reveals many aspects of the policymaking process between the Management Council, the Executive Yuan, provincial agencies, and other levels of government. Other items of interest are communications between the council and non-governmental organizations and individuals, and records on land use, landownership, land policies, investment priorities, and stockholder rights.

Chapter 17

Taiwan Provincial Legislature Library
台灣省議會圖書館

I. Provincial Legislature and County and Municipal Governments

The Taiwan Provincial Legislature was established soon after retrocession in 1946. When the Nationalist government fled to Taiwan in 1949, provincial authorities faced a dilemma: how could it administer Taiwan, when there was now a "national" government controlling only Taiwan? Overlaps, redundancies, and conflicts became a problem between the "central" and the "provincial" authorities. Unlike the Legislative Yuan, which had constitutionally mandated authority, the provincial legislature had only the rights of suggestion and supervision.

Following retrocession, the provincial legislature underwent three phases of development. The first Taiwan Provincial Legislature (Taiwan sheng canyi hui 台灣省參議會) was formed in May 1946 and functioned until December 1951. Many of the functions and procedures of the legislature were established during this chaotic period, such as the supervision of state-owned enterprises. Second, between December 1951 and June 1959 the Provisionary Taiwan Provincial Legislature (Taiwan sheng linshi canyi hui 台灣省臨時省參議會) was formed and established committees on civil administration, financial reconstruction, agriculture and forestry, education, and communications. The temporary legislature also established a working group on state-owned enterprises. The present Taiwan Provincial Legislature (Taiwan sheng yihui 台灣省議會) was inaugurated in June 1959.

Four main types of documents are held at the Taiwan Provincial Legislature Library (Taiwan sheng yihui tushuguan 台灣省議會圖書館):

1. Legislative business (*yishi lu* 議事錄): basic records of legislative business, including statements and hearings. These records remain restricted.
2. *Legislative Gazette* (*Yihui gongbao* 議會公報): published since 1953, the *Gazette* is a weekly record of legislative events, including policy reports, hearings, resolutions, and correspondence between the legislature and government organizations.
3. Fact-finding trips: reports on forestry and agriculture, the food supply, finance, state monopolies, reconstruction, state-owned industries, education, and civil administration.
4. Campaign literature and memoirs: this collection is limited.

In addition to records of the legislature, the collection at the library also includes documents from the Taiwan provincial government and other agencies. These include policy planning and implementation reports, and written correspondence between provincial government agencies and the legislature.

Similar to the provincial government, county and municipal governments have executive and

155

legislative branches. The executive branches produce county and municipal government gazettes and annual reports. The legislative branches also produce legislative gazettes and legislative records. These documents are stored at individual local government agencies and local libraries as well as the provincial legislature library.

II. Foreign Exchange and Foreign Trade Council of the Executive Yuan, 1956–68 (Xingzheng yuan, Waihui maoyi shenyi weiyuanhui 行政院外匯貿易審議委員會)

The Foreign Exchange and Foreign Trade Council controlled Taiwan's foreign trade policies from 1956 to 1968. In general the council steered Taiwan from an import-substitution to an export-based industrial strategy. The formation of the council was an attempt to streamline jurisdiction over foreign trade and foreign exchange. Before the creation of the council, at least twenty ministries, bureaus, working groups, and other central and provincial government agencies shared jurisdiction over foreign trade and exchange.

The Foreign Trade and Foreign Exchange Council had broad authority over foreign trade and foreign exchange policies, allocation and use of foreign currencies, allocation and distribution of American aid, and coordination of trade and exchange policies among all levels of government. Committee members included the minister of finance, the minister of economics, the secretary of the American Aid Utilization Council (Mei yuan yunyong weiyuanhui mishu zhang 美援運用委員會秘書長), the executive secretary of the Economic Stabilization Council of the Executive Yuan, a representative from the central bank, the bureau chief of the Central Trust Bureau, two representatives from the Taiwan provincial government, and two representatives from the Bank of Taiwan. The committee met weekly to discuss foreign trade and foreign exchange policies.

Similar to the Control Council, the Foreign Trade and Foreign Exchange Council organized working groups. These groups focused on imports, exports, foreign exchange, and other matters. There were also research groups made up of scholars and experts to study specific problems and submit reports and recommendations. These groups covered such issues as export foreign exchange rates and imports trends.

Most documents from the council consist of records of the weekly committee meetings. These meetings considered the reports and recommendations from working groups, communications from government agencies, and petitions from individuals and organizations. In all there were around 600 weekly meetings. The holdings of the provincial legislature library begin with meeting no. 67 and end with no. 608. The location of the records of the remaining weekly meetings remains unclear.

The weekly committee reports consist of reports on foreign exchange figures from the previous week, correspondence and requests from other government agencies (such as the Ministry of Economic Affairs), petitions and suggestions from individuals and groups such as private industries, same-trade associations, and chambers of commerce, surveys and reports from working groups, and surveys by committee members.

Chapter 18

Party Historical Commission of the Guomindang and Other Collections on Taiwan
國民黨黨史會

Records held by the Party Historical Commission of the Guomindang (Guomindang, Dangshi hui 國民黨黨史會) are organized into several major groups. Along with the general documentary collection, archival material is also organized into several additional categories such as topical collections ("special organization archives"), gazettes, periodicals, newspapers, audiovisual materials, and oral histories.

Documents on economic history are divided according to period. Records dating to 1924–36 consist mainly of newspaper clippings on economic issues. Documents from the second period, 1937–45, include organizational charters and reports from central and local agencies. These include the Ministry of Economic Affairs, National Resources Commission, Agricultural Bureau, Materials Bureau, the China Industrial Company, China Silk Company, Ministry of Agriculture and Forestry, Central Agricultural Experiment Center, Central Forestry Experiment Center, Central Fisheries Experiment Center, Central Stock-Raising Experimental Center, Ministry of Food Stocks, Warehouse Engineering Administration Bureau, and China Industrial Cooperative Association.

The special organization archives has five separate collections: Shanghai Huanlong Road Collection (*Shanghai Huanlonglu dang'an* 上海環龍路檔案, 1914–23), Hankou Collection (*Hankou dang'an* 漢口檔案, 1926–27), First Five Central Departments Collection (*Zhongyang qianwubu dang'an* 中央前五部檔案, 1924–27), Central Political Conference Collection (*Zhongyang zhengzhi huiyi dang'an* 中央政治會議檔案, 1924–26, 1926–37), and the Supreme Defense Council (*Guyofang zuigao weiyuanhui dang'an* 國防最高委員會檔案, 1939–47).

The First Five Central Departments Collection contains over 16,000 items. Those from the Merchants Department (one of the five departments) number 2,021 items, such as documents on organization, conferences, finance, regulations, disputes, plans, reports, correspondence, and personnel.

The collection of central government gazettes includes the *Industrial and Commerce Gazette* (*Gongshang gongbao* 工商公報), *Water Conservancy News* (*Shuili tongxun* 水利通訊), *Beijing Trademark Gazette* (*Beijing shangpiao gongbao* 北京商標公報), and *Accounting News* (*Zhuji tongxun* 主計通訊). Among the local gazettes are publications from Shandong, Anhui, Jiangxi, Jiangsu, Qingdao, Hebei, Henan, Guizhou, Yunnan, Hubei, Fujian, and Guangdong.

Legislative Yuan (1952 to Present)
立法院

The Legislative Yuan (Lifa yuan 立法院) is one of the two representative bodies of the Nationalist government. The Legislative Yuan was established in 1926. When the Nationalist government retreated to Taiwan in 1949, the Legislative Yuan, along with other representative bodies, suspended elections of new mainland representatives.

The Legislative Yuan was (and is) empowered to deliberate and approve laws, budgets, and treaties. While there is no doubt that the executive branch dominated policymaking up to the 1990s, government leaders did utilize the Legislative Yuan as a forum for debate of major issues. In addition, individuals and private organizations addressed petitions and grievances to the Legislative Yuan.

The Legislative Yuan had broad formal powers. It had authority to make laws, approve budgets, declare martial law, extend amnesty, approve foreign treaties, declare war, approve peace treaties, extend approval of the prime minister and president of the Control Yuan, draft constitutional amendments, provide emergency aid to provincial and local governments, and mediate disputes between the central government and local governments.

The Legislative Yuan was organized into three levels: the legislature (*quanyuan weiyuanhui* 全院委員會), permanent committees (*changshe weiyuanhui* 常設委員會), and special committees (*tebie weiyuanhui* 特別委員會). The permanent committees included those on domestic affairs, foreign policy, national security, economics, finance, budget, education, communications, frontier policies, overseas Chinese, judiciary, and law.

The records of the Legislative Yuan are published and stored at the Legislative Yuan and other major libraries in Taiwan. These records are published in five publications:

1. *Legislative Yuan Gazette* (*Lifa yuan gongbao* 立法院公報): published twice weekly, the gazette is the basic record of the activities of the legislature and its committees and statements by legislators. In addition, the publication contains petitions and important correspondence between government branches.

2. *Legislative Yuan Press Release* (*Lifa yuan xinwen'gao* 立法院新聞稿): released nightly; highlights major events for journalistic purposes.

3. *Law Special Collection* (*Falü'an zhuanji* 法律案專輯): designed for the legal profession; records deliberations and decisions.

4. *Loose-leaf Law Collection* (*Huoye falü* 活頁法律): records all laws passed by the legislature and signed by the president.

5. *Legislative Yuan News Bimonthly* (*Yuan wen banyue kan* 院聞半月刊): begun in 1973, reports on foreign visitors, legislative conferences, symposia, and trips.

Customs Service Archival Storehouse
海關圖書資料庫

In 1987, customs authorities formed a preparatory task force for the establishment of a customs museum. By 1991 the task force had collected some 2,000 items related to the history of the Customs Service. Almost all Customs Service documents were published. The following collections are available at the Archival Storehouse (Haiguan tushu ziliao ku 海關圖書資料庫):

1. Bureau of Taxation (Zong shuiwui si 總稅務司: 38 volumes containing documents from 1860 to 1949; includes seven volumes of *Documents Illustrative of the Origins, Development, and Activities of the Chinese Customs Service.*
2. Foreign Trade Records of the Republic of China (Zhonghua minguo haiguanhuayang maoyi zongce 中華民國海關華洋貿易總冊): volumes from 1902 to 1935 (missing: 1906, 1907); overviews of imports and exports; and reprints by Academia Historica based on information that came to Taiwan with the Nationalist government in 1949.
3. Annual Statistical Records of Foreign Trade (Haiguan zhongwai maoyi tongji niankan 海關中外貿易統計年刊): records from 1947 to 1949 with information on tariff rates, products, and shipping.
4. Chinese Import and Export Annual Statistics (Zhongguo jinkou maoyi tongji niankan 中國進出口貿易統計年刊): 1949 to 1988.
5. Republic of China Taiwan Monthly Import Statistics (Zhonghua minguo Taiwan diqu jinkou tongji yuebao 中華民國台灣地區進口統計月報): 1989 to 1993.
6. Republic of China Taiwan Monthly Export Statistical Records (Zhonghua minguo Taiwan diqu chukou tongji yuebao 中華民國台灣地區出口統計月報): 1989 to 1993.
7. Chinese Import and Export Statistical Monthly (Zhongguo jinchukou maoyi tongji yuebao 中國進出口貿易統計月報): volumes from May 1948; January, June, 1951; July and August 1946; April 1947.
8. Annual Reports of the Customs Service (Guanwu nianbao 關務年報): begun in 1977.

In addition, the Archival Storehouse has a large collection of microfilmed documents relating to the Chinese Customs Services. There are currently 111 rolls of microfilm incorporating statistical series, special series, miscellaneous series, service series, office series, inspectorate series, the maritime customs, and decennial reports.

National Chengchi University's Social Sciences Information Center:
Documents from Labor and Business Associations After 1945
國立政治大學社會科學資料中心

In 1958, the Activities Center for Private Organizations in the Republic of China (Zhonghua minguo minzhong tuanti huodong zhongxin 中華民國民眾團體活動中心) created the Collected Information on National Private Organizations (*Quanguo geji minzhong tuanti yilanbiao ziliao* 全國各級民眾團體一覽表資料). The center collected material from private organizations, including information on founders, membership, organizational charters, project plans, budgets, financial reports, meeting records, as well as publications. These records have been turned over to National Chengchi University's Social Sciences Information Center and are open to the public.

The entire collection is approximately 150 volumes and contains information on 230 national, provincial, and local commercial and industrial organizations. There is also information on Overseas Chinese trade associations. Most of the data date from after 1950 and detail membership backgrounds such as academic achievements and membership in political parties.

The documents contain information on fifteen national-level organizations and 91 provincial organizations. The collection contains a great deal of information on around 110 groups registered with the city of Taipei.

National Taiwan University's Three People's Principles Center:
Personal Papers of Li Guoding (K. T. Li)
國立台灣大學：李國鼎檔案

Li Guoding (李國鼎) held a variety of government positions: he was secretary of the Council on U.S. Aid, minister of economics, minister of finance, and minister without portfolio. He was intimately involved in the economic development of Taiwan after 1949. His personal papers include memos, conference records, reports, student dissertations, as well as notes from his graduate study at Oxford University. These papers are organized in two volumes.

Broadly speaking the papers are organized topically: politics, economic development, trade, finance, American assistance and loans, agriculture, fisheries, timber, stockraising, water conservancy, energy, transportation and communication, land use, urban development, industrial development, investment, business management, technology, education, population control, mainland China affairs, foreign firms, the Guomindang, taxation, state-owned enterprises, public housing, and pharmaceuticals. These documents represent the breadth of Li Guoding's interest in economic development issues.

Other Thematic Documentary Collections and Publications

I. Native-Place Associations (同鄉會) in Taiwan After 1945

Many government workers and businessmen emigrated to Taiwan from the mainland after 1945. Many of these immigrants formed associations based on common place of origin. The exodus from the mainland after the Nationalist government retreated to Taiwan in 1949 accelerated the formation of such groups. In 1992 there were still some 650 registered native-place associations. The leadership of most of these associations was (and is) composed of men from the commercial and business sectors.

Three levels of government have jurisdiction over native-place associations: the Interior Ministry, the Taiwan Provincial Social Bureau, and the social bureaus of county and municipal governments. Formal registration information is available at all three levels of government.

According to the Electronic Overview of Information and Documents of Executive Agencies of the Republic of China (*Zhonghua minguo xingzheng jiguan dianzi ziliao dangzonglan* 中華民國行政機關電子資料檔總覽), the Ministry of Interior currently maintains a database entitled Documents of Information on National Social Groups (*Quanguoxing shehui tuanti ziliao dang'an* 全國性社會團體資料檔案). These documents record basic information on social organizations such as formal title, statement of purpose, secretariat, location, and date of establishment. This information, however, was designed for official use and requires official approval. Access to this information for research purposes is possible, but difficult.

Information on native-place associations is more accessible from county and municipal agencies. For instance, the Taipei municipal government maintains basic information on native-place associations. There is no standardized procedure for archival storage at these local institutions, and older records have been vulnerable to damage.

Native-place associations regularly publish newsletters. Such newsletters record annual meetings and often include information on activities, loans, job placement, job training, and investments. Many of these newsletters can be found in major libraries on Taiwan.

II. Historical Documents on the Development of Taiwan's Fertilizer Industry, 1945–53

The fertilizer industry was one of the three industries targeted by the Nationalist government for development in Taiwan after 1945. In 1947, the fertilizer industry produced 15 percent of the fertilizer needed in Taiwan, but after 1980 Taiwan's fertilizer industries produced enough for export. There is a broad array of historical sources available on the development of Taiwan's fertilizer industry.

The first group of important documents on the development of the fertilizer industry was produced by the Nationalist government as it planned Taiwan's administration after 1945. Documents stored in the Materials Department (Wuzi si 物資司) include Reports on Taiwan's Industry and Mining (*Taiwan gongkuang shiye kaocha baogao* 台灣工礦事業考察報告), Outline of Cooperation on Joint Management of Taiwan Province's Industrial and Mining Between the National Resources Council of the Ministry of Economics and the Taiwan Provincial Executive Government Office (*Jingji bu ziyuan weiyuanhui, Taiwan sheng xingzheng zhangguan gongshu heban Taiwan sheng gongkuang shiye hezuo dagang* 經濟部資源委員會, 台灣省行政長官公署合辦台灣省工礦事業合作大綱), Reports on Policies by the Taiwan Provincial Executive Government Office, Work Reports on the Fertilizer Industry, May 1946 (*Taiwan sheng xingzheng zhangguan gongshu shizheng baogao, feiliao gongye gongzuo jianbao* 台灣省行政長官公署施政報告, 肥料工業工作簡報), Work Report of the Taiwan Fertilizer Corporation, November 1947 (*Taiwan feiliao youxian gongsi gongzuo baogao* 台灣肥料有限公司工作報告), Conference Record of the First Executive and Oversight Committee Meeting of the Taiwan Fertilizer Corporation, January 1947 (*Taiwan feiliao youxian gongsi chuangli hui diyi ci dongjianhui huiyi jilu* 台灣肥料有限公司創立會第一次董監會會議紀錄), and the Charter of the Taiwan Fertilizer Limited Corporation, April 1947 (*Taiwan feiliao youxian gongsi zhangcheng* 台灣肥料有限公司章程). These documents have been published in Chen Wuzhong and Chen Xingtang, eds., *Taiwan guangfu he guangfu hou wunian shengqing* 台灣光復和光復後五年省情 (Taiwan province at retrocession and five years later) (Nanjing: Nanjing chubanshe, 1989). Information from this period can also be found in government gazettes, as well as in Japanese documents stored at the Central Library Taiwan Branch and the Institute of Modern History, Academia Sinica. The Japanese collection includes agricultural surveys, government gazettes, and almanacs. Yilan County's Cultural Center also has a small collection concerning the Taiwanese fertilizer industry.

Because Taiwan's fertilizer industry was under joint provincial and central government control after 1945, the archives of the National Resources Council, Taiwan Area Productive Industries Control Council, and the Economic Stabilization Council all have documents related to the fertilizer industry.

Publications

I. Banking (After 1945)

After 1945 banks in Taiwan were controlled by either the central government or local governments. In addition, banks were differentiated by function. For example, some banks were designated to cater to export-import transactions; other banks specialized in agricultural loans.

In general, banks put out three types of publications: annual reports, monthly or quarterly publications, and commemorative publications. Annual reports typically contained general economic data and particular information on the individual bank, including its history and organization, the scope of business, a record of major events, philanthropic activities, financial reports, officers, and branches.

Commemorative issues date back to the period of Japanese administration. Examples include *Taiwan yinhang ershi nian nianzhi*台灣銀行二十年年誌 (Twenty years of the Bank of Taiwan) and *Taiwan yinhang sishi nian nianzhi* 台灣銀行四十年年誌 (Forty years of the Bank of Taiwan; rep. 1993). These publications cover the history of the bank, its organization, and its business activities in Taiwan, Japan, China, Manchuria, Southeast Asia, India, Europe, and the United States. Examples of commemorative issues after 1945 are *Zhanghua shangye yinhang liushi nian shi* 彰化商業銀行六十年史) (History of sixty years of the Zhanghua Commercial Bank) (1967); *Diyi yinhang bashi nian* 第一銀行八十年 (Eighty years of the First Bank) (1979), *Jiaotong yinhang bashi nian* 交通銀行八十年 (Eighty years of the Bank of Transportation) (1987), and *Taibei shi yinhang ershi nian* 臺北市銀行二十年 (Twenty Years of the Taipei Municipal Bank) (1989).

Periodicals published by banking institutions contain information on economic and financial theory, reports, technical issues, and literary essays. One such publication is the *Taiwan yinhang jikan* 台灣銀行季刊 (Bank of Taiwan quarterly), first published in 1947 and dedicated to scholarly discussion of economic issues facing Taiwan. The Bank of Taiwan has also published special issues dedicated to specific economic problems and economic sectors such as mining, water conservancy, fertilizers, land use, timber, insurance, and electrification.

The Bank of Taiwan also publishes the *Taiwan yinhang Taiwan jingji jinrong yuebao*台灣銀行台灣經濟金融月刊 (Bank of Taiwan economic and financial monthly) (1965–), which replaced *Taiwan jingji dongtai jianbao* 台灣經濟動態簡報 (Summary of economic trends in Taiwan), published since 1961. The monthly contains articles on economic and financial issues, scholarly works, reports, translations of articles from abroad, book reviews, surveys, chronologies, and statistics.

Other examples of periodicals from national-level banks are *Huanan yinhang yuekan* 華銀銀行月刊 (Bank of South China monthly), published since 1951, the First Commercial Bank's *Yiyin yuekan* 一銀月刊, published since 1956, and the Cooperation Exchequer's *Today's Co-operation Exchequer*(*Jinri heku* 今日合庫), published since 1975.

Publications from specialty and local banks include the Bank of Communication's *Chanye jinrong* 產業金融; the China Agriculture Bank's *Nongye jinrong luncong*農業金融論叢, published since 1979; and the China Import-Export Bank's *Shuchuru jinrong shuangyuekan* 輸出入金融雙月刊. Local banking institutions are typically cooperatives or affiliated with agricultural and fishery associations. Two publications produced by these banks are *Jiceng jinrong* 基層金融, published since 1970, and *Xinyong hezuo* 信用合作, published since 1984.

II. State-Owned Enterprises

State-owned enterprises encompass a wide variety of industries, and many publish periodicals devoted to contemporary industry developments as well as historical accounts. Examples of the latter genre are *Taidian ershi nian shi* 台電二十年史 (The twenty-year history of Taiwan Electrical Power) and *Taiwan dianli fazhan shi* 台灣電力發展史 (The history of Taiwan Electrical Power Development).

Publications from other state-owned enterprises include the China Petroleum Corporation's *Zhongguo shiyou zhi* 中國石油志 and *Sishi nianlai zhi Zhongguo shiyou gongsi* 四十年來之中國石油公司; *Taitang shi nian* 台糖十年, published by the Taiwan Sugar Corporation every decade since 1955; the Taiwan provincial government's Materials Bureau's overview of its operations, T*aiwan sheng wuzi ju yewu jingying gaikuang* 台灣省物資局業務經營概況 (1964), The ninetieth-anniversary history of the China Merchants Steamship Company, *Zhaoshang ju jiushi nian jinian* 招商局九十週年紀念 (1962); the Ministry of Telecommunication's historical summary of Chinese telecommunications, *Zhongguo dianxin ji* 中國電信紀 (1971), and its centennial history of telecommunications, *Dianxin yibainian jinian* 電信一百週年紀念; the Railroad Bureau's similar *Zhongguo tielu chuangjian ba nian shi* 中國鐵路創建百年史 (1981), the Highway Bureau's review of four decades, *Gonglu ju sishi nian* 公路局四十年 (1986); and, not to be missed, *Jilonggang jian'gang bainian jinian wenji* 基隆港建港百年紀念文集 (One-hundredth anniversary of the port of Keelung) (1984).

Part III

READING BUSINESS AND ECONOMIC HISTORY

DOCUMENTS OF REPUBLICAN CHINA

Chapter 19

How to Read Republican Period Documents[1]

by Zhang Wode 張我德

I. Major Types of Republican Documents

This essay offers a brief introduction to the different types of official government documents used during the Republican Period. It concentrates on document structure, vocabulary, and commonly used forms of punctuation, sectioning, and headings. From 1912 to 1942, the Chinese government approved seven sets of regulations containing formulas for official documents. These regulations established formal documentary nomenclature and function. Meanwhile, some document types that remained outside the official taxonomy but continued to be generated by governmental bureaus in accordance with past practice gained informal acceptance by the state.

On January 30, 1912, the Republic of China Provisional Government in Nanjing promulgated China's first regulation to formally systematize government communications. The regulation stipulated five types:

1. *ling* 令 (sometimes called *yu* 諭): "order" or "decree"—downward communications sent from higher to lower government offices or from government offices to private citizens;

2. *zi* 咨: "lateral communications"—communications between organs of equal status;

3. *cheng* 呈: "petition"—documents sent from lower to higher government offices or from private citizens to government officials;

4. *shi* 示: "proclamation"—announcements sent from a government office to the public. Note: laws established by a resolution in the upper house of the legislature (Canyiyuan 參議院) and announced directly by the president were called *bugao* 布告 (sometimes mistakenly written *gongbu* 公布);

5. *zhuang* 狀: "documents of certification"—used for administrative appointment or reward.

---

[1]This is an edited translation of Professor Zhang's multipart article, "Zenyang yuedu minguo shiqi de gongwen" 怎樣閱讀民國時期的公文 (How to read official documents of the Republican era), *Beijing dang'an shiliao* 北京檔案史料 (Beijing historical archival materials), no. 5 (1987), 69–74; no. 6 (1987), 63–74; no. 7 (1987), 67–75; no. 8 (1987), 64–70; no. 9 (1988), 65–75; and no. 10 (1988), 72–76.

In addition, the 1912 regulations required that all nonclassified documents from the president or the ministries be published in the government gazette (*gongbao* 公報). Unless otherwise specified, the directives of nonclassified documents went into effect in Beijing on the fifth day after their proclamation and outside Beijing on the fifth day after the arrival of the gazette.

The new regulations placed the president on a commensurate level with other officials. Hence, all former imperial document types used by the emperor, such as decree (*zhi* 旨), proclamation or mandate (*zhao* 詔), ordinance (*gao* 誥), command (*chi* 敕), and edict (*yuzhi* 諭 旨), were abolished, as were palace memorials (*zouzhe* 奏折) and routine memorials (*tiben* 題 本). The regulations further simplified the highly complex system of communication between government bureaus by reducing the number of document types to one or, at most, two (except for special categories such as foreign affairs). Except for a brief interlude when Yuan Shikai attempted to restore the monarchy in 1914–16, the 1912 regulations established the basis for document forms throughout most of the Republican period. However, subsequent laws entailed minor additions or changes.

On November 6, 1912, Yuan Shikai issued new procedures for official documents (*Gongwenshu chengshi ling* 公文書程式令). Yuan expanded the power of the provisional president by allowing him to promulgate laws and regulations without first seeking approval from the legislature. These laws and regulations were referred to by the term *jiaoling* 教令 (command).

The new regulations divided the category of *ling* (令 order) into several more precise subcategories: *ling* 令 (*zongtongling* 總統令, *yuanling* 院令, and *buling* 部令), *weirenling* 委任 令, *xunling* 訓令, *zhiling* 指令, and *chufenling* 處分令.

1. *ling* 令:
   a. *zongtongling* 總統令: "executive order" or "presidential order"—used by the president to promulgate laws and international treaties, issue commands (*jiaoling* 教令), announce the national budget, and appoint and dismiss high- and middle-ranking officials;
   b. *yuanling* 院令: "council order"—used by the State Council to address certain important matters;
   c. *buling* 部令: "ministerial order"—used by central government ministries to promulgate certain important matters;

2. *weirenling* 委任令: "appointment order"—used by high-level officials (including the president) to appoint lower-ranking officials to certain posts;

3. *xunling* 訓令: "instructions"—used by high-level officials (including the president) to convey instructions to subordinates;

168

4. *zhiling* 指令: "directive"—an instruction in response to a petition or request by subordinate officials;

5. *chufenling* 處分令: instructions given by administrative bureaus to nongovernment agencies concerning specific affairs.

In addition, *zi* 咨 (lateral communication) became a term exclusively used for communications between the president, State Council, and the upper house. All other communications between organs in a nonhierarchical relationship were henceforth referred to as *gonghan* 公函 (official letter). All governmental proclamations directed at the general public were subsumed under the rubric of *bugao* 布告 (later sometimes called *tonggao* 通告), and official replies to petitions generated from nonstate groups or individuals were called *pi* 批 (official reply).

On May 26, 1914, Yuan Shikai again exercised his *jiaoling* power to redefine the forms and parameters of official documents. Earlier that month, he renamed the State Council, from Guowu yuan (國務院) to Zhengshi tang (政事堂), and made the secretary of state (*guowu qing* 國務卿) his de facto personal secretary. These changes, as well as the creation (or revival) of imperial documentary forms, signaled his future intention to restore a monarchical system—with the State Council to resemble the Qing Grand Council (Junji chu 軍機處) and the secretary of state to act as the functional equivalent of the grand councilor (*shouxi junji dachen* 首席軍機大臣).

Yuan's Presidential Documents:

1. *celing* 策令: an order used to appoint or dismiss civilian and military officials and to confer rank and other honors;

2. *shenling* 申令: a mandate used to proclaim new laws, commands (*jiaoling*), treaties, budgets, and instructions to officials;

3. *gaoling* 告令 (used like *bugao* 布告): proclamations directed at the general public;

4. *piling* 批令: a mandate used to reply to petitions from subordinate officials;

5. *zi* 咨: a lateral communication, as between the president and the Legislative Yuan (Lifa yuan 立法院).

Documents used by the State Council and the secretary of state in communicating with ministries (and *yuan*) and provincial governments (during Yuan's presidency):

1. *fengji* 封寄: a document used by the secretary of state to transmit a personally received presidential order (*yu* 諭) to ministries and provincial governments;

2. *jiaopian* 交片: similar to *fengji*, but used only for brief dispatches to ministries;

3. *gonghan* 公函: a document used for consultation, sent by the secretary of state to ministries and provincial governments;

4. *zi* 咨: a document used by the State Council in reply to petitions from ministries and high-level local government offices.

These categories make it clear that the primary task of the State Council was to transmit the orders (*yu* 諭) of the president to central and local government organs. In this sense, the *fengji* served the same function as court letters (*jixin* 寄信) during the Qing dynasty. Meanwhile, the *jiaopian*, a form of communication used within the capital during the Qing, was also revived.

Documents Used by Government Offices and the People:

1. *xiang* 詳: "detailed report"—a document sent by a subordinate to his superior (originally used during the Ming and Qing dynasties);

2. *chi* 飭: an order or instruction from a superior to his subordinate (equivalent to the *zha* 札 used during the Qing dynasty);

3. *zichen* 咨陳: an upward-moving document from the highest-level local government offices to central ministries (cf. *zicheng* 咨呈: a document used by provincial governments and ministries when communicating with the State Council);

4. *pi* 批: a reply to a petition from a subordinate official or nonstate groups or individuals;

5. *bing* 稟: a petition from the people to the government (used during the Qing dynasty for similar purposes) or one from a subordinate official to a superior);

6. *cheng* 呈: originally used exclusively by high officials in writing to the president.

Following Yuan Shikai's death in June 1916, minor modifications were made to the rules for government documents. These changes represented a move back to the original document forms promulgated by Dr. Sun Yat-sen's Nanjing Provisional Government in 1912. Later, in June 1928 a government revision approved structural alterations allowing official documents to be written with greater use of the vernacular, sectioned into paragraphs, and clarified with punctuation. Furthermore, a distinction between intra-governmental petitions and those sent to the government from the people was established: the former retaining the label *cheng* 呈, and the latter were called *zhuang* 狀. Five months later these changes were revoked. In the aftermath, little attention was paid to revising document forms until 1942. In June of that year, telegrams (*dianbao* 電報) and express mail letters in lieu of a telegram (*kuaiyou daidian* 快郵代電, or simply *daidian* 代電) were incorporated as formal document types.

Besides officially sanctioned document forms, other types of documents were used between various government bureaus. These were collectively called *zati* 雜體 (miscellaneous forms) and included different forms:

1. *shouyu* 手諭: "hand edict"—a downward communication containing instructions or some kind of notification sent by the head of a bureau to his subordinates within the same bureau. In exceptional cases, *shouyu* were also used to send communications directly to a subordinate bureau for the sake of convenience;

2. *qiancheng* 簽呈: "strip petitions"—an upward communication used within a bureau by a subordinate to offer proposals or request instructions from the bureau head (these were written on thin strips called *qiantiao* 簽條, hence the name). In exceptional cases, *qiancheng* were sent directly to a superior bureau;

3. *zhecheng* 折呈: "folded petitions"—a less formal petition than a *cheng* 呈, *zhecheng* were written on folded white paper and did not have to conform to the rule that petitions limit their scope to only one issue. *Zhecheng* were used to deal with more complex matters. Usually, the author discussed the content with the addressee (his superior) and handed it to him to be used as a written record. It was more personal than formal;

4. *shuotie* 說帖: "prospectus" or "opinion petition"—similar to the *zhecheng*, *shuotie* were folded white documents either personally given to a superior by his subordinate or submitted as an appendix to a formal petition. In *shuotie,* the subordinate expressed in detail his opinion or put forward a suggestion regarding some matter;

5. *jielüe* 節略: "brief memorandum"—an upward document reporting a matter to a superior.

II. Structure of Official Documents (gongwen 公文)

Gongwen (official documents) extend back to the Qin dynasty (221–206 B.C.E.). Unlike ordinary prose, *gongwen* have a fixed form chosen according to the relationship of the author to the recipient, as well as the type of matter addressed and the purpose of the document. Generally speaking, the majority of *gongwen* were written by functionaries of low educational attainment who merely followed strict guidelines in filling in the document with the relevant content. For this reason, *gongwen* are often clumsily written, and sometimes laden with seemingly incoherent wording and non sequiturs.

Structure of Official Directives, Replies, and Telegrams

Both directives (*zhiling* 指令) and replies (*pi* 批) were used to convey instructions to a subordinate in response to a petition or request.

In a *zhiling* 指令, the author would clearly state his bureau, the type of document (i.e., *zhiling*), and the document number on the first line. This would be followed by the name of the recipient on the second line, situated below the author's name to reflect the recipient's lower rank. On the third line, the author would use an opening statement expressing the subject of the original petition. The proceeding text usually began with the ideographs *cheng* and *xi*, either in consecutive order (*chengxi* 呈悉) or set apart with a word or phrase in between (*cheng* . . . *xi* 呈 . . . 悉). The author would indicate the end of the text with the term *ciling* 此令 ("hence this order").

The *pi* 批 followed the same guidelines, only substituting the word *pi* 批 for *zhiling* 指令 at the beginning of the text and *cipi* 此批 for *ciling* 此令 at the end.

The structure of telegrams (*dianbao* 電報) was also simple. Telegrams began with the recipient's official title and name followed by either the salutation *jian* 鑒, if sent to a superior or an equal, or *lan* 覽, if sent to a subordinate. At the end of the text came the sender's official title and name followed by the date. Unlike other document forms, telegrams used a rhyming code (*yunmu* 韻目) to denote the date. The rhyming code developed out of officially sanctioned rhyming schemes that Qing dynasty scholars had to learn in order to compose the required poems on the civil service examinations. These rhyming schemes were arranged in a rhyming directory (*yunshu* 韻書) that formed the basis of the rhyming code table (*yunmu dairi biao* 韻目代日表).

The symbols of the twelve Earthly Branches (dizhi 地支) were often used to show the time or month of the dispatch. The Earthly Branches, in the ascending order of the 12 months, are 子 (*zi*), 丑 (*chou*), 寅 (*yin*), 卯 (*mao*), 辰 (*chen*), 巳 (*si*), 午 (*wu*), 未 (*wei*), 申 (*shen*), 酉 (*you*), 戌 (*xu*), and 亥 (*hai*).

Telegrams often end with the character *yin* 印 (seal). This marker means that the original draft of the telegram had an official seal affixed. The character *kou* 叩 (as in *koushou* 叩首, to kowtow) occasionally appears after the name of the sender as an expression of deference. One may also observe the character *mi*, written 秘 or 密 (secret), indicating the secret nature of the communication. Lastly, a blank space in a sentence on a telegram can represent a show of respect for the person or organization that follows (as in correspondences of the dynastic period, discussed below in Section III).

Placement of Quotations

The use of quoted passages (excerpts from other documents) in official communications saved the recipient the time and effort he might spend consulting the files for relevant information. In theory, this dividend translated into greater bureaucratic efficiency. However, if quotations were appended at each link of the documentation process, the reader might have to wade through layer after layer of excerpts before ascertaining the objective of the document at hand. Accumulated citations from previous documents could result in unnecessary repetition that hampered the efficiency of the system.

How to Distinguish Direct Quotation Markers

Quoted passages in official documents are often structured so that quotes are contained within quotes, often up to several layers. On first sight, it may be difficult to establish the interrelationship between them. However, if one can master a "special" vocabulary, the task can be accomplished.

The beginning of a passage from a received document (*laiwen* 來文) is usually announced by the opening quotation marker *kai* 開 or *cheng* 稱, or sometimes *baogao* 報告. Generally speaking,

1. *kai* 開 begins a quote from a superior or equal;

2. *cheng* 稱 begins a quote from a subordinate;

3. *baogao* 報告 is used when a superior quotes a report from a subordinate.

These opening quotation markers are commonly preceded by *nei* 內, as in *neikai* 內開 or *neicheng* 內稱 ("what is listed therein . . ."), or by the name of the type of document being quoted, as in *chengcheng* 呈稱, *zikai* 咨開, *lingkai* 令開, or *hankai* 函開.

Conversely, the combinations *dengyin* 等因, *dengyou* 等由, *dengqing* 等情, and *dengyu* 等語 function as closing quotation markers. More specifically:

173

1. *dengyin* 等因 ends a quote received from a superior;

2. *dengyou* 等由 ends a quote received from an equal;

3. *dengqing* 等情 ends a quote received from a subordinate;

4. *dengyu* 等語 ends a quote containing a law (*faling* 法令), regulation (*zhangcheng* 章程), a report from a subordinate, or an oral statement.

If more than one passage is being quoted at a time, the character *ge* 各 (each) is inserted in front of these markers (i.e., *ge dengyin* 各等因, *ge dengyou* 各等語, etc.). After the 1930s, official documents began to employ the term *yunyun* 云云 as a closing quotation marker, most likely under the influence of contemporary newspaper and periodical writing styles. Most occurrences of *yunyun* appear in communications from nongovernmental organizations to government offices. Examples:

1. 令開 <u>quoted text</u>. 等因

2. 咨開 <u>quoted text</u>. 等由 (or 等因)

3. 呈稱 <u>quoted text</u>. 等情

Markers That Indicate Who Is Being Quoted

Before beginning a quote from a previously received document, the sender had to state clearly the bureau from which it originated. This required another marker in front of the bureau name indicating the relationship between the sender and the official who sent the original document to him. This type of marker has several forms:

1. *feng* 奉: when the received document came from a superior (some government bureaus, and especially nongovernmental organizations, used the more humble term *qiefeng* 竊奉);

2. *zhun* 准: when the received document came from an equal;

3. *ju* 據: when the received document came from a subordinate;

4. *jiaoxia* 交下 (sometimes *faxia* 發下): when an order was received from a superior official;

5. *chen* 陳: occasionally used when quoting a subordinate or a statement by a private citizen.

Note that both *feng* 奉 and *zhun* 准 correspond to the opening quotation marker *kai* 開, and *ju* 据 to *cheng* 呈, although it was not uncommon to omit *kai* 開 or *cheng* 呈. Whereas *feng, zhun,* and *ju* are sometimes used by themselves, they frequently have a character in front, such as *an* 案 (record, case), meaning that the ensuing quote has relevance to a filed record or past case (or merely to balance the sentence by the inclusion of an extra syllable, i.e., *anfeng* 案奉, *anzhun* 案准, *anju* 案据; or a time word like *xian* 現 or *zi* 兹 (now), *qing* 頃 (just now), or *qian* 前 (previously) (i.e., *xianfeng* 現奉, *qingzhun* 頃奉, *qianju* 前据, etc.). Examples:

1. (案) 奉 <u>bureau name</u> 令開 <u>quoted text</u>. 等因

2. (頃) 准 <u>bureau name</u> 咨開 <u>quoted text</u>. 等由 (or 等因)

3. (前) 據 <u>bureau name</u> 呈開 <u>quoted text</u>. 等情

"Transitional" and "Arrival" Terms

Official documents use the transitional terms *fengci* 奉此, *zhunci* 准此, and *juci* 據此 after the closing quotation marker to lead the reader from the quoted passage into the proceeding text related to the quote. The term *fengci* 奉此 is used after a quote from a superior and thus generally follows *dengyin* 等因 (e.g., 等因。奉此,); *zhunci* 准此 is used after a quote from an equal and thus generally follows *dengyou* 等由 (e.g., 等由。准此), except when an equal wishes to express respect for his colleague and chooses *dengyin*; and *juci* 據此 is used after a quote from a subordinate and generally follows either *dengqing* 等情 or *dengyu* 等語 (e.g., 等情。據; or 等語。據此). A transitional term is set apart from its respective closing quotation marker by a period unless the received document contains an enclosure. In this case, an explanation of the enclosure is inserted between the closing quotation marker and the transitional term.

Some documents also include a term denoting that the document from which a quotation is culled has arrived. This term comes directly after the closing quotation marker and before any enclosure description or transitional term. The two terms most commonly used are (1) *dao* 到, followed by an abbreviation of the author's bureau (i.e., *dao ting* 到廳, *dao shu* 到署), and (2) *qianlai* 前來. When this kind of term is added, the transitional term is commonly omitted. Some officials, for the sake of simplicity, would omit both terms. Some examples:

1. (案) 奉 <u>bureau name</u> 令開 <u>quoted text</u>. 等因. 奉此...

2. (頃) 准 <u>bureau name</u> 咨開 <u>quoted text</u>. 等由 (or 等因). 准此...

3. (前) 據 <u>bureau name</u> 呈開 <u>quoted text</u>. 等情. 據此...

Summary or Paraphrase Markers

In some official documents, the writer may have paraphrased or outlined essential points instead of copying sections of a received document verbatim. In such cases, the passage is often preceded by characters such as *yi* 以, *guanyu* 關於, and *wei* 為 (instead of opening quotation markers such as *kai* 開 or *cheng* 稱).

Moreover, terms such as *zai'an* 在案 (*ge zai'an* 各在案 if more than one in succession), *you'an* 有案, and *zaijuan* 在卷 were used at the end of the summary of previous cases to indicate that the said previous case(s) was on file. Similar markers include *ju . . . yian* (据 . . . 一案), *zhun . . . yian* (准 . . . 一案), and *yiju . . . lüecheng* (以据 . . . 略稱). The choice of these terms had no relation to the rank of the persons involved (in contrast to closing quotation markers). This type of summarizing was primarily used in replies (*fuwen* 復文) or in situations where a summary provided a more adequate or succinct explanation than the original document.

Lingshu Ci 領述詞

If a section of a document does not contain a quote from a received document but directly leads into an explanation of the situation at hand or cites a certain theory or convention, the author would provide a cue word called a *lingshu ci* 領述詞. *Lingshu ci* can be divided into four categories: *qie* 竊 or 切, *cha* 查, *zhao* 照, and *zi* 茲.

1. *qie* 竊 means "in private" or "secret." In official documents it acts as an expression of humility and is usually found in petitions, although occasionally it is written in lateral communications and letters to equals as a show of respect. Some variations on *qie* include *qiewei* 竊維, *qieyi* 竊以, *qiecha* 竊查 , and *qie'an* 竊按:
   a. *qie* 竊: when used alone it generally acts as an introductory particle without any independent meaning. Sometimes *qie* is followed by the author's name or the name of the bureau from which he is sending the document;
   b. *qiewei* 竊維 and *qieyi* 竊以 introduce the author's line of reasoning or the basis for an assertion. *Qiewei* (*wei* as in 思維, thinking) is similar to "我想 . . ." in modern spoken Mandarin; the *yi* 以 in *qieyi* 竊以 means "because" or "for this reason";

176

   c. *qiecha* 竊查 and *qie'an* 竊按 introduce a situation in which the author can check (*cha* 查) a case or written record. What comes next is not a direct quote from a document, but a brief summary by the author.

2. *cha* 查 is used widely in situations in which a record, law, theory, or fact can be looked up. It can be found in any section of a document and is neutral in terms of superior-subordinate usage. Variations on *cha* include *ancha* 案查, *juancha* 卷查, *fucha* 伏查, *jincha* 謹查, *zuncha* 遵查, *fucha* 復查, *zicha* 茲查, *xiancha* 現查, and *weicha* 惟查:

   a. *ancha* 案查 and *juancha* 卷查 mean that the author has checked a case or record on file;

   b. *fucha* (伏查) and *jincha* 謹查 indicate that the author has checked a case or record on file, with the added expression of respect or humility appropriate to an upward document;

   c. *fucha* (復查) (sometimes also *youcha* 又查, *zaicha* 再查, or *gengcha* 更查): when in a complicated matter a sequence of records has been checked, *fucha* 復查 announces each cited document after the first;

   d. *zuncha* 遵查: used in a petition when summarizing a file that a superior had previously ordered checked;

   e. *fucha* (復查), *xiancha* 現查, and *zicha* 茲查 are used to state that the author already has the record in question;

   f. *weicha* 惟查 is used at a transitional point in the passage (*wei* 惟 means "however," "but").

3. *zhao* 照 means "clear" or "known." It is frequently used in combinations, for example, *zhaode* 照得 and *anzhao* 案照, and primarily utilized in downward documents. In rare instances, *anzhao* 案照 can also be found in lateral communications.

   a. *zhaode* 照得 has no substantive meaning. It precedes a statement that is common knowledge. If required, it can be roughly translated as "As everyone knows . . ." or "It is very clear that . . . ";

   b. *anzhao* 案照 has approximately the same meaning as *zhaode*, but is less forceful or authoritative in tone. The two are more or less interchangeable.

4. *zi* 茲 means "now" or "at present." It is usually used in the final section of a document.

Conclusion and Imperative Terms

The function of a conclusion term is to point out that a situation has already been explained above. These terms are found in the concluding sections of the document (thus the situation need not be repeated) and what follows is usually an explanation of the purpose of the document or a demand/request of the recipient. Conclusion terms can be divided into three categories based on the hierarchical relationship of sender and receiver:

1. *zifeng qianyin* 茲奉前因, *fengling qianyin* 奉令前因, or *yuanfeng qianyin* 緣奉前因 is used when instructions, orders, or any communication had been received from a superior;

2. *zhunzi qianyou* 准咨前由, *zhunhan qianyou* 准函前由, or *zizhun qianyou* 茲准前由 is used when a letter or lateral communication had been received from an equal. Sometimes, in order to express respect for the author of the received document, the official used *zhunzi qianyin* 准咨前因;

3. *jucheng qianqing* 據呈前情 or *ziju qianqing* 茲據前情 is used when a document had been received from a subordinate.

In addition, the term *weici* 為此 is used exclusively for downward documents (i.e., *ling* 令, *bugao* 布告, etc.). On some occasions, as in a relatively short document, transitional terms (*fengci* 奉此, *zhunci* 准此, *juci* 据此) are used to sum things up.

Imperative terms indicate that the following text is an order or request and therefore generally appear in the concluding section. They consist of characters like *yang* 仰, *qing* 請, *ken* 懇, *qi* 祈, *xi* 希, or *fan* 煩. They are often preceded by such auxiliary verbs as *hexing* 合行 (to a subordinate, e.g., 合行令仰), *xiangying* 相應 (to an equal, e.g., 相應函請), or *lihe* 理合 (to a superior, e.g., 理合呈請). Here, *hexing*, *xiangying*, and *lihe* all mean "should." In a downward document, these auxiliary verbs can be omitted (e.g., *yangji zunzhao* 仰即遵照).

Appellation Terms 稱謂詞

Official documents are filled with different appellations and titles not regularly found in other written materials. Below are a number of examples:

1. *jun* 鈞: originally functioning as a unit of weight in ancient times (30 catties or 15 kg), in Republican period documents *jun* was used as a respectful form of address to a superior governmental organ (e.g., *junfu* 鈞府, *junyuan* 鈞院, *junting* 鈞廳, etc.), an official of higher rank (e.g., *junzhang* 鈞長 and *junzuo* 鈞座—*zuo* [seat] symbolized a high official's position in the imperial court and became a general term for the highest-ranking officeholders during the Republic), an order or instruction of a superior (e.g., *junming* 鈞命, *junling* 鈞令, *junshi* 鈞示, *junyu* 鈞諭, etc.), or a superior's decision on a matter (e.g., *juncai* 鈞裁,

junduo 鈞奪, *junhe* 鈞核, etc.). Telegrams to one's superior or equal frequently employed the term *junjian* 鈞鑒 as a salutation;

2. *da* 大: used as a prefix to refer to high central government organs (e.g., *dafu* 大府, *dabu* 大部) or lateral communications received from an equal (e.g., *dazi* 大咨, *dahan* 大函);

3. *gui* 貴: a term of respect for a recipient who is an equal (e.g., *guibu* 貴部, *guiju* 貴局, *guizhuxi* 貴主席, *guiyuanzhang* 貴院長, *guixianzhang* 貴縣長, etc.);

4. *gai* 該: "the said . . ."—a substitute term used to refer to a subordinate or a third party (e.g., *gaibu* 該部, *gaiju* 該局, *gaifu* 該府, *gaixian* 該縣, *gaibuzhang* 該部長, etc.);

5. *er* 爾: sometimes used as a pronoun by a superior addressing a subordinate or a government official addressing private citizens;

6. *bi* 敝: a term of humility used in lateral communications to refer to one's own bureau or oneself (e.g., *biting* 敝廳, *biju* 敝局, *bitingzhang* 敝廳長, *bijuzhang* 敝局長, etc.);

7. *shu* 屬: added by a subordinate as a prefix to his own bureau in a communication to his immediate superior (e.g., *shuju* 屬局, *shuhui* 屬會, *shusuo* 屬所, etc.);

8. *zhi* 職: a term used by a subordinate official to refer to his own bureau in a document to a superior (e.g., *zhiting* 職廳, *zhixian* 職縣, etc.);

9. *ben* 本: used in lateral and downward documents to refer to the author's own bureau (e.g., *benyuan* 本院, *benting* 本廳, *benbu* 本部, etc.) and/or the person responsible for the document in that bureau (e.g., *benyuanzhang* 本院長, *benbuzhang* 本部長, etc.). On April 18, 1931, the Nationalist government stipulated that *ben* 本 be used exclusively to refer to one's own bureau in all upward, lateral, and downward documents, thereby abolishing terms like *bi* 敝, *shu* 屬, and *zhi* 職. Nevertheless, *bi, shu*, and *zhi* continued to appear in government communications in spite of the new regulation;

10. *xian* 憲: rarely seen in Republican documents. In the Qing period *xian* was a term of respect for superior officials, including the rank of prefect (e.g., general-governor = *duxian* 督憲, prefect = *fuxian* 府憲, etc.).

III. Punctuation and Sectioning

Use of Quotation Marks

Before the 1930s and even up to the 1940s, most official documents continued to use character combinations like the ones mentioned above as quotation markers. However, symbols different but equivalent to Western-language quotation marks gradually began to gain wider use.

Elevation

One pre-Republican convention observed in official documents was for bureaucrats to begin a new line at the same level or a certain number of spaces higher than the regular text when writing the name of a superior or an important bureau, etc. This represented a show of respect and deference. In Republican documents some elements of this practice remained. For instance, the proper name of a superior bureau was moved to the top of the following line. An indirect reference to a superior bureau might receive the same treatment. However, depending on the relationship of the two bureaus involved, the indirect reference might only be separated from the preceding text by a blank space or just written as a natural continuation of the text. As a sign of respect, the names, official titles, statements, and actions of superior officials might also be elevated to the top of the next line.

Rules for Sectioning of Text and Quotes

Regulations formulated by the Ministry of Education in 1930 stipulated that documents over ten lines should be divided into paragraphs. According to the new rule, the first line of each paragraph began at the third space down, and every other line of the section began at the top. In addition, all quoted passages of over two lines were divided into a new section, with the first line indented five spaces (starting at the sixth), and every other line of the quote began at the fourth space down. If the quoted passages were relatively long, they too were to be divided into paragraphs according to the same formula. Each paragraph of the quote began with an opening quotation mark, the closing quotation mark coming only at the end of the entire quote (note: all secondary quotes within the primary quote were not further indented). After the closing quotation mark, the closing quotation marker (*dengyin* 等因, *dengqing* 等情, *dengyou* 等由, *dengyu* 等語) was placed at the top of the next line.

Chapter 20

Documents on Wu Yunchu's Enterprises:
Introduction and Glossary
吳蘊初企業檔案

Wu Yunchu, a native of Jiading county, Jiangsu province, was the founder of the Tien Chu Ve-tsin Manufacturing Company (Tianchu weijing zhizao chang 天櫥味精製造廠 [Heavenly Kitchen Monosodium Glutamate Manufacturing Company]), with headquarters in Shanghai and a branch in Hong Kong; the Tien Yuen Electro-Chemical Works (Tianyuan dianhua chang 天原電化廠); the Tien Lee Synthetic Nitrogen Products Company (Tianli danqi zhipin chang 天利氮氣製品廠); the Tien Sheng Ceramic Works (Tiansheng taoqi chang 天盛陶器廠); and other chemical enterprises. Wu and his contemporary Fan Xudong (范旭東), the founder of the Chiu Ta Salt Refining Company (Jiuda jingyan gongsi 久大精鹽公司) and the Yung-Li Chemical Industries (Yongli huaxue gongye gongsi 永利化學工業公司) in Tianjin, were often referred to as "the Northern Fan and the Southern Wu" (北范南吳).

Born in 1891 into a poor family, Wu had no schooling until the age of thirteen. After studying for two years in a private academy, he entered the Shanghai Foreign Language School (Shanghai guangfang yanguan 上海廣方言館). Subsequently, he studied chemistry in the Ministry of Army's Shanghai Munitions Special School (Lujun bu Shanghai haibing gongxue tang 陸軍部上海兵工學堂) and returned to the school to teach after graduating in 1911.

When the Shanghai Munitions School closed in 1913, Wu went to Wuhan to work as a laboratory technician in the Hanyang Iron & Steel Works (Hanyang gangtie chang 漢陽鋼鐵廠). He was appointed brickyard manager of the Hanyang Iron & Steel Works one year later. In 1915, he was invited to Tianjin to establish a nitric alkali works (xiaojian chang 硝鹼廠). After the effort failed, he went to work for the Tianjin Mint as a laboratory technician. The following year he returned to Hankou to work for the Hanyang Arsenal Works (Hanyang binggong chang 漢陽兵工廠), first as head of its physical chemistry section and then as chief of its pharmaceutical section.

In 1921 Wu Yunchu entered a partnership with Song Weicheng (宋偉臣), a capitalist who had opened the Xiechang Match Factory (Xiechang huochai chang 燮昌火柴廠), to establish the Chichang Nitric Alkali Works (Chichang xiaojian gongsi 熾昌硝鹼公司) in Hankou. With Song providing the capital and Wu the technical leadership, the company produced materials necessary for manufacturing matches. In the same year, Wu Yunchu went to Shanghai and established the Chichang New Ox-Glue Works (Chichang xinniu pijiaochang 熾昌新牛皮膠廠) to produce the glue needed to manufacture matches. At the time, monosodium glutamate, a profitable condiment produced in Japan, attracted Wu's attention. In 1922 he found a way to mass-produce monosodium glutamate at low cost. In the following year when Zhang Yiyun (張逸云), a Shanghai condiment businessman, opened the Tien Chu Ve-Tsin Manufacturing Company, Wu Yunchu was appointed manager of the company. Their Buddhist Hand (Foshou 佛手) brand of monosodium glutamate

181

competed well with its Japanese counterpart. With the movement to boycott Japanese goods, Tien Yuen products became increasingly popular in China and Southeast Asia. Consequently, the value of the company's annual output increased from 100,000 yuan a year to over one million yuan. In 1927 annual profits reached several hundred thousand yuan, with a daily output of 1,600 pounds.

According to the initial agreement between Wu and Zhang Yiyun, Wu received 0.10 yuan for every pound of monosodium glutamate produced by the company, a lucrative reward that earned him a monthly income of 2,000 yuan. Within a few years he accumulated tens of thousands of yuan, with which he bought shares of Tien Yuen and eventually became both its manager and majority stockholder.

Wu Yunchu paid attention not only to chemical production but also to research. In 1928 he founded the China Institute of Chemical Industry (Zhongguo huaxue gongye yanjiusuo 中國化學工業研究所) and chaired its board of directors. The Tien Yuen Electro-Chemical Works provided funds for the institute to conduct chemical experiments to meet the needs of the company and the chemical industry at large. Wu Yunchu also supported the publication of *Huaxue gongye* 化學工業 (Chemical industry), the first journal of its kind in China. Because of his work in chemical research, Wu was elected vice president of both the Chinese Chemical Engineering Association and the General Federation of Chinese Industry and nominated as a director of the Shanghai Chemical Materials Guild.

From profits made in the Tien Chu Ve-Tsin, Wu Yunchu opened the Tien Yuen Electro-Chemical Works in 1929 to produce hydrochloric acid, caustic soda, bleach, and other chlorine-based products. Previously, all the materials for making monosodium glutamate had been imported from Japan. Wu's purpose in opening the Tien Yuen Works was to provide Tien Chu with domestically manufactured materials. Tien Yuen means "raw materials for the Tien Chu Company." Within several years the capitalization of the Tien Yuen Electro-Chemical Works increased from 200,000 yuan to 1.05 million yuan and output grew sixfold.

In 1932, the Tien Chu Ve-Tsin Manufacturing Company was forced to reorganize due to speculation by Zhang Yiyun's heir. Wu used the opportunity to increase his shareholding position and gained control of the company. He expanded the scale and variety of production by establishing the No. 2 and No. 3 branches of the Tien Yuen Works.

During the 1933 boycott of Japanese goods, he bought a fighter/trainer plane for 120,000 yuan, which he named "Tien Chu" and donated to the Chinese Aviation Society. An advertising campaign trumpeting this "patriotic donation of planes" boosted sales at home and abroad. Profits in Southeast Asia increased over 300,000 yuan in that year. In July 1935 Wu Yunchu reorganized Tien Chu into a limited liability company and increased its capitalization. That year he also founded the Tien Sheng Ceramic Works. Previously, China had to rely on imports for its acid and alkali containers. The newly established Tien Sheng Works had a capacity to produce acid- and alkali-resistant containers in sufficient amounts to meet domestic needs.

In 1936 Wu founded the Tien Lee Synthetic Nitrogen Products Company to produce ammonia with hydrogen, a byproduct from the Tien Yuen Works. With additional equipment, the Tien Lee Company soon started to produce nitric acid. Apart from the newly collected shares and the profits made by the Tien Chu Company, Wu Yunchu also obtained large amounts of capital from the government-affiliated Kincheng Banking Corporation (Jincheng yinhang 金城銀行).

After the outbreak of war with Japan in 1937, Wu Yunchu moved equipment from the Tien Chu Company and the Tien Yuen Works to Sichuan. The rest of his enterprises, which remained in Shanghai, were either destroyed in the war or operated under German names to avoid seizure. Meanwhile, Wu founded a branch of the Tien Chu Ve-Tsin Manufacturing Company in Kowloon, Hong Kong, then still under British rule. In 1939 Wu added an acid and alkali department to the Kowloon branch in order to make it self-reliant in the production of hydrochloric acid. The branch works was seized by the Japanese when they attacked Hong Kong after Pearl Harbor, but Wu managed to transport important equipment to Sichuan.

In Chongqing, the Tien Yuen Works and the Tien Chu Company resumed production in 1940 of monosodium glutamate, hydrochloric acid, caustic soda, and bleach. A shortage of funds made it necessary to bring in additional investment. By 1942 the Kincheng Banking Corporation held 60 percent of the Tien Yuen Works' (Sichuan) shares. In 1943 the National Resources Commission also invested in the Tien Yuen Works. After the war Wu Yunchu re-established his enterprises in Shanghai.

Wu Yunchu held a series of important positions in the National Government. He was a member of the National Economic Commission, the National Resources Commission, the National Political Consultative Council, and the Planning Committee of the Ministry of the Economy. He also chaired the National Industry Association.

After 1949 Wu Yunchu assumed a variety of offices in the People's Republic of China. He became a member of the East China Military and Administrative Committee, a member of the Shanghai Municipal People's Government, vice chairman of the Shanghai Association of Industry and Commerce, and chairman of the Shanghai Guild of Chemical Material Industry. Wu also founded the Yunchu Public Welfare Foundation (Yunchu gongyi jijinhui 蘊初公益基金會). He died on October 15, 1953.

The documents in this chapter are stored in the Shanghai Municipal Archives. Two volumes of these documents have been published by the archives under the title *Wu Yunchu qiye shiliao* 吳蘊初企業史料 (Historical materials on Wu Yunchu's business enterprises) (Shanghai: Dang'an chubanshe, 1989). The volumes consist of documents from the Tien Chu Ve-Tsin Manufacturing Company and the Tien Yuen Electro-Chemical Works.

These documents reveal aspects of the relationship between the state and a privately operated company, the Shanghai Tien Yuen Electro-Chemical Works. Document 1, for instance, is the authorized regulations of the company. Article 2 of the document, in particular, shows that the company regulations were reviewed and approved by the responsible government department (in this case, the Ministry of Finance), and that the company received assistance from the government in the form of a tax exemption.

Documents 2 and 3 concern the Shanghai Tien Yuen Electro-Chemical Works' petitions for an increase in the salt quota. In November 1928 the company obtained approval from the Ministry of Finance for an annual tax exemption on 14,000 piculs of salt used in its production. Document 2 is a response to the company's application for an additional 34,000 piculs of salt annually, accompanied by a tax exemption. The document indicates that the Ministry of Finance refused to increase the company's salt quota for two reasons: (1) the company had installed only 40 of the planned 120 electrolyzers, and (2) it was difficult to know whether trial production would be successful. It is important to remember that salt production, transportation, and sale were government monopolies administered by the Ministry of Finance. The Ministry of Industry and Commerce did not have jurisdiction over salt affairs and taxation. When it received the Tien Yuen Company's petition for a larger salt allotment and a tax exemption, it had to communicate with the Ministry of Finance regarding the company's petition. Document 2 is a communication from the Ministry of Industry and Commerce, forwarding the decision of the Ministry of Finance. Document 3, on the other hand, is an approval from the Ministry of Finance for an increase of 28,560 piculs in the company's salt quota. It also instructs the company where to obtain the allotted salt. Documents 2 and 3 reveal an important aspect of the state's control of the economy. This is expressed in the contrast between the rejection of the first application and the approval of the second, and the fact that the Salt Administration's Songjiang assistant district inspector (Songjiang yunfu 松江運副) had to inspect the electrochemical company's 40 newly installed electrolyzers before approval was granted.

Document 10 is an express-mail letter in lieu of a telegram, and Document 11 is an official letter to the company issued by the Chemical Industry Department of the National Resources Commission. The National Government's control of the economy during World War II can be seen in various sections of these documents, such as the statement in Document 10 that the budget for purchases from American aid projects should be presented to the Supreme National Defense Council via the Executive Yuan, and Document 11's reference to Chiang Kai-shek's order to the Natural Resources Commission to draw up a three-year plan.

Document 12 is a draft of an official letter by the Tien Yuen Electro-Chemical Works to the Bureau for Settling Enemy and Puppet Regime Properties in the Jiangsu, Zhejiang, and Anhui Areas. The bureau had previously demanded that the company pay 283,088,200 yuan for the goods and materials left in the electrochemical works by the Japanese. In the document, the company asks the government to exclude from payment items that could not be purchased—clear evidence of the state's control over the private sector.

This chapter introduces ten types of documents, including 註冊章程 (*zhuce zhangcheng*: authorized regulations), 訓令 (*xunling*: decree), 批文 (*piwen*: official reply to a subordinate body), 呈文 (*chengwen*: petition), 令 (*ling*: command), 呈文稿 (*chengwen'gao*: draft for a petition), 通知 (*tongzhi*: notice), 函 (*han*: letter), 代電 (*daidian*: an official letter sent by express mail in lieu of a telegram), and 公函稿 (*gonghan'gao*: draft for an official document).

Document 1 (vol. 2, p. 5)

The Authorized Regulations of the Tien Yuen Electro-Chemical Works Co., Ltd.
天原電化廠股份有限公司奉核准章程

This document contains the authorized regulations of a private enterprise (註册章程). Phrases such as "奉 . . . 核准," "給照," and "免納 . . . 税" are commonly found in this type of record. The document stipulates the company name, official approval, business scope, location, and announcement method.

奉准	fèngzhǔn	to receive authorization (i.e., authorized), authorize, approve
本	běn	this, one's own
電化廠	diànhuàchǎng	electro-chemical works
股份	gǔfèn	stock share
有限公司	yoǔxiàn gōngsī	limited company
蒙	méng	receive
核准	hézhǔn	to approve; approval
鹽酸	yánsuān	hydrochloric acid
漂粉	piǎofěn	bleach
燒鹼	shāojiǎn	caustic soda
試辦期	shìbàn qī	initial trial period
免納 . . . 税	miǎnnà . . . shuì	to exempt from taxation
電解法	diànjiěfǎ	electrolysis
股東會	gǔdōng huì	shareholders' meeting

由 . . . 議決	yóu . . . yìjué	let . . . deliberate and decide
展期	zhǎnqī	extension
函告	hán gào	inform by letter
公告之	gōnggào zhī	announce it

Document 2 (vol. 2, pp. 6–8)

The Ministry of Industry and Commerce's Decree Concerning the Tien Yuen Works' Petition for an Increase in the Quota of Tax-Exempted Salt
工商部關于天源電化廠請求增加鹽額并免稅的訓令

This document is a decree (訓令) issued by a superior to a subordinate. The format of the cover page of Document 2 was designed for the convenience of processing. It provides us with valuable information. The words at the top of the page indicate that this was a document received by the Shanghai Tien Yuen Electro-Chemical Company. The bottom of the page is where the serial number for the document (as with all incoming documents) should have been entered. The left margin is the place for the serial number of the incoming decree, as well as the date it was received. The first column on the right is the summary of the document, the end of which is marked by the word 由 *you*, a conventional word to conclude the synopsis. The section (附件 *fujian*) at the bottom of the right-hand corner is kept blank, showing that there was no appendix attached to the document.

A few more words about the cover page: when sending a document like this, the Ministry of Industry and Commerce simply filled in the name of the addressee at the top and the subject summary in the first column on the right. The three other columns for 擬辦 (decision recommendation), 決定辦法 (final decision), and 備考 (special note) were intended for the receiving agency. Normally, a middle- or low-rank official, manager, or staffer suggested a decision and then a person of higher rank gave approval.

This document is largely a quotation by the Ministry of Industry and Commerce of a lateral communication from the Ministry of Finance, starting from 內開：查天原 in the third line of the main text and ending with 咨復查照等因 in the last line of the next page. In the quotation, the Ministry of Finance refers to the Tien Yuen Works' case (查天原 . . . 有案) and quotes a report from the Salt Administration's Songjiang assistant district inspector (復稱：該廠 . . . 等語).

Vocabulary items commonly found in this type of documents include 令飭, 令仰, 知照, 轉, 核辦, 批示, and 屬實.

訓令	xùnlìng	decree
事由	shìyóu	(a conventional phrase used in official documents) main subject (of a communication)

准	zhǔn	(a conventional word to acknowledge receipt of a communication from an equal) "have received" or "according to (a document) that we have received (from . . .)"
咨覆	zīfù	reply in the form of a lateral communication
該廠	gāichǎng	this factory, the said factory
增用鹽斤	zēngyòng yánjīn	to increase salt used (in production)
請免稅	qǐng miǎnshuì	to apply for a tax exemption
令飭	lìngchì	order
知照	zhīzhào	notify; notified; take note of
由	yóu	(a conventional word to end a summary of a document)
為 . . . 事	wéi . . . shì	(a common phrase for subject summary; in this case, it briefly indicates the purpose of the document, that is, to notify the Tianyuan Works in the form of an order)
令知	lìngzhī	order . . . to know; notify in the form of an order
查 . . . 在案	chá . . . zài'àn	we find that (used to introduce something at the beginning of a document; the word "cha" is often used to refer to previous cases on record)
前據 . . . 等情	qiánjù . . . děngqíng	according to the previous . . . ; we have formerly received . . . from . . . regarding . . .
呈	chéng	petition

新購	xīn'gòu	recently purchased
轉咨	zhuǎnzī	send a letter of lateral communication to (the Ministry of Finance) on behalf of (the Tien Yuen Works); in historical documents the word 轉 is often used to indicate that the incoming document was not processed by the receiving agency; instead it was forwarded to another agency for handling; 轉 is often used in such verb combinations as 轉令, 轉呈, 轉飭, 轉知, 轉函, etc.
財部	cáibù	Ministry of Finance
繼續免稅	jìxù miǎnshuì	to continue to exempt from taxation
咨請	zīqǐng	to ask in the form of an official lateral communication
核辦	hébàn	to examine (a case, etc.) and act acoordingly; to consider and carry out accordingly
知照	zhīzhào	to notify, take note of
茲准 . . . 在案	zīzhǔn . . . zaì'àn	now we have received (a reply from the Ministry of Finance) on our record; according to the received . . . on our record
咨復	zīfù	to reply in the form of a lateral communication
內開	neìkāi	(often used to introduce the content of a received document; it can be translated as "it reads")
查 . . . 有案	chǎ . . . yǒuàn	find . . . on record (the phrase is often used to refer to an old case)

189

年額	niáné	annual quota
前經核准	qiánjīng hézhǔn	was previously approved after examination
援例	yuánlì	in accordance with a precedent
當	dāng	should, ought to
以 . . . 是否屬實	yǐ . . . shìfǒu shǔshí	regarding whether . . . is true or not
令飭	lìngchì	order . . . to do something
松江運副	Sōngjiāng yùnfù	Salt Administration's Songjiang assistant district inspector
詳查具復	xiángchá jùfù	to investigate carefully and submit a reply
電槽	diàncáo	eletrolyzer
復稱 . . . 等語	fùchēng . . . děngyǔ	(beginning and ending quotation signposts denoting a quote culled from the reply [fù] of the Songjiang assistant district inspector), a reply, stating " . . . "
本部	běnbù	this, our office (here it refers to the Ministry of Finance)
以 . . . 之案	yǐ . . . zhī'àn	the case regarding . . .
事閱	shìyuè	this (matter) has passed . . .
出品	chūpǐn	product
優良	yōuliáng	excellent
銷場	xiāochǎng	market
暢旺	chàngwàng	smooth and brisk
均難預計	jūnnán yùjì	both are difficult to predict

至	zhì	as to, as for, with regard to
須俟 . . . 個月	xūsì . . . gèyuè	should wait for . . . months
自可	zìkě	naturally it may be
從緩	cónghuǎn	be postponed
經	jīng	already
令飭	lìngchì	(the subject of this order is the Ministry of Finance)
俟 . . . 後	sì . . . hòu	wait until . . .
撿同	jiǎntóng	report together with, accompanied by
再行核辦	zàixíng hébàn	to examine further, then handle accordingly
在案	zài'àn	(this signpost marks the end of the Ministry of Finance's reference to a case on record)
茲准前因	zīzhǔn qiányīn	now based on the above situation
相應 . . . 咨復	xiāngyìng . . . zīfù	(the Ministry of Finance) accordingly reply in the form of a lateral communication
查照	cházhào	reference; please take a note of . . . for future reference
等因	děngyīn	(a signpost used to mark the end of a quotation from the communication of a superior [here it is signaling the end of the Ministry of Industry and Commerce's quotation of the Ministry of Finance's lateral communication])
准此	zhǔncǐ	according to this, therefore, accordingly

合行	héxíng	should
令仰	lìngyǎng	instruct /order (someone to do something)
此令	cǐ lìng	(a conventional phrase to end a decree)

Document 3 (vol. 2, pp. 9–10)

The Ministry of Finance's Approval of a Request from the Tien Yuen Electro-Chemical Works for an Increase in Its Salt Quota
財政部核准天原電化廠增加鹽額

This document is an official reply to a subordinate body (批). The big characters on the right of the document indicate that it was issued by the Ministry of Finance. The smaller characters on the same line give the category code of the document (鹽字) and its serial number. 鹽字 indicates that the document concerns salt affairs. The second line from the right specifies the addressee of this reply—the Tien Yuen Electro-Chemical Works. The characters 事由 in the third line initiate a summary of the document, which ends with the word 由 in the fifth line. This is followed by a summary in the sixth and seventh lines of the Tianyuan Works' petition to the Ministry presented on March 22, 1937, which also ends with the word 由. The official reply concludes with the conventional phrase 此批 (hereby this reply is given).

In the main text, the document first recounts how the Tien Yuen Works' case has been processed. It was first examined by the former Inspectorate of the Salt Gabelle in Songjiang District (淞江稽核分所). Then the Directorate-General of Salt Administration passed on its report to the Ministry of Finance. The Ministry of Finance instructed that the Tien Yuen Works obtain the salt allotment from the North Huai River area. In addition, it also instructed the Directorate-General of Salt Administration to forward the order to the Songjiang Salt Administration and the Lianghuai (region to the north and south of the Huai River) Salt Administration.

Phrases regularly used in this type of document include 應與照准 and 此批.

事由	shìyóu	subject, content (signpost preceding a summary of the content of a communication)
核准 . . . 由	hézhǔn . . . yóu	(this signpost brackets the summary of the document's content)
工鹽	gōngyǎn	industrial salt
用額	yòngé	amount used, quota
市担	shìdàn	picul (a unit of weight; = 0.05 ton)

配運	pèiyùn	to allocate and transport
仰即知照	yǎng jí zhīzhào	you should immediately take a note of it (a common phrase used in instructions or orders to let subordinates know the result of the document process)
迅賜核准	xùncì hézhǔn	to grant a quick examination and approval
呈悉	chéngxī	the petition is known, noted
業經 . . . 勘明屬實，由 . . . 轉報到部	yèjīng . . . kānmíng shǔshí, yóu . . . zhuǎnbào dàobù	(used to indicate the flow of a document's transmission)
松江稽核分所	Sōngjiāng jīhé fēnsuǒ	Inspectorate of the Salt Gabelle in the Songjiang District
勘明	kānmíng	investigate, survey
鹽務總局	yánwù zǒngjú	The Directorate-General of Salt Administration
轉報	zhuǎnbào	report on behalf of (the Inspectorate of the Salt Gabelle in the Songjiang District)
到部	dàobù	arrived at the ministry (here the Ministry of Finance)
覆核	fùhé	re-examine
無異	wúyì	the same as
連	lián	together with
應予照准	yīng yǔ zhàozhǔn	should be given approval accordingly
向 . . . 配運	xiàng . . . pèiyùn	to purchase and transport the alloted amount from . . .
除 . . . 外, 仰即知照	chu . . . wài, yǎng jí zhīzhào	in addition to (instructing the Directorate-General of Salt Administration) you should (also) note this

轉飭	zhuǎnchì	to pass on the order; order on behalf of (the Ministry of Finance); to in turn order
松江兩淮管理局	Sōngjiāng-Liǎnghuai guǎnlǐjú	(collective term referring to the Songjiang Salt Administration and the Lianghuai Salt Administration)
此批	cǐpī	(a conventional phrase used to mark the end of a written instruction)
政務次長	zhèngwù cìzhǎng	administrative vice minister
代拆	dàichāi	open (a letter, etc.) on somebody's behalf
代行	dàixíng	act on someone's behalf

Document 4 (vol. 2, p. 11)

Tien Yuen Electro-Chemical Works' Petition
to the Ministry of Industry for a Tax Exemption
天原電化廠呈請實業部准免出品稅

Document 4 is a petition (呈) submitted by a private enterprise to a ministry. This type of document begins by indicating the party presenting the petition (具呈人), followed by a summary of the document using the formula 呈為 . . . 事 (This petition is a request concerning the matter of . . .) or 呈為復請 . . . 事 (This petition is a request, again, concerning the matter of . . .). The document ends with the formula 謹呈 (petition sincerely presented to . . .), indicating to which authority the petition was presented.

Much of the first half of this document is the Tien Yuen Works' quotation of the instruction from the Ministry of Industry, which begins with 批開 and ends with 此批等因. This quotation in turn contains another quotation (i.e., the report of the Review Committee for Industry Rewards [報告 . . . 等語]).

Phrases commonly found in these documents include 具呈人, 呈請, 復請, 仰懇, and 俯賜.

實業部	shíyè bù	the Ministry of Industry
具呈人	jùchéng rén	the party presenting the petition
呈為 . . . 事	chéngwèi . . . shì	(a common formula used to summarize the content of a petition; this phrase normally appears at the beginning of a document or quotation [also written 呈為 . . . 由])
復請	fùqǐng	to request again
准免 . . . 稅	zhǔnmiǎn . . . shuì	approval of the tax exemption for
陳明	chénmíng	to state clearly
緣由	yuányóu	reason

仰懇俯賜	yǎngkěn fǔcì	respectfully request you to grant us
查照	cházhào	to consult, refer to
獎勵辦法 奉...批開	jiǎnglì bànfǎ fèng ... pīkāi	a method of reward, a means of rewarding according to the instruction of (opening quotation mark for the Ministry of Industry's instruction; the quotation ends with "此批 ... 等因")
鈞部	jūnbù	your ministry (Ministry of Industry)
呈悉	chéngxī	petition is noted (the ministry noted the petition from the Tien Yuen Works)
查此案	chá cǐàn	having examined this case (here 查 means that the author consulted how the case had been processed)
前据	qiánjù	according to a previous (report from ...); have already received ...
獎勵工業審查 委員會	jiǎnglì gōngyè shěnchá wěiyuánhuì	Review Committee for Industry Rewards
該廠所製...等語	gāichǎng suǒzhì ... děngyǔ	(a summary report from the Review Committee for Industry Rewards)
尚屬	shàngshǔ	can be considered
純淨	chúnjìng	pure, clean
尚未	shàngweì	not yet
外埠	wàibù	other ports
毋庸	wúyōng	need not
擬准	nǐzhǔn	to propose to accept, approve
以...為限	yǐ ... wéixiàn	to set ... as the limit

若干	ruògān	a certain amount
擔	dàn	picul (a unit of weight; = 0.05 ton)
由 . . . 定之	yóu . . . dìngzhī	to be determined by . . .
等語	děngyù	here ends (the Ministry of Industry's quotation of the report of the Review Committee for Industry Rewards)
當經 . . . 復核	dāngjīng . . . fùhé	at that time to be re-examined by
本部	běnbù	our ministry (Ministry of Industry)
如所擬辦理	rú suǒnǐ bànlǐ	to be handled as proposed
咨請	zīqǐng	send a communication requesting . . .
據呈前情	jùchéng qiánqíng	based on the above situation in your petition; having received the petition regarding the above issue
應俟 . . . 後再行	yìngsì . . . hòu zàixíng	should wait until . . . and then
到部	dàobù	reach the ministry (Ministry of Industry)
等由	děngyóu	(signpost signaling end of quotation [here indicating Tien Yuen's quotation of the Ministry of Industry's instruction])
奉此	fèngcǐ	having received this (from here on, the writer begins to explain Tien Yuen Works' situation)
伏查	fúchá	now we find (伏 is a self-deprecatory word)
敝	bì	this (a self-deprecatory word)
明文	míngwén	stipulated in writing
運銷	yùnxiāo	transportation and sale

三友實業社	sānyǒu shíyè shè	Sanyou Industrial Company
改良場	gǎiliáng chǎng	(silkworm) improvement farm
埠	bù	port
承銷	chéngxiāo	undertake sales of the product
不一而足	bùyī'érzú	by no means an isolated case
消納	xiāonà	to take in for consumption
苟	gǒu	if
有 ... 之虞	yǒu ... zhīyú	there will be the danger of
供過于求	gōngguòyúqiú	supply exceeds demand
陳明緣由	chénmíng yuǎnyóu	to state the situation clearly
復請	fùqǐng	to petition again
出品税	chūpǐn shuì	production tax
并	bìng	and
俯賜	fǔcì	graciously grant (a decision; a respectful phrase for an inferior to describe the action of granting [a decision or something] from a superior; similar phrases are 俯准 give [your] gracious approval, 俯允 grant [your] gracious permission, 俯示 give [your] gracious instruction)
奉批前因	fèngpī qiányīn	based on the received instruction concerning the above situation; having received instruction regarding the above issue
理合	lǐhé	ought to, should

具文	jùwén	to prepare a document
呈請	chéngqǐng	to petition for; present to . . . for
鑒核施行	jiànhé shīxíng	to appraise and execute
謹呈	jǐnchéng	sincerely presented to (this phrase is normally followed by the name of the recipient)

Document 5 (vol. 2, p. 12)

The Ministry of Industry's Directive to the Tien Yuen Electro-Chemical Works
實業部致天原電化廠令

This document is a directive (指令) given by a higher authority to a subordinate concerning the latter's petition. At the beginning of the document is the category code of the document (工字), indicating that it concerns the industrial sector, and the serial number (第3446號). According to the format and formula of this type of document, it starts with the word 令, signifying to whom the directive is given. This is followed by the specific instruction, which is initiated by the phrase 為令行事 (for the purpose of performing an order), and concluded with 此令 (order is hereby given). Words frequently used in such an instruction include 為令行事, 查, 准此, and 此令.

為令行事	wéilìng xíngshì	to perform an order (this phrase is used to indicate the purpose of the document)
查 . . . 各在案	chá . . . gè zài'àn	(we) find . . . all on the record
該公司 . . . 一案	gāigōngsī . . . yian	the case of . . . regarding this company
業經	yèjīng	already
咨准	zīzhǔn	have received a lateral communication from (the Ministry of Finance; 准 indicates a quotation or reference to a document from an agency of the same bureaucratic standing or without subordinate relation; it does not mean approval or permission)
准 . . . 展長一年 免税	zhǔn . . . zhǎncháng yīnǐan mǐanshùi	to approve tax exemtion for . . . to be extended for one year
專制權	zhuānzhì quán	patent right
運輸費	yùnshū fèi	transport expenses

均毋庸議	jūnwúyōngyì	neither needs to be discussed
茲准	zīzhǔn	now having received (a lateral communication from the Ministry of Finance)
節稱	jiéchēng	an abbreviated version states . . .
自 . . . 起 . . . 為止	zì . . . qǐ . . . weízhǐ	begin from . . . and end in . . .
扣	kòu	to deduct
填發	tiánfā	to issue
此令	cǐlìng	order is hereby given; hence this order
附	fù	enclosed, attached

Document 6 (vol. 2, p. 13)

Tien Yuen Electro-Chemical Works' Petition to the Ministry of Industry (Draft)
天原電化廠致實業部呈(稿)

This document, like Document 4, is a petition (呈) submitted by a private enterprise to a ministry. However, being a draft, it omits information on who is submitting the petition (具呈人). Unlike Document 4, this document begins with a detailed summary of the purpose of the petition (呈為呈請 . . . 事). Words commonly found in these documents include 具呈人, 復請, 仰懇, and 俯賜.

瞬已屆滿	shùnyǐ jièmǎn	has expired quickly
懇請賜予	kěnqǐng cìyǔ	earnestly request . . . to favor us with . . .
續減	xùjiǎn	to extend a reduction
咨商	zīshāng	to send a communication in order to consult
核定	hédìng	to ratify after examination
以利	yǐlì	in order to benefit
維 . . . 生存	wéi . . . shēngcún	to safeguard the survival of
竊查 . . . 在案	qièchá . . . zài'àn	we humbly find . . . on record
仰荷	yǎnghè	it should be respectfully appreciated that . . .
航輪	hánglún	steamboat
暨	jì	and
一等	yīděng	one grade
茲查	zīchá	we now find . . .

亦將屆滿	yìjiāng jièmǎn	will also expire
不景氣	bùjǐngqì	depression, slump
傾銷	qīngxiāo	to dump
益烈	yìliè	keener, more competitive
一跌再跌	yīdiēzàidiē	(the prices) continue to drop
受創頗深	shòuchuǎng pōshēn	to suffer a heavy loss
輒以	zhéyǐ	often because
激昂	qí áng	very high
故	gù	therefore
不借 . . . 實難	bùjiè . . . shínán	without . . . it would be difficult to
掙扎	zhēngzhá	struggle with difficulty
圖存	túcún	for survival
所有 . . . 緣由	suǒyǒu . . . yúanyóu	all the reasons why . . .
伏乞賜予	fúqǐ cìyǔ	respectfully beg (you) to graciously grant us
實為公便	shíwéi gōngbiàn	indeed just and expedient

Document 7 (vol. 2, p. 14)

The Ministry of Industry's Reply to the Tien Yuen Electro-Chemical Works' Petition
實業部致天原電化廠批文

This document is an official instruction in response to a subordinate body's petition (批文). In introducing the addressee, the instruction uses 原具呈人 (the original party presenting the petition) rather than 批 (an official reply to). This document gives only a summary reference to the Tien Yuen Works' petition rather than a detailed quotation of the original petition.

Basically, the purpose of this document is to forward the decision of the Ministry of Railroads to the Tien Yuen Works. Most of it is the Ministry of Industry's quotation of the Ministry of Railroads' lateral communication (案准貴部 . . . 查照等由). In this quotation, the Ministry of Railroads refers back to a lateral communication from the Ministry of Industry (据獎勵 . . . 見覆 等由).

In referring to the Ministry of Industry, the Ministry of Railroads uses the word 貴, a respectful form for addressing another institution when there is no subordination involved. Words commonly found in this type of document include 呈悉, 案准, 應與照准, 此批, and 再行通知.

依據	yījù	in accordance with
分咨 . . . 兩部	fēnzī . . . liǎngbù	send separate communications to the two ministries (of . . .)
開	kāi	state (term often used to introduce the content of a quotation)
案准	ànzhǔn	according to the case on our records, according to (a received lateral communication) in our records
貴部	guìbù	your ministry (Ministry of Industry; 貴 is an honorific term)
據 . . . 議決	jù . . . yì jūe	in accordance with the deliberation and decision of . . .

見覆   jiànfù   to receive a reply (見覆 = 見復; in classical Chinese, 見 is often used as a reflective pronoun before a verb to refer to oneself)

到部   dàobù   reach (our) ministry (Ministry of Railroads)

通令各路   tōnglìng gèlù   issue an order to each railroad

相應咨復   xiāngyīng zīfù   to reply accordingly by lateral communication

准此   zhǔncǐ   according to the received document

再行通知   zàixíng tōngzhī   will notify again

仰即遵照   yǎngjí zūnzhào   should immediately follow this order

Document 8 (vol. 2, p. 15)

The Ministry of Industry's Notice to the Tien Yuen Electro-Chemical Works
實業部致天原電化廠通知

This is a notice (通知) issued by the government to a private enterprise. The category code (工字) indicates that the document concerns industry. The document first specifies the addressee of the notice with the formula "通知 . . ." (this is to notify), followed by a review of the current state of affairs, starting with 查 (we note that). It concludes with the conventional phrase 特此通知 (hereby this notice is given).

The basic purpose of the document was to inform the Tianyuan Works of the Ministry of Communications' decision. It is largely a detailed quotation of the reply from the Ministry of Communications (from 案准貴部 to 咨請貴部轉飭遵照辦理等因). In this quotation, the Ministry of Communications first refers to a lateral communication from the Ministry of Industry and then quotes the report from the China Merchants' Steam Navigation Company, Ltd., regarding the Tien Yuen Works' case. This quote begins with a reference to the Tien Yuen Works and ends by asking the Ministry of Communications to pass on its decision to Tien Yuen through the Ministry of Industry.

Words often found in such a notice are 經 . . . 方可, 將 . . . 始可, 仰, 剋日, 為要, 等情, and 特此通知.

工字第 . . . 號	gōngzì dì . . . hào	communication serial number
查 . . . 在案	chǎ . . . zài'àn	(we) find . . . on record
呈請 . . . 一案	chéngqǐng . . . yīàn	petition regarding the case of . . .
各節	gèjiē	all the details
批飭	pīchì	to sanction
貴部	guìbù	(an honorific reference to the Ministry of Industry)

等由	děngyóu	(here signifies the end of the Ministry of Communications' reference to the Ministry of Industry's lateral communication [Industry # 8991])
到部	dàobù	reach (our) ministry (Ministry of Communications)
本部	běnbù	our, this ministry (Ministry of Communications)
招商局	zhāoshāngjú	China Merchants' Steam Navigation Company, Ltd. (initially 商辦輪船招商 [總]; beginning in 1932, it was called the 國營招商局)
裝運	zhuāngyùn	to pack and transport, to load and ship
自當...為	zìdāng . . . wéi	should naturally consider . . . as . . .
有效期間	yǒuxiào qījiān	period of validity
惟	wéi	however
覓...作保	mì . . . zuò bǎo	find . . . to be the guarantor
經...方可	jīng . . . fāngkě	can do something only after . . .
殷實	yīnshí	substantial
商號	shānghào	business establishment
應將...後,始可	yīngjiāng . . . hòu, shǐkě	should wait until after having done . . . , then can start to . . .
承運	chéngyùn	carry
手續	shǒuxù	formality, procedure
辦妥	bàntuǒ	finish doing something properly

奉令前因, 理合	fènglìng qiányīn, lǐhé	with the decree regarding the above situation, (we) should . . . ; having received a decree regarding the above issue, we are duty bound (to do something)
抄附	chāofù	enclosed is a copy of . . .
呈請鈞部轉咨 . . . 令飭	chéngqǐng jūnbù zhuǎnzī . . . lìngshì	petition to your ministry (Ministry of Communications) to send a lateral communication (to the Ministry of Industry) asking it to issue a decree (to the Tien Yuen Works)
等情	děngqíng	(used by a superior to acknowledge communication by inferior, followed by 據此 (here it marks the conclusion of the petition)
據此	jùcǐ	upon receipt of this document, according to this document that we have received, consequently
相應	xiāngyìng	correspondingly, accordingly
咨請貴部轉飭	zīqǐng guìbù zhuǎn shì	send a lateral communication to ask your ministry (Ministry of Industry) to decree . . . on our behalf
又	yòu	in addition
印花	yìnhuā	stamp, stamp duty, stamp tax
仰補繳	yǎng bǔjiǎo	you should make a deferred payment
特此通知	tècǐ tōngzhī	hereby this notice is given

Document 9 (vol. 2, p. 16)

Letter from Wu Zhaohong to Wu Yunchu
吳兆洪致吳蘊初函

This is a personal letter (函) written by Wu Zhaohong (吳兆洪), head of the National Resources Commission Secretariat. It opens with the salutation "... 大鑒," and concludes with 敬上 (yours respectfully). In this type of document, vocabulary items such as 惟為, 擬煩, and 為荷 are common.

大鑒	dàjiàn	salutational formula for a letter
關於...一事	guānyú ... yīshì	as for ... (this affair), regarding ...
收購	shōugòu	purchase
參加合辦	cānjiā hébàn	joint partnership with
本會	běnhuì	this commission (the National Resources Commission)
籌辦	chóubàn	make arrangements for
惟	wéi	however
為便查考起見	wèi biàn chákǎo qǐjiàn	for the convenience of future reference
擬煩	nǐfán	intend to trouble (you)
負債表	fùzhàibiǎo	liabilities list
過會	guòhuì	send to the commission (the National Resources Commission)
以資	yǐzī	so that, so as to
存案	cún àn	keep on record

為荷	wéihè	we should be very much obliged
籌安	chóuān	good luck; take care
敬上	jìngshàng	respectively yours

Document 10 (vol. 2, pp. 17–18)

The National Resources Commission's Telegram
to the Tien Yuen Electro-Chemical Works
資源委員會致天原電化廠代電

This is an official letter sent by express mail in lieu of a telegram (快郵代電 or 代電). On the bottom of the document is the category code (. . . 字) and the blank to enter a serial number. In the right margin is an area for the date and time it was received (年 . . . 月 . . . 日 . . . 時到). On the top of the right column is a summary of the document (事由). The lower right column shows that an appendix is attached. The second column 擬辦 (proposed response, action recommendation) reflects that the document was to be transferred to the Sichuan Branch of the Tien Yuen Electro-Chemical Works for examination and reply (note that the characters in this column were entered by the Tien Yuen company, not by the National Resources Commission). The big characters in the middle column indicate that this was an express mail letter sent by the National Resources Commission. According to the small characters in the column, the category code and serial number for the document is 資36第10671, and it was sent on July 17, 1941. On the bottom of the first page we find the seal of the National Resources Commission. The main body of the document is written in the format of an official letter.

Words often used in such a letter include 見復, 結案, and 即希 . . . 為荷.

附件	fùjiàn	appendix
擬辦	nǐbàn	to intend to execute or manage
美貸	měidài	American loan
動支	dòngzhī	to put to use, employ, draw on
見復	jiànfù	to reply (to me)
代電	dàidiàn	an official letter sent by express mail in lieu of a telegram
截至	jiézhì	up to
業經	yèjīng	already

212

預算	yùsuàn	budget
呈 A 轉 B	chéng A zhuǎn B	reported to A and then A submitted it to B
追加	zhuījiā	to make an addition
核算	hésuàn	calculate
完竣	wánjùn	completed
亟宜清理	jí yí qīnglǐ	urgently needs to be put in order or sorted out
轉帳	zhuǎnzhàng	transfer accounts
結案	jié'àn	to conclude the case
相應	xiāngyìng	correspondingly, accordingly
檢奉	jiǎnfèng	to respectfully present
氮氣	dànqì	nitride
清單	qīngdān	detailed list
察收	cháshōu	to check upon receipt
核對	héduì	to check
列帳	lièzhàng	bookkeeping
匯率	huìlù	exchange rate
彙辦	huìbàn	to collect data and take care of
午	wǔ	(this character is used to indicate the 7th month)
篠	xiǎo	(this character is used to indicate the 17th day of the month)
清單	qīngdān	detailed list of items that serves as a statement, a statement of account

213

Document 11 (vol. 2, p. 19)

An Official Letter from the Chemical Industry Department of the National Resources Commission to the Tien Yuen Electro-Chemical Works
資源委員會化工組致天原電化廠函

This document is an official letter (公函). The first line on the right indicates that the letter was sent on the order of Chiang Kai-shek. To show respect to Chiang Kai-shek and the Tien Yuen Electro-Chemical Works, the document starts a new line (lines 2 and 4) when referring to them. Since the company was not subordinate to the Chemical Industry Department of the National Resources Commission, the latter used 貴 in addressing the former. In the last column we find the seal of the Department and the date that the letter was written.

In official government letters the following usages are regularly employed: 奉 . . . 諭, 限 . . . 以前, 擬定, and 為荷.

奉 . . . 諭	fèng . . . yù	(we) have received the order from . . .
委員長	wěiyuánzhǎng	commission chairman (here refers to Chiang Kai-shek)
限 . . . 以前	xiàn . . . yǐqián	to set . . . as the deadline
擬定	nǐdìng	to draw up (a plan)
原定計劃	yuándìng jìhuà	the original plan
較切實際	jiào qiè shíjì	relatively practical
詳盡	xiángjìn	detailed
計劃書	jìhuàshū	plan; a set of plans
彙編	huìbiān	compilation
此致	cǐzhì	this (letter) is hereby sent to
啓	qǐ	to inform, write

Document 12 (vol. 2, pp. 20–21)

A Letter from the Tien Yuen Electro-Chemical Works to the Finalization Office of the Bureau for Settling Enemy and Puppet Regime Properties in the Jiangsu, Zhejiang, and Anhui Areas (Draft)
天原電化廠致蘇浙皖區敵偽產業處理局結束辦事處函 （稿）

This document, like the previous one, is an official letter, but as a draft, it shows places where editing was done, such as in the third line on page 1 and the first line on page 2. On the right margin of page 1 is the date when the letter was dispatched (February 8, 1947). On the top of the page are the blanks for the category code and the serial number. The first column on the right indicates that this was a draft dispatch by the Tien Yuen Electro-Chemical Company. The second column gives information on (1) the addressee's name: the Finalization Office of the Bureau for Settling Enemy and Puppet Regime Properties in the Jiangsu, Zhejiang, and Anhui Areas; (2) the type of document: official letter; and appendix: none. The third column includes (1) a summary of the document, concluded with the conventional word 由; (2) the name of the author and the date on which the document was drafted, examined, finalized, copied, sealed, and dispatched. The fourth column gives information on (1) the number of the letter as an outgoing document of the company; (2) the manner it was sent (delivered); and (3) the number of it as an incoming document (to the addressee).

The main part of the document was written in accordance with the format and formula of official letters, as discussed above. Since this is a draft, there is no seal. We only see the words "place for the seal of the president of the company." Phrases regularly found in this type of letter include 敬啟者, 案查, 特再函達, and 此致.

發文稿	fāwén'gǎo	draft dispatch
收文機關或 　個人之名稱	shōuwén jīguān huò 　gèrén zhī míngchēng	name of the institution or person 　receiving the document
文別: 函	wénbié: hán	type of document: letter
附件: 無	fùjiàn: wú	appendix: none
擬稿: (人名/時間)	nǐgǎo: (rénmíng/shíjiān)	drafted: (name/time)

核定: (人名/時間)	hédìng: (rénmíng/shíjiān)	examined and finalized: (name/time)
繕正: (人名/時間)	shànzhèng: (rénmíng/shíjiān)	copied: (name/time)
封發: (人名/時間)	fēng fā: (rénmíng/shíjiān)	sealed and dispatched: (name/time)
發文字號:... 字第...號	fāwén zìhào:... zì dì...hào	category number for the outgoing dispatch
遞寄辦法:送	dìjì bàn fǎ: sòng	method of delivery: deliver in person
發文日期:	fāwén rìqī:	date of dispatch: February 8, 1947
歸檔:...字第...號	guīdǎng:...zì dì...hào	to be filed under: code...number...
敬啓者	jìngqǐzhě	I have the honor to inform you (opening phrase in correspondence)
案查	ànchá	it appears from the record that, we find on our record
接奉	jiēfèng	to receive (from a superior)
鈞局	jūnjú	your bureau (Settling Enemy and Puppet Regime Properties in the Jiangsu, Zhejiang, and Anhui Areas
滬清丙字	hù qīng bǐngzì	category code
第...號	dì...hào	number for the document
以敝廠...繳款 等由	yǐ bìchǎng...jiǎokuǎn děngyóu	(this is the summary of notice 50226)
敵遺	díyí	left by the enemy
收歸國有	shōuguī guóyǒu	to be taken over by the state, be nationalized
估價單	gūjià dān	list of estimated assessment, value
囑	zhǔ	to enjoin, advise, urge

剋日	kèrì	immediately
到局	dàojǔ	reach our Bureau for Settling Enemy and Puppet Regime Properties in the Jiangsu-Zhejiang-Anhui Area
單列	dānliè	itemized in the list
原委	yuánwěi	how something happened from beginning to end; circumstances, details
迄今	qìjīn	up to this day
未蒙賜復	wèiméng cìfù	have not been favored with a reply, have not been granted your gracious reply
為日已久	wéi rì yǐjiǔ	it has been a long time
特再函達	tè zài hándá	to especially send you another letter; we therefore send you a letter again
參照	cānzhào	in light of; consult, refer to
數額	shùé	amount
繳付	jiǎofù	to make payment
無任公感	wúrèn gōnggǎn	to express appreciation for facilitating official affairs; "we are extremely grateful for . . ."

Chapter 21

Documents on Liu Hongsheng's Match Enterprises:
Introduction and Glossary
劉鴻生企業檔案

Liu Hongsheng (or Liu Hung-sheng; also known as O. S. Lieu, 1888–1956) was one of the most prominent and successful entrepreneurs of the Republican period. Liu was involved in many industries, such as mining, cement, wool, and banking. Liu's singular success in match manufacturing earned him the accolade "King of Matches" (*huochai dawang* 火柴大王).

Liu attended St. John's College (later St. John's University) in Shanghai for one year. He married the daughter of Yeh Cheng-chung (Ye Chengzhong 葉澄衷, 1840–99), a pioneer in Chinese match manufacturing and owner of the Xiechang Match Company (Xiechang huochai gongsi 燮昌火柴公司). Later, Liu established the Hung Sung Match Company (Hongsheng huochai gongsi 鴻生火柴公司) in 1924. In 1927 Liu traveled to Europe and the United States to study Western business practices. Although this selection of documents focuses on Liu's efforts to create a joint-venture company in the match industry, Liu was interested in joint ventures in other industries as well.

Chinese match manufacturing, like many indigenous industries, blossomed during World War I. After the war, however, Chinese manufacturers were hampered by continued domestic as well as international obstacles. Foreign competitors in match manufacturing, especially Swedish and Japanese firms, were armed with superior capital and technology, and Chinese manufacturers were also less competitive in terms of economies of scale. Moreover, they faced transportation bottlenecks, political instability, and labor strife.

In 1927 Liu Hongsheng and fellow Chinese manufacturers responded to their eroding competitive edge by forming a trade association (*tongye gonghui* 同業公會), and by petitioning the local government and the new National Government for relief. On one front, Liu negotiated mergers with the Yingchang (熒昌) and Zhonghua (中華) match companies. This effort culminated in the formation in 1930 of the China Match Company (Da Zhonghua huochai gongsi 大中華火柴公司), which accounted for one-quarter of total match production in China. On another front, Liu and fellow manufacturers petitioned the government for a trade association–run monopoly (*gongmai* 公賣). However, manufacturers and the government could not agree on whether the government or the private firms would run the monopoly. The scheme also faced vigorous protests from Western manufacturers and governments. Liu's vision of a national match combination did not come to fruition until 1936.

The following selections illustrate Liu's efforts to create a larger and more Western-style match company from existing companies. They also show how Liu attempted to involve the government in managing the domestic market in order to circumvent foreign competition. For basic biographical information on Liu Hongsheng, see Howard Boorman, ed., *Biographical*

Dictionary of Republican China. (New York: Columbia University Press, 1968), 3: 398–400; *Minguo renwu dacidian* 民國人物大辭典 (Biographical dictionary of the Republican period) (Shjijiazhuang: Hebei renmin chubanshe, 1991), p. 1457; *Zhongguo renming dacidian: dangdai renwujuan* 中國人名大詞典：當代人物卷 (Chinese biographical dictionary: contemporary personages) (Shanghai: Shanghai cishu chubanshe, 1992), p. 570; Li Shengping, ed., *Zhongguo jinxiandai renming dacidian* 中國近現代人名大辭典 (Biographical dictionary of Chinese in modern times) (Beijing: Zhongguo guoji guangbo chubanshe, 1989), p. 179; *Who's Who in China,* 5th ed. (Shanghai: China Weekly Review, 1932), p. 167; Zhang Qifu and Shu Heng, eds., *Huochai dawang Liu Hongsheng* 火柴大王劉鴻生 (Liu Hongsheng, the King of Matches) (Henan: Henan renmin chubanshe, 1990, 1993); Liu Nianzhi, *Shiyejia Liu Hongsheng zhuanlüe: huiyi wode fuqin* 實業家劉鴻生傳略－回憶我的父親 (Brief biography of industrialist Liu Hongsheng: reminiscences of my father) (Beijing: Wenshi ziliao chubanshe, 1982); and *Liu Hongsheng qiye shiliao* 劉鴻生企業史料 (Historical materials on Liu Hongsheng's enterprises) (Shanghai: Shanghai renmin chubanshe, 1981), pp. 473–93. For information on the match industry during the Republican period, see He Simi, "Jindai Zhongguo huochai gongye de fazhan" 近代中國火柴工業的發展(西元一八六七至一九三七) (Modern development of the Chinese match industry, 1867–1937), in *Guoshiguan guankan* 國史館館刊 (Journal of Academia Historica) 16 (1994): 89–114; *Zhongguo jindai jingjishi lunzhu tiyao* 中國近代經濟史論著提要 (Abstracts of works on modern Chinese economic history) pp. 342–45; and Sherman Cochran, "Three Roads into Shanghai's Market: Japanese, Western, and Chinese Companies in the Match Trade, 1895–1937," in Frederic Wakeman and Yeh Wen-hsin, eds., *Shanghai Sojourners* (Berkeley: University of California Press, 1992), pp. 35–75.

The following documents are from the Economic Research Institute of the Shanghai Academy of Social Sciences, ed., *Liu Hongsheng qiye shiliao* 劉鴻生企業史料 (Historical sources on Liu Hongsheng's business enterprises) (Shanghai: Shanghai renmin chubanshe, 1981). The original documents are housed at the Economic Research Institute of the Shanghai Academy of Social Sciences (Shanghai shehui kexueyuan jingji yanjiusuo 上海社會科學院經濟研究所).

Document 1 (vol. 2, p. 25)

Letter from Liu Hongsheng to Chen Yuanlai
劉鴻生致陳源來函

In general, a Chinese letter contains three main sections: salutation (such as 大鑒 *dajian*, 鈞鑒 *junjian*, and 閣下 *gexia*), body, and closing. The body of the letter is further divided into an opening phrase (such as 久違雅教 *jiuwei yajiao* or 時深懷念 *shishen huainian*), a courtesy expression (such as 茲者 *cizhe*, 茲因 *ciyin*, or 茲將 *cijiang*), the substance of the letter, and a courtesy expression to signal the end of the letter (such as 耑此 *duanci* or 奉覆 *fengfu*). The closing section of the letter is divided into a greeting (such as 敬頌大安 *jingsong da'an*) and a signature. The salutation, opening phrase, courtesy expression, greeting, and signature all denote, with some variations, the type of correspondence and the relationship between sender and reader. Not all letters necessarily conform to the standard formulas. The editors of the letters from which these selections were taken saw fit to dispense with many formulaic courtesy expressions and greetings. For more information, see James C. P. Liang, Lloyd Haft, and Gertie Mulder, *Business and Correspondence Chinese* (Dordrecht, Holland: Foris Publications, 1983).

Chen Yuanlai was in Kōbe, Japan, when Liu wrote to him.

神户	shénhù	Kōbe
函	hán	letter
弟	dì	I (conventionally used by a speaker or writer to refer to himself)
鑒于	jiànyú	in view of
聯合事業	liánhé shìyè	joint enterprise, trust, combine
與夫	yǔfū	and moreover
吾國	wúgúo	my country (China)
火柴業	huǒchái yè	match industry
不振	bù zhèn	unable to prosper, backward

以為	yǐwéi	in order to; to consider, think
欲圖	yù tú	attempt to, want to
同業	tóngyè	same trade or business
大規模	dà guīmó	large-scale
方能	fāng néng	only (until) then can . . .
是以	shìyǐ	therefore, hence; by this means
秋間	qiūjiān	during the autumn
合併	hébìng	merger
當經	dāngjīng	already
討論委員會	tǎolùn wěiyuánhuì	discussion committee
大綱	dàgāng	outline
議決	yìjué	to deliberate and decide
嗣	sì	thereafter
遂致	suì zhì	then causing it to . . . ; consequently
益甚	yì shèn	increasingly serious
岌岌可危	jíjí kěwēi	in imminent danger
滬	hù	Shanghai
籌議	chóuyì	to deliberate, arrange, settle
抵制之策	dǐzhì zhī cè	strategies for resistance
因之	yīnzhī	thereby
不容或緩	bùróng huò huǎn	must not be delayed

221

致書	zhìshū	send a letter
舊案	jiù'àn	former proposal, former issue
邀天下之幸	yāo tiānxià zhī xìng	to be extremely fortunate
私圖之心	sī tú zhī xīn	for selfish purposes
壟斷	lǒngduàn	to monopolize
從大處遠處著想	cóng dà chù yuǎn chù zhuóxiǎng	to take into account all factors and consider the long term
大局	dàjú	overall situation
惠予	huìyǔ	to be so kind as to give
俾	bì	so that
樹 . . . 基礎	shù . . . jīchǔ	establish . . . foundation
穩固	wěngù	stabilize; stable, solid
瑞商	ruìshāng	Swedish merchants
則幸甚矣	zé xìng shèn yǐ	thus, I would be extremely grateful

Document 2 (vol. 2, p. 26)

Letter from Chen Yuanlai to Liu Hongsheng
陳源來自神户復劉鴻生函

Chen Yuanlai's reply (from Kōbe) to Liu Hongsheng's letter of January 3, 1930.

復	fù	to answer, to reply
捧讀	pěngdú	to read with reverence
台函	táihán	your (esteemed) letter
祇悉壹是	zhī xī yīshì	respectfully noted everything
際此 . . . 時期	jìcǐ . . . shíqī	at this time of . . .
商戰	shāngzhàn	trade war
劇烈	jùliè	fierce
資愈厚者力愈洪	zī yù hòu zhě lì yù hóng	those with the most resources have the most power
進展	jìnzhǎn	development
而圖存立	ér tú cúnlì	. . . and seek survival
民生	mínshēng	the people's livelihood
日用必需之品	rìyòng bìxū zhī pǐn	daily necessities
迄	qì	so far, up till now
既 . . . 且	jì . . . qiě	both . . . and . . .
分立各不相謀	fēnlì gè bù xiāngmóu	isolated from each other and without cooperation

慨然	kǎirán	with deep feeling
高謀勝算	gāomóu shèngsuàn	clever and superb calculation and planning
利國福民	lìguó fúmín	to benefit the nation and the people
光明正大	guāngmíng zhèngdà	guileless and aboveboard
無既	wújì	deeply
一德一心	yīdé yīxīn	with one heart and one mind, with one idea and will
力謀	lìmóu	to make every effort to
尊擬	zūnnǐ	your venerable drafts
付	fù	to turn over to
務期	wùqī	to be sure to do something, make sure to do something
妥協	tuǒxié	to compromise and accommodate
一致	yīzhì	unanimity, consensus
尤所欣幸	yóu suǒ xīnxìng	particularly fortunate and overjoyed
敝處	bìchù	my humble place (company)
趨前候教	qūqián hòujiào	hasten to await your instructions
接談	jiētán	interview
是荷	shìhè	would be grateful if . . .

Document 3 (vol. 2, p. 27)

Letter from Jia Shiyi to Liu Hongsheng
國民政府財政部司長賈士毅致劉鴻生函

董君	dǒngjūn	Mr. Dong
惟	wéi	but
公賣	gōngmài	monopoly
略得梗概	lüè dé gěnggài	having received the gist of the plans
參照	cānzhào	to refer to, consult; in light of
通例	tōnglì	general practice
酌採	zhuó cǎi	to adopt after deliberation
擬就	nǐ jiù	completed formulation (of a draft); to draw up
草案	cǎo'àn	a draft
一、		(this horizontal stroke in a Qing or Republican document is often used to initiate an item in a list; it does not necessarily have anything to do with numbering)
專賣	zhuānmài	monopoly
委托	wěituō	to entrust
公會	gōnghuì	association, union, league, society
章程	zhāngchéng	charter, rule, regulation

225

權責	quán zé	rights and responsibilities
具體	jùtǐ	specific, concrete
以	yǐ	because of
利害	lìhài	advantages and disadvantages; benefit and loss
細目	xìmù	detailed items
合同	hétong	contract, agreement
抄奉	chāo fèng	to copy and respectfully present to you
即乞察照	jí qǐ cházhào	please immediately note
字樣	zìyàng	wording
尚待	shàng dài	awaiting
斟酌	zhēnzhuó	deliberation and adjustment
獨占	dúzhàn	monopoly, to monopolize
抵觸	dǐchù	in contravention of, in conflict with
以 . . . 名義	yǐ . . . míngyì	in (under) the name of, in the capacity as
措詞	cuòcí	wording of a letter
轉旋之餘地	zhuǎnxuàn zhī yúdì	room to maneuver
附奉	fùfèng	send the enclosed to you
率陳	shuài chén	to state frankly
臆見	yìjiàn	personal assumption, a hypothesis, personal ideas (which are usually not true or sound)
為荷	wéihè	would be grateful for . . .

Document 4 (vol. 2, p. 28)

Appendix A: Outlines of the Conditions Governing the Match Monopoly (extracts)
(附一) 火柴專賣辦法大綱 (摘錄)

賣買權	mài mǎi quán	right to buy and sell; sales monopoly
專屬于	zhuān shǔyú	belongs exclusively to
説明	shuōmíng	explanation
規定	guīdìng	to stipulate
所屬	suǒshǔ	to belong . . . to
以為	yǐwéi	take as, is regarded as
根本	gēnběn	base, basis, foundation,
執行	zhíxíng	to implement, to carry out
政府所設之 . . . 官署	zhèngfǔ suǒ shè zhī . . . guānshù	agency established by the government
主管	zhǔguǎn	to take charge of
主管 "X" 官署	zhǔguǎn "X" guānshǔ	the government agency/agencies that is/are in charge of X
事項	shìxiàng	affair, matter
調查	diàochá	to investigate; investigation
平價	píngjià	to regulate prices
招商	zhāoshāng	to invite merchants
包賣	bāomài	to have exclusive selling rights

承辦	chéngbàn	to undertake
監督	jiāndū	to supervise; supervision
權利	quánlì	rights
義務	yìwù	obligation
另定之	lìng dìng zhī	to be decided separately
係 . . . 之意	xì . . . zhīyì	it means that
官督商辦	guāndu shāngbàn	supervised by the government and managed by businessmen
由	yóu	up to
自行	zìxíng	by itself, automatic
設廠	shè chǎng	establish factories
供不應求	gòng bùyìng qiú	demand exceeds supply
但以 . . . 為限	dàn yǐ . . . wéi xiàn	only within the limits of . . .
現有	xìanyǒu	now existing
張本	zhāngběn	advanced arrangements
但書	dànshū	proviso
並非	bìngfēi	is not
輸入	shūrù	to import
進口	jìnkǒu	to import
海關	hǎiguān	customs, maritime customs
盡數	jìnshù	the entire amount, completely
寄存	jìcún	to store temporarily

附設	fùshè	affiliated, attached
指定	zhǐdìng	to appoint, assign; assigned, designated
倉庫	cāngkù	warehouse
酌量	zhuóliàng	to consider
需給	xū jǐ	supply and demand
按照	ànzhào	on the basis of
次第	cìdì	order, sequence
平均	píngjūn	average, on the average
由...收買	yóu ... shōumǎi	purchased by ...
供過于求	gòng guòyú qiú	supply exceeds demand
倘	tǎng	in case, if
提出	tíchū	to make delivery of goods
轉運	zhuǎnyùn	to transfer, convey, forward
搬運之費	bānyùn zhī fèi	cost of transportation
該	gāi	the said (merchant)
明白	míngbái	clearly, publicly
暗中	ànzhōng	secretly, indirectly
不得已	bùdéyǐ	no alternative but to, to have to

Document 5 (vol. 2, pp. 29–30)

Appendix B: Temporary Regulations Granting the Match Trade Association Monopolistic Rights (extracts)
(附二) 委託火柴公會賣買火柴暫行章程 (摘錄)

施行	shīxíng	to execute, carry out, put into operation
得照	dé zhào	can follow in accordance with
經理	jīnglǐ	to manage
承銷	chéngxiāo	contract to sell
只准	zhī zhǔn	only allow
總會	zǒnghuì	federation of trade unions
既	jì	since, as
即	jí	then, accordingly
一個以上	yīgè yǐshàng	more than one
若不如此	ruò bù rúcǐ	if it is not so
競銷	jìngxiāo	to compete for markets
成立	chénglì	to establish
隨時	suíshí	at any time
派員	pài yuán	to dispatch officials
故宜	gù yí	hence it is appropriate
主管官署	zhǔguǎn guānshǔ	government office in charge, responsible office

檢查	jiǎnchá	to inspect
帳目	zhàngmù	accounts
免致	miǎnzhì	so as not to
爭議	zhēngyì	dispute(s)
行政	xíngzhèng	administration
除...外	chú ... wài	except ...
委託	wěituō	to entrust
期滿	qīmǎn	to expire
估價	gūjià	to appraise, assess the price of
儲存	chǔcún	to store
墊款	diànkuǎn	to advance money; money advanced
國庫	guókù	state treasury
核定	hédìng	to check and decide
協商法	xiéshāng fǎ	(method of) consultation and negotiation
純益	chúnyì	net profit
即	jí	namely
報酬	baòchǒu	pay, reward
開支	kāizhī	expenses, expenditure
有損	yǒusǔn	decrease, harm
假定	jiǎdìng	arrange or assume for the time being
以待	yǐdài	so as to wait for

三成	sānchéng	30 percent (each 成 = 10%)
改良	gǎiliáng	to improve
支配	zhīpèi	to allocate, use, spend

Document 6 (vol. 2, p. 31)

Appendix C: Chinese-Swedish Treaty (extracts concerning monopolies)
(附三) 中瑞條約中與專賣有關之條文

廢止	fèizhǐ	abolish
行商	hángshāng	Cohong merchants (in 1720, Chinese merchants in Canton formed a trade monopoly called the Cohong (公行))
獨占	dúzhàn	to monopolize
始得	shǐde	only . . . can
諾威	nuòwēi	Norway
臣民	chénmín	subjects (i.e., of a state, kingdom, empire, etc.)
輸出入品之賣買	shū chū rù pǐn zhī màimǎi	the import or export trade
限制	xiànzhì	restrictions
阻礙	zǔài	to hinder, impede

Document 7 (vol. 2, p. 32)

Appendix D : Chinese-French Treaties (extracts concerning monopolies)
(附四) 中法條約中與專賣有關之條文

特權	tèquán	privileges
商事會社	shāngshì huìshì	trade union or association
獨占業	dúzhàn yè	monopolies
境內	jìngnèi	within the boundaries
設置	shèzhì	establish
亦	yì	and, also
團體	tuántǐ	organization
查	chá	it is found that, we find that
國民政府	guómín zhèngfǔ	National Government
關稅	guānshuì	customs duty

Document 8 (vol. 2, p. 33)

Letter from Lu Hongji to Liu Hongsheng
國民政府財政部陸鴻吉致劉鴻生函

一節	yījié	regarding the matter of . . .
達覽	dálǎn	to have received and read
兹	zī	now
遵囑	zūnzhǔ	as requested
附奉	fùfèng	to enclose and send (to you)
司長	sīzhǎng	head of the department
改正	gǎizhèng	to revise
當局	dāngjú	the authorities
推誠	tuīchéng	to display sincerity
有 . . . 之慮	yǒu . . . zhīlù	to be concerned over something
慎之于始	shènzhī yú shǐ	to be cautious from the beginning
美僑商業	měiqiáo shāngyè	American merchant businesses (in China)
與 . . . 有違	yǔ . . . yǒuwéi	does not comply with . . .
合眾國	hézhòngguó	republic (here referring to the United States)
任便	rènbiàn	freely, without interference
杜	dù	to prevent
包攬	bāolǎn	to monopolize

235

把持	bǎchí	to dominate
權限	quánxiàn	rights
貴	guì	your (honorific)
特派交涉員	tèpài jiāoshèyuán	specially appointed negotiator (in foreign affairs), special commissioner of the Ministry of Foreign Affairs stationed in a certain province
擅用	shànyòng	to do something without authorization
勢必	shìbì	certainly will
國際糾紛	guójì jiūfēn	international dispute(s)

Chapter 22

Documents on Rong Zongjing's Textile Enterprises: Introduction and Glossary
榮宗敬企業檔案

Rong Zongjing (also known as Yung Tsung-ching and T. K. Yung, 1873–1938), popularly known as the "Flour and Textile King of China," was a prominent industrialist during the Republican period. Rong and his brother Rong Desheng 榮德生 (1875–1952) earned a prominent place among Chinese industrialists. By 1922, their flour factories' production accounted for one-third of the total production capacity of all Chinese flour manufacturers.

Rong Zongjing received his education at a traditional private academy (*si shu* 私塾) before his rise in the flour and textile industries. Rong also apprenticed at a native bank (*qianzhuang* 錢莊) for four years and later worked at a modern bank in Shanghai. Before his entrance into flour and textiles, Rong and his friends established a modern bank.

The following selections demonstrate the ambivalent relationship between a prominent industrialist and the government. Rong Zongjing played a very public role in the movement to boycott Japanese goods in the 1920s. Such campaigns benefited Rong's enterprises immensely, and Rong encouraged state intervention on behalf of Chinese manufacturers. Rong also urged officials to take measures to ensure supplies of raw materials to Chinese manufacturers. One will find Rong less sanguine about the state's role in the economy when his textile manufacturing plants fell into debt in the 1930s and became targets of government seizure.

Biographical information on Rong can be found in Xu Youchun, ed., *Minguo renwu dacidian* 民國人物大辭典 (Biographical dictionary of the Republican period) (Shijiazhuang: Hebei renmin chubanshe, 1991), pp. 1344–45; *Zhongguo renming dacidian: lishi renwu juan* 中國人名大詞典：歷史人物卷 (Chinese biographical dictionary: historical personages) (Shanghai: Shanghai cishu chubanshe, 1990), p. 422; Li Shengping, ed., *Zhongguo jinxiandai renming dacidian* 中國近現代人名大辭典 (Biographical dictionary of Chinese in modern times) (Beijing: Zhongguo guoji chubanshe, 1989), p. 500; *Who's Who in China*, 5th ed. (Shanghai: China Weekly Review, 1932), p. 287; *Zhongguo jindai jingjishi lunzhu tiyao* 中國近代經濟史論著提要 (Abstracts of works on modern Chinese economic history) (1949–85), pp. 340–41; and Yang Xu, *Rongshi xiongdi: yidai dashiyejia chuangye fengyunlu* 榮氏兄弟：一代大實業家創業風雲錄 (The Rong brothers: an account of a generation of great industrialists) (Shenzhen: Haitian, 1993). A selection of documents from Rong family enterprises has been published in *Rongjia qiye shiliao: Maoxin, Fuxin, Shenxin xitong* 榮家企業史料：茂新、福新、申新系統 (Historical sources on the Rong family business enterprises: Mow Sing & Foh Sing flour mills and Sung Sing cotton mills), 2 vols. (Shanghai: Shanghai renmin chubanshe, 1980).

Document 1 (vol. 2, p. 37)

Letter from Rong Zongjing to Ye Chucang and Ma Chaojun
榮宗敬致葉楚傖、馬超俊函

葉楚傖	Yè Chǔcāng	member of the Jiangsu Provincial Government Council and concurrently head of the provincial Construction Department; also acting head of the Guomindang Central Worker's Department
馬超俊	Mǎ Chāojùn	influential GMD leader; as of July 1927 head of the National Government Labor Bureau
實業	shíyè	industry
萌芽	méngyá	embryonic state
時局	shíjú	current political situation
視	shì	compare
蓋	gaì	(an initial article) for, because, in fact
頻仍	pínréng	frequent
產額	chǎn'é	volume of production, output
阻梗	zǔgěng	blockage, gridlock
花貴紗賤	huāguì shājiàn	expensive raw cotton, cheap cotton yarn
使然	shǐrán	has caused it to be so
查	chǎ	(we) find; to examine

難保	nánbǎo	one cannot say for sure
貪圖重利	tāntú zhònglì	to covet great profit
採辦	cǎibàn	to purchase
棉荒	miánhuāng	cotton shortage
何所恃	hé suǒshì	what would they rely on
夫	fū	in this instance (a character used to begin a statement)
豈淺鮮	qi qiǎnxiān	would it be unimportant
用特函達	yòngtè hándá	this special correspondence to (someone); for this particular reason send a letter to (someone); I thereby especially write you a letter
公端	gōngduān	you (an honorific term used when addressing one's superior)
可否	kěfoǔ	I wonder if I may . . .
明令	mínglìng	formal decree
俾	bǐ	in order to, so that
垂絶	chuíjué	endangered, near-extinction
苟延	gǒuyán	to linger on, perpetuate, continue
利賴之	lìlaì zhī	dependent on that (favorable action)

Document 2 (vol. 2, p. 38)

Letter from Rong Zongjing to Ma Chaojun
榮宗敬致馬超俊函

馬超俊	Mǎ Chāojùn	still director (until December 1928) of National Government Labor Bureau; from June 1928 also member of the Guangdong Provincial Government Council and concurrently head of the provincial Agricultural and Industry Department and head of the provincial Construction Department
支	zhī	count (n); a measurement of quality (in textiles), the higher the number, the better the quality
雙股線	shuānggǔ xiàn	two-ply thread
抵制	dǐzhì	to boycott, resist
閣下	géxià	Your Excellency
國貨	guóhuò	native goods (Chinese merchandise)
統計	tǒngjì	to count, calculate; statistics
稅厘	shuìlí	transportation tax
求過于供	qiú guòyú gòng	demand exceeds supply
徒托空言	tú tuō kōngyán	to depend merely on empty words
提倡	tíchàng	to promote, advocate
于無形	yú wúxíng	not noticeable

諒	liàng	I expect, I think, I suppose
高明	gāomíng	your honor
以為然	yǐwéi rán	to agree with it
再有請者	zài yǒu qǐng zhě	I have a further request; furthermore
外粉	wàifěn	imported flour
驚人	jīngrén	frightening
承	chéng	to be indebted, be granted a favor
暨	jì	and
徵收	zhēngshōu	to collect, levy
進口稅	jìnkǒushuì	import tariff
冀	jì	to hope
惠	huì	to benefit
實非淺鮮	shí fēi qiǎnxiān	considerably
曉諭	xiǎoyù	to make known to all by proclamation
禁銷	jìnxiāo	to ban the sale of, prohibit sales of
是以	shìyǐ	therefore, by this means, hence
銷路	xiāolù	a sale, a market
日有起色	rì yǒu qǐsè	to improve steadily
維護	wéihù	to protect, safeguard
暢銷	chàngxiāo	to be in great demand, have a ready market
侵入	qīnrù	invasion, encroachment

Document 3 (vol. 2, p. 39)

Letter from Rong Zongjing to Ma Chaojun
榮宗敬致馬超俊函

反日	fǎnrì	anti-Japanese
空氣	kōngqì	air, atmosphere
彌漫	mímàn	to spread, envelop, cover
非特 . . . 且	fēitè . . . qiě	not only . . . but also
外交	wàijiāo	foreign relations, foreign policy
後盾	hòudùn	to back up, show support for
已歸平淡	yǐ guī píngdàn	returned to a normal level, cooled down
商號	shānghào	shop, store
竟	jìng	unexpectedly, actually
粵	yùe	Guangdong
呆滯	dāizhì	idle, inactive
道路傳聞	dàolù chuánwén	rumors, hearsay
憑信	píngxìn	to rely upon; reliable, believable, well-founded
素仰	sùyǎng	to have always admired, to have always looked up to
熱心	rèxīn	enthusiastic, eager, ardent
黨國	dǎngguó	the party and the nation

242

濟案	jǐ'àn	May 3, 1928, conflict between Chinese and Japanese troops in the city of Ji'nan
未解	wèijiě	unresolved
外患	wàihuàn	foreign aggression
方滋	fāngzī	growing unabated
堅持到底	jiānchí dàodǐ	firmly persist to the end
最後勝利	zuìhòu shènglì	eventual victory

Document 4 (vol. 2, p. 40)

Letter from Xue Mingjian to Rong Zongjing
薛明劍致榮宗敬函

接洽	jiēqià	to take up a matter with, arrange with, consult with
晨間	chénjiān	dawn, early morning
實業部	shíyèbù	Ministry of Industry (in charge of industry, commerce, mining, and agriculture, founded December 12, 1930)
稚老（吳稚暉）	Zhìlǎo	Wu Zhihui, member of the GMD Central Political Council
汪（精衛）	Wāng	Wang Jingwei, head of the Executive Yuan
孔（祥熙）	Kǒng	Kong Xiangxi, finance minister
檢收	jiǎnshōu	to receive and examine
晤	wù	to meet
主筆	zhǔbǐ	editor-in-chief
云云	yúnyún	etc.

Document 5 (vol. 2, p. 41)

Letter fom Rong Zongjing to Chiang Kai-shek
榮宗敬致蔣介石函

竊查	qièchá	I (we) find that
民商	mínshāng	(here refers to the businessman himself); I as a private businessman
不景氣	bùjǐngqì	economic depression
金融	jīnróng	finance, financial situation
周轉	zhōuzhuǎn	turnover, circulation
不靈	bùlíng	ineffective
乞予	qǐ yǔ	just beg you to grant
在案	zài'àn	on record
惟	wéi	but
據呈	jùchéng	to receive a petition
採取	cǎicǔ	adopt
草擬	cǎonǐ	to draft
整理	zhěnglǐ	to put in order, sort out, adjust
方針	fāngzhēn	policy, guiding principle
棉統會	miántǒnghuì	one of the many special agencies under the jurisdiction of the National Economic Council; established in 1933 to promote and regulate cotton-related endeavors

著手	zhuóshǒu	to begin something, set about something
報章	baòzhāng	newspapers
競載	jìng zǎi	to compete in reporting (news)
有謂	yǒuwèi	some say that . . .
資産	zīchǎn	asset
估計	gūjì	to estimate, assess
完竣	wánjùn	to complete, finish
收歸官有	shōuguī guānyǒu	seizure by the state; to be nationalized
流言所及	liúyán suǒjí	as far as the rumors go
駭人聽聞	hàirén tīngwén	what one hears is shocking and appalling
商股	shānggǔ	privately owned shares
暫感	zàn'gǎn	to temporarily feel
是以	shìyǐ	therefore
救濟	jiùjì	relief
以維營業	yǐ wéi yíngyè	in order to stay in business
重心固在乎	zhòngxīn gù zàihu	the emphasis is certainly on . . .
要求更止乎	yāoqiú gèng zhǐhū	the request particularly concerns only . . .
初無整理之可言	chū wú zhěnglǐ zhī kěyán	no reason to speak of fixing at the beginning
此中消息	cǐzhōng xiāoxi	the inside story, the information has come to light
令人寒慄	lìngrén hánlì	to cause one to shudder in terror
方克有濟	fāng kè yǒujì	only then can (the matter) be of help

荷	hè	to receive
實部	shíbù	Ministry of Industry and Commerce
官息	guānxī	official news
流于	liúyú	to degenerate, change for the worse
宰割之嫌	zǎigē zhī xián	to be suspicious of being partitioned
脆弱之基	cuìruò zhī jī	fragile foundation
自相聚訟	zìxiāng jùsòng	to argue and fight among ourselves
外敵虛入	wàidí xūrù	attacked from without when weak from within
又何以當	yòu héyǐ dāng	how can we withstand
年邁力衰	niánmài lìshuāi	old and infirm
流言蜂起	liúyán fēngqǐ	rumors abound
景況日非	jǐngkuàng rì fēi	situation deteriorating daily
重出	chóngchū	to re-emerge, come out of retirement
以資	yǐzī	as a means of
在民商	zài mínshāng	to be a private businessman; I as a private businessman
鞠躬盡瘁	jūgōng jìn cuì	to give one's all
又何敢辭	yòu hégǎn cí	how can I dare shirk my responsibility
伏維	fúwéi	(a self-deprecatory reference to begin a statement addressing a superior)
國本	guóběn	foundation of the state

夙著勛勞	sù zhù xūnláo	your long-standing and much noted meritorious service
呼籲無門	hūyù wúmén	no response to my appeals
蕪呈	wúchéng	superfluous appeal
冒瀆萬機	màodúwànjī	I dare to presume upon your heavy workload
伏乞	fúqǐ	to humbly beg
亮察	liàngchá	for your perusal
俯加	fǔjiā	to deign to give, graciously give
日月之出，爝火自息	rìyuè zhī chū juéhuǒ zìxī	if you act, the rumors will disappear by themselves
正朝野之視聽	zhèng cháoyě zhī shì tīng	so as to clarify matters to the government and the public
拯實業于水火	zhěng shíyè yú shuǐhuǒ	to rescue industries from disaster
感沐宏德	gǎn mù hóngdé	to be deeply grateful
迫切	pòqiè	urgently
實深待命	shí shēn dàimìng	to sincerely wait for orders

Document 6 (vol. 2, p. 42)

Letter from Rong Zongjing to Kong Xiangxi
榮宗敬致財政部長孔祥熙函

感受	gǎnshòu	to be affected by, experience, feel
呈請	chéngqǐng	petition to a higher authority for consideration or approval
鈞	jūn	(honorific) you or yours
不察	bùchá	not to examine, look into, or scrutinize
貿然	maòrán	rashly, hastily, without careful consideration
越俎代庖	yuè zǔ dài páo	to exceed one's functions and meddle in others' affairs
非維 . . . 抑且	fēiwéi . . . yìqiě	not only . . . but also
濫用	lànyòng	abuse, misuse, use indiscriminately
職權	zhíquán	power or authority of office
以 . . . 而言	yǐ . . . éryán	so far as . . . is concerned
何來 . . . 之可能	hé lái . . . zhī kěnéng	how is . . . possible
固甚于昔	gù shènyú xī	certainly more than in the past
苟獲	gǒu huò	if obtained
稍加憐惜	shāo jiā liánxī	to have a little pity for
在所可卜	zàisuǒ kěbǔ	the result can be predicted
用心所在	yòngxīn suǒzài	the real motive

必具勝算	bì jù shèngsuàn	must have a strategy to ensure success
敬祈	jìngqí	to respectfully request
根據事實	gēnjù shìshí	on the basis of facts
早佈	zǎobù	to announce soon
卓見	zhuōjiàn	outstanding opinion, brilliant idea

Chapter 23

Documents on Chambers of Commerce and Same-Trade Associations: Introduction and Glossary
商會和同業公會經濟檔案

Associations of merchants and businessmen have a long history in China. Their scope and function adapted to rapid economic and social change after 1800. In general, merchant and business organizations developed from native-place associations (*huiguan* 會館) into same-trade associations (*tongye gonghui* 同業公會) and then into chambers of commerce (*shanghui* 商會). However, older organizations persisted and existed side by side with the newer forms.

The number of geographic-based trade associations decreased after the mid-nineteenth century, as the economic role of native-place associations was gradually assumed by same-trade associations, often led by merchants who traded with foreign merchants. As these trade associations expanded, native-place membership requirements lapsed. As the scope of the associations expanded from the narrowly defined regional relations, their ability to enforce their regulations also decreased.

Although the same-trade associations' expansion impaired their ability to influence merchants by coercion, it reflected a combination of motivations for joint action. Trade wars, especially against better-financed, larger, technologically superior, and foreign government–backed merchants, were among the reasons why merchants found it advantageous to organize into same-trade associations. Several of the documents from Liu Hongsheng's match-manufacturing enterprises reflect this trend. (See Chapter 21.)

Many same-trade associations found it advantageous to create increasingly larger organizations. These relatively large groups did not replace the smaller groups but acted as umbrella organizations to increase political or commercial leverage when necessary. These umbrella groups, so-called 集成行會 (*jicheng xinghui*), were formed by same-trade associations of different regions. Their function was to mediate disputes between members, research general economic conditions, and provide trade and investment information. Moreover, these umbrella groups also participated in administering and organizing local affairs such as bridge repair and charitable works. A few of these groups even acquired the right of taxation to support their activities.

In 1904 the Qing government encouraged the organization of chambers of commerce. The chambers of commerce did not replace smaller trade associations but transcended restrictions based on geography and same-trade affiliations. An important motivation for creating chambers of commerce was to develop relationships with the newly created government bodies designed to foster economic development during the late Qing. The relationship between chambers of commerce and state agencies, sometimes cooperative, often contentious, continued into the Republican period. Throughout this period, the major responsibilities of the chambers were to develop trade and protect merchant interests. For further information, see Tang Lixing, *Shangren yu Zhongguojinshi shehui* 商人與中國近世社會 (Merchants and modern Chinese society) (Zhejiang: Renmin chubanshe, 1993), pp. 276–91; and Pan Junxiang et al., eds., *Jindai Zhongguo guoqing toushi: guanyu jindai Zhongguo jingji, shehui de yanjiu* 近代中國國情透視—關于近代中國經濟、社會的研究 (Modern Chinese national conditions: research on modern Chinese economy and society) (Shanghai: Shanghai shehui kexueyuan chubanshe, 1992).

Document 1 (vol. 2, pp. 45–49)

The Shanghai Silk Trade Association's Letter to the
Shanghai Chamber of Commerce Requesting a Ban
on the Importation of Artificial Silk
上海市綢緞同業公會致上海市商會函

This is an official letter from the Shanghai Silk Trade Association. We have previously seen the format, formulas, and vocabulary typical of this type of document. Here we examine the cover page for such a document. In the right margin is the incoming document number given by the Shanghai Chamber of Commerce and the date on which it was received (June 10, 1946). The large characters in the upper middle column read "the Shanghai Silk Trade Association," showing that the document used the association's stationery for official dispatches. In the center of the middle column is the 文別 (*wenbie*: type of document) stating that this is an official letter sent by the Shanghai Silk Trade Association to the Shanghai Chamber of Commerce. The lower middle column indicates that the letter was sent on June 8, 1946, and its number is 79. The 附件 (*fujian*: appendix) section in the lower right column reads 如文, that is, "as stated in the document." The trade association's seal is found on the lower middle part of the cover page.

The summary line (*shiyou*: 事由) on the first page of the letter indicates that it concerns a request for a prohibition on the importation of artificial silk from abroad. From the conclusion on the fifth page, we know that the main purpose of the communication was *yongte luhan fengda jixi chazhao* 用特錄函奉達即希查照, that is, "to copy the letter [from . . .] and forward it [to the Shanghai Chamber of Commerce] for your reference." Hence the major portion of this letter is a long quotation of another letter, beginning from *qiezi rikou* 竊自日寇 on the first page and ending with *bingying zhizhi dengqing* 屏營之至等情 on the fourth page.

Note that there were a few copying errors and corrections in this letter. To ensure the integrity of the letter, corrections were marked with authenticating stamps.

玻璃綢	bōlí chóu	artificial silk
同業公會	tóngyè gōnghuì	trade association
敬啓者	jìngqǐzhě	I beg to inform you (an opening phrase in letters to initiate communication about a given matter)

案據	ànjù	according to a communication on file, according to a received (letter from . . .) in our records
敝會	bìhuì	my humble association (the Shanghai Silk Trade Association)
函稱	hánchēng	as the letter states
竊	qiè	my humble self (a term of modesty used when addressing a superior)
日寇	rìkòu	Japanese invaders
奔潰	bēnkuì	to flee, run away; defeated
擁擠	yǒngjǐ	crowded, packed
商肆	shāngsì	store, shop
觸目皆是	chùmù jiē shì	can be seen everywhere, ubiquitous
變本加厲	biàn běn jiā lì	to become aggravated
素崇虛榮	sù chóng xūróng	to always worship vanity
樂購	lè gòu	to enjoy purchasing
定購	dìnggòu	to order (goods)
美匯	měihuì	American currency
震駭	zhènhài	astounding
威懾	wēishè	to terrorize
莫若	mòruò	nothing is more than
繅絲廠	sāosīchǎng	reeling mill
蠶農	cánnóng	silkworm raiser, sericulturist
生計	shēngjì	livelihood, means of livelihood

查	chǎ	we find that . . .
斐聲歐美	fěishēng ōu měi	to enjoy fame in Europe and America
價值甚鉅	jiàzhí shèn jù	extremely high value
方今	fāngjīn	at present
重光	chóngguāng	to recover (lost territory)
建設肇始	jiànshè zhàoshǐ	construction has just started
非 . . . 不可	fēi . . . bùkě	must, to have to
爭取外匯	zhēngqǔ wàihuì	win over foreign currencies
充裕國庫	chōngyù guókù	to replenish the national treasury
聽	tīng	to allow, let
傾銷	qīngxiāo	to dump (goods)
排擠	páijǐ	to push aside, squeeze out, elbow out
陷於破產	xiànyú pòchǎn	to fall into bankruptcy
勢有必然	shìyǒubìrán	inevitable trend; certainly will
謹剖	jǐn pōu	to analyze sincerely
於下	yúxià	as follows
暴日	bàorì	cruel Japanese
略入	lüèru	to invade; invasion
伏莽遍地	fúmǎng biàndì	bandits everywhere
採伐作薪	cǎifá zuòxīn	to cut down for firewood
飼料	sìliaò	forage, fodder, feed
成本	chéngběn	cost

得未曾有	déwèi céngyǒu	unprecedented
舶來	bólái	imported
副產品	fùchǎnpǐn	by-product
廢物	fèiwù	waste material, trash
與之競爭	yǔzhī jìngzhēng	to compete with it
精煉	jīngliàn	to refine
印花	yìnhuā	printed (cloth); a revenue stamp
費時甚久	fèishí shènjiǔ	extremely time-consuming
手續繁複	shǒuxù fánfù	complicated procedure
不賴人力	bùlài rénlì	not to rely on human power
成本至低	chéngběn zhìdī	production cost is low
望洋興嘆	wàng yáng xìngtàn	to feel powerless and frustrated
限制綦嚴	xiànzhì qíyán	strict restriction
稅則	shuìzé	tax regulations
不外乎	bùwàihū	nothing more than
塞漏卮	sāi lòuzhī	to stop up a leak
維國產	wéi guóchǎn	to protect national products
用意至善	yòngyì zhìshàn	good intention
該	gāi	this, that, the said
江海關	jiānghǎiguān	Shanghai Maritime Customs
公佈	gōngbù	to promulgate
輸入	shūrù	to import

遺漏	yílòu	to omit, leave out
所不解者	suǒ bùjiě zhě	that which is difficult to understand
進口商	jìnkǒu shāng	importer
詭以...之名	guǐ yǐ ... zhīmíng	to use the name of falsely
人造膠質	rénzào jiāozhì	manmade fiber, artificial fiber
相朦混	xiāng ménghùn	to deceive
由...所成	yóu ... suǒchéng	made out of, consists of
名異	míngyì	different in name
實同	shítóng	similar in essence
公允	gōngyǔn	just and fair
模塑質	mósù zhì	plasticity
可造型的	kě zàoxíng de	formable
可塑造的	kě sùzào de	moldable
人造松香	rénzào sōngxiāng	synthetic resin
透明	tòumíng	transparent
薄膜	bómó	membrane, film
彫塑	diāosù	molding
魚目混珠	yúmù hùn zhū	to pass off the sham as genuine
藉免	jímiǎn	so as to evade
苟不	gǒubù	if not
勢必	shìbì	will inevitably
與...相抵牾	yǔ ... xiāng dǐwǔ	to conflict with

工潮	gōngcháo	workers' movement
澎湃	péngpài	in an upsurge
迄今未已	qìjīn wèiyǐ	not cease until now
底薪	dǐxīn	basic salary, wages
生活指數	shēnghuó zhǐshù	cost-of-living index
相乘	xiāngchéng	to multiply each other
空前危機	kōngqián wēijī	an unprecedented crisis
摧殘	cuīcán	devastation
故特籲請	gùtèyùqǐng	hereby appeal for
立許	lìxǔ	to grant prompt permission to
以維 . . . 生計	yǐwéi . . . shēngjì	in order to maintain the livelihood of
職工	zhígōng	staff and workers
不勝迫切	bùshèng pòqiè	extremely urgent
屏營之至	bǐngyíng zhīzhì	in anxious expectation (of the superior to handle affairs) (this phrase usually appears at the end of a document from a subordinate)
等情	děngqíng	(used to acknowledge a communication of an inferior; here the long quotation ends)
到會	dàohuì	to reach (the Shanghai Chamber of Commerce)
纖維	xiānwéi	fiber
有干禁令	yǒugān jìnlìng	to violate the prohibition

色澤	sèzé	color and luster
遠非...所可倫比	yuǎnfēi ... suǒ kě lúnbǐ	cannot be compared with
無法倖存	wúfǎ xìngcún	cannot survive
瀕於絶滅	bīnyú juémiè	on the verge of extinction
行將	xíngjiāng	to be about to
據函前情	jùhánqiánqíng	having received a letter regarding the above issue; based on the content of the above letter
除...外	chú ... wài	in addition to . . . , besides . . .
備文	bèiwén	to prepare a document
樣本	yàngběn	sample
晉京	jìnjīng	to enter the capital city
阻遏	zǔ'è	to thwart
用特	yòngtè	I thereby especially . . .
錄函	lùhán	to copy a letter
奉達	fèngdá	have the honor to inform
即希查照	jíxī cházhào	please note clearly
為荷	wéihè	grateful, obliged

Document 2 (vol. 2, pp. 50–53)

A Letter from the Xiangxing Export Company to the Shanghai Chamber of Commerce Asking for Assistance with a Petition for Exemption from Duties on the Imported Artificial Silk Components of Exported Silk Clothing
祥興出口商行致上海市商會函

This is a letter to the Shanghai Chamber of Commerce. The summary reference sheet provides useful information about the document. The words on the top of the page indicate that this is the Shanghai Chamber of Commerce's synopsis sheet. The top of the first line on the right shows the date when the document was received (February 14). The upper middle part of the line tells us the institution from which it was received (the Xiangxing Export Company). The lower middle part of the first line indicates the type of document (letter). The bottom of the line shows that there is no appendix attached. The second line from the right is a summary of the document (*shiyou* 事由), which ends with the conventional word *you* 由. The third line, 擬辦 (*juban*: recommended action), records the measures that a departmental secretary of the Chamber of Commerce recommends or proposes to take. Here the recommended action is 轉呈 (*zhuancheng*: petition [to the Inspectorate of the Shanghai Maritime Customs] on behalf of [the Xiangxing Export Company]). This recommendation is as the letter requested.

商會	shānghuì	chamber of commerce
摘由單	zhāiyóudān	synopsis sheet
出口商行	chūkǒu shānghāng	export trading company
轉函	zhuǎnhán	to pass on a letter
江海關	jiānghǎiguān	Shanghai Maritime Customs
補征...稅	bǔzhēng ... shuì	to impose insufficient duties
迅予豁免	xùnyù huòmiǎn	to grant prompt exemption
懇請貴會轉呈...	kěnqǐng guìhuì zhuǎnchéng	beg your Shanghai Chamber of Commerce to petition on our behalf (to the Ministry of Finance and the

		Inspectorate of Shanghai Maritime Customs)
稅務司	shuìwùsī	Commissioner of Customs, Inspectorate of Customs
竊商人等	qiè shǎngrén děng	we humble businessmen (similiar phrases are 民等、商等、敝商、民商、敝民)
太平洋戰事	tàipíngyáng zhànshì	the Pacific War
即告停頓	jígào tíngdùn	was promptly suspended
本業	běnyè	this trade or business
同人	tóngrén	colleagues
莫不	mòbù	there is none who is (does) not
慶幸	qìngxìng	to rejoice
共謀復業	gòngmóu fùyè	to work together to restore a business
此誠	cǐ chéng	this is indeed
挽回	wǎnhuí	to retrieve, redeem
良機	liángjī	good opportunity
溯...自...以來	sù...zì...yǐlaí	ever since ...
事匪易易	shì fěi yìyì	it is not an easy matter
差幸	chāxìng	barely satisfactory
手工藝品	shǒugōngyì pǐn	handicrafts
徵收	zhēngshōu	to impose, collect (a levy, etc.)
詎	jù	(interjection of surprise) who could have expected that ...
出於意料	chūyú yìliào	contrary to one's expectation

261

繡花	xiùhuā	embroidery
重稅	zhòngshuì	heavy taxation
業經	yèjīng	already
淪陷區	lúnxiàn qū	(Japanese-)occupied areas
囤積	túnjī	to hoard for speculation
獲致	huòzhì	to receive, accumulate, accrue
厚利	hòulì	large profits
愈...益	yù...yì	the more ..., the more
綢貨	chóuhuò	silk goods
繁多	fánduō	in great numbers and variety
一經	yījīng	as soon as, once, immediately after
報關	bàoguān	to declare something at customs
重重	chóngchóng	to be beset with (difficulties)
稍一失當	shāo yī shīdàng	with slightly improper handling
不特...尚且	bùtè...shàngqiě	not only ... but also
罰金	fájīn	fine
有...之慨	yǒu...zhīkǎi	to sigh with a deep feeling about
左右為難	zuǒyòu wéinán	in a dilemma
為數極少	wéishǔ jíshǎo	very few in number
抑且	yìqiě	moreover
應市	yìngshì	to meet the demand of the market
起而代之	qǐ ér dài zhī	to replace

自阻銷路	zì zǔ xiāolù	to block one's own sale
瀝陳	lìchén	to state sincerely
俯察下情	fǔchá xiàqíng	investigate conditions at lower levels; gracious consideration of our humble situation
體恤商艱	tǐxù shāng jiān	to understand and sympathize with our businessmen's difficulties
實為感禱	shíwéi gǎndǎo	indeed grateful
藉蘇民困	jièsū mínkùn	so as to relieve the distress of the masses
實為感禱	shíweí gōngdǎo	earnestly grateful for your favor (a conventional phrase closing a letter asking for a favor)
此上	cǐshàng	hence respectfully present to . . .

Document 3 (vol. 2, p. 54)

The Shanghai Chamber of Commerce's Joint Draft for a Petition to the Ministry of Finance and for an Official Letter to the Inspectorate of the Shanghai Maritime Customs for the Exemption of Duties on Artificial Silk Components of Exported Silk Clothing
上海市商會致財政部呈文〔稿〕
上海市商會致江海關稅務司函〔稿〕

This is a joint draft for two separate documents with the same content (i.e., a petition to the Ministry of Finance and an official letter to the Inspectorate of the Shanghai Maritime Customs), both concerning an exemption from duties on artificial silk components of exported silk clothing. The dual function of the draft is indicated by the top of the line in the right margin. The middle of the line is a summary of the document in the formula ". . . 由," and at the bottom of the line is the category number of the document, 第1073號, which is under the category of "ordinary" (*pu* 普). The line in the left margin shows the date on which the draft was written (February 15, 1946), the name of the person who wrote it, and the name of the copier and proofreader.

Although the main part of the document was drafted for both a petition and an official letter, the differences between the two types of documents can be seen in the formula used in each case: the former starts with the opening phrase *cheng wei chengqing shi* 呈為呈請事 ("This petition is a request concerning the matter of"), whereas the latter begins with *jing qi zhe* 逕啓者 ("I beg to inform you"); upon reviewing the issue and past communication the former uses the phrase *lihe . . . chengqing* 理合 . . . 呈請 ("dutifully petition for"), while the latter employs *xianging . . . handa* 相應 . . . 函達 ("correspondingly send you this letter"); and the former concludes with the phrase *yangqi jun bu jianhe* 仰祈鈞部鑒核 ("respectfully request your Ministry to examine and approve the petition"), whereas the latter ends with *jixi gui guan chahe* 即希貴關察核 ("your Customs' checkup and approval will be appreciated"). The word 鈞 is used to refer to the higher authorities, but 貴 to an institution or person when there is no subordination involved. Expressions of gratitude also differ between the two types of documents. The petition uses *shi wei gongbian* 實為公便 ("truly both just and expedient"; "truly grateful for your gracious favor"), whereas the latter uses *shi ren gongyi* 實級公誼 ("truly appreciate your friendly assistance"). Another difference is reflected in the use of phrases for addressing receivers: *jincheng* 謹呈 ("written respectfully to") in the petition to a superior agency and *cizhi* 此致 ("hereby this letter is sent to") in the official letter to an agency of the same rank or without subordinate distinctions.

云云	yúnyún	stands for the omitted part of a quoted letter from the Xiangxing Export Company; when this draft was copied as a formal document, the omitted part would be included in full; it is not uncommon to find such use of 云云 in document drafts
至	zhì	until (indicates that when this draft was copied to become a formal document, the omitted part would be copied up to this point; specifically, the part between 即告停頓 and 而符政府獎勵 would be fully copied)
符...之旨意	fú ... zhī zhǐyì	in accordance with someone's order
等語	děngyǔ	(signpost for ending a quotation or a reference to a document from an inferior institution; here it indicates the end of the quotation from the Xiangxing Export Company's letter)
到會	dàohuì	reached the Chamber (Shanghai Chamber of Commerce)
完過	wánguò	have paid, have finished
返還稅項	fǎnhuán shuìxiàng	categories of taxes to be returned
角逐	jiǎozhú	to contend with
市場	shìchǎng	market
當茲	dāngzī	at present
戰後復興	zhànhòu fùxīng	postwar restoration
恢復元氣	huīfù yuánqì	to regain one's strength
基於上述理由	jīyú shàngshù lǐyóu	for the above-mentioned reasons

似	sì	it seems that . . .
再行	zài xíng	again, once more
轉致	zhuǎnzhì	to cause, result in
阻抑外銷	zǔyì wàixiāo	to thwart the sale abroad
准予	zhǔnyǔ	to agree to do something
行知	xíngzhī	to issue an official document
呈部	chéngbù	petition to the ministry (Ministry of Finance)

Document 4 (vol. 2, pp. 55–56)

Reply from the Inspectorate of the Shanghai Maritime Customs to the Shanghai Chamber of Commerce Regarding the Exemption from Duties Imposed on Artificial Silk Components of Exported Silk Clothing

江海關稅務司函復上海市商會

This document, as indicated by the cover page, is an official letter from the Inspectorate of the Shanghai Maritime Customs (ISMS). The first column on the right is a detailed summary of the document written in the formula "... 由"; the bottom of the column is left blank, indicating that there is no appendix attached. The second column 擬辦 (*niban*: recommended action) is for the convenience of the addressee's internal staff to record action recommendations. In this case, the Shanghai Chamber of Commerce (SCC), not the ISMC, enters this column. Here the recommended action is *zhuanzhi* 轉知: notify (the Xiangxing Export Company) on behalf of (the ISMS). The line in the left margin indicates the document number (no. 198) and the date on which it was received. The letter was written using the format of an official letter.

From a reference in a later document, we can infer that the date of this document is February 25, 1946.

In the document the ISMC paraphrases instead of using a direct quotation when referring to letter no. 1073 from the SCC. The paraphrasing begins with a brief reference to the Xiangxing Export Company's letter to the SCC (以據 ... 等語), then goes on to the ISMS's request (函囑察核 ...), and ends with 等由. From 准此 on, the ISMC begins to enunciate what should be done with the case.

函復關於 ... 辦法	hǎnfù guānyǔ ... bànfǎ	a reply in the form of a letter regarding the regulations of ...
轉口	zhuǎnkǒu	in transit
業經奉令	yèjīng fènglìng	to have already respectfully received a decree
廢止	fèizhǐ	to abolish
所有 ... 一律	suǒyǒu ... yīlù	all ... without exception

查照轉知	chǎzhào zhuǎnzhī	to note and make known in turn, take official notice and notify (the Xiangxing Export Company) on our behalf
以 . . . 等語	yǐ . . . děngyǔ	(brackets a summary of the letter from the Xiangxing Export Comapany to the Shanghai Chamber of Commerce)
函請轉呈	hánqǐng zhuǎnchéng	to request by letter to petition on their behalf
函囑	hánzhǔ	to enjoin by letter
察核	cháhé	to examine and decide
等由	děngyóu	(followed by zhǔncǐ; refers to a communication by officials of equal standing or of slightly inferior rank; here it signifies the end of the reference to the SCC's letter no. 1073)
准此	zhǔncǐ	on receipt of the above (used between equals), according to this (letter); accordingly, therefore
係屬	xìshǔ	is considered as
本關	běnguān	this customs office (the Shanghai Maritime Customs)
層奉 . . . 令	céngfèng . . . lìng	to receive an order handed down (here from the Ministry of Finance)
准函前由	zhǔnhán qiányóu	having received the letter regarding the above issue; based on/in accordance with the received letter concerning the foregoing affairs

相應函復	xiāngyìng hánfù	to reply correspondingly in the form of an official letter
查照	cházhào	to take notice, note this
轉知	zhǔanzhī	to notify (a third party), make it known in turn

Document 5 (vol. 2, p. 57)

The Shanghai Chamber of Commerce's Letter Responding
to the Xiangxing Export Company (Draft)
上海市商會復祥興出口商行函〔稿〕

This document is the draft of an official letter from the Shanghai Chamber of Commerce (SCC) to the Xiangxing Export Company concerning the latter's petition for an exemption from duties imposed on artificial silk components of exported silk clothing. This letter is written on the same kind of draft sheet as Document 3, with its summary and number in the right margin and the date (February 26), drafter's name (a personal seal), and the name of the copier and proofreader in the left margin.

Like Document 3, the handwriting in this document is very cursive and sometimes illegible. Generally speaking, draft documents used cursive more often than formal documents.

准 . . . 函復	zhǔn . . . hánfù	based on a reply letter from . . . ; to receive a reply letter from . . .
前據來函	qiánjù láihán	according to your previous letter, having received your letter
將 . . . 一項	jiāng . . . yīxiàng	regarding the issue of . . .
等情	děngqǐng	(here it signifies the end of a reference to the Xiangxing Export Company's letter)
即經 . . . 去後, 兹	jíjīng . . . qùhòu, zī	after (document processing), now . . .
分別呈函	fénbié chénghán	to send the petition and letter respectively
公函	gónghán	official letter
略開	lüèkāi	(this is followed by a direct, though abridged, quotation of a segment of the said document)

等由	děngyóu	(here it signifies the end of the quotation of the ISMC's letter no. 198, which begins with 查輸入本口)
原料	yuánliào	raw materials
合先	héxīan	the first right thing to do is . . .
備函轉達	bèihán zhuǎndā	to prepare a letter and pass it on

Document 6 (vol. 2, pp. 58–59)

The Ministry of Finance's Approval of the Exemption from Duties Imposed on Artificial Silk Components of Exported Silk Clothing
財政部批復上海市商會

This document is an official reply from the Ministry of Finance to the Shanghai Chamber of Commerce (SCC) concerning the latter's petition. In the right margin is the date when the SCC received the document as well as the incoming document number assigned by the SCC.

In the previous chapter we examined the format and vocabulary of this type of document. As indicated at the top of the first column on the right, the opening formula for this type of document is "... 批" (*pi:* "an official reply from ... "). The bottom of the column shows when the document was written and its category number (an outgoing document from the ministry concerning customs affairs). In the following two lines is a summary of the document (*shiyou* 事由), followed by the phrase in the middle of the page specifying to whom the reply is made (批 ...) and a summary of the petition received. The main content of the reply starts with 呈悉 (*chengxi:* the petition has been received). On the lower part and across the right margin of both the cover page and the following page is the ministerial seal.

所稱	suǒchēng	the so-called, what is called
應由	yīngyóu	ought to be done by
逕向	jìngxiàng	directly
洽辦	qiàbàn	to contact and deal with someone about something
原訂 ... 之辦法	yuándìng ... zhī bànfǎ	the original regulation concerning ...
經於 (date) 令飭	jīngyú (date) lìngchì	It is on our record that on (date) we
轉令 ... 在案	zhuǎnlìng ... zàiàn	ordered one person to convey the order to another person
仰知照	yǎng zhīzhào	please take official note of it

Document 7 (vol. 2, pp. 60–61)

A Decree from the Ministry of Economic Affairs to the
Shanghai Chamber of Commerce Regarding Abolition of Export Duty
經濟部致上海市商會訓令

This document is a decree issued to a subordinate organ. In the right margin is the date when the document was received (September 23, 1946). On the bottom of this margin is the incoming document number (9-35). The first column on the right contains the title "... 訓令" (*shunling*: a decree by) and its number as an outgoing document, as well as the date when it was dispatched (September 20, 1946). The following line is a summary of the decree in the formula "... 由." The second line from the left indicates the receiver of the decree. The main part of the document reviews the case, beginning with with the phrase "案奉 ... 開" (it is on record that we have received ..., stating) and concluding with the phrase "合行令仰遵照" (we should carry out the order in accordance with) followed by the phrase "等因," which marks the end of a quotation from a communication from a superior (in this case, the Executive Yuan).

Note that this document contains two layers of quotation. The outer layer is the Ministry of Economic Affairs' quotation of the Executive Yuan's decree no. 1236, which begins with 案奉國民政府 and ends with 除分令財政部外, 合行令仰遵照。 等因. The inner layer is the Executive Yuan's quotation of the National Government's decree no. 335 (starting with 國防最高委員會 and ending with 除令交立法院外, 令行遵照。等因).

The decree concludes with "此令" (hereby this decree is issued). Vocabulary items regularly found in this type of document include "案奉," "開," "合行," and "此令."

案奉	ànfèng	it is on record that we have received
開	kāi	to state
國防最高委員會	gúofáng zùigāowěiyuánhuì	Supreme National Defense Council
先予施行	xiānyǔ shīxíng	to authorize then implement first
立法院	lìfǎyùan	Legislative Yuan
立法程序	lìfǎ chéngxù	legislative procedure

除令交 . . . 外	chú lìngjiāo . . . wài	in addition to turn over (the case) to (the Legislative Yuan)
合行令仰遵照	lìngxíng lìngyǎng zūnzhào	we should issue an order, please act in accord with it (here 令行 seems a copying error for 合行 [should])
除分令財政部外	chǔ fēnlìng cǎizhèngbù wài	in addition to issuing a separate order to the Ministry of Finance
合行	héxíng	it is therefore necessary
轉飭遵照	zhuǎnchì zūnzhào	to pass on an order for you to obey, issue an order as instructed and please accordingly

Document 8 (vol. 2, p. 62)

The Shanghai Chamber of Commerce's Letter to
Shanghai Same-Trade Associations (Draft)
上海市商會致上海各同業公會函(稿)

This is a draft of the Shanghai Chamber of Commerce's letter to twenty-one same-trade and same-industry associations announcing the Ministry of Economic Affairs' decree regarding exemption from export duties. The document follows the format and formulas of an official letter, starting with 逕啓者 (I beg to inform you) and concluding with 此致 (sincerely yours). Yet, as we have seen in Document 3, this type of draft letter does not identify the sender's name since it was for internal use. In the right margin is a summary of the letter in the formula ". . . 由," as well as the number of the document. In the left margin is the date of the draft (September 24, 1946) and the names of drafter and proofreader. In the top margin is stamped *shan* 繕, indicating that this draft was to be copied.

云云至	yúnyún zhì	(see glossary in Document 3)
下會	xiàhùi	came down (to the Shanghai Chamber of Commerce)
用特	yòngtè	for this special purpose
錄令函達	lùlìng hándá	to copy the decree and send it to you by letter
週知	zhōuzhī	to make known to all
土布	tǔbù	handwoven cloth
毛巾被毯	máojīn bèi tǎn	towel coverlet
內衣	nèiyī	underwear
織造	zhīzào	weavings
化妝品	huàzhuāngpǐn	cosmetics

地毯	dìtǎn	carpet
皂燭	zàozhú	soap and candle
汽燈	qìdēng	gas lamp
油墨	yóumò	printing ink
花邊抽繡	huābiān chōuxiù	lace trimming
飛花	fēihuā	jacquard
洋裝	yángzhuāng	Western garments
草帽	cǎomào	straw hat
針織工業	zhēnzhī gōngyè	knitting industry
造紙	zàozhǐ	papermaking
造漆	zàoqī	paint production
桐油	tóngyóu	tung oil
蛋	dàn	egg
苧麻	zhùmá	ramie
腸衣輸出	chángyī shūchū	sausage-casing export
搪磁	tángcí	enamelware
熱水瓶	rèshuǐpíng	thermos bottle
調味粉	tiáowèi fěn	condiment, seasoning

Document 9 (vol. 2, pp. 63–67)

A Letter to the Shanghai Commercial Association
致上海市商業聯合會公函

This document is a letter from a business association to the Shanghai Commercial Association, urging the latter to petition the government to promptly enact labor laws. The author of the letter is unknown. Although this document is much longer than the others in this chapter, its format and vocabulary are similar. The letter resembles an internal draft since there is neither seal nor author's name.

聯合會	liánhéhuì	an association
速訂	sùdìng	to stipulate promptly
勞動法規	láodòng fǎguī	labor laws
竊維	qièwéi	we think . . . (an auxiliary word used in the beginning or middle of a sentence to begin a statement)
列邦	lièbāng	various foreign nations
勞動爭議	láodòng zhēngyì	labor dispute
約分	yūefēn	can be roughly divided into
任意之和解	rènyì zhī héjiě	reconciliation
公斷	gōngduàn	arbitration
發達	fādá	to develop; developed
雙方各舉	shuāngfāng gèjǔ	each side elects respectively
代表	dàibiǎo	representative

調查	diàochǎ	to investigate
倘...再	tǎng ... zài	if ... then
以解決之	yǐ jiějué zhī	in order to solve
後又改前制	hòu yòu gǎi qiánzhì	later change the previous practice
另選	lìngxuǎn	to elect another
給以	gěiyǐ	to grant, give
判定	pàndìng	judgment; to judge
強制	qiángzhì	forced
新西蘭	Xīnxīlán	New Zealand
行之最久	xíng zhī zuìjiǔ	the most effective practice for the longest period
不偏不黨	bùpiān bùdǎng	impartial
由...選	yóu ... xuǎn	elect from, choose from
除...外, 餘	chú ... wài, yú	in addition to ... , all others
從事	cōngshì	to conduct, be engaged in
倘...即	tǎng ... jí	if ... then
勸告	quàngào	exhortation
不服	bùfú	to refuse to obey
控訴	kòngsù	to accuse, submit a complaint
審判官	shěnpàn guān	a judge
總督	zǒngdū	governor (governor-general)
任命	rènmìng	to appoint

最高法院	zuìgāo fǎyuàn	the Supreme Court
推事	tuīshì	a judge
推薦（荐）	tuījiàn	to recommend
判決案	pànjué àn	decision of the court
絕對	juéduì	absolutely
拘束	jūshù	binding
效力	xiàolì	force
凡	fán	every, any, all
一經 . . . 即	yījīng . . . jí	as soon as, once, immediately after
同盟	tóngméng	joint
罷工	bàgōng	to strike; a (labor) strike
閉鎖	bìsuǒ	to picket, close
工場	gōngchǎng	factory
兩事	liǎngshì	two things, two matters
前者	qiánzhě	the former
. . . 之利在於	. . . zhīlì zàiyú	the advantage of . . . lies in
自由調處	zìyóu tiáochǔ	to arbitrate freely
其終也	qízhōngyě	in the end, the disadvantage
每啓 . . . 之弊	měiqǐ . . . zhībì	often brings about the malfeasance of
久延不決	jiǔyán bùjué	procrastination
後者	hòuzhě	the latter

在乎	zàihū	to depend on (whether . . .), consist in; to care, mind
早決	zǎojué	early solution; to decide early
爭端	zhēngduān	dispute
其末也	qímòyě	in the end; the disadvantage
易貽 . . . 之譏	yìyí . . . zhījī	likely to give ground for ridicule
專斷	zhuānduàn	arbitrary
不公	bùgōng	unfair
兩者	liǎngzhě	both
互有優劣	hùyǒu yōulüè	each has its strong and weak points
欲定	yùdìng	if desirable to settle
要視 . . . 耳	yàoshì . . . ěr	should depend on
國情	guóqíng	national conditions
在初	zàichū	initially, at first
僅見於	jǐnjiànyú	is found only in
刑律	xínglù	criminal law
違警律	wéijǐnglù	laws governing police violations
頒	bān	to promulgate
工會條例	gōnghuì tiáolì	labor union regulations
載明	zǎimíng	to put in writing clearly
細釋其意	xìshì qíyì	to interpret the meaning carefully
係採 . . . 之法	xìcǎi . . . zhīfǎ	to adopt the method, means of

仲裁	zhòngcái	to arbitrate
與...略同	yǔ . . . lüètóng	roughly the same as
仍寓...之意	réngyù . . . zhīyì	still imply that, still contain the meaning that
公共安寧	gōnggòng ānníng	public order
惟	wěi	however
已逾三載	yǐyú sānzǎi	has been over three years
先之	xiānzhī	first
繼之	jìzhī	subsequently
共推	gòngtuī	together elect or choose
第三者	dìsānzhě	a third party (to a dispute, etc.)
終之	zhōngzhī	finally
官廳	guāntīng	local authorities
固極明顯	gùjí míngxiǎn	undoubtedly obvious
轉折既多	zhuǎnzhé jìduō	full of twists and turns
需時自久	xūshí zìjiǔ	certainly time-consuming
風潮	fēngcháo	unrest
頓呈...之象	dùnchéng . . . zhīxiàng	immediately present an appearance of
參証	cānzhèng	put in the light of
酌定	zhúodìng	to deliberate and formulate a decision
庶於	shùyú	so as to
維持	wéichí	to keep, maintain, preserve
兩有裨益	liǎng yǒu bìyì	of benefit to both

慎審	shènshěn	cautious
改訂	gǎidìng	to reformulate, rewrite
種類綦繁	zhǒnglèi qífán	of great variety
斷非	duànfēi	absolutely not
竟其功	jìng qí gōng	to accomplish the task
參酌	cānzhuó	to consider a matter in the light of
詳定	xiángdìng	to draw up detailed (regulations)
日趨精密	rìqū jīngmì	become increasingly precise
智識有限	zhìshí yǒuxiàn	limited in knowledge
有 . . . 必要	yǒu . . . bìyào	there is the necessity to
補充教育	bǔchōng jiàoyù	to augment education
尚焉	shàng yān	of great value, important
衰老病亡	shuāilǎo bìng wáng	to become old and feeble, and die
在所不免	zài suǒ bùmiǎn	cannot be avoided
顧	gù	and, accordingly
勞工儲蓄	láogōng chǔxù	workers' savings
保險	bǎoxiǎn	insurance
按年遞增	ànnián dìzēng	to increase year by year
失業漸多	shīyè jiànduō	an increase in unemployment
須圖安插之方	xū tú ānchā zhī fāng	to find a means of assigning jobs
公共介紹所	gōnggòng jièshào suǒ	public agency for (job) placement

移民	yímín	migration, immigration, emigration; immigrants
墾殖	kěnzhí	to reclaim and cultivate wasteland
凡此諸端	fáncǐ zhūduān	all these items
無一非	wúyīfēi . . .	all are (literally, "not a single one is not")
際茲	jìzī	at present, presently
大局甫定	dàjú fǔdìng	the overall situation has settled
早日頒行	zǎorì bānxíng	issue early for enforcement
收 . . . 之效	shōu . . . zhīxiào	produce the effect of . . .
考	kǎo	to examine
萌芽	méngyá	to germinate
產業革命	chǎnyè gémìng	Industrial Revolution
機械	jīxiè	machinery
手工業	shǒugōngyè	handicraft industry
企業家	qǐyè jiā	entrepreneur
不能立足	bùnéng lìzú	difficult to keep a foothold
遂致	suìzhì	therefore, resulting in
資本	zīběn	capital
集中於	jízhōng yú	to concentrate, accumulate
少數	shǎo shù	a small number of, a few, a minority of
物價	wùjià	commodity prices
所入薪貲	suǒrù xīnzī	salary, income

無以為生	wúyǐ wéishēng	cannot eke out a living
相激相蕩	xiāngjīxiāngdàng	to agitate each other, stimulate each other
階級之戰鬥	jiējí zhī zhàndòu	class struggle
以起	yǐqǐ	start
稍異於是	shāoyì yúshì	slightly different from that
尚乏	shàngfá	still lack
向受	xiàngshòu	to suffer from all along
帝國主義	dìguózhǔyì	imperialism
漸見衰落	jiànjiàn shuāiluò	to decline gradually
既...復...	jì...fù...	already...again...
協定性質	xiédìng xìngzhì	in the nature of an agreement
幼稚工業	yòuzhì gōngyè	young industries
幾無以自存	jīwú yǐ zìcún	almost cannot survive
應以...為度	yīngyǐ...wéidù	should not exceed the limit of
折耗	zhéhào	to lose money
勢將	shìjiāng	certainly will, be bound to
閉歇	bìxiē	to close down
流離失所	liúlí shī suǒ	to become destitute and homeless
足貽	zúyí	enough to affect adversely
社	shè	society
內外交困	nèiwài jiāokùn	beset with difficulties at home and abroad
奔濤駭浪	bèntāo hàilàng	a perilous situation

隱憂	yǐnyōu	hidden danger
預為防範	yùwéi fángfàn	to take precautions aganst
遵循	zūnxún	to adhere to, comply with

Document 10 (vol. 2, pp. 68–76)

Draft Regulations for Industrial and Commercial Associations in Beiping
北平市工商同業公會章程準則草案

準則	zhǔnzé	standard, criterion
草案	cǎoàn	a draft
總則	zǒngzé	general rules, general principles
暫行條例	zànxíng tiáolì	provisional regulations
定名為	dìngmíng wéi	to be named as
某業	mǒuyè	a certain trade, industry
以 . . . 為宗旨	yǐ . . . wéi zōngzhǐ	take . . . as the aim
施行	shīxíng	to put into effect, implement
事務所	shìwùsuǒ	institution, office
任務	rènwù	mission, task
如左	rúzuǒ	as follows
關於 . . . 事項	guānyú . . . shìxiàng	the affairs concerning . . .
主管官署	zhǔguǎn guānshǔ	government office in charge
委辦	wěibàn	entrust someone to handle some task
調查研究	diàochá yánjīu	to investigate and study
興辦	xīngbàn	to initiate, establish

公益	gōngyì	public welfare
弊害	bìhài	harm, corrupt practice
矯正	jiǎozhèng	correction
必要時	bìyàoshì	when necessary
維持	weíchí	to sustain
配給	pèijǐ	ration, allocation
所揭	suǒjīe	promulgated, announced by
宗旨	zōngzhǐ	aim, purpose
所列	suǒlìe	listed by
係指...而言	xìzhǐ...éryán	is in regard to
左列各款	zuǒlìe gèkuǎn	the following items or subsections
共同	gòngtóng	collectively, together
收買	shōumǎi	to purchase
販賣	fànmài	to sell
保管	bǎoguǎn	to take care of
燃料	ránliào	fuel
審議	shěnyì	examination and deliberation; discussion
調節	tiáojíe	to regulate, adjust
債務擔保	zhàiwù ānbǎo	debt guarantee
取締	qǔdì	to proscribe, ban
行號	hánghào	business establishments, shops
主體人	zhǔtǐrén	legal entity, owners

情事	qíngshì	circumstances, situation
褫奪公權	chǐduó gōngquán	to deprive of civil rights
除名	chúmíng	to remove someone from the rolls
破產	pòchǎn	to go bankrupt, become insolvent
復權	fùquán	to restore (civil) rights
行為能力	xíngwéi nénglì	capacity
發言權	fāyánquán	right to speak
表決權	biǎojúequán	right to vote
權數	quánshù	amount/number of rights
以...作比例	yǐ...zuò bǐlì	in proportion to/with
繳納	jiǎonà	to pay
會費	huìfèi	membership fee
盡...義務	jìn...yìwù	to fulfill...obligation(s)
遵守	zūnshǒu	to abide by
欠繳	qiànjiǎo	to owe a payment of
警告	jǐnggào	to give a disciplinary warning
予以...處分	yǔyǐ...chǔfèn	to give the punishment of
入會	rùhùi	admission to the union
志愿書	zhìyuànshū	application form
會員証	hùiyuán zhèng	membership certificate
無故出會	wúgù chūhùi	to withdraw from the association without reason

商店解散	shāngdiàn jiěsàn	dissolution of a store
商店倒閉	shāngdiàn dǎobì	closing of a store
聲敘理由	shēngshù lǐyóu	to state the reason
填具	tiánjù	to fill out
出會書	chūhùishū	form for withdrawal from the union
認可	rènkě	to approve; approval
委託書	wěituōshū	a certificate entrusting someone to do something
改派	gǎipài	to reappoint
亦同	yìtóng	also the same
解任	jiěrèn	to be relieved of office
事由	shìyóu	cause, reason
致 . . . 者	zhì . . . zhě	someone who incurs (something)
妨害	fánghài	to impair, be harmful to
名譽	míngyù	reputation
信用	xìnyòng	credit
充任	chōngrèn	to act as, serve as (i.e., an official)
理事	lǐshì	director
監事	jiānshì	supervisor
無記名	wújìmíng	secret ballot
連舉法	liánjǔfǎ	election from the lower levels
當選	dāngxuǎn	(be) elected

候補	hóubǔ	alternative, expectant
逾	yú	to exceed, go beyond
理事長	lǐshìzhǎng	chairman of the board of directors
常務理事	chángwù lǐshì	standing members of the board of directors
行使	xíngshǐ	to exercise (a right, power, etc.)
左列職權	zuǒliè zhíquán	the following functions and powers

Chapter 24

Documents on National Government Economic Agencies:
Introduction and Glossary
國民政府經濟部會

This chapter contains two documents from key central government economic agencies during the Nanjing Decade (1927–37). These records reflect the central government's effort to coordinate national economic projects.

The National Economic Council (Quanguo jingji weiyuanhui 全國經濟委員會) was established in 1933 after a two-year preparatory phase and was subordinate to the National Government (Guomin zhengfu 國民政府). The council was designed to function as a cabinet-level coordinating agency for economic affairs and was composed of heads of the Ministries of Interior, Finance, Transportation, Industry, Education, and other departments and agencies with jurisdiction over economic development.

Although designed to centralize economic planning, the council's vast array of responsibilities inevitably engendered administrative overlap, conflict, and confusion. First, the council was responsible for the planning and authorization of national economic "reconstruction" and development. Second, it was responsible for approving budgets for economic projects. Finally, it was expected to undertake specific projects directly, such as highway construction, agricultural development, waterworks, education, and health care. After the National Economic Council was dissolved following the outbreak of the Sino-Japanese War in 1937, its functions were assumed by the Ministry of Economic Affairs and other agencies.

The Huai River Control Commission (Daohuai weiyuanhui 導淮委員會) was established in 1929. The commission was directly under the jurisdiction of the National Government. Later, in 1934, the Huai River Control Commission came under the jurisdiction of the National Economic Council. The commission wielded wide authority in managing the Huai River. All central, provincial, and local agencies, as well as military organizations based in the valley, were formally under the administrative control of the Huai River Control Commission.

The functions and structure of agencies such as the National Economic Commission and the Huai River Control Commission reflect the attempt by the Nationalist regime to enhance central authority and central coordination of national economic development. Both efforts met with varying degrees of success.

Document 1 (vol. 2, pp. 79–93)

Report of the Secretariat of the National Economic Council
經濟委員會秘書處報告

This document is a long draft report. From the different handwriting styles, we can see that it was copied by several persons and that other persons marked insertions and corrections during the preparation and review process.

It has a reference page recording the process of preparation and approval as an outgoing document. This page was not sent out. Instead, it was kept by the organization that produced the document for future reference. The letterhead reveals that the Secretariat of the National Economic Council (Quanguo jingji weiyuanhui mishu chu 全國經濟委員會秘書處) originated the document. In the upper right corner the document is identified as a 便函 (*bianhan*: informal letter). The recipient of the informal letter was Ye Chucang (1887–1946), then secretary-general of the Nationalist Party Central Executive Committee (Zhongguo guomindang di si jie zhongyang zhixing weiyuanhui 中國國民黨第四屆中央執行委員會). The term 事由 (*shiyou*: subject) indicates the purpose of the correspondence. A section member (*keyuan* 科員), a section chief (*kezhang* 科長), and the secretary-general approved the document. This document was commissioned (*jiaoban* 交辦) and drafted (*nigao* 擬稿) on January 16, 1934. It was copied (*shanxie* 繕寫) and sealed and sent (*fengfa* 封發) on the same day. Finally, the document number is given to the left of the dates.

無不	wúbù	all without exception, invariably
視為	shìwéi	to see as, regard as
均	jūn	without exception, all
以為	yǐwéi	as
籌劃	chóuhuà	to deliberate and plan
總樞紐	zǒng shūniǔ	most pivotal agency
頒佈	bānbù	to promulgate, to issue

條例	tiáolì	regulations, rules, ordinances
任命	rènmìng	to appoint (someone to office)
指定	zhǐdìng	to appoint, assign, designate
負有...全責	fùyǒu . . . quánzé	to assume full responsibility
促進	cùjìn	to promote, press forward, urge to proceed; promotion
生計	shēngjì	means of livelihood, livelihood
允宜	yǔnyí	ought to be, should be
慎重	shènzhòng	cautious, careful, prudent
訂定	dìngdìng	to draw up beforehand
籌備	chóubèi	to prepare, arrange
簡則	jiǎnzé	general regulations
規定	guīdìng	to stipulate; rule, regulation
應辦	yīngbàn	should attend to
事務	shìwù	work, routine; general affairs
令派	lìngpài	to appoint by decree
前後	qián-hòu	from beginning to end, altogether
計約	jìyuē	approximately
修正	xiūzhèng	to revise, amend, correct
直隸	zhílì	to be directly subordinate to
取銷	qǔxīao	to abolish
委員長制	wěiyuánzhǎng zhì	in the commission the chief exercises leadership in everything

改設	gǎishè	to re-establish
常務委員	chángwùwěiyuán	standing committee member
職掌	zhízhǎng	duty, responsibility, function
審核	shěnhé	to examine and approve
經費	jīngfèi	funds, budget
核定	hédìng	to check and ratify, appraise and decide
監督	jiāndū	to supervise, control
指導	zhǐdǎo	to guide and direct
特定	tèdìng	specially designated, specific, specified
實施	shíshī	to put into effect, implement, carry out
重派	chóngpài	to reappoint
蒞會	lìhuì	to be present at a meeting
就職	jiùzhí	to assume office
即於	jíyú	then, accordingly
是日	shìrì	that day
宣告	xuāngào	to declare, proclaim
成立	chénglì	to establish
再加	zàijiā	in addition
先後	xiānhòu	successively, one after another
以期	yǐqī	so as to expect
前途	qiántú	future, the prospect
共圖	gòngtú	to pursue jointly, seek together

努力	nǔlì	to make great efforts, try hard
期內	qīnèi	within the time period
曾	céng	have already
召開	zhàokāi	to convene
嗣	sì	hereafter, subsequently
宗旨	zōngzhǐ	aim, purpose
分別	fēnbié	separately
進行	jìnxíng	to carry out, implement
基於	jīyú	because of, in view of
事業	shìyè	enterprise, undertaking
需要	xūyào	requirement, needs; to need
應有	yīngyǒu	due, proper, deserved
組織	zǔzhī	organization
逐漸	zhújiàn	gradually
擴充	kuòchōng	to expand, strengthen, augment
計	jì	to count, compute, calculate
審議	shěnyì	deliberation and discussion
公路	gōnglù	highway, road
工程	gōngchéng	engineering
衛生	wèishēng	sanitation, health
教育	jiàoyù	education
農村建設	nóngcūn jiànshè	rural reconstruction

專處	zhuānchù	special department
設施	shèshī	facilities
實驗	shíyàn	experiment, test
迨至	dàizhì	to wait until
原有	yuányǒu	pre-existing, original
暫仍其舊	zàn réng qíjiù	to remain temporarily as it used to be
賡續	gēngxù	to continue; continuously, successively
改稱	gǎichēng	to change the name
以符名實	yǐ fú míng shí	so that the name accords with reality
以農立國	yǐ nóng lì guó	a nation based on agriculture
盛衰	shèngshuāi	prosperity and decline, rise and fall
國本	guóběn	the foundation of a country
以專	yǐ zhuān	in order to focus
責成	zéchéng	responsibility; to charge somebody with a task
人煙稀少	rényān xīshǎo	sparsely populated
寶藏	bǎozàng	precious (mineral) deposits
亟	jí	urgently
宜	yí	should, ought to
籌議	chóuyì	to plan and discuss
開發	kāifā	to develop, open up
以便	yǐbiàn	so that, so as to

就近	jiùjìn	at the nearest convenient place
接洽	jiēqià	to take up a matter with, consult
剿匪	jiǎofěi	to attack (communist) bandits
收復	shōufù	to recover, recapture
亟待	jídài	to demand urgently, need badly
切實	qièshí	feasible, practical, realistic
比年	bǐnián	recent years
生產	shēngchǎn	to manufacture, produce
事業	shìyè	an enterprise, undertaking
多成	duō chéng	many became
凋敝	diāobì	depressed, languished
力圖	lìtú	to try hard to, strive to
振作	zhènzuò	to exert oneself, display vigor
以裕	yǐyù	in order to enrich
民生	mínshēng	people's livelihood
所在	suǒzài	place; herein lies . . .
統籌	tǒngchóu	to plan as a whole, to plan comprehensively
救濟	jiùjì	to relieve; relief
統制	tǒngzhì	to control; control
辦有成效	bàn yǒuchéngxiào	attended to with desirable effects
當	dāng	ought, should, must

再	zài	again, once more
推而廣之	tuī ér guáng zhī	to promote widely
專設機構	zhuānshè jīgòu	an ad hoc organization
以收 . . . 之效	yǐ shōu . . . zhī xiào	in order to receive . . . benefit
迄今	qìjīn	up to now
僅有	jǐnyǒu	merely, only
規畫	guīhuà	to plan, prepare
若欲	ruò yù	if desired
有待	yǒudài	to await, remain (to be done)
著手	zhuóshǒu	to set about, start
較久	jiàojiǔ	comparatively long
可言	kěyán	to speak of
爰	yuán	hence, consequently
分段	fēnduàn	broken up in paragraphs
略述如此	lüèshù rúzǔ	to describe briefly as follows
築造	zhùzào	to construct
於 . . . 起	yú . . . qǐ	from . . . on, beginning from
先	xiān	first, begin with
蘇	sū	Jiangsu province
浙	zhè	Zhejiang province
皖	wǎn	Anhui province

298

聯絡	liánluò	to connect; connected, connecting; to have contact
督造	dūzào	to supervise and construct
經	jīng	as a result of, after
規定	guīdìng	rule, regulation; to stipulate
標準	biāozhǔn	standard, criterion
單價	dānjià	unit price
並決定	bìng juédìng	and decide
撥借	bōjiè	to grant a loan to
基金	jījīn	funds
以助	yǐzhù	so as to help
包含	bāohán	to include
滬杭	hùháng	from Shanghai to Hangzhou
京蕪	jīngwú	from Nanking to Wuhu
蘇嘉	sūjiā	from Suzhou to Jiaxing
長宣	chángxuān	from Changxing to Xuancheng
京杭	jīngháng	from Nanking to Hangzhou
杭徽	hánghuī	from Hangzhou to Anhui
先後	xiānhòu	one after another
通車	tōngchē	open to traffic
籌備處	chóubèi chù	preparatory office
擬具 . . . 計劃	nǐjù . . . jìhuà	to draw up a plan about . . .

路線	lùxiàn	route
概算	gàisuàn	budget estimate
採納	cǎinà	to adopt, accept
議決案	yìjuéàn	a resolution
豫	yù	Henan province
鄂	è	Hubei province
贛	gàn	Jiangxi province
湘	xiāng	Hunan province
依據	yījù	basis, foundation
工程圖、表、書類	gōngchéng túbiǎo shūlèi	project map, chart, book, and the like
支配	zhīpèi	to allocate, arrange; allocation
擬訂	nǐdìng	to draw up, draft
工款	gōngkuǎn	construction fund
幹	gàn	main line, main artery
支	zhī	branch line, feeder line
互通	hùtōng	open both ways
路面	lùmiàn	road surface, pavement
訓練	xùnliàn	to train
材料	cáiliào	material
調查	diàochá	to investigate; investigation
考察	kǎochá	to inspect, examine, study
油田	yóutián	oilfield

水災	shuǐzāi	flood
移交	yíjiāo	to turn over, transfer
工程處	gōngchéng chù	engineering department
工振局	gōngzhèn jú	work relief bureau
歸併	guībìng	to merge into
工務所	gōngwù suǒ	bureau of public works
幹堤	gàn dì	main embankment
培修	péixiū	to repair
以防	yǐfáng	in order to prevent
泛濫	fànlàn	to flood, overflow; inundate
沿	yán	along
淮	húai	Huai River
堤岸	dì'àn	embankment
涵洞	hándòng	culvert
以資	yǐzī	as a means of
蓄	xù	store up, save up
洩	xiè	to let out, discharge
浚治	jùnzhì	to dredge
潮	cháo	tide
水閘	shuǐzhá	water gate
障	zhàng	to block, obstruct
潮汛	cháoxùn	seasonal tide

倒灌	daòguàn	to flow backward
興...之利	xīng ... zhī lì	to promote the benefit of
灌溉	guàn'gài	to irrigate
航運	hángyùn	shipping
黃	huáng	the Huang River (Yellow River)
洛	luò	the Luo River
沙	shā	the Sha River
穎	yǐng	the Ying River
凡	fán	all
田畝	tiánmǔ	farmland
畝	mǔ	unit of area = 0.0667 hectare
洪水	hóngshǔi	flood
兼	jiān	simultaneously, concurrently
水位	shuǐwèi	water level
沿江一帶	yánjiāng yīdài	the region along the Yangtze River
完固	wán gù	to be completed and strengthened
重演	chóngyǎn	to recur, repeat
氣象	qìxiàng	weather, climate; meteorology
水文(學)	shuǐwén (xue)	hydrology
地質	dìzhì	geology
徵集	zhēngjí	to collect
規劃	guīhuà	plan, program

堤工	dīgōng	dike (embankment) construction
堤款	dīkuǎn	fund for dike construction
奉命	fèngmìng	to act under orders, receive orders
接辦	jiēbàn	to take over control
鄂省	èshěng	Hubei province
保管	bǎoguǎn	to take care of
專款	zhuānkuǎn	special fund
督責	dūzé	to supervise and encourage
勘	kān	to investigate, survey
估	gū	to estimate, appraise
歲修	suìxiū	annual repairs
赶(趕)於	gǎnyú	hurry (to do something) by . . . , quickly complete by . . .
中旬	zhōngxún	the second ten days of a month
方	fāng	short for cubic meter
標價	biāojià	the marked price
盛漲	shèngzhǎng	sudden and quick rise
防汛	fángxùn	flood prevention
事宜	shìyí	affairs, matters, the necessary arrangements
截至 . . . 止	jiézhì . . . zhǐ	by (a specified time)
閱	yuè	to pass through, experience (e.g., 閱七月: for seven months, seven months have passed)

自管	zìguǎn	self- (local) management
因是	yīnshì	therefore, for this reason
餘款	yúkuǎn	surplus funds
興工	xīnggōng	to initiate construction, start work
金水建閘計劃	jīnshuǐ jiànzhá jìhuà	Jinshui Floodgate Project
業已	yèyǐ	already
見諸實施	jiànzhū shíshī	to bring into effect
猶	yóu	just as, like; still
須	xū	to need, require
略事	lüèshì	to make slight . . .
經辦	jīngbàn	to handle, deal with
國聯	guólián	League of Nations
商定	shāngdìng	to decide through consultation
呈奉	chéngfèng	respectfully submitted
行政院	xíngzhèng yuàn	Executive Yuan
照辦	zhàobàn	to act as planned or proposed
實為	shí wéi	truly is
技術	jìshù	technology, skill, technique
開端	kaīduān	beginning
隸屬於	lìshǔyú	subordinate to, under the jurisdiction of
細菌	xìjūn	bacterium, germ
化學	huàxué	chemistry

製藥	zhìyào	to manufacture medicine
寄生蟲	jìshēngchóng	parasite
衛生工程	wèishēng gōngchéng	public health project
模型	móxíng	model
幻燈片	huàndēngpiàn	a slide
實驗室	shíyànshì	laboratory
檢疫	jiǎnyì	quarantine
事權	shìquán	rights and responsibilities
收回	shōuhuí	to regain, recover
霍亂	huòluàn	cholera
防治	fángzhì	prevention and treatment
舉辦	jǔbàn	to conduct, carry out
環境	huánjìng	environment, surroundings
流行病	liúxíngbìng	communicable disease, epidemic disease
盛行	shèngxíng	rampant, everywhere
瘧疾	nuèjí	malaria
撲滅	pūmiè	to stamp out, exterminate, wipe out
住血蟲病	zhùxuèchóngbìng	schistosomiasis
各省	gèshěng	each province
公路衛生組	gōnglù wèishēng zǔ	mobile health unit
群眾	qúnzhòng	the masses
助產	zhùchǎn	midwifery

功用	gōngyòng	function, use; effect
挽回	wǎnhuí	to retrieve
利權	lìquán	economic rights
地方	dìfāng	local; location, place
淞滬戰區	sōng-hù zhànqū	war zone between Wusong and Shanghai
善後	shànhòu	to deal with the aftermath
此外	cǐwài	besides, in addition, moreover
在先	zàixiān	formerly, in the past
面積	miànjī	area
分配	fēnpèi	distribution
租佃	zūdiàn	tenancy
關係	guānxi	relationship
金融	jīnróng	finance, banking
消費	xiāofèi	to consume
運輸	yùnshū	to transport; transportation
慎	shèn	careful, cautious
密	mì	meticulous, carefully considered
合作社	hézuòshè	cooperative
徵詢	zhēnxún	to seek the opinion of, consult
專家	zhuānjiā	expert, specialist
藉便	jíbiàn	in order to, so as to
農振	nóngzhèn	agricultural development

貸	dài	loan
蠶桑	cán sāng	sericulture
輔助	fǔzhù	to assist
原種	yuánzhǒng	original breed, primary breed
義大利	yìdàlì	Italy
交	jiāo	to breed, mate
雜種	zázhǒng	hybrid, crossbreed
土種	tǔzhǒng	indigenous breed
指導	zhǐdǎo	to direct, guide
飼養	sìyǎng	to raise, rear
綜	zōng	to put together, sum up
繼往開來	jìwǎng-kāilái	to carry on the heritage so as to pave the way for future generations
一應	yīyīng	all
貫通	guàntōng	to have a thorough knowledge of
重複	chóngfù	to duplicate, repeat
衝突	chōngtū	conflict
遺漏	yílòu	to omit
凌亂	língluàn	in disorder, in a mess, in confusion
弊	bì	disadvantage, harm

Document 2 (vol. 2, pp. 94–104)

Decree from the National Government to the Huai River Control Commission
國民政府訓令導淮委員會

Whereas Document 1 is a final draft of an outgoing document kept in the originating agency, Document 2 is an incoming document received by one agency from another. The summary sheet for this document records how the document was processed by the receiving agency, in this case, the Huai River Control Commission.

The upper right corner identifies the originating agency 來文機關 (*laiwen jiguan*) of the document as the National Government (Guomin zhengfu 國民政府). The document type 文別 (*wenbie*) indicates that the document was a decree (*shunling* 訓令). The summary sheet also indicates that the document, after it had been received by the Huai River Control Commission, was distributed to the General Office's Number 1 Section, the Engineering Office, and the Land Office (all subordinate offices of the Huai River Control Commission). The recommended response (*qianni banfa* 簽擬辦法) was to present it to leaders for perusal, but it is not clear whether the Engineering Office and the Land Office read it or not since only the General Office entered a reading date.

The next sheet is the cover page from the National Government. It went out with the original document. Its format was designed for the convenience of processing. Except for the 事由 and 附件 sections, all other items on the sheet were for the addressee agency to use for processing. But the Huai River Control Commission used its own processing sheet to record how the decree from the National Government was handled.

The document consists of two parts: the decree itself and two attachments. The purpose of the decree was to relay to the Huai River Control Commission two regulations regarding unification of water control agencies. The main text of the decree is largely a quotation of a letter from the GMD Central Political Council, and begins with 查統一全國水利行政一案 (*cha tongyi quanguo shuili xingzheng yi an*) and ends with 函達查照辦理等由(*handa chazhaobanli dengyou*). The quoted portion describes the origin of the two regulations.

Unlike Document 1, which was a draft, this decree was a formal document. You may recall that there were a few insertions, deletions, and corrections in the draft. This document, too, was marked with some corrections. One difference here is that corrections and changes were accompanied by square stamps. The use of these stamps was to show to the addressee that these changes were made with proper approval. Draft documents normally did not have such stamps.

統一	tǒngyī	to unify
綱要	gāngyào	an outline, sketch
辦法	bànfǎ	means, method
查照辦理	cházhào bànlǐ	to act accordingly
遵照	zūnzhào	to obey, conform to, comply with, act in accordance with
為 . . . 事	wéi . . . shì	in the matter of . . . ; for the purpose of . . .
函開	hánkāi	to state in a letter
查 . . . 一案	chá . . . yīàn	we find the case regarding . . .
前經	qiánjīng	already, previously
屆	jiè	(numerary adjunct for periodic events)
原則	yuánzé	principle
交	jiāo	to assign, hand over
規畫	guīhuà	plan, program
實施	shíshī	to put into effect, implement
暫	zhàn	temporarily
歸	guī	to belong to
統籌辦理	tǒngchóu bànlǐ	to be dealt with simultaneously by a single government agency
擬具	nǐjù	to draw up
呈核	chéng hé	to submit for review
嗣	sì	subsequently
據	jù	based on, according to

擬呈	níchéng	to draw (something) up and submit it
會擬	huìnǐ	to draw up jointly
進行	jìnxíng	to carry out, implement
會呈	huìchéng	joint petition or report; to present or report jointly
復經	fùjīng	again through; after . . . again
相應	xiāngyìng	should; correspondingly
撿同	jiǎntóng	to put together
函達	hándá	to inform through an official correspondence
等由	děng yóu	(conventionally used in official communications immediately after a quotation from a letter by an agency of the same [or inferior] rank)
自應	zìyīng	certainly should, of course should
照辦	zhàobàn	to act accordingly, comply with, act upon
除...外	chú . . . wài	except, besides
函復	hánfù	to reply via official letter
分行	fēnxíng	to send document(s) separately
合行	héxíng	to act in concert (sometimes also "it is therefore necessary . . .")
抄發	chāofā	to copy and send out
原附件	yuánfùjiàn	the original and attached documents
令仰該會遵照	lìng yǎng gāi huì zūnzhào	your council will be guided by these instructions

校對	jiàoduì	proofreader
監印	jiānyìn	an official in charge of the official seal
中央	zhōngyāng	the central government
水利	shuǐlì	water conservancy
總機關	zǒng jīguān	chief agency
主辦	zhǔbàn	to take charge of, sponsor
事宜	shìyí	relevant matters
流域	liúyù	river valley
一律	yīlù	without exception, all
接收	jiēshōu	to take over, receive
統籌支配	tǒngchóu zhīpèi	to plan and manage by a single government agency
分別	fēnbié	separate, separately
建設廳	jiànshètīng	provincial department of reconstruction
主管	zhǔguǎn	to be in charge of
縣	xiàn	county
受	shòu	to be subject to
指揮	zhǐhuī	to direct, command
關涉	guānshè	concerning, involving, related
以上	yǐshàng	more than
各	gè	each, every

部會	bùhuì	ministry and council (committee, commission) of the central goverment, the various departments of the central government
組織法	zǔzhī fǎ	rules of organization, bylaws
涉及	shèjí	to involve, relate to
修改	xiūgǎi	to revise, modify
統	tǒng	all
集中	jízhōng	to centralize
地形測量	dìxíng cèliáng	topographic survey
水文測驗	shuǐwén cèyàn	hydraulic survey
直接	zhíjiē	direct, directly
治導	zhìdǎo	to regulate, control
有著者	yǒuzhuózhě	those that obtained funds
仍	réng	still
某	mǒu	a certain, so-and-so
統轄	tǒngxiá	to exercise control over, to govern
歲修	suìxiū	annual construction
防汛	fángxùn	flood prevention
國庫	guókù	national treasury
大宗	dàzōng	a large amount
籌畫	chóuhuà	to deliberate and plan
附加稅	fùjiāshuì	surtax

特定	tèdìng	specific, specified, specially designated
用途	yòngtú	use, function
撥歸	bōguī	to allocate . . . for . . .
另	lìng	other, another, separate
英	yīng	England
庚款	gēngkuǎn	Boxer indemnity
專款	zhuānkuǎn	special funds
儀器	yíqì	instrument, equipment
延聘	yánpìn	to employ, engage, appoint
歸併	guībìng	to incorporate into, merge into
核轉	hézhuǎn	to transmit an official document to a higher body after perusal
轉發	zhuǎnfā	to transmit
照舊	zhàojiù	as before

Chapter 25

Documents on Taiwan's Economic Development and the ROC Government: Introduction and Glossary
中國政府與台灣經濟發展

The Qing government ceded control of Taiwan and the Pescadores in 1895 to Japan, as a part of the Treaty of Shimonoseki that ended the First Sino-Japanese War (1894–95). Japan administered Taiwan from 1895 to 1945.

Before the end of the Second Sino-Japanese War (1937–45), the government of the Republic of China sought and received assurances from the Allied Powers that Japan would return Manchuria, Taiwan, and the Pescadores to China after the war. As a result, the ROC Government formed investigation committees under the Central Planning Bureau (Zhongyang sheji ju 中央設計局) in April 1944 to prepare for the takeover of Manchuria and Taiwan after the war.

The Taiwan Investigation Committee (Taiwan diaocha weiyuanhui 臺灣調查委員會) was headed by General Chen Yi 陳儀 and was responsible for drafting a plan for the takeover. Document 1 is a draft plan that General Chen submitted to his superiors. It indicates the interest taken by the ROC Government in the economic, financial, industrial, mining, and agricultural development of Taiwan after the war.

The end of the Sino-Japanese War and the Pacific War did not bring tranquillity to Taiwan. Political tension, social friction, and economic instability contributed to an uprising on February 28, 1947 (the "2-2-8 Incident"). In the harsh suppression that followed, thousands of Taiwanese were killed. In 1949 the ROC government, defeated on the mainland, made Taiwan its base for "national recovery."

Documents 2–7 illustrate the dire economic situation the ROC government, industrialists, and businessmen faced on Taiwan immediately after the government retreated to the island. Problems included inadequate infrastructure, lack of capital and technology, and political instability. These documents show patterns of communication between the official and private sectors of the economy: between manufacturers and officials, and between trade associations and the government. These documents also reflect how different segments of the ROC government addressed economic issues. Executive agencies, legislative committees, and publicly owned enterprises all had different roles in, and often differing perspectives on, Taiwan's economic recovery and development.

Document 1 (vol. 2, pp. 107–21)

Draft Outline for the Takeover of Taiwan
臺灣接管計劃綱要草案

This selection is from a formal draft outline prepared by the Taiwan Investigation Commission. It was submitted in October 1944.

接管	jiēguǎn	to take control over
中央設計局	zhōngyāng shèjìjú	Central Planning Bureau
臺灣調查委員會	táiwān diàochá wěiyuánhuì	Taiwan Investigation Commission
主任委員	zhǔrèn wěiyúan	director, chairman
擬	ní	to draw up, prepare a draft
呈	chéng	to submit, present

Section 1: General Rules 通則

設施	shèshī	facilities, administrative measures
實行	shíxíng	to carry out, implement
國父	guófù	father of the country (Sun Yat-sen)
遺教	yíjiào	teachings handed down
秉承 . . . 訓示	bǐngchéng . . . xùnshì	to follow the instructions of . . .
總裁	zǒngcái	director-general of the Guomindang (Chiang Kai-shek)
力謀	lìmóu	to make every effort to work for

315

福利	fúlì	material benefit, well-being
剷除	chǎnchú	to root out, eradicate
敵人	dírén	enemy
勢力	shìlì	power, influence
消極	xiāojí	negative, unfavorable
當	dāng	ought, should, must
注重	zhùzhòng	to lay stress on, pay attention to
掃除	sǎochú	to wipe out
肅清	sùqīng	to eliminate, mop up
反叛	fǎnpàn	to revolt, rebel
革除	géchú	to abolish, get rid of
舊染	jiùrǎn	old customs and practices
壓制	yāzhì	suppression, restraint
腐敗	fǔbài	corruption
貪污	tānwū	misappropriation of public funds
苛稅	kēshuì	exorbitant taxes
酷刑	kùxíng	cruel and savage torture
等	děng	and so forth
吸鴉片	xī yāpiàn	to smoke opium
惡習	èxí	pernicious habit, evil ways
安定	āndìng	to stabilize, maintain
秩序	zhìxù	order, stability

積極	jījí	positive, favorable
強化	qiánghuà	to strengthen, consolidate
行政機關	xíngzhèng jīguān	administrative organ
增強	zēngqiáng	to enhance, improve, strengthen
效率	xiàolù	efficiency
預備	yùbèi	to prepare
實施	shíshī	to put into effect, implement
憲政	xiànzhèng	constitutional government
建立	jiànlì	to establish, set up
民權	mínquán	civil rights, civil liberties
基礎	jīchǔ	basis, foundation
以...為原則	yǐ...wéi yúanzé	based on the principle that . . . , in accordance with the principle of . . .
根絶	gēnjué	to stamp out, eradicate, exterminate
榨取	zhàqǔ	to squeeze, extort
原有	yuányǒu	(what) one had before, original, previous
生產能力	shēngchǎn nénglì	production capacity
勿使	wùshǐ	not to allow, prohibit
停頓	tíngdùn	to stop, halt; stagnate
衰退	shuāituì	to fail, decline
其...除外	qí...chúwài	not including, excluding, except
違法	wéifǎ	to break the law; illegal

病民	bìngmín	to harm people
所得	suǒdé	what one gets, that which one gets
利益	lìyì	interest, benefit, profit

Section 5: Fiscal Revenue 財政

佔領	zhànlǐng	occupation; to occupy, capture
時代	shídài	time, age, epoch, period
稅收	shuìshōu	tax revenue
收入	shōurù	income, revenue, earnings
廢止	fèizhǐ	to abolish, annul
其餘	qíyú	others, the rest, the remainder
均	jūn	without exception, all
暫	zàn	for the time being, temporarily
照舊	zhàojiù	as before, as usual, as of old
徵收	zhēngshōu	to levy, collect
逐漸	zhújiàn	gradually
專賣	zhuānmài	monopoly
國營事業	guóyíng shìyè	state-owned (and/or -operated) enterprise
亦	yì	also, too
地方	dìfang	local; locality
財政	cáizhèng	finance; fiscal
中央	zhōngyāng	central authorities

給予	gěiyǔ	to give, grant, bestow
相當	xiāngdāng	considerable, suitable, appropriate
補助	bǔzhù	subsidy, assistance (usually financial)
不立	bùlì	does (is) not set up or established
預算	yùsuàn	budget
收支	shōu-zhī	revenue and expenditure
報告	bàogào	report
緊急	jǐnjí	emergency
支付	zhīfù	payment
權	quán	power, authority
會計	kuàijì	accounting, bookkeeping
審計	shěnjì	an audit; to audit
簡便	jiǎnbiàn	simple, convenient
暫行	zànxíng	provisional, temporary
辦法	bànfǎ	way, manner, means; measure
俟	sì	once after
秩序	zhìxù	order, sequence
正式	zhèngshì	formal, official

Section 6: Finance and Banking 金融

| 中央銀行 | zhōngyāng yínháng | Central Bank of China |
| 發行 | fāxíng | to issue (currency, stock, bonds, etc.) |

印有	yìnyǒu	printed along with
地名	dìmíng	place-name
法幣	fǎbì	China's national currency from November 1935 to August 1948
貨幣	huòbì	money, currency
以下	yǐxià	the following
簡稱	jiǎnchēng	be called for short, abbreviated
舊幣	jiùbì	old currency
兌換率	duìhuànlù	exchange rate
期間	qījiān	time period
流通	liútōng	to circulate; circulation
按	àn	on the basis of, in accordance with
法定	fǎdìng	legal, statutory
逾期	yúqī	to exceed the time limit; after the valid period
一概	yīgài	one and all, without exception
作廢	zuòfèi	to become invalid
鈔票	chāopiào	paper money
查明	chámíng	to find out, ascertain
額	é	amount
若干	ruògān	a certain number or amount
市面	shìmiàn	business, market
為限	wéixiàn	to be within the limit of, not exceed

抗戰	kàngzhàn	War of Resistance Against Japan (1937–45)
黃金	huángjīn	gold
比價	bǐjià	exchange rate
準備金	zhǔnbèijīn	reserve fund, reserves
財產	cáichǎn	property
充作	chōngzùo	to serve as, act as
償還	chánghuán	compensation, indemnity; to pay back
基金	jījīn	fund
不足	bùzú	insufficient
賠償	péicháng	to compensate, pay for; reparations
媾和	gòuhé	to make peace
負擔	fùdān	to shoulder a burden
債務	zhàiwù	debt, liabilities
公債	gōngzhài	government bonds
社債	shèzhài	company bonds
募集	mùjí	to raise, collect
清理	qīnglǐ	to settle (accounts, etc.), put in order, clear up
救濟	jiùjì	to relieve; relief
監督	jiāndū	to supervise, control
調整	tiáozhěng	to adjust, regulate, revise
改組	gǎizǔ	to reorganize

| 必要時 | bìyàoshí | when necessary |
| 停業 | tíngyè | to cease doing business, close down |

Section 7: Industry, Mining, and Commerce 工、礦、商業

所有	suǒyǒu	to own, possess
合有	héyǒu	jointly owned
接收	jiēshōu	to take over
正當	zhèngdàng	legitimate, legal
民營	mínyíng	privately operated
宣戰	xuānzhàn	to declare war
官有	guānyǒu	government-owned
公有	gōngyǒu	publicly owned
移轉	yízhuǎn	to transfer
私有	sīyǒu	privately owned, private
視同	shìtóng	to regard as
沒收	mòshōu	to confiscate, expropriate
維持	wéichí	to keep, maintain, preserve
恢復	huīfù	to resume, restore, renew
開發	kāifā	to develop, open up
資金	zījīn	fund
四聯總處	sìlián zǒng chù	Joint Board of the Four Banks (the Central Bank of China, the Bank of China, the Bank of Communications, and the

322

Farmers' Bank of China; it was the ROC Government's highest financial agency and under the direct control of Chiang Kai-shek from July 1937 to October 1948)

統籌	tǒngchóu	to plan as a whole
貸放	dàifàng	to loan out
物資	wùzī	goods and materials
人力	rénlì	manpower
預先	yùxiān	in advance, beforehand
資產	zīchǎn	property, capital, assets
掌握	zhǎngwò	to control; control
核定	hédìng	to check and ratify
福利	fúlì	material benefits, welfare
增進	zēngjìn	to enhance, promote
儘可能	jǐnkěnéng	as much as possible
內地	nèidì	inland, interior, hinterland
管制	guǎnzhì	control
土產	tǔchǎn	local products
銷路	xiāolù	market
處理	chǔlǐ	to handle, deal with, dispose of
經營	jīngyíng	to manage, run
民生主義	mínshēng zhǔyì	People's Livelihood (one of Sun Yat-sen's Three Peoples' Principles)

實業計劃	shíyè jìhuà	Industrial Plan (set out by Sun Yat-sen)
配合	pèihé	to cooperate, coordinate
合理	hélǐ	rational, reasonable, equitable
盟國	méngguó	allied countries (i.e., China's allies in World War II)
中立國	zhōnglìguó	neutral countries
經營人	jīngyíngrén	manager
協商	xiéshāng	to consult, talk things over, negotiate
歡迎	huānyíng	welcome
友邦	yǒubāng	friendly nations
投資	tóuzī	investment; to invest
技術	jìshù	technology
充分	chōngfèn	fully, amply

Section 9: Transportation and Communication 交通

郵電	yóudiàn	postal service and telecommunications
臨時	línshí	temporary, provisional
總機關	zǒngjīguān	central office, pivotal organ
統一	tǒngyī	to unify, centralize
原狀	yuánzhuàng	status quo ante, original condition
部門	bùmén	government departments
補充	bǔchōng	to replenish, supplement

器材	qìcái	equipment, material
租購	zūgòu	to rent and purchase
輕便鐵路	qīngbiàn tiělù	light railway
電信	diànxìn	telecommunications
橋樑	qiáoliáng	bridge
修復	xiūfù	to repair, restore, renovate
護路	hùlù	to patrol and guard a road or railway
警衛	jǐngwèi	security guard
產權	chǎnquán	property right
糾紛	jiūfēn	dispute
先行	xiānxíng	beforehand, in advance; to go ahead (to do something)
公布	gōngbù	to promulgate, announce, publish
保障	bǎozhàng	to ensure, guarantee, safeguard
獎勵	jiǎnglì	to encourage and reward

Section 10: Agriculture 農業

農	nóng	agriculture, farming
林	lín	forestry
漁	yú	fishing (industry)
牧	mù	livestock raising
權益	quányì	rights and interests

耕作	gēngzuò	cultivation, farming
種籽	zhǒngzǐ	seed
牲畜	shēngchù	livestock
農具	nóngjù	farm implements, farm tools

Section 11: Society 社會

登記	dēngjì	to register; registration
人民團體	rénmíntuántǐ	public organization
實際情況	shíjì qíngkuàng	actual situation
解散	jiěsàn	to dissolve, disband
革命	gémìng	revolutionary; revolution
忠烈	zhōngliè	patrotism; martyrdom
事蹟	shìjī	deed, achievement
表彰	biǎozhāng	to commend, praise
安置	ānzhì	to settle, arrange for
撫卹	fǔxù	to comfort and compensate a bereaved family
肥料	féiliào	fertilizer
輔導	fǔdǎo	to guide, train
查戶	cháhù	to check on a household
取保	qǔbǎo	to get a guarantor
墊發	diànfā	to advance (money)

承辦	chéngbàn	to handle, undertake
供銷	gòngxiāo	supply and marketing
社會福利	shèhuì fúlì	social welfare
習俗	xísú	custom, convention
禮節	lǐjié	courtesy, etiquette, protocol
國際善後總署	guójì shànhòu zǒngshǔ	United Nations Rehabilitation and Relief Agency (UNRRA), 1943–47
密切	mìqiè	close, intimate
聯繫	liánxì	contact, connection
工振	gōngzhèn	to rejuvenate industry
農振	nóngzhèn	to rejuvenate agriculture (i.e., by providing farmers with better working conditions as a form of relief)

Section 16: Land Management 土地

收歸	shōuguī	to return to, take back . . .
國有	guóyǒu	to nationalize
原業主	yuányèzhǔ	original proprietor
憑證	píngzhèng	certificate, voucher
地籍	dìjí	land registry
散失	sànshī	to scatter and disappear; missing
補正	bǔzhèng	remedy, correction
平均地權	píngjūn dìquán	equalization of land rights
耕者有其田	gēngzhě yǒu qí tián	land to the tiller

Document 2 (vol. 2, pp. 122–30)

Meeting Minutes of the Taiwan Area Production Enterprises Management Council (October 3, 1951)
臺灣區生產事業管理委員會會議紀錄

生產事業 管理委員會	shēngchǎn shìyè guǎnlǐ wěiyuǎnhuì	Production Enterprises Management Council
站在...立場	zhànzài ... lìchǎng	to keep the stand of ...
董事會	dǒngshìhuì	board of directors
似乎	sìhu	it seems; as if
不甚	bùshèn	not very
協調	xiétiáo	harmonious, coordinated, consonant with
現象	xiànxiàng	phenomenon
收支	shōuzhī	revenue and expenditure
相抵	xiāngdǐ	to offset, balance
催繳	cuījiǎo	to press for payment
盈餘	yíngyú	surplus, profit
週轉	zhōuzhuǎn	to circulate, transfer, turn over
自行	zìxíng	by oneself, of one's own accord
動用	dòngyòng	to draw upon, put to use
繳納	jiǎonà	to pay, hand over
切實	qièshí	sincerely, earnestly

為...起見	wéi . . . qǐjiàn	for the purpose of, in order to, for the sake of
美援	měiyuán	American aid
相對基金	xiāngduì jījīn	counterpart funds
撥付	bōfù	to appropriate a sum of money
擴充	kuòchōng	to expand
增產	zēngchǎn	to increase production
私人資本家	sīrén zīběnjiā	private-sector capitalist
態度	tàidù	attitude, approach
著眼	zhuóyǎn	to see from the angle of
固定資產	gùdìng zīchǎn	fixed assets
折舊	zhéjiù	depreciation
成本	chéngběn	production cost
盈虧	yíng-kuī	profits and losses
一針見血	yī zhēn jiàn xiě	to cut to the heart of the matter
殊深遺憾	shū shēn yíhàn	extreme and profound regret
匯率	huìlù	exchange rate
後果	hòuguǒ	consequence, aftermath
不堪設想	bùkān shèxiǎng	too dreadful to contemplate
物價	wùjià	commodity prices
波動	bōdòng	to undulate, fluctuate
絕	jué	absolutely

不止	bùzhǐ	more than, not limited to
反而	fǎn'ér	on the contrary, instead
要點	yàodiǎn	main points
自力更生	zìlì gēngshēng	self-reliance
利害	lì-hài	advantages and disadvantages
決策	juécè	an adopted policy, a decision
越少越好	yuèshǎo yuèhǎo	the fewer the better
令出多門	lìngchū duō mén	government decrees originating from many different agencies (causing confusion)
無所適從	wú suǒ shì cóng	not knowing what to follow, to not know what to follow
國策	guócè	state policy
違背	wéibèi	to violate, go against, run counter to
查賬	cházhàng	to audit accounts
不勝應付	bùshèng yìngfu	more than what can be handled, too much to be dealt or coped with
逃避	táobì	to escape, evade, shirk
不得不	bùdé bù	to have no choice but to, have to
巧變花樣	qiǎo biàn huāyàng	to cleverly play tricks
業務	yèwù	business
責備	zébèi	to reproach, blame
官價	guānjià	official price

相去過遠	xiāng qù guò yuǎn	the difference is significant
迎刃而解	yíng rèn ér jiě	to readily solve any problem
虧損	kuīsǔn	loss, deficit
補貼	bǔtiē	subsidy
協理	xiélǐ	to assist in the management (of an enterprise); an assistant manager
所得稅	suǒdéshuì	income tax
稅捐稽征處	shuìjuān jīzhēng chù	a tax office
交涉	jiāoshè	to negotiate
抵繳	dǐjiǎo	to repay a debt with goods of equivalent value
預繳	yùjiǎo	to pay in advance
樟樹	zhāngshù	camphor tree
事非得已	shì fēi dé yǐ	there is no other choice
繳庫	jiǎokù	to pay to the state treasury
巡迴	xúnhuí	to make a circuit of, to tour
團	tuán	group
待遇	dàiyù	wages, salary; the manner of treating people
現款	xiànkuǎn	ready money, cash
服務不週	fúwù bùzhōu	unsatisfactory service
貸款	dàikuǎn	loan, credit
來源	láiyuán	source

頭寸	tóucùn	cash
固然	gùrán	no doubt, of course
明瞭	míngliǎo	to understand, be clear about
處境	chǔjìng	the circumstance one faces
窘迫	jiǒngpò	predicament, difficulty
勉為其難	miǎn wéi qí nǎn	to try to do a hard task (as well as one can)
供(貢)獻	gòngxiàn	to contribute
不妨	bùfáng	there is no harm in, might as well
書面	shūmiàn	in written form
透過	tòuguò	by means of, through

Document 3 (vol. 2, pp. 131–32)

**The Economic Commission of the Legislative Yuan's Request to
the Procedural Commission to Include Bicycle Manufacturers' Petition on the Agenda**
（立法院）經濟委員會函請程序委員會將自行車進口一案列入議案

經濟委員會	jīngjì wěiyuánhuì	Economic Commission
中華民國 　全國工業總會	zhōnghuámínguó 　quánguó gōngyè zǒng huì	National Industrial Association of the 　Republic of China
請願書	qǐngyuànshū	petition
換購	huàngòu	to purchase through an exchange of goods, 　barter
日製	rìzhì	manufactured in Japan
自行車	zìxíngchē	bicycle
災害	zāihài	catastrophe, calamity
轉請	zhuǎnqǐng	to pass on the request to, ask on behalf of
採納	cǎinà	to accept, adopt
議案	yì'àn	proposal, motion
受文者	shòuwénzhě	addressee, receiver
程序	chéngxù	procedure
列席	lièxí	to attend a meeting (but without the right 　to speak or vote)
爰	yuán	hence, thereupon
提報	tíbào	to put forward or submit (a report to . . .)

相應	xiāngyìng	correspondingly, consequently
覆請查照	fùqǐng cházhào	to reply requesting reference to (the document); take a note of . . . for future reference
公決	gōngjué	to decide by the majority
據聞	jùwén	it is reported, it is said
攸關	yōuguān	(it) concerns
推舉	tuījǔ	to choose, elect
民瘼	mínmò	people's misery
無微不至	wú wēi bú zhì	meticulously, in every possible way
扶植	fúzhí	to foster, assist
不遺餘力	bù yí yúlì	to spare no effort, do one's utmost
謹	jǐn	sincerely, respectfully
懇	kěn	to request, beseech
確立	quèlì	to establish
遭受	zāoshòu	to suffer, be subjected to
打擊	dǎjī	to hit, strike, attack; to give a blow to
就 . . . 言之	jiù . . . yánzhī	speaking of . . . ; as for . . .
必需品	bìxūpǐn	necessities
獨佔	dúzhàn	to monopolize
心所謂危	xīn suǒ wèi wēi	worried about the so-called critical situation
萬萬不可	wàn wàn bùkě	absolutely cannot

倘	tǎng	if, supposing, in case
突破	tūpò	to break through, surmount
惡例	èlì	a bad precedent
把握	bǎwò	assurance, certainty
戰線	zhànxiàn	battlefront, the front
韌度	rèndù	toughness, tenacity, endurance
脆弱	cuìruò	fragile, frail, weak
蹶	júe	to fall, suffer a setback
邏輯	luójí	logic
三角貿易	sānjiǎo màoyì	triangular trade
有關各方	yǒuguān gèfāng	the relevant (departments), the concerned parties
國計	guójì	national economy
肥料	féiliào	fertilizer
祗祈	zhīqí	respectfully requests
召集	zhàojí	to convene, assemble, summon
商討	shāngtǎo	to deliberate, discuss
橡膠	xiàngjiāo	rubber
製革	zhìgé	to process hides; tannery
塗料	túliào	coating, paint
油漆	yóuqī	paint

Document 4 (vol. 2, pp. 133–40)

**Minutes of the Taiwan Region Enterprises Management Council Meeting
on the Sale of Public Enterprises (June 11, 1953)**
台灣區生產事業管理委員會出售公營事業檢討會紀錄

公營事業	gōngyíng shìyè	publicly operated enterprise
林源	línyuán	forest resource
電源	diànyuán	power source
水源	shuǐyuán	source of water
水泥	shuǐní	cement
紙業	zhǐyè	paper industry
肥料	féiliào	fertilizer, manure
工礦	gōngkuàng	industrial and mining enterprises
農林	nónglín	farming and forestry
分售	fēnshòu	to sell separately
整售	zhěngshòu	to sell as a whole
抑	yì	or
所屬	suǒshǔ	that which is subordinate
搭配	dāpèi	to arrange in pairs or groups, to select, match
固	gù	admittedly, no doubt
兼顧	jiāngù	to give consideration to several things

權益	quányì	rights and interests
耕地	gēngdì	cultivated land
統計	tǒngjì	statistics, count
收益	shōuyì	profit
消息靈通	xiāoxī língtōng	well-informed
閉塞	bìsè	uninformed, isolated
簡便易行	jiǎnbiàn yìxíng	simple and easy to implement
耕者有其田	gēngzhě yǒu qí tián	land to the tiller
地價	dìjià	land price
補償	bǔcháng	to make up for, compensate
除掉 . . . 外	chúdiào . . . wài	besides, in addition to
民股	míngǔ	private shares
法團股	fǎtuángǔ	corporate shares
超過	chāoguò	to exceed, surpass, overtake
夾雜	jiāzá	to be mixed up with, be mingled with
官股	guāngǔ	government share
減除	jiǎnchú	to subtract, deduct
省議會	shěngyìhuì	provincial assembly
國策	guócè	the state's basic policy, national policy
置於	zhìyú	to place in, arrange, establish
另行	lìngxíng	separately
解決	jiějué	to solve, resolve, settle

何項方式	hé xiàng fāngshì	what kind of method
執行	zhíxíng	to carry out, execute, implement
鳳梨	fènglí	pineapple
當前	dāngqián	present, current
磚瓦廠	zhuānwǎchǎng	brickyard
遍佈	biànbù	spread all over
聯營	liányíng	joint operation
扞格	hàn'gé	to conflict; incompatible
且多責難	qiě duōzé nàn	to incur censure from various quarters
完竣	wánjùn	to complete
分營	fēnyíng	to operate separately
屆時	jièshí	when the time comes
輔導	fǔdǎo	to give guidance in study or training
自任	zìrèn	to do something by oneself, to handle by oneself
標售	biāoshòu	to sell by tender
中標人	zhòngbiāorén	the winning bidder; tender
抵充	dǐchōng	to compensate for, pay in lieu of cash
賬面	zhàngmiàn	account book
難免出入	nánmiǎn chūrù	it is difficult to avoid discrepancies
底價	dǐjià	minimum price, base price
酌予	zhuóyǔ	to act according to one's judgment

338

糖業	tángyè	sugar industry
為...所執有	wèi ... suǒ zhíyǒu	held by, owned by
左右	zuǒyòu	control, influence
相宜	xiāngyí	suitable, fitting, appropriate
所持	suǒchí	what one holds or owns
純粹	chúncuì	pure, unadulterated; solely
情勢	qíngshì	situation, circumstances
判斷	pànduàn	to judge, decide, determine
必樂於	bì lèyú	to be happy to, take delight in
先予	xiānyǔ	to give priority to
至於	zhìyú	as for, as to

Document 5 (vol. 2, pp. 141–47)

Draft Measures for Reforming the Regulation of Foreign Exchange and Trade
改革現行外匯貿易管理辦法試擬

協進會	xiéjìnhuì	mututal assistance association
電送	diànsòng	to send by telegram
試擬	shìnǐ	tentative draft
略以	lüèyǐ	summarized as
素有研究	sùyǒu yánjiū	have always been learned in, to be knowledgeable about
座談會	zuòtánhuì	forum, symposium
參照	cānzhào	to consult, refer to; in light of
擬存備參考	nǐcún bèi cānkǎo	to intend to file for reference
錄附	lùfù	to make a copy of and enclose herewith
結匯證	jiéhuìzhèng	certificate for purchasing or selling of foreign exchange (from/to state banks)
匯入匯款	huìrùhuìkuǎn	incoming remittance
外資	wài zī	foreign capital
僑資	qíaozī	capital (funds) of overseas Chinese
收款人	shōukuǎnrén	payee
結售	jiéshòu	to sell
等額	děngé	an equal amount

保險費	bǎoxiǎnfèi	(insurance) premium
匯出匯款	huìchū huìkuǎn	outgoing remittance
流通	liútōng	circulation; to circulate
分割	fēngē	to cut apart, break up, carve up
轉讓	zhuǎnràng	to transfer possession of, change hands
依⋯決定之	yī ... juédìngzhī	to decide on the basis of ...
供求	gōngqiú	supply and demand
抵押	dǐyā	mortgage
折扣	zhékòu	discount, rebate
隨時	suíshí	at any time, at all times
市價	shìjià	market price
兌付	duìfù	cash (a check, etc.)
新台幣	xīn tāibì	New Taiwan Dollar (NT)
專人	zhuānrén	special person
蒐（搜）集	sōují	to search out, collect, gather
資料	zīliào	data, material
發行	fāxíng	to issue, release
儲存	chǔcún	to store up
窺知	kuīzhī	to learn (of an event)
機關	jīguān	office, organ, body
列報	lièbào	to tabulate and report to a higher body
精密	jīngmì	precise, accurate

編製	biānzhì	to work out, draw up
奢侈品	shēchǐpǐn	luxuries
分類	fēnlèi	to classify, sort; classification
附	fù	enclosed herewith
具	jù	to have, possess
余額	yú'é	remaining sum, balance
滿額	mǎn'é	to fulfill quota
追加	zhuījiā	to add to (the original amount)
登記	dēngjì	to register; registration
合格	hégé	qualified, up to standard
陸續	lùxù	one after another, in succession
限定	xiàndìng	to limit, restrict
擇定	zédìng	to decide, choose, fix, set
貿易界	màoyìjiè	trade circles
專業化	zhuānyèhuà	specialization
章則	zhāngzé	rules, regulations, constitution
鮮青果	xiān qīngguǒ	fresh fruit
凡	fán	every, any, all
報價	bàojià	quoted price
行情	hángqíng	quotations (market), prices
動態	dòngtài	trends, developments
責成	zéchéng	to instruct (someone to fulfill a task)

列表	lièbiǎo	to tabulate, arrange in tables or columns
抽查	chōuchá	selective examination, spot check
分析	fēnxī	analysis; to analyze
明瞭	míngliǎo	clear; to understand
決策	juécè	policy decision
魚苗	yúmiáo	(fish) minnows
一律	yīlù	all, without exception
初審	chūshěn	initial examination
一併	yībìng	to handle together
彙編	huìbiān	to compile
視	shì	to take . . . into consideration
頭寸	tóucùn	cash
丁款	dīngkuǎn	Section D
撥配	bōpèi	to allocate, appropriate, set aside
藉以	jièyǐ	so as to
製成品	zhìchéngpǐn	manufactured goods
與民爭利	yǔ mín zhēng lì	to compete with the people for profits
靈活反應	línghuó fǎnyìng	to reflect flexibility
逕向	jìngxiàngs	straight, directly, straightaway
收取	shōuqǔ	to collect
現行	xiànxíng	currently in effect, in force
匯率	huìlù	foreign exchange rate

趨於單一	qū yú dānyī	to reach a unified (exchange rate)
貶值	biǎnzhí	to depreciate, devalue; depreciation
受阻	shòuzǔ	to be impeded or hindered
旺盛	wàngshèng	vigorous, exuberant
頂讓	dǐngràng	to let someone have something at a fair price; transfer
無形絕跡	wúxíng juéjì	disappeared without a trace
坐享...之利	zuòxiǎng ... zhīlì	to sit idly and enjoy the profit
廉價	liánjià	low price
讓出	ràngchū	to give up, give way
展其報負	zhǎn qí bàofù	to give free play to one's aspiration
大展鴻圖	dàzhǎn hóngtú	to realize one's ambition
盈余	yíngyú	surplus, profit
所得	suǒdé	income, advantage, gains
可望	kěwàng	hopefully; expected to
所失	suǒshī	loss, disadvantage
暴漲	bàozhǎng	prices soared, prices skyrocketed
一目了然	yī mù liǎorán	to be clear at a glance
產地	chǎndì	place of production, producing area
漏動	lòudòng	loophole
杜塞	dùsāi	to stop up, block up

劃一	huàyī	standardized, uniform
既除	jìchú	have got rid of something already
對內競爭	duìnèi jìngzhēng	internal competition

Document 6 (vol. 2, pp. 148–58)

The Ministry of Finance Processing Group's Meeting Minutes
Concerning Taiwan's Textile Industry
財政部加工組關於臺灣紡織工業檢討會紀錄

鑒於	jiànyú	in view of, in consideration of
顯著	xiǎnzhù	marked, remarkable
履行	lǚxíng	to observe, comply with
獲致	huòzhì	to gain, obtain, achieve
冊首	cèshǒu	beginning of a volume
檢驗局	jiǎnyànjú	Bureau of Inspection
物資局	wùzījú	Bureau of Goods and Materials
中信局	zhōngxìnjú	Central Trust of China
遠東	yuǎndōng	the Far East (Textile Company)
六和	liùhé	Six Harmonies (Textile Company)
纖維	xiānwéi	fiber
紡紗	fǎngshā	to spin . . . into yarn
印染	yìnrǎn	printing and dyeing
雍興	yōngxīng	Yongxing (Textile Company)
亦	yì	also, too
原棉	yuánmián	raw cotton
外匯	wàihuì	foreign exchange

信用	xìnyòng	credit and reputation
盡失	jìnshī	exhausted, finished, lost
越南	yuènán	Vietnam (South Vietnam)
力謀	lìmóu	to try hard to, strive to
反響	fǎnxiǎng	repercussion, echo, reverberation
駐	zhù	to be stationed in (an institution functioning abroad)
參事（處）	cānshìchù	councillor (council)
如期交貨	rúqī jiāohuò	to deliver goods on schedule
專程	zhuānchéng	special trip
如次	rúcì	as follows
僑商	qiáoshāng	overseas Chinese merchant
深恐	shēnkǒng	to be very afraid
雙重	shuāngchóng	dual, twofold
幾經	jǐjīng	go through . . . several times
業已	yèyǐ	already
前功盡棄	qiángōng jìn qì	all that has been achieved is spoiled
罰款	fákuǎn	to impose a fine
多賴	duōlài	to be very much dependent
前此	qiáncǐ	previous, preceding
採購	cǎigòu	purchase
承	chéng	be indebted (to someone for a kindness)

不特 . . . 而	bùtè . . . ér	not only . . . but also
訪問團	fǎngwèntuán	visiting mission
經 . . . 乃得	jīng . . . nǎidé	can . . . only after
水災	shuǐzāi	flood, inundation
不可抗拒	bùkě kàngjù	irresistible
延期	yánqī	to postpone, defer, put off
非正式	fēizhèngshì	unofficial, informal
公証行	gōngzhènghàng	notary organization
何辭以對	hé cí yǐ duì	what pretext can be given
亦屬有利	yì shǔ yǒulì	to also be favorable
珍惜	zhēnxī	to treasure, value, cherish
布疋	bùpǐ	cloth
欠交	qiànjiāo	to owe, be behind with delivery (or payment)
承辦	chéngbàn	to undertake
中和	zhōnghé	Zhonghe (Textile Company)
中央信託局	zhōngyāng xìntuōjú	Central Trust of China
商定	shāngdìng	to decide through consultation
分攤	fēntān	to share
承製	chéngzhì	to undertake to manufacture
務求	wùqiú	must be sure to; by all means
如數交貨	rúshù jiāohuò	delivery in full

立即	lìjí	immediately
承織	chéngzhī	to undertake to weave
漿紗機	jiāngshājī	sizing machine
應洽	yīngqià	should make arrangements with
倘...則	tǎng ... zé	if . . . then
承擔	chéngdān	to bear, undertake, assume
虧損	kuīsǔn	loss, deficit
專案	zhuān'àn	a special case
記載	jìzǎi	to put down in writing, record
予以扣回	yǔ yǐ kòuhuí	to deduct
紡錠	fǎngdìng	spindle
飭	chì	put in order; orderly
一貫作業	yīguàn zuòyè	integrated operation (in factories)
優先	yōuxiān	(first) priority
織布廠	zhībùchǎng	textile mill
針織廠	zhēnzhīchǎng	knitting mill
細紗	xìshā	fine yarn
核結外匯	hé jié wàihùi	to ratify and to apply for purchase of foreign exchange (from state banks)
標購	biāogòu	to purchase by bidding
投標	tóubiāo	to submit a tender, enter a bid
二班制	èrbānzhì	two-shift system

易感疲勞	yì gǎn pỉláo	to fatigue easily
效率自低	xiàolù zìdī	efficiency is certainly low
三班制	sānbānzhì	three-shift system
迅即洽 . . .	xùnjí qià . . .	to arrange promptly with
淡季	dànjì	slack season, off-season
美援會	měiyuánhuì	American Aid Association
先行撥借	xiānxíngbōjiè	to appropriate the loan first
旺季	wàngjì	peak period, business season
週轉	zhōuzhuǎn	to transfer; turnover, circulation
人造棉紡業	rénzàomián fǎng yè	rayon fiber yarn industry
均感困難	jūn gǎn kùnnan	to be equally difficult
韓國	hánguó	Korea (South Korea)
迄今	qìjīn	up to now
餘數	yúshù	remainder
欠佳	qiànjiā	not good enough, not up to the mark
違約	wéiyuē	to break a contract
依約	yīyuē	according to the contract
可予貸借	kě yǔ dàijiè	may be granted a loan
幅寬太狹	fúkuān tài xiá	the width of cloth is too narrow
織景	zhījǐng	picture-weaving
蠶絲	cánsī	natural silk
混紡	hùnfǎng	blending

不敷需要	bùfū xūyào	to be insufficient for need
東南亞	dōngnányà	Southeast Asia
中東	zhōngdōng	the Middle East
瑞典	ruìdiǎn	Sweden
西德	xīdé	West Germany
購存	gòu cún	to purchase for storage
預為儲備	yùwéi chǔbèi	to store beforehand
退稅	tuìshùi	to refund taxes; tax rebate
外銷專戶	wàixiāo zhuānhù	specialized firms for sale abroad
另撥專款	lìng bō zhuānkuǎn	to appropriate special funds separately
墊付	diànfù	to pay on behalf of someone for reimbursement later
按 . . . 計息	àn . . . jìxī	to calculate interest according to
檢驗證書	jiǎnyànzhèngshū	certificate of inspection
研擬	yán nǐ	to study and then draw up

Document 7 (vol. 2, pp. 159–65)

Joint Reply from the Ministry of Economic Affairs and the Ministry of Finance to the Executive Yuan Regarding the Case of the Tangrong Ironworks
經濟、財政兩部關於監察院糾正唐榮救濟案的聯合申複書

This document is a reply jointly drafted by the Ministry of Finance and the Ministry of Economic Affairs. When a case needed to be processed by more than one government organization, documents were often prepared and issued jointly by two or more organs, with one organ as the principal sponsor (*zhuban danwei* 主辦單位) and the other(s) as collaborating sponsor(s) (*xieban danwei* 協辦單位). The usual procedure was for the principal sponsor to prepare a preliminary draft and then discuss it with the collaborating unit(s). Once agreement was reached over the draft, a final version was sent out in the name of two or more government organs.

The printed letterhead 經濟部會稿 (*Jingji bu huigao*) indicates that this was a joint-draft reference sheet prepared by the Ministry of Economic Affairs. In the item for the principal processing unit (主辦單位) in the first line from the right, the Ministry of Economic Affairs was entered. The collaborating unit for this draft was the Ministry of Finance. The addressee (*shouwenzhe* 受文者) for the document was the Executive Yuan. An appendix (*fujian* 附件) is attached as stated in the document (*ruwen* 如文). All officials who were involved in the processing and approval of the document signed their names on this reference sheet. In the middle of the sheet are the official seals of the two ministries.

The small characters in brackets in the right margin tell us that there are two copies for the same draft. This copy was filed in the Ministry of Economic Affairs (*ci gao cunzai Jingjibu* 此稿存經濟部).

會稿	huìgǎo	joint draft
監察院	jiāncháyùan	the Control Yuan
糾正	jiūzhèng	to correct, redress, rectify
唐榮鐵工廠	tángróng tiegōngchǎng	Tangrong Ironworks
擬具	nǐjù	to draft, draw up
敬祈	jìngqí	to request respectfully

全銜	quánxián	full name of an official title
救濟	jiùjì	to relieve, succor, relief
疏於	shūyú	to be negligent in
會計師	kuàijìshī	accountant
尚無	shàngwú	still lack
明文	míngwén	to stipulate in explicit terms
干預	gānyù	to interfere, intervene
現行法令	xiànxíng fǎlìng	existing laws and decrees
奈	nài	but
惡化	èhuà	to deteriorate, worsen
不尋常	bùxúncháng	unusual, uncommon, extraordinary
擴張過度	kùozhāng gùodù	to overexpand
公司法	gōngsīfǎ	company law
取締	qǔdì	to outlaw, ban, suppress
殊欠完備	shūqiàn wánbèi	very incomplete
為謀...計	wèimóu . . . jì	in order to strive for
轉投資	zhuǎn tóuzī	to transfer the investment
主管機關	zhǔguǎn jīguān	responsible government agency, the authorities concerned, the agency or agencies in charge
...得派員	. . . dé pàiyuán	can send personnel
證券商	zhèngquànshāng	stockbroker

逾格	yúgé	to exceed the limit, depart from usual practice
暫緩	zànhuǎn	to postpone
已瀕	yǐ bīn	on the verge of
照認	zhàorèn	to undertake to do something . . . ; accordingly
滯納金	zhìnàjīn	fine for delayed payment
積極性	jījíxìng	initiative, enthusiasm
制頒	zhìbān	to stipulate and promulgate
尚具 . . . 可能	shàngjù . . . kěnēng	there is still the possibility of
被迫	bèipò	to be compelled, be forced to, be constrained
究應	jiūyīng	how exactly should (one do someth
牽此涉彼	qiāncǐ shèbǐ	to involve the various parties affec each other
關連廣泛	guānlián guǎngfàn	to be extensively connected
均將蒙受	jūn jiāng méngshòu	will all suffer (losses)
因果循環	yīnguǒ xúnhuán	the cycle of cause and effect
不堪設想	bùkān shèxiǎng	dreadful to contemplate
夏秋之際	xià qiū zhī jì	during summer and autumn
倒風頗盛	dǎofēng pō shèng	the practice of going bankrupt pr
值 . . . 之難關	zhí . . . zhī nánguān	at the critical juncture of
已呈	yǐchéng	already present

任令	rènlìng	to let something go unchecked
勢將激盪	shìjiāng jīdàng	will inevitably arouse
波瀾	bōlán	great waves, billows
爰	yuán	and thereupon
清償	qīngcháng	pay off
債務人	zhàiwùrén	debtor
處分權	chǔfèn quán	rights to deal with (a matter)
淨值	jìngzhí	net value
承諾	chéngnùo	promise
財源	cáiyuán	financial source
龐雜	pángzá	disorderly, numerous and jumbled
勢採	shìcǎi	will certainly adopt
展延	zhǎnyán	to extend
旨在	zhǐzài	the purpose lies in . . . ; for the purpose of . . .
消滅	xiāomìe	to extinguish, destroy, eliminate
債權	zhàiquán	creditor's right
所負	suǒfù	(the money) owed
料款	liàokuǎn	payment for material
貨款	huòkuǎn	payment for goods
聯袂而來	liánmèi'érlái	to come together
坐索	zuòsuǒ	to demand (payment of a debt)

355

匡計	kuāngjì	rough calculation, estimate
鉅大	jùdà	huge
力所不逮	lì suǒ bùdǎi	ability falling short of one's wishes
尤恐	yóukǒng	particularly afraid
視聽	shìtīng	public opinion
有違	yǒuwéi	to go against
本旨	běnzhǐ	original aim
磋商	cuōshāng	to consult, exchange views
外銷	wàixiāo	for sale abroad
鋼筋	gāngjīn	reinforcing bar
續訂	xùdìng	to continue to order
加發	jiāfā	to send out more (goods)
核屬可行	hé shǔ kěxíng	to be considered feasible
備查	bèichá	to file for future reference
比照	bǐzhào	according to
一成	yīchéng	one-tenth
迺經	nǎijīng	therefore, as a result of (someone's effort)
為...起見	wèi ... qǐjiàn	in order to
攤還	tānhuán	to pay back in installments
牌價	páijià	list price
債權人	zhàiquánrén	creditor
至為沉重	zhì wéi chénzhòng	(the burden) is extremely heavy

總動員法	zǒng dòngyuán fǎ	general mobilization law
以其為	yǐ qí wéi	as it is
實績	shíjī	actual accomplishment
未便	wèibiàn	inconvenient, not suitable for
債戶	zhàihù	debtor
基於	jīyú	because of, in view of
會商	huìshāng	to consult
資負	zīfù	assets and liabilities
維持營運	wéichí yíngyùn	to keep the business in operation
事宜	shìyí	the matters concerned
須得 . . . 始能	xūdé . . . shǐnéng	can . . . only after getting something done
債信已失	zhàixìn yǐshī	has lost one's credit
紛起	fēnqǐ	to come one after another
索債	suǒzhài	to demand payment of a debt
糾紛	jiūfēn	dispute
先決條件	xiānjué tiáojiàn	prerequisite, precondition
墊款	diànkuǎn	to advance money to be paid back later
祇 (只)	zhǐ	only, merely
二途	èrtú	two methods
可循	kěxún	can be followed
介入	jièrù	to interfere
維持現狀	wéichí xiànzhuàng	to maintain the status quo

行使	xíngshǐ	to exercise, perform
銀根較緊	yín gēn jiǎo jǐn	the money market is quite tight
週轉欠靈	zhōuzhuǎnqiànlíng	to have insufficient cash to meet needs
救濟令	jiùjìlìng	relief order
合...規定	hé...guīdìng	in conformity with the provision
援用	yuányòng	to quote, cite, invoke
受理	shòulǐ	to accept and hear a case
類同之...例	lèitóngzhī...lì	a similar precedent in
重建程序	chóngjiàn chéngxù	reorganization procedures
在所難免	zài suǒ nánmiǎn	can hardly be avoided
事端	shìduān	disturbance, incident
殊非...之道	shūfēi...zhīdào	not at all a way to...